The *Wind* from *Vulture Peak*

The *Wind* from *Vulture Peak*

The Buddhification of Japanese Waka in the Heian Period

Stephen D. Miller
translations with Patrick Donnelly

East Asia Program
Cornell University
Ithaca, New York 14853

The Cornell East Asia Series is published by the Cornell University East Asia Program (distinct from Cornell University Press). We publish books on a variety of scholarly topics relating to East Asia as a service to the academic community and the general public. Standing Orders, which provide for automatic notification and invoicing of each title in the series upon publication are accepted.

Address submission inquiries to CEAS Editorial Board, East Asia Program, Cornell University, 140 Uris Hall, Ithaca, New York 14853-7601.

Cover Design: Adam B. Bohannon
Cover Calligraphy: Eiichi Okamoto, Michi *("Path"), from the author's collection.*

Number 166 in the Cornell East Asia Series
Copyright © 2013 by Stephen D. Miller and Patrick Donnelly. All rights reserved.
ISSN: 1050-2955
ISBN: 978-1-933947-86-0 hardcover
ISBN: 978-1-933947-66-2 paperback
Library of Congress Control Number: 2012953208

This book is dedicated to my mentor and friend

William R. LaFleur

CONTENTS

vii

ACKNOWLEDGMENTS

The twelfth-century Tibetan mind-training practice known as *lojong* contains fifty-nine aphorisms, one of which is "be generous to everyone." The meaning of this particular aphorism is that one should be grateful even to those people and situations that presented themselves as obstructions to your own progress on the path. In the many years that this project on Buddhist *waka* has occupied my mind and my time, I have faced numerous obstacles that seemed to be, at the time, insurmountable. Thankfully, many institutions, teachers, family members, colleagues, students, friends, lovers, and a spouse (who'd have thought *that* would be possible?) came to my aid, and it is to them that these words of thanks are directed.

I won't dwell upon the people, places, and events that made me who I am before college (though there were many, like the inimitable Sue Stork-Garcia, for whom I feel great fondness and gratitude), but it is to Harold Wright and Gordon Grigsby at Ohio State University who sparked my initial interest in Buddhism and poetry that I am most grateful, while Diantha Rau and Patti Koelsch soothed my frantic soul with their wisdom. At Columbia University, Cathy Benton and Neil Gross put up with my lack of self-confidence, while Chris Collins cheerfully bore its brunt at home. At UCLA, Linda Chance, Jan Bardsley, Laura Miller, Jackie Stone, Sarah Lubman, and Leo Ching were confidants and strength-givers as I tried to evolve myself into a scholar. I'll never adequately be able to express how much their friendship has meant; in recent years Linda and Jackie in particular assisted me with this project in countless ways.

In its earliest stages, this project was nourished by the encouragement of William R. LaFleur, who over the decades also came to be its heart-mind (*kokoro*). The Japan Foundation provided time and money first in the form of a dissertation fellowship, and later with a research fellowship; without this generosity I would never have discovered the

Japanese scholarship on my topic. Eiichi Okamoto exhibited profound patience over many years as I pelted him with questions about Japanese language and culture; Ishihara Kiyoshi was extremely tolerant of my infelicities with the Japanese language as I tried to pose adequately polite questions about his own research on *shakkyō-ka*.

At the University of Colorado, Laurel Rasplica Rodd (friend, housemate, and colleague since my days at the University of Michigan) has never wavered in her support for this book, or for me as a person and a scholar; it isn't possible to exaggerate the extent and efficacy of her advocacy. Greg Rodd has also been a great listener-friend, as well as a consummate reader-editor of the earliest drafts of this book. Without the many ways Steve Snyder and Linda White have loved and nourished me over the years (the dinners! the conversations!) I strongly doubt whether I could have reached this happy point. I'd also like to thank Lynn Parisi, Susan Schmidt, and Bud Coleman for their considerable friendship in Boulder and after. To George Bealer (who called me up out of the blue to say "let's be friends!"), Keith Gresham (not just George's spouse, but a true friend in his own right), and Marcia Yonemoto (thank you for Boston and for unconditional love and humor), I am inexpressibly grateful for unfaltering kindness. To Minori Murata I can only bow in profound respect, for patience, food, and love over the years at Quince Avenue and since. And to my "first" Japanese friend, Takayuki Kida, thank you for saying *hi* in the *ryokan ofuro* in Kyoto, and for faithful friendship when I was illiterate and uncommunicative, from early days to the present. Thanks also to Judith Simmer-Brown—sangha sister/mother, mentor, friend, and a model of kindness, compassion, and intellectual vigor whom I feel honored to know.

At the University of Massachusetts, I have benefitted immensely from the emotional and academic and support of Amanda Seaman, Sean Gilsdorf, Bruce Baird, and Jeanne Hardy, while Enhua Zhang, David Schneider, and Zhijun Wang have taught me the meaning of collegiality. I can only hope in the future to return the support I received from all of them. A heartfelt thank you to Sharon Domier, our indefatigable librarian, who has never failed to answer a question of mine. From what I can tell, she is a magician cloaked in a librarian's clothing. Julie Hayes has been as kind to me as any Chair/Dean could possibly be, and Bill Moebius in turn. The intellectual and emotional encouragement Julia Demmin gave me during the completion of this book was literally indispensible. Karen Smyers, newfound old friend, showed me unconditional love and lent invaluable editing skills—may you live forever! Dori Digenti, whom I have known since our wayward days in Kyoto, has continued to be my friend in life, in the sangha, and in a shared love of Japan; I am so thankful to have made my home in her neighborhood. Thank you to Elizabeth Oyler, Andrew Macomber, Bobby Luckhardt, Kim McNelly, Robert Khan, Ethan Segal, Jane Hirshfield, Chase Twichell, Henry Lyman, and Cheryl Crowley, as students, friends, readers, and colleagues for whom any person and scholar would be thankful.

I will always be indebted to Laura Kaufman's understanding of Japan, of Buddhism, of practice, of scholarship, and of, well, everything. I doubt I could repay one-tenth of the kindness she has shown, but hope to, in this and subsequent lifetimes.

The love, compassion, brotherhood, and friendship Larry Schourup has shown me since we met in Columbus, Ohio in 1972 is of such depth that I could never repay him, though he is precisely the kind of person who would never desire repayment. Thank you, too, to Isao Sano for showing Larry and me both what devotion is.

To the love of my life and my spouse, PSD, I'm hopelessly and helplessly speechless. You have taken my breath away ever since we met (online!) in 2002, and continue to do so today. I wouldn't be what I am today without you. Thank you for loving me and letting me love you.

Patrick Donnelly and I are grateful to the editors of the journals and anthologies in which versions of these translations appeared previously: *Bateau, Cha: An Asian Literary Journal, Circumference, eXchanges, Inquiring Mind, Gallery of Readers Anthology, Kyoto Journal, Mead, Metamorphoses, New Plains Review, NOON: The Journal of the Short Poem, The Drunken Boat, Literature and Literary Theory, Poetry International* and *Zone 3*.

Finally, I would like to thank the editors and staff of the Cornell East Asia Series for their generous assistance in all stages of this publication.

Stephen D. Miller
South Deerfield, 2011

Each sentience is brief, is it not?
Therefore I'm trying to record whatever
I can of the instantly squandered present
so I can say in stone-plain words
what sentience is.

Rules: Tell the truth. No decoration. Remember death.

— Chase Twichell

Nothing is ever really lost, or can be lost,
No birth, identity, form—no object of the world.
Nor life, nor force, nor any visible thing;
Appearance must not foil, nor shifted sphere confuse thy
        brain.
Ample are time and space—ample the fields of Nature.
The body, sluggish, aged, cold—the embers left from earlier
        fires,
The light in the eye grown dim, shall duly flame again;
The sun now low in the west rises for mornings and for
        noons continual;
To frozen clods ever the spring's invisible law returns,
With grass and flowers and summer fruits and corn.

— Walt Whitman

if the wind
            from Vulture Peak

had not blown
            my sleeves inside-out—

would I have found
            the jewel

inside the reverse
            of my coat?

                    — Sōjō Jōen

1 INTRODUCTION

In the twelfth century, court *waka*—that most orthodox of genres—became the vehicle by which Japanese writers brought their literary and spiritual aspirations together in a new way. The shift they made from the practices of their cultural past, and the new mindset that was formed as a result of this shift, is the story of this study.

Several questions arise when we delve into the intersections of the literary and the religious—specifically, the intersections of *waka* poetry (a short thirty-one-syllable poem) as a genre of Japanese literature and Buddhist poetry as a category of that genre. The first question focuses upon the "shift" mentioned above. Japanese and Western scholars seem to agree that there was a change that occurred in the orientation of poetry during the twelfth century, when writers began to apply certain Buddhist philosophical concepts that had come to pervade various aspects of Heian life to the skill of writing *waka*. The poetry and prose of Fujiwara no Shunzei (1114–1204) is usually cited as the best evidence for this shift. This study will show that Shunzei's "new" approach to *waka* was in fact the culmination of a synthesis that began in the Nara period (710–784), gave birth to new literary expressions in the mid to late Heian period (784–1185), and came to fruition under Shunzei's direction in the compilation of the seventh imperial poetry anthology (*Senzaiwakashū* [hereafter *Senzaishū*], 1188), when he created two new independent books of *waka* called "Shakkyō-ka" (*uta/waka* on the teachings of the Buddha Śākyamuni) and "Jingi-ka"

I

(*waka* on *kami* matters).[1] It is the *waka* of the former kind that will be the focus of this study.[2]

A second, and more general, question pertains to the manner in which *waka* maintained its generic qualities in terms of topic, meter (syllabics), diction, rhetoric, and tone, after it began to accommodate the philosophical ideas of a soteriological religion like Buddhism. A thirty-one-syllable poem hardly seems the kind of genre that would— or *could*—explicate or embody these complex religious ideas.

A third question pertains to the venue in which Buddhist *waka* came to be compiled. While Buddhist *waka* appear in various kinds of anthologies, this study analyzes the evolution of Buddhist *waka* that were included within the imperial poetry anthology (*chokusenwakashū* [hereafter *chokusenshū*]) during the second half of the Heian period.[3] As a literary project that originated by decree from the sovereign Daigo (r. 897–930) in the early tenth century, the *chokusenshū* was initiated as a public forum for the display of court poetry, and because it originated from the emperor himself, it was grounded, in the tenth century at least, in a *kami*-centered worldview, making it an unlikely repository for *waka* on nonnative (i.e., Buddhist) themes.

Finally, questions arise concerning particular Buddhist and Buddhist-related concepts that comprised the world of ideas during the Heian period. Were there certain concepts that may have contributed to the appearance of Buddhist *waka* more than others? Was the conflation of Buddhism and poetry that is said to have occurred during the twelfth century a result of an ongoing discussion

---

1. When referring to the kind, or sub-genre, of *waka*, *shakkyō-ka* will appear in italics with no capital letter. When I am referring to a book of *shakkyō-ka*, it will appear as "Shakkyō-ka." *Kami* refers to the native Japanese "gods."

2. I will not take up *jingi-ka* in this study, but such poems were the subject of a recent MA thesis (2010) by Christina Olinyk at the University of Massachusetts, Amherst entitled "Poems of the Gods of the Heaven and the Earth: An Annotated Translation of the Jingi-ka Book of the *Senzaishū*."

3. For the purposes of this study, unless indicated otherwise, the word "waka" and "poem/poetry" will be used interchangeably and will refer to all aspects of its appearance in an anthology: that is, its headnote (*kotobagaki*) or topic (*dai*), the thirty-one-syllable poem, and the poem's attribution.

of these concepts or the result of certain kinds of experience to which the imperial court opened itself at that time?

WHAT'S AT STAKE

The questions posed above form the core of this study: the evolution of Buddhist *waka* from the time of the *Man'yōshū* (ca. 759) to the *Senzaishū* (1188), the specific nature of the shift concerning *waka* that occurred in the twelfth century, the preservation of *waka*'s courtliness as it assimilated Buddhist ideas, and the religious, philosophical and literary ideas that formed a conceptual locus out of which Buddhist *waka* could arise.

The impetus for this work arose from William LaFleur's groundbreaking study of the Buddhist values that were assigned to literary works and the literary values that were assigned to the Buddhist teachings. *The Karma of Words* presented scholars with a new paradigm of Japanese medieval history, Buddhist philosophy, and literature in several genres. LaFleur's claim that "the arc of Japan's medieval experience" should rightly begin with the compilation of Kyōkai's *Nihonkoku genpō zen'aku ryōiki*, or *Nihon ryōiki* (ca. 810–824), in the early part of the Heian period (784–1185), challenged previous periodization schemes by both Western and Japanese scholars that located the medieval in the political sphere.[4] Likewise, his discussion of Fujiwara no Shunzei (1114–1204), medieval *waka* and Tendai Buddhist doctrines paved the way for other studies—mostly notably Edward Kamens's translation and study of the *Hosshin wakashū* and Rajyashree Pandey's work on Kamo no Chōmei—to explore Japanese Buddhist poetry in more detail.[5]

---

4. William R. LaFleur, *The Karma of Words* (Berkeley and London: University of California Press, 1983), 9.

5. Edward Kamens, *The Buddhist Poetry of the Great Kamo Priestess: Daisaiin Senshi and Hosshin wakashū* (Ann Arbor: The Center for Japanese Studies, University of Michigan, 1990). Rajyashree Pandey, *Writing and Renunciation in Medieval Japan: The Works of the Poet-Priest Kamo no Chōmei* (Ann Arbor: The Center for Japanese Studies, University of Michigan, 1998).

This study, however, does not focus on either "the medieval arc" of Japanese literary history or upon a particular work or poet, but rather upon the development of a particular sub-genre of poetry that came to be called *shakkyō-ka*. In *The Karma of Words*, LaFleur wrote the following about court *waka* and Buddhism: "In Shunzei's view, a poem is Buddhist not because it has hidden within it an allusion to a scripture or an unambiguously sacred source, but because the trajectory back to that source itself produces a rejection of the distinction between sacred and profane literatures."[6] This is a provocative idea, not only because of what it reveals about Shunzei, poetry, and Buddhism, but also because of what it does not reveal: if Shunzei *did* believe that poetry was not Buddhist because of its allusions and references, then why did he feel compelled to create an independent book of *shakkyō-ka*— *waka* that clearly allude to sacred Buddhist sources—in the *Senzaishū*? If court *waka* did not need Buddhist appurtenances to be Buddhist, then why was it necessary to compile poems that were known by this time as *shakkyō-ka* (*waka* on the teachings of the Buddha)?

The aim of this study is to look carefully at the kinds of poems Japanese poets considered Buddhist—or compiled in such ways as to become Buddhist—as a means of clarifying how the Japanese came to regard the *waka* as holding salvific power. The principal argument of this study will be that while the writing of *waka* on Buddhist themes provided a familiar literary format whereby the aristocracy could select those teachings that were best suited for its literary sensibilities, the compilers of the imperial poetry anthologies were also selective about the arrangement of these poems. Because *waka* on Buddhist themes needed to fulfill their duties as courtly poems at the same time that they represented some aspect of the compiler's interpretation of the Buddhist teachings, they occupied at once two epistemological realms—the literary and the religious. As a mediator of these two realms, *waka* on Buddhist themes would eventually contribute significantly to the concept known as *kadō soku butsudō* (the path of poetry is none other than the path of the Buddha).

---

6. LaFleur, *The Karma of Words*, 95–96.

AVENUES OF INTERROGATION

The primary pathway through which the idea that "the path of poetry is none other than the path of the Buddha" may be understood is to examine the gradual evolution of *waka* on Buddhist themes that led to that statement. During the era of the *Man'yōshū*, the *chokusenshishū* (imperial *kanshi* anthologies) in the early 800s, the *Kokinwakashū* (hereafter *Kokinshū*, 905) and the *Gosenwakashū* (hereafter *Gosenshū*, 951), it was not at all clear that *waka* would ever become the kind of genre that dealt with Buddhist occasions or Buddhist texts, much less Buddhist concepts. Unlike many Western literatures that expressed Christian ideas in poetic form very early in their histories, Japanese poetry did not find a way to express feelings and thoughts about Buddhist teachings until almost five hundred years after the introduction of Buddhism to Japan in 538. While we do find poems on Buddhist-related topics (character- or narrative-based, rather than on themes related to the teachings) during this era, it was not until the early eleventh century that a group of *waka* on Buddhist themes was compiled in the *Shūiwakashū* (hereafter *Shūishū*, ca. 1005–1007), the third imperial poetry anthology after the *Kokinshū* and the *Gosenshū*.

During the period of this evolution from the late 600s to the late 1100s, the compilers of the imperial anthologies, my focus here, seemed unsure at times what to call or where to include these *waka*. In the *Shūishū*, the compiler or compilers (which remains unclear) included them, without any titular designation, within the book of Laments ("Aishō-ka"). In the *Goshūiwakashū* (hereafter *Goshūishū*, 1086) the fourth imperial anthology, the compiler subcategorized nineteen *waka* on Buddhist themes within a book of "Miscellaneous Poems" (Zōka) calling them "Shakkyō." In the fifth and sixth imperial anthologies, *Kin'yōwakashū* (hereafter *Kin'yōshū*, 1126–1127) and *Shikawakashū* (hereafter *Shikashū*, 1151) *waka* on Buddhist themes lost their "Shakkyō" title, though their location in books of "Miscellaneous Waka" did not change. Uncertainties about naming *waka* on Buddhist themes were not definitively resolved until the seventh imperial anthology, *Senzaishū*, in which for the first time the compiler created an independent book of Buddhist *waka* called "Shakkyō-ka." From this point forward, such books appeared in every subsequent imperial anthology up to and including the final one completed in 1439. The five imperial anthologies during which this evolution took place, from the *Shūishū* through the *Goshūishū*, *Kin'yōshū*, *Shikashū*, and *Senzaishū*, must therefore comprise the main focus of this study, though it will also be helpful to examine poetry on Buddhist topics before the *Shūishū*, when the role and development of such poems was still unclear.

Questions of terminology and categories are a recurring issue that is central to this study. These problems of terminology concerning *waka* on Buddhist themes are not merely confined to the realm of semantics. As many cognitive scientists have shown, what something is named and how it is categorized are deeply connected with our epistemological interpretations of the world, and have effective consequences thereafter. That these poems were not given any categorical distinction in the earlier eras of Japanese literary history, then later compiled as a variety of *aishō-ka* (lament), *zōka* (miscellaneous poem), and finally designated as *shakkyō-ka* (poems on the teachings of the Buddha), signals the gradual resolution of an internal tension among court poets. The primary causes of this tension had been uncertainty about the appropriateness of *waka*—a poetic form believed to have been transmitted from the *kami*—for Buddhist expression, as well as the appropriateness of the imperial anthologies—a representation of the imperial *mandala*, if you will—as a repository for such poems. Though definitive responses to such tensions did not occur at one specific time in history, in any single genre of literature, or with the support of any one Buddhist teaching, we will be able to point to certain temporal, literary, and religio-philosophical moments as signposts for understanding the process by which the literary and Buddhist religious spheres eventually conflated.

It will also be important to this study to examine the strategies by which poets and compilers maintained the courtliness of the *waka* form. This will entail a close look, not only at the internal projects of the poems themselves, but also the strategies of association and progression within the sequences in which the poems appear, and by which their meanings were amplified. As the overarching task of this study is to track the development of a new subgenre of *waka*, the chapters progress chronologically. It will be helpful occasionally to refer to *waka* on Buddhist themes in other kinds of anthologies (personal [*shisenshū*] and private [*shikashū*]) as well as poetry competitions (*utaawase*) and one-hundred-poem sequences (*hyakushu-uta*), but the imperial anthologies will be the principal focus. It will be especially important to demonstrate how compilers of the imperial poetry anthologies schematically organized sequences of Buddhist *waka*, in some cases, as poetic reconstructions of the Buddhist path (J: *michi*, C: *tao*; S: *mārga*) and in other cases as *tableaux vivants* of certain themes, the organization of sūtra chapters, pertaining to certain kinds of Buddhist occasions, or even alluding to the relationship among authors to whom the poems were attributed. Close readings of individual poems in all of the anthologies during which this evolution took place will demonstrate how a variety of teachings were used to support the process by which compilers and poets came to write court *waka* on Buddhist themes, and how, eventually, these poems were granted status equal to other categories of court *waka*.

It will be important as we begin to establish a working vocabulary with which to describe the "modes" and "modalities" of poetry, to examine previous Japanese scholarship on the topic of Buddhist *waka* and *shakkyō-ka*, to ascertain the religiosity of both *waka* and Buddhist *waka*, to clarify terms and categories, and finally to describe our translation strategies and goals.

MODES AND MODALITIES

It is important not to lose sight of the courtly nature of *waka* on Buddhist themes. It has become unfashionable and ethnocentric to discuss *waka* as the Japanese version of the Western lyric poem, and this study will not do so. However, it would not be helpful to dissociate that which is *lyric* from the *waka*. Whether a poem arises from or is prompted by a public, social, or personal occasion, it can have lyric qualities—that is, it can express and/or evoke feelings (the hallmark of lyric poetry): it may simultaneously fill its personal and public responsibilities (such as taking a role in a poetry competition). The characteristics of the lyric mode are that it is often grounded in sensually specific vocabulary (imagery—but also pertaining to the other four senses), and that its focus tends toward subjectivity rather than objectivity. But the lyric is not the only mode in play: there are two other modes, narrative and meditative, which also play important roles in any given poem. In the case of reading *waka*, the narrative layer is often provided by either the headnote or the topic, by which the anthologizer provides readers with a "story" element often lacking in the poem proper: where and when the poem was composed, the person or people involved in the occasion (in addition to, in some cases, the author), and the situation that prompted its writing.[7] The narrative "predicament," as one poet calls it, does not need to be complex to qualify as a narrative: waiting for a lover or observing the cherry blossoms were common narrative predicaments for court poetry, which Buddhist poems would adapt or transform. (In the case of *waka* based on a topic rather than a headnote [often more generous in its information], frequently there is still a narrative element, either implied by the fact that the topic has been assigned, by someone [usually] other than the author, or appearing in the poem itself.) Reading *waka* or *shakkyō-ka* sequentially in an imperial poetry anthology, the narrative provided by the headnote or topic to a single poem is enhanced when read in conjunction with the previous and following headnote/topic and poem. When the anthologizer wished to create a longer or more complex narrative, as in the case of the *Shūishū*, poems were arranged in such a way as to imply that story. By such strategies, poets and anthologizers circumvented the inherent

---

7. This discussion on modes draws upon a critical essay on Stephen Dunn's poem "The Reverse Side" by Patrick Donnelly. Donnelly's three-part designation of poetic modes is different from the traditional distinction of lyric, narrative, and dramatic. See <http://www.answers.com/topics/the-reverse-side-poem-6>. Accessed January 15, 2009.

narrative limitations of *waka*, and ensured that the narrative mode—essential to ground the poem in a specific reality—was in place to support the overall poetic project. Often when these poems were written, the recipient(s) understood the narrative context; it was later that the missing narrative element needed to be supplied by the anthologizer.

Finally, with the emergence of *waka* on Buddhist themes, a third poetic mode becomes more prominent: the meditative. Deployment of the meditative mode does not necessarily designate poetry that is contemplative or provoked by meditative discipline, though it could include both of those qualities. In the West, the label "meditative poetry" is often given to either to the metaphysical poets of seventeenth-century England or the mystical poetry of Rumi or William Blake. More recently, meditative poetry has also been associated with American poets like Gary Snyder and Allen Ginsberg. However, the meditative *mode*, rather than meditative *poetry*, is characterized by the way it focuses "on working out an idea or a philosophical argument or considers the *meaning* of narrative, in ways that appeal primarily to the intellect."[8] Narrative belongs to the realm of facts, events, and other specifics that the poet may inflect toward the lyric or meditative modes, or toward both in varying degrees. While the lyric mode expresses and evokes feeling, usually strong feeling, the meditative mode is focused upon and characterized by logic, instruction, reasoned argument or debate (internal or external).

It is important to emphasize that these three poetic modes usually do not function alone, but together to support any particular poem's project. If a mode *does* appear alone without the support of either of the other modes, or if one of the modes is excessively amplified, the poem may fail outright, or an aesthetic imbalance of the kind Ono no Komachi (early Heian period) created in her famous *hito ni awamu* poem (*Kokinshū* 1030) can result:

---

8. Patrick Donnelly, "How the Narrative, Lyric, and Meditative Modes of Poetry Combine in Hybrid Modes—and Why," unpublished manuscript.

人に逢はむ月のなきには思をきてむねはしり火に心やけをり

hito ni awamu / tsuki no naki ni wa / omoiokite / munehashiribi ni / kokoro yakeori

> I need to see him,
> and there's no moon—
>   love's brazier
> fires my sleepless breasts,
> my heart burning and breaking—

>   — Ono no Komachi[9]

Though this *waka* does hint at a narrative predicament (the lover will not come) the extreme emphasis on the metaphor of burning, viewed narrowly in terms of deployment of the modes, results in an almost claustrophobic lyric-overload. The poem does not seem set in any particular narrative space; it is performed almost solely within the realm of the speaker's obsessive feelings—exactly the danger of any poem that seems to exclude all modes but the lyric. There are readers with an appetite for lyric excess, but this poem's strategies must have seemed excessive even to the Japanese compiler, since it was not included among the love poems or even among the love poems in one of the Miscellaneous books.[10] Poems with Buddhist themes would also, on occasion, express strong feeling, but in various ways they took steps to distance themselves from the destructive or delusionary influence of passion (most especially the kind on display in Komachi's poem): one such strategy was deployment of the intellectualizing influence of the meditative mode.

A poem that leans heavily upon the meditative mode is this one by Kūya, from the *Shūishū* Buddhist *waka* sequence:

---

9. Kojima Noriyuki and Arai Eizō, eds., *Kokinwakashū*, in *Shin Nihon koten bungaku taikei* [hereafter SNKBT], vol. 5 (Tokyo: Iwanami Shoten, 1989), 313.

10. The fact that Komachi's poem was written in an uneven metric of 6, 7, 6, 7, 7 syllables probably explains why it was included in the book of "Miscellaneous Forms" (Zattei) in the *Kokinshū*.

一度も南無阿弥陀仏と言ふ人の蓮の上にのぼらぬはなし
hitotabi mo / namu amida bu to / iu hito no / hachisu no ue ni / noboranu wa nashi[11]

LEFT ON THE MARKETPLACE GATE

> among those who call
> the Name
> even one time

> there are none
> who won't reach
> the top of the lotus leaf

> — Kūya Shōnin[12]

The compiler(s) have supplied a narrative element in the headnote, whereby Kūya (903–972) is understood to have posted the poem on the marketplace gate for others to see, but the poem itself emphasizes its meditative argument: to "call / the Name / even one time" has salvific power. (The "Name" in our translation functions as a synecdoche for *Namu Amida Bu[tsu]*, embedded in the poem itself, the actual *mantra* for which Kūya advocates.) Many Western readers would probably regard, and then dismiss, this poem as didactic, but this would be misguided. Didacticism, as LaFleur has said, needs to be grounded in the "history of ideas" prevalent at the time the poem was written.[13] It is more helpful for the purposes of this study to recognize the didactic impulse as one symptom or characteristic of the meditative mode, which makes such poems appeal more to the intellect than the emotions (without completely neglecting the latter). Poets

---

11. According to Ishihara Kiyoshi, this poem also appears in the *setsuwa* collection *Kokonchomonjū*. Ishihara Kiyoshi, *Shakkyō-ka no kenkyū* (Kyoto: Dōhōsha, 1980), 62.

12. Further discussion as well as the original source for this poem can be found in Chapter 3, 82 and 123–125.

13. LaFleur, *The Karma of Words*, 18.

wishing to deemphasize, for religious reasons, the passions of the lyric mode would have found the cooler temperatures of the meditative mode particularly useful. Kūya's poem is indeed instructive, one of the principal characteristics of the meditative mode, and downplays whatever emotional aspects the poem's predicament might have had in a different treatment. Moreover, Japanese readers did not view *waka* that displayed a tendency to guide or instruct with disdain in the mid-tenth century or for several centuries to come. Once the compilers created a literary space for *waka* with such a project, they became a part of the courtly tradition and the imperial poetry anthology. We will come to see which of the three poetic modes is deployed, and which predominates in any particular poem with Buddhist themes, may be seen as an important component of how that poem relates or responds to (or in some cases even seems to express conflict with) the Buddhist teachings.

Unlike a mode, which for our purposes describes how language is used and what its effects are, a *modality* for Buddhist *waka* may be described as having two components: (1) the spiritual source upon which the poem is based, and (2) the social reality to which it speaks. The modalities of importance to this study are heavenly/courtly, soteriological/courtly, and soteriological/monastic. A heavenly/courtly modality derives its spiritual sustenance from the world of the *kami* (heavenly) and speaks to the social reality of the imperial court. The primary—though not the only—mode of this modality is lyric. (This modality was preceded by one which will be of less importance to this study, but which we may call heavenly/tribal.) The second modality, soteriological/courtly, derives its spiritual support from the Buddhist promise of salvation, but maintains its orientation toward the values of the imperial court. The third modality, soteriological/monastic, retains the spiritual concerns of the second modality—that is, from Buddhist soteriology—but speaks to the social reality of the monastic complexes (and their teachings) that became increasingly prevalent in the beliefs of the imperial court. The primary—though not the only—mode of this modality is meditative. While the courtly modality primarily utilizes the images, diction, and themes of court *waka* as they were established in the *Kokinshū,* the monastic modality *may* use some of those aspects, but also uses diction, images, and themes obtained from a particular Buddhist context. It may be assumed that both modalities have some kind of soteriological motivation behind them though the extent to which a poem was composed with that in mind might have differed considerably from poet to poet.

PREVIOUS JAPANESE SCHOLARSHIP ON BUDDHIST *WAKA* AND *SHAKKYŌ-KA* AND THE PROBLEM OF TERMINOLOGY

Most Japanese scholars refer globally to the Buddhist *waka* in the third through seventh anthologies as "*shakkyō-ka*."[14] Compounding the problem of whether or not a *waka* can be called a *shakkyō-ka* if it is not found in a book of the same name is the fact that Japanese scholars also use other rubrics in an attempt to describe the exact nature of these poems. One of the most common (and overlapping) terms for *shakkyō-ka* based upon a passage of text or a chapter title or a sūtra title is *hōmon-ka* (*waka* on the Dharma gate). Other terms include *kyōshi-ka* (*waka* on the essence or import of a scriptural passage or text, very similar to *hōmon-ka*), *kyōri-ka* (*waka* on a Buddhist doctrine or principle), and *Bukkyō-ka* (*waka* on the teachings of Buddhism). A review of some of the Shōwa-era scholarship that has shaped the study of *shakkyō-ka* demonstrates many different responses to problems of terminology and typology.

Two of the earliest scholars from the Shōwa era to address the topic of "*shakkyō-ka*" were Fukui Kyūzō in 1934 and Sakaguchi Genshō in 1935.[15] Fukui's work appeared in *Tanka kenkyū* under the title "Shakkyō waka ni tsukite." In his article, Fukui presents a short history of what he calls both "*shakkyō waka*" and "*shakkyō-ka*,"

---

14. I will use quotations around the word "*shakkyō-ka*" if a scholar or scholars tends to use that word as a homogenizing rubric for all *waka* on Buddhist themes.

15. A six-volume collection of Buddhist *waka* entitled *Shakkyō kaei zenshū* was also published in 1934 (and reprinted in 1978). As the title suggests, the editors and compilers used the word *shakkyō-ka* indiscriminately for any poem considered to have a Buddhist theme. Takakusu Junjirō, Fukui Kyūzō et al, eds., *Shakkyō kaei zenshū* (Tokyo: Tōhō Shuppan, 1934 [1978]).

starting with the famous Kataokayama *waka* attributed to Shōtoku Taishi, some *waka* on Buddhist themes from the *Man'yōshū,* and the *bussokuseki-ka* (poems on the footprints of the Buddha) at Yakushi-ji.[16] He ends his article with brief mentions of Dōgen (1200–1253), Musō Kokushi (1275–1351), and Eisai (1141–1215) as well as the fourteenth and seventeenth imperial anthologies *Gyokuyōshū* (1313–1314) and *Fugashū* (1344–1346), but makes no effort to contextualize any of the poems he identifies. He prefaces his history with assertions about "our ancestors" (*wareware ga sosen*) of the Japanese "people" or "nation" (*kokumin*), stressing the role that the Japanese played in aestheticizing Buddhism: "our ancestors were the people who ... aestheticized (*geijutsuka shita*) Buddhism."[17] This is followed later in the article with another nationalistic reference to the Saishō-ō-kyō and Ninnō-kyō Sūtras that existed "in my country as essential to [preserving] the nation-state" (*kokka hon'i no waga kuni ni*).[18] In the end, Fukui's article is little more than a polemic about the accomplishments of Japanese poets and what value these accomplishments held for the *kokumin.* However, it did at least attempt to identify the kinds of poems that might be regarded as "*shakkyō-ka*," though he made no attempt to define the rubric.

Sakaguchi Genshō devotes considerable space to Buddhist *waka* in his work *Nihon Bukkyō bungaku josetsu,*[19] without the nationalistic tone of Fukui's article. In the Preface to his section on Buddhist *waka,* Sakaguchi points to three general areas of inquiry with which he is concerned. First, "he does not want to forget" (*wasuretakunai*) the particular "social circumstances" (*shakaiteki jōsei*) that led to the reflection of "a single Buddhist ideology" (*hitotsu no Bukkyōteki shisō*) in literature. Second, he says he will consider how Buddhist doctrines (*kyōri*) in literature ought to be categorized (*dono hanchū*

---

16. Shōtoku Taishi's poem will be discussed in Chapter 3, while the *Man'yōshū waka* and the *bussokuseki-ka* will be discussed in Chapter 2.

17. Fukui Kyūzō, "Shakkyō waka ni tsukite," *Tanka kenkyū* (April 1934), 316.

18. Ibid., 319.

19. Sakaguchi Genshō, *Nihon Bukkyō bungaku josetsu* (Tokyo: Keibunsha, 1935, reprinted by Kokusho Kankōkai, 1972), 231–258.

ni zokuseshimu beki ka), meaning apparently not only the doctrine but also the kinds of literature. Third, he states that he is interested in how the "content of Buddhist ideology" (*Bukkyō no shisō naiyō*) that is reflected in literature developed over time *or* how a single work (of literature) that reflects Buddhist ideology induced a certain "flavor" (*aji*), or effect.[20]

Like Fukui, Sakaguchi's approach is chronological: he starts with poetry in the *Man'yōshū* and the *bussokuseki-ka* of Yakushi-ji, but does not regard them as *shakkyō-ka*. In a separate section titled "Shakkyō-ka no hatten" (The Development of *Shakkyō-ka*), Sakaguchi separates the rubric *shakkyō-ka* from the Nara period and assigns it to the Heian period instead.[21] He identifies the "characteristics" (*tokushoku*) of poems in the *Shūishū*, and passes judgment on the *shakkyō-ka* in the *Goshūishū*, saying that its compiler, Fujiwara no Michitoshi (1047–1099), still did not have a clear idea of what kind of poetry belonged there.[22]

Sakaguchi also focused upon the role of Tendai Buddhism, and in particular that of Ryōgen (912–985), abbot of Enryaku-ji, in reviving the temple complex on Mount Hiei and the influence that such a revival might have had on composing *waka* on Buddhist themes. Sakaguchi closes his section on *waka* and Buddhism with a brief analysis of a few "*shakkyō-ka*" in the *Kin'yōshū* and the *Shikashū* as well as a slightly longer analysis of a few poems in the independent books of "Shakkyō-ka" in the *Senzaishū* and the *Shinkokinshū*.[23]

Two scholars from the 1950s who addressed *shakkyō-ka* were Sekiguchi Sōnen (1952) and Hori Ichirō (1955). Sekiguchi's article, "Shakkyō-ka ron" (Discussion on *Shakkyō-ka*) appeared in the journal *Bungei kenkyū*.[24] Here the author proposed a bipartite typology of *shakkyō-ka* that was influential on some scholars later because, for the first time, it targeted the "problem" (*mondai*) of religiosity and

---

20. Sagakuchi, 1–2..
21. Ibid., 236.
22. Sakaguchi, 238–241 and 243–245.
23. Ibid., 243–254.
24. Sekiguchi Sōnen, "Shakkyō-ka ron," *Bungei kenkyū* 10 (June, 1952), 20–26.

aesthetics as they applied to Buddhist *waka*.[25] Sekiguchi's solution was to designate two broad categories that he called *daieiteki na uta* (topical *uta*) and *taikenteki na uta* (experiential *uta*).[26] For Sekiguchi the most successful *shakkyō-ka* were those that were able to "join" (*ketsugō*) these two categories (topical and experiential) whereby the "lyric flavor" (*jojōmi*), and thus its aesthetic value, were preserved in the emotions of the author as they related to the poem's topic (*daiei*). Sekiguchi concludes with the judgment that the *shakkyō-ka* in the *Shinkokinshū* (1206) more successfully fused these two aspects than the *shakkyō-ka* in the *Senzaishū*.[27]

In an article from the journal *Indogaku Bukkyōgaku kenkyū* in 1955, Hori Ichirō returned to the historical process by which "*shakkyō-ka*" came to be formed.[28] Already addressed by both Fukui and Sakaguchi, the historical development of "*shakkyō-ka*" was well known by this time, yet Hori claimed he would take a perspective that regarded these poems as a "problem of Buddhist history" (*Bukkyō-shi no mondai*) rather than "the problem of literary history" (*bungaku-shi no mondai*).[29] This four-page article does not give him room in which to address this distinction. Hori focuses his attention on the Buddhist diction and themes of poems from the era of the *Man'yōshū* to the *Shūishū*, placing more emphasis on the earlier anthology. He is careful to make a distinction between "Buddhist *waka*" and "*shakkyō-ka*," a distinction that occurred sometime after Saichō composed his *anokutara sanmyaku sanbodai* poem (the fifth poem [1920] in the "Shakkyō-ka" book of the *Shinkokinshū*), but other than pointing out the new category of "Shakkyō" poems in the *Goshūishū* in his first sentence (a point to which he does not return), he does not speculate further about the significance of different terminology.

The first scholars to present more complex typologies of Buddhist

---

25. Ibid., 22.

26. Ibid.

27. Ibid., 26.

28. Hori Ichirō, "Shakkyō-ka seiritsu no katei ni tsuite," *Indogaku Bukkyōgaku kenkyū* vol. 3, no. 2 (March 1955): 11–15.

29. Ibid., 12.

waka were Yamada Shōzen in 1953 and Okazaki Kazuko in 1963. Both authors, like Fukui and Sakaguchi, homogenize all Buddhist *waka* under the umbrella term "*shakkyō-ka*," but their typologies do attempt to elucidate certain characteristics of those poems. Yamada's typology was presented, without much lasting effect on later scholars, in an article entitled "Kyōshi-ka no seiritsu (The Formation of *Kyōshi-ka*)" published in *Buzan gakuho* in 1953.[30] Yamada used the term *kyōshi-ka* (sūtra *shakkyō-ka*) before Okazaki did, but within the article itself substituted it with the term *hōmon-ka* (poems on the Dharma gate), which in contemporary scholarship is often used as an alternative term for *shakkyō-ka*. The overlapping meanings of the three terms Yamada uses within his article are not easy to resolve. Perhaps this confusion was due in part to the unsettled nature of identifying terminology for Buddhist *waka* in the Heian period, but it is also possible that Yamada had not yet worked out his typology to its full extent.[31]

Yamada's tripartite typology consists of the following: (1) *hōmon-ka* (indistinguishable from *kyōshi-ka*), (2) *waka* composed on the occasion of Buddhist services, lectures, and ceremonies (*butsuji hōe*), and (3) poems on the reflections and feelings of religious wonderment when a poet is faced with the profundity of the Buddhist teachings (*Bukkyōteki jukkai / eitan*).[32] For Yamada's second type (more an explanation than actual name), Okazaki uses the word *hōen-ka* (about which I will say more next), but the definitions provided by both scholars are indistinguishable. The same holds true for Yamada's third type of *shakkyō-ka*—again an explanation rather than a rubric—and Okazaki's fourth type: *jukkai(-ka)*. The only term not used in Yamada's typology but found in Okazaki's is *kyōri-ka*.

Okazaki's four-part typology was unveiled in a seminal article for *shakkyō-ka* studies in 1963 called "Shakkyō-ka kō: hachidaishū o

---

30. Yamada Shōzen, "Kyōshi-ka no seiritsu," *Buzan gakuho* 2 (November 1954): 131–142.

31. Kubota Jun concurs with the *Bukkyō jiten* definition of *hōmon-ka*, which, in essence, defines them as *kyōshi-ka*. "Hōmon-ka to shakkyō-ka," *Kyōten*, vol. 6 of *Nihon bungaku to Bukkyō* (Tokyo: Iwanami Shoten, 1994), 257–258. *Hōmon-ka* also refers to the book of Buddhist *imayō* in the *Ryōjin hisho* (1179).

32. No single term is provided for this category.

chūshin ni" (A Consideration of *Shakkyō-ka*: With a Focus on the First Eight Imperial Anthologies).[33] The typology she presents is: (1) *kyōri-ka* (doctrinal *shakkyō-ka*), (2) *kyōshi-ka* (scriptural *shakkyō-ka*), (3) *hōen-ka* (covenant *shakkyō-ka*), and (4) *jukkai* (reflective *shakkyō-ka*).[34] We may notice overlap in this typology: *kyōshi-ka* is often used to refer to poems on Buddhist doctrine (*kyōri-ka*) while *jukkai-ka* are often indistinguishable from *hōen-ka*. Okazaki's typology has become the most prevalent used by reference works such as *Waka daijiten* and *Bukkyō bungaku jiten*,[35] but some scholars and reference works either skip or modify her typology altogether. For example, the *Nihon koten bungaku daijiten* refers only to *hōmon kyōri no uta* (poems on Dharma scripture and doctrine) without reference to the rest of Okazaki's typology. Finally, it needs to be emphasized that the terms used for these types of *shakkyō-ka* were created by modern *waka* scholars, and did not appear in the collections of Heian imperial anthologies.[36]

Kyōshi-ka (sūtra *shakkyō-ka*) in Okazaki's typology refers to *shakkyō-ka* based specifically on Buddhist scriptures. Under this type she places both *shakkyō-ka* based upon the general import of what is preached in the scriptures or on concepts from them. She also included *waka* based on topics that utilize the metaphors and parables in the scriptures, a short passage or verse from the scriptures, or are based upon the meaning of an individual chapter of a scripture. (For such poems, this information can frequently be found in the *kotobagaki* (headnote) and/or *dai* [topic], if there is one.)

Kyōri-ka (doctrinal *shakkyō-ka*), according to Okazaki, are *shakkyō-ka* based upon the principal doctrines preached in Buddhism

---

33. Okazaki Kazuko, "'Shakkyō-ka kō: hachidaishū o chūshin ni," *Bukkyō bungaku kenkyū* (Kyoto: Hōzōkan, 1963), 79–118.

34. These are my translations for each term.

35. *Waka daijiten* [hereafter WDJ] 2nd edition (Tokyo: Meiji Shoin, 1989), 460; *Bukkyō bungaku jiten*, 1st edition (Tokyo: Tōkyōdō Shuppan, 1980), 133–137.

36. *Jukkai-ka*, for example, is related to *eikai*, a term first used as a type of *kanshi*, or Chinese poem, in the second of the three imperial poetry anthologies of the early ninth century, while *kyōshi-ka* first appears as a term in a *hyakushu-uta* from 1355. (WDJ, 475 and 231).

in general as well as the import of more specialized Buddhist terms. Examples she offers are *waka* with *kotobagaki* or *dai* such as "[poems] composed on *gachirinkan*" (contemplation on the full moon disk), a Shingon practice, or "[composed on] the essence of the 'wisdom that recognizes the equality of all' when composing poems on the *tathāgatas* of the five wisdoms" (*byōdōshōchi*).

According to Okazaki, *hōen-ka* (covenant *shakkyō-ka*) are *shakkyō-ka* composed on the occasion of memorial ceremonies, lectures and readings on the scriptures, pilgrimages to temples, monasteries, and sacred sites, as well as on the feelings of joy and felicitation that arise during those occasions. These *shakkyō-ka* are the type that express a covenant (*kechien*) with the Buddhadharma. However, they can also express the sociality of a given occasion.

The fourth and final type of *shakkyō-ka* Okazaki proposes is *jukkai(-ka)*, *waka* that arise from the desire to express one's longing for salvation, ambition to seek the Dharma on the path, reflections on one's impermanent body, and revelations of religious feelings (thus, reflective *shakkyō-ka*). She characterizes such poems as more emotional in tone than the other four types, and as most often expressed after or as the result of an inspirational occasion.

Okazaki's definition of the word *shakkyō* (Buddhist teachings) is useful because she connects it immediately to *shakkyō-ka*: "'Shakkyō' ordinarily means the teachings of the Buddha—in other words, Buddhism. On the occasions when [compilers] collected Buddhist-related *waka* in collections of *waka*, the [*waka*] sometimes formed a category called 'shakkyō.' We call the *waka* of this category *shakkyō no waka* or *shakkyō-ka*."[37] Most notable about Okazaki's definition is its detailed categorization schema, one that will be important in this work. The advantage of this definition of *shakkyō-ka* is that it is neither vague nor all-inclusive, that it forms a relationship with (*ni kansuru*) the Buddhist teachings, without ever defining exactly what

37. Okazaki, "Shakkyō-ka kō," 79. It should be noted that the first appearance of the word *shakkyō* in a Japanese document is in an entry for the year 716 (Reiki 2) in the *Shoku Nihongi* (compiled 794–796). *Nihon kokugo daijiten*, 2nd edition, vol. 6 (Tokyo: Shogakkan, 2001), 1142.

that connection is. The definition is, however, also ahistorical in that it includes all *waka* on Buddhist themes after the *Shūishū* in the same category of "*shakkyō-ka.*"

Finally, as the author of the only full-length study of *shakkyō-ka*, Ishihara Kiyoshi deserves considerable credit for the extent of his research, though much is archival rather than theoretical. *Shakkyō-ka no kenkyū* (*Research on* shakkyō-ka) covers the *shakkyō-ka* in the third through eighth imperial poetry anthologies, as well as the *Hokke-kyō nijūhappon-ka* (*shakkyō-ka* on the twenty-eight poems on the Lotus Sutra) by Shunzei, Saigyō (1118–1189), and Jien (1155–1225).[38] Here Ishihara presumed that all of the poems he analyzed were *shakkyō-ka* whether they appeared in a *shakkyō-ka* book or not. For the most part, Ishihara's methodology was to trace the sūtra, doctrine, or occasion upon which a *waka* was composed and to link that source with his explication of the poem. He did not consider the poems he examined within the broader courtly context of the *waka* genre nor did he consider them as poems that were connected in any way to *waka* that proceeded or succeeded them in a sequence of poems. He presumed that the Buddhist source provided all the information necessary to understand the poem. Occasionally he also discussed rhetorical techniques used within a poem, but his primary effort was to provide a direct lineage from text, doctrine, or occasion to the "*shakkyō-ka*" in question.

In the Introduction to *Shakkyō-ka no kenkyū*, Ishihara noted that a "precise definition" (*meikaku na teigi*) of *shakkyō-ka* had not theretofore been presented. In order to redress this situation, Ishihara provided ten categories (*hanchū*) about which *shakkyō-ka* have been composed, though he later admitted there is both categorical imprecision and overlap among these. All of his categories (the Buddha, the various Buddhas and bodhisattvas, Buddhist doctrine, sūtra references, Buddhist occasions [*gyōji*], monks and nuns, temples and monasteries,

---

38. Ishihara, *Shakkyō-ka no kenkyū*, 1980. All appearances of the term "Lotus Sutra," as well as the names of all other Buddhist sūtras, will not be italicized in this study. The word "Sutra" without a long mark over the "u" refers only to the Lotus Sutra and the Heart Sutra. All other sūtra names have a long mark over the "u."

Buddhist contemplation of nature, Buddhist sentiments, Buddhist morals derived from nature) can be found in modern dictionary and encyclopedia entries for the term "*shakkyō-ka*," but Ishihara added one that is not: the category of Buddhist experience (*Bukkyō taiken*). Ishihara divided each chapter of his study (except for the sequences of Lotus Sutra chapter poems) into two principal kinds: "*shakkyō-ka*" that he called *taiken-ka* ("*shakkyō-ka*" based on personal experience) and those that he called *daiei-ka* ("*shakkyō-ka*" based on topics).[39] Within this broad categorical division Ishihara also employed Okazaki's original typology—*kyōri-ka, kyōshi-ka, hōen-ka,* and *jukkai,* but the larger distinction he drew was between topic and experience.

Ishihara is correct that we can detect a broad division of Buddhist *waka* or *shakkyō-ka* into two types—what he calls *daiei-ka* or *taiken-ka* (what I will call "scriptural" and "occasional"), but this sort of classification system is not entirely useful until after the *Shūishū*. What the dual classification system does provide, though, is an explanation for *waka* of sentiment that sometimes appear to have little or no connection to the actual teachings of Buddhism. To imply that there is no overlap between these two kinds of "*shakkyō-ka*" is also to overstate the importance of the categories: the words "occasional" and "scriptural" can describe one aspect of the poems' projects, but many other factors must be taken into consideration to fully characterize those projects.

JAPANESE *WAKA*: OF RELIGIOUS ROOTS?

The problems of Buddhist *waka* must be considered in conjunction with the larger issue of religious—that is, *kami*-centered—*waka* in general. The ancient myths that account for *waka*'s first appearance, and the usages to which such poetry was put, were reiterated throughout Japanese history in various religious, literary, and historical

---

39. In a footnote, Ishihara says his bipartite distinction was borrowed from Asaka Keiu, but this is a mistaken attribution. The correct attribution is Sekiguchi Sōnen in his "Shakkyō-ka ron," 21.

documents, but during the Nara period, and perhaps much later, the myths themselves were believed to make up part of Japan's national history.[40]

The origins of *waka* in the mytho-historical legends were first related in Chapter 20 of the *Kojiki* (compiled in 712).[41] Here it was said that Susano-o no Mikoto, the unruly brother of the Sun Goddess, Amaterasu Ōmikami, composed a song (*uta*), thought to be Japan's oldest poem.[42] In time, these songs *generated from* the *kami* would become the *waka* that were created as encomiums and supplications and *presented to* the *kami* during certain rituals. Examples of these Shintō *waka* (later called *jingi-ka*) can be found throughout the ancient, classical and medieval periods up to the final poem in the last imperial poetry anthology *Shinzokukokinwakashū* (completed in 1439). These Shintō-themed poems preceded their Buddhist companions, eventually called *shakkyō-ka*, by several hundred years, but together they express in poetic form the various "worlds" of Japanese religion.

Religious Worlds and Cultural Porosity

The concept of "worlds" in religious studies was most fully developed by William E. Paden in *Religious Worlds: The Comparative Study of Religion*. While Paden uses the word "worlds" to refer to different religions in the world, this concept can be expanded to refer to the various "worlds" that exist within one religion, as he understands religion to be "aspectual or multidimensional." He writes, "Religion can involve feeling and mystical experience, but also political, institutional structure. It may be about nature and it may be about self. It is expressed in symbols and ideas, but also in

---

40. Sakamoto Tarō, *The Six National Histories of Japan*, John S. Brownlee, trans. (Vancouver and Tokyo: UBC Press and the University of Tokyo Press, 1991), 51–56.

41. Donald L. Philippi, trans., *Kojiki* (Princeton and Tokyo: Princeton University Press and the University of Tokyo Press, 1968), 91.

42. As one of the footnotes to this chapter says, "This song, the first in both the *Kojiki* and the *Nihon Shoki*, has traditionally been regarded as the oldest Japanese poem." Ibid.

acts and rites; in art, and also in philosophies."[43] This perspective takes into account both the dynamic and static aspects of a religion, and describes literary space—"in art"—in which religious worlds can also be identified.

In applying the word "worlds" to the realms of experience found not only in religion but also in religious literature, we must ask what these worlds are and how they function. Here Paden is quite specific:

> The idea of world helps mediate the ideas of difference and commonality. In spite of their differences, religious worlds have in common certain general forms of mythic and ritual behavior. ... Religious language and behavior are not just beliefs and acts *about* the world, but actual ways through which a world comes into being. So the idea of worlds deals with the realm of particular historical matrices, yet also allows us to see typical or analogous ways by which worlds are constructed.[44]

The benefit of this characterization to the study of Buddhist *waka* is apparent in several ways. First, *waka* with Buddhist content are different in various ways and, therefore, not homogenous. One of the most obvious differences between individual Buddhist *waka* is the bipartite distinction created by Sekiguchi Sōnen between those that are based upon the *sentiment* of a religious occasion or experience and those that focus on a *teaching* (written, ritualistic, etc.) of Buddhism. This "world" may be referred to as a poem's religious environment. Second, the use of both religious and/or poetic (secular) diction can bring forth a religious world because of the intrinsic power of words themselves. This aspect of a poem's "world" is supported in Japan first by the concept of *kotodama* (word spirit) and then later the concept of *kyōgen kigo* (wild words and specious phrases), the latter formula drawn from an appeal that the Chinese poet Po Chü-i made

---

43. William E. Paden, *Religious Worlds: The Comparative Study of Religion* (Boston: Beacon Press, 1994), 12.

44. Ibid., 54

to accompany a copy of his poems presented to a Buddhist temple and used frequently throughout Japan's medieval period to justify the writing of secular verse. Third, *waka* with Buddhist content, poetic sequences in which they are found, and *shakkyō-ka* were composed and formulated at specific times in history. While it is not always possible to locate the origins (and thus the ultimate meaning, if such a thing is possible) of a Buddhist *waka*, it is possible to provide readings of the sequences in order to discover what sort of "world" the entire sequence is meant to convey, if any.

Helpful here also is the concept of porosity. One dictionary defines Japanese religion "as a coverall term to indicate the amorphous, shared elements of religious belief and practice ... where the 'walls' between religions tend to be porous."[45] Porosity is a concept used primarily in the sciences, but which can be adapted here to refer not only to the porosity between religions (*kami* faith and Buddhism, for example), but also between Buddhism and Japanese culture and society. Since Buddhism was not a religion native to Japan, we can speak of "walls" between it and Japanese culture. A highly porous society allows more nonnative practices and beliefs to thrive among and synthesize with native culture, while a less porous society prevents those same practices and beliefs from gaining strength within the culture.

According to this analogy, the porosity of the wall between native Japanese culture and Buddhism is subject to political and social vicissitudes in different historical eras. The early poems of the *Man'yōshū*, for example, show a lesser degree of porosity (fewer Buddhist elements) than do its later poems. The same is true for the porosity in the Kana Preface (*Kanajo*) to the *Kokinshū*, the first imperial anthology of Japanese *waka*. There we find native beliefs—what today we call Shintō, "the way of the gods"—girding the foundations of *waka* poetry and the imperial anthology project, with no evidence that Buddhism existed in the world of the Japanese court at all. On the other hand, there is a much higher degree of porosity in the seventh imperial anthology, *Senzaishū*, in which there are numerous

---

45. *Harper-Collins Dictionary of Religion*, 1st edition (San Francisco, 1995), 555.

references to Buddhism in its Preface and a new and independent book of Buddhist poetry for the first time.

THE RELIGIOUS WORLD OF KI NO TSURAYUKI'S *KANAJO*

The next five sections of this Introduction will theorize how Ki no Tsurayuki's conception of *waka,* that it possessed the capacity to transform the affairs of the world, would later become a conception of *waka* that possessed the capacity to transform one's desires (the cause of suffering) into a vehicle of salvation. For such a change to occur there had to be an understanding (realized or not, foregrounded or not) of the Buddhist conception of "no-self." This change in perspective can be explained with reference to what Buddhists call the five *skandhas.* The teachings of the five *skandhas* themselves may not have been widely taught in Heian Japan, but such teachings did pervade the Mahāyāna. The eventual conflation of *waka* and Buddhist enlightenment that characterizes twelfth century poetics could only have occurred if poets actually began to believe before that time that the teachings of self (*waka* poet desiring personal expression) could be transformed into the teachings of no-self (what we might characterize as "poet-less *waka*").

In the Preface (*Kanajo*) to the *Kokinshū,* its author Ki no Tsurayuki (884?–946?) wrote, "It is poetry which, without effort, moves heaven and earth, stirs the feelings of the invisible gods and spirits, smoothes the relations of men and women, and calms the heart of fierce warriors."[46] If the words "God," "Zeus," or "Shiva" were substituted here for "poetry" (*uta*) no reader would mistake the religious nature of this statement. However, in this context the word *uta*—a word synonymous with *waka*—carries the same kind of spiritual power. From a Western point of view, one does not expect the kind of power

---

46. Laurel Rasplica Rodd with Mary Catherine Henkenius, *Kokinshū: A Collection of Poems Ancient and Modern* (Princeton: Princeton University Press, 1984), 35.

that is usually reserved for religious texts like the Bible, the Buddhist sūtras, the Qur'an, and the Torah to be attributed to a literary form. But if we understand Tsurayuki correctly, Japanese poetry, short in form though it may be, has the awesome ability to regulate the existential conditions of life, maintain order in the physical world and affect the "gods and spirits" who, in turn, affect the lives of people. This assertion can be compared to the efficacy of a prayer, incantation, or *mantra* that mediates between the world of otherness and the world of "us-ness."

In the next two sentences of the *Kanajo*, Tsurayuki provides some "historical" context for the origins of poetry: "Such songs came into being when heaven and earth first appeared. However, legend has it that in the broad heavens they began with Princess Shitateru, and on earth with the song [*uta*] of Susano-o no Mikoto."[47] Here we understand that Japanese poetry not only affects the "gods and spirits" but also originates from them. Japanese people can "stir[s] the feelings of the invisible gods and spirits" because they were granted that power when they received and began to write in the 31-syllable *waka* form.

Tsurayuki further claims that Susano-o no Mikoto standardized *waka* on earth by determining that it should be comprised of thirty-one syllables. At this point in the Preface, the link between deities and human/*waka* is complete, yet Tsurayuki further tightens the connection by claiming that in recent times—"since the Nara period"—poetry has spread throughout the land. How was this accomplished? "In that era [Nara] the sovereign must truly have appreciated poetry, and during his reign Kakinomoto no Hitomaro of the Senior Third Rank was a sage of poetry. Thus rulers and subjects must have been one."[48] This statement places *waka* firmly in the creative hands of humans, since the sovereign was regarded as a *kami* descendant of Susano-o no Mikoto and those deities who preceded him.

The reason for this extended foray into the origins of *waka* poetry

---

47. Ibid. Susano-o no Mikoto, brother of the Sun Goddess, was on earth as a human incarnation of the deities from whom he was descended.

48. Ibid., 42.

is not to claim that all Japanese poetry is religious; it is not. What may be asserted, however, is that according to this mythology all *waka* are felt to partake of their *kami* origins. This is perhaps the reason, one speculates, that when the *kami*-sovereign Daigo (r. 897–930) commanded Tsurayuki and three other men of the court to compile the first anthology of Japanese *waka*, Tsurayuki reached back into Japan's early myths as told in *Kojiki* and *Nihongi* to provide the *gravitas* necessary for the task at hand.[49]

The final book of poems in the *Kokinshū* that Laurel Rodd translates as "Court Poetry" supports these statements of Tsurayuki. As Rodd writes, these poems "are a collection of poems and songs used in court rituals and religious ceremonies."[50] They are this, but there is also a short section of less courtly songs from the eastern provinces. Due to the presence of these eastern songs, it is difficult to argue for a thematic arc of religiosity that stretches from the *Kanajo* to the final poems in the book. However, the fact that most of the "court poems" are used in "court rituals and religious ceremonies" can be offered as further evidence of the relationship between *waka* and *kami* faith.

Finally, of crucial importance to the spiritual roots of Japanese poetry is the term *kotodama,* word spirit. Many literary scholars have pointed to *kotodama* as an example of the essential nondualistic nature of religion and literature in Japan. For example, Konishi Jin'ichi writes about the preclassical tradition: "There remained no distinction between literature and religion; both narratives and song drew on kotodama, the concept of words as incantatory and divine, so that poets not only transmitted meaning but imparted a sense of the supernatural."[51] Gary Ebersole supports this claim: "Song was sung and poetry recited not only for aesthetic pleasure but as a means of ordering and controlling potentially dangerous aspects of the world.

---

49. In addition to Ki no Tsurayuki, the other three compilers were Ki no Tomonori, Ōshikochi no Mitsune, and Mibu no Tadamine (all of the late ninth and early tenth centuries).

50. Ibid., 23.

51. Konishi Jin'ichi, *A History of Japanese Literature, Volume One: The Archaic and Ancient Ages,* Aileen Gatten and Nicholas Teele, trans. (Princeton: Princeton University Press, 1984), 61.

This sense of the efficacy of poetic language in and of itself survived until much later in Japanese history and was prominent in the Heian and Kamakura periods."[52]

The poetic language to which both Konishi and Ebersole refer is the language of Yamato, the native language of Japan. *Kotodama* does not reside in the Chinese language. The poetic forms in which we find either the word *kotodama* or an expression of its meaning run the gamut from *kagura uta* (songs of the *kami*) to the *chōka* (long poem), but it is clear that *kotodama* had its origins in songs and its effectiveness was later carried over into the *waka* poetic form as well. Ebersole feels that "the best known literary reference to the magical power of poetry ... is found in Ki no Tsurayuki's Japanese Preface to the *Kokinshū*. ..."[53] As we have seen, it is clear from the Preface that Tsurayuki thought *waka*—a court poetic form—was derived from the *kami* and, as such, contained their presence and their power. There is no mistaking the fact that the wellspring from which *waka* poetry came was spiritual in nature. The concept of *waka-as-kotodama* probably never disappeared completely from the consciousness of Japanese poets, but the increasingly social nature of the *waka* enterprise most likely overwhelmed this older notion, and gave birth to a style more satisfactory to the needs of the men and women of the court. The fascination with seasonal rhythms so common in early *Man'yōshū* poetry began to align itself with poets' desires to display their literary skills. In other words, a poet's desire for his or her beloved or for celebrating the seasonal changes became inseparable from the need to express that desire in a fixed poetic form.

For the concept of *waka-as-michi* to develop within the poetry tradition, poets needed to discard (or, at least, seem to discard) their desire for worldly success. They needed to understand how this desire or any other desire led to their own suffering and the suffering of others. The impetus for these discoveries came from the Buddhist temple complexes and their teachings, from governmental inequities,

---

52. Gary Ebersole, *Ritual Poetry and the Politics of Death in Early Japan* (Princeton: Princeton University Press, 1989), 19.

53. Ibid.

from the excruciating pressure of social prosperity as well as from the internal acknowledgement (supported by Buddhist teachings in a way that *kami*-centered worldview had not) that worldly success was short-lived and transient. So while some members took the drastic measure of leaving the court for the religious life, others sought comfort in the possibility that they could transform the worldly into the religious, by transforming the social and literary practice of composing *waka* into an increasingly religious practice.

Waka-as-*Michi*

In her analysis of the role of Buddhism in Japanese literature, Rajyashree Pandey clearly presents the historical arc by which *waka*, above all other literary forms, came to represent the artistic ideal to which one could apply the same kind of practice and discipline (*shugyō*) that one would need to attain the Buddhist ideal of enlightenment.[54] Her survey of the development of *waka* into a *michi* and *waka* as religious practice visits most of the primary participants in the discourse: Princess Senshi, Fujiwara no Shunzei, Myōe Shōnin (1173–1232), Mujū Ichien (1226–1312), and Shōtetsu (1381–1459). Each of these writers contributed to the ongoing philosophical discussion that conflated the worldly and the religious, the samsaric and the nirvanic, and the artistic and the Buddhist. Rather than reiterate Pandey's analysis, however, it might be more useful here to speculate about how the mechanism of conflation evolved on an experiential level. If poets were going to write *waka* on Buddhist themes, believing that the experience would expedite their salvation, they needed to go beyond the conceptual—needed to experience how this conflation worked on an organic and personal level. Of course, it must have been useful to understand that the Tendai three truths (*santai*) conflated the provisional and the absolute producing the middle way (*chū*) or that the Shingon concept of enlightenment in this very body (*sokushin*

---

54. Pandey, *Writing and Renunciation in Medieval Japan,* 9–55.

jōbutsu) conflated the enlightened self with the unenlightened self, but how might such knowledge have been applied to the process of elevating the writing of a court poem of thirty-one syllables to a spiritual practice?

One answer to this question lies in the Buddhist description of the linear psychological process by which the self (that is, the unenlightened self) perpetuates its existence. Known as the five *skandhas*, the description of this process is a useful conceptual tool for comprehending how the men and women of the Heian court probably perceived the origins of suffering. However, the five *skandhas* can also be used to demonstrate how a Buddhist practitioner might thwart the perpetuation of an unenlightened self for the goal of enlightenment. The five *skandhas* may or may not have been a topic of discussion among the laymen and laywomen of the court, but they were fundamental to the teachings of Buddhism as they were understood throughout Asia. In order for us to comprehend how the writing of *waka*—and the writing of Buddhist *waka* in particular—might eventually serve as a path to salvation, we must first comprehend how it was considered to be an obstacle. It will be helpful to address this problem by explicating the five *skandhas* as *process* rather than as *concept*.

THE FIVE *SKANDHAS*

Found in both the Sutta (S: Sūtra) Pitaka as well as the Abhidhamma (S: Abhidharma) Pitaka of the early Pāli texts, the five *skandhas*, or aggregates, are usually defined as the factors of which a person or self (*pudgala*) is comprised, but also as the factors which cause suffering (S: *duhkha*).[55] In what is usually considered to be the first sermon the Buddha delivered about the Four Noble Truths, the *Samyutta nikāya*, he says, "And this is the Noble Truth of Sorrow. Birth is sorrow, age is sorrow, disease is sorrow, death is sorrow; contact

---

55. I will use the Sanskrit word *skandha* in my own writing, but will not replace the Pāli word with the Sanskrit where it appears in quotations. Hereafter, Pāli words will be designated with a "P" and Sanskrit words with an "S" followed by the word.

with the unpleasant is sorrow, separation from the pleasant is sorrow, every wish unfulfilled is sorrow—in short all the five components [aggregates] of individuality are sorrow."[56]

In addition to the Four Noble Truths, the doctrine of the five *skandhas* is used to explain the inherent selflessness (*ānatman*) of a person. As Mathieu Boisvert explains, "[The five *skandhas*] must not be mistaken for a permanent entity since beings are nothing but an amalgam of ever-changing phenomena."[57] In this regard, the five *skandhas*, which are ultimately impermanent, are not so much factors of a person or self as they are "processes or events with which one is constituted that one needs to understand in order to achieve Enlightenment."[58]

According to Boisvert, the five *skandhas* "are variously translated as matter or form (S and P: *rūpa*); sensation, emotion or feeling (S and P: *vedanā*); recognition or perception (P: *saññā*; S: *samjñā*); karmic activity, formation, or force (P: *sankhāra*; S: *samskāra*); and consciousness (P: *viññāna*; S: *vijñāna*)."[59] He goes on to explain that the standard translations need to be viewed with a critical eye since they can mean more than one thing in the early Pāli texts. While it is certainly important to contextualize the usage of the five *skandhas* in the original texts, it is also important for Western readers to be diligent about their own presuppositions when it comes to words like "emotion," "perception," and "formation," which may carry connotations in English that they do not have in Pāli or Sanskrit.

In essence, the five *skandhas* are an explanation for how the self continually reconfirms its existence: according to this understanding, it is through such continual reconfirmation that we come to believe in the mistaken idea of a permanent self. The *skandhas* are divided into two parts: the first *skandha* belongs to the body and the second

---

56. W. M. Theodore de Bary, ed., *The Buddhist Tradition in India, China, and Japan* (New York: The Modern Library, 1969), 16.

57. Mathieu Boisvert, *The Five Aggregates: Understanding Theravāda Psychology and Soteriology* (Delhi: Sri Satguru Publications, 1997), 4.

58. Sue Hamilton, *Identity and Experience: The Constitution of the Human Being According to Early Buddhism* (London: Luzac Oriental, 1996), xxiv.

59. Boisvert, *The Five Aggregates*, 4.

through fifth *skandhas* belong to the mind. The reconfirmation of the self is explained in the following way.

First, the *skandha* of "form" can be understood either as the body or as matter that exists apart from the body. In this particular *skandha*, there is no psychophysical reaction either in one's mind or to the world around it.

The second *skandha*—"sensation, emotion, or feeling"—is more adequately translated by the first of these terms than either "emotion" or "feeling." The second *skandha* is more concerned with the initial sensations experienced either by the body alone or the body upon some matter or form. Sensation is nothing more than the initial interplay between a body and some matter—in other words, that which is gained through our senses. At this point of the encounter, the mind has not yet appeared and has made no evaluation or judgment of what it has experienced or seen; it is simply processing the light and sound waves in the eye and ear, touch and taste sensations on the skin and tongue, and olfactory sensations in the nose. The traditional teachings of the *skandhas* identify this *skandha* as what Boisvert calls a "bifurcation point."[60] This is the point at which craving *can* arise. It is not, however, "the only causal factor involved in the production of craving."[61]

With the third *skandha*, the body and the mind have their first opportunity to interact in a very fundamental way toward what the body has sensed. Traditionally, the perception *skandha* is expressed in three ways: with pleasure, with displeasure, or with neither pleasure nor displeasure, that is, neutrally. In the sense that this *skandha* is interpretive of the previous *skandha*—sensation— it is an "interpretation of reality that [is] not conducive to insight and that generate[s] obsessions."[62] It should be noted that there are both unwholesome and wholesome perceptions, and it is to the unwholesome perceptions that the previous sentence refers. If one were to replace unwholesome perceptions with wholesome perceptions

---

60. Ibid., 71.
61. Ibid., 72.
62. Ibid., 89.

(perceptions of impermanence, suffering, and selflessness), one could avoid the generation of "craving, aversion, clinging and becoming, all of which fall under the next aggregate: *sankhāra* [S: *samskāra*]."[63]

All of what we ordinarily think of as falling under the definition of emotion and feeling in Western psychology falls under the fourth *skandha*, *sankhāra* (Pāli) or *samskāra* (Sanskrit), in this schema, frequently translated as "mental formations." It is here that we fully develop our attachments and aversions. At this point, whether consciously or not, the self pursues or avoids certain aspects of the world, whereas in the previous *skandha* the perception is a more provisional, corporeal interpretation. If one were to replace the unwholesome perceptions with wholesome perceptions, then the fourth *skandha* would not generate itself.

Volitional activity is an essential part of the fifth and final *skandha*, translated as "consciousness." At this point, the self actively pursues, and arranges its activities around, that which it has identified as positive and avoids that which it has identified as negative. Since neutrality, or "ignorance" as it is known in Buddhism, is also a position that one can take toward the world, the mind can also pursue a stance in which one consciously ignores the world or something in it. However, this still constitutes a reaction as distinguished from enlightened nonattachment. Because of the active nature of this *skandha*, the rebirth of the entire five-*skandha* process is regenerated.

In Japan, the *skandhas* were introduced primarily through the Kusha school of the Nara period.[64] However, the *skandhas* also played a role in other schools' sutras and texts, many of which were significant to Japanese Buddhism.[65] Texts such as the *Mo-ho chih-kuan* (J: *Makashikan*) by Chih-i, the Lotus Sutra, and Aśvagosha's *Daijō kishin ron* (The Awakening of Faith) all contain references to

---

63. Ibid.

64. Richard Bowring, *The Religious Traditions of Japan 500-1600* (Cambridge: Cambridge University Press, 2005), 99–100. Bowring prefers the word "seminar" or "traditon" instead of "school."

65. Junjiro Takakusu, *The Essentials of Buddhist Philosophy* (Honolulu: University of Hawaii Press, 1947), 72–73.

the five aggregates (sometimes also called the five components). In the *Mo-ho chih-kuan*, Chih-i refers to the *skandhas* in his explanation of something the mind must engage with, in three of the four *samādhis* (constantly walking meditation, part walking/part sitting meditation, and neither walking nor sitting meditation).[66] In the Lotus Sutra, the five aggregates appear in at least two chapters: Chapter 3, Parable (*Hiyubon*) and Chapter 14, Comfortable Conduct (*Anrakugyōbon*). In Chapter 3, the gods Indra and Brahmā recount the Buddha's first turning of the dharma-wheel, where, they say, he "turned the Dharma-wheel of the four truths, / With discrimination preaching the dharmas, / The origination and extinction of their five collections [*skandhas*]."[67] In Chapter 14, the *skandhas* are referred to as the "Māras of the five *skandhas*" with which the Buddha's "saints and sages do battle."[68] And in the *Daijō kishin ron* (*The Awakening of Faith*), Aśvaghosha says that in order to enter the realm of Suchness, one must examine "the five components" which may be "reduced to matter (object) and mind (subject)."[69] These examples leave no doubt that the members of court knew the concept of the five *skandhas* at this time to the extent that they read or heard the sūtras.

THE FIVE *SKANDHAS* AND THE *KANAJO*

In the schema to which they belong, the five *skandhas* describe the process by which attachments to a permanent self and the world

---

66. See Daniel B. Stevenson and Neal Donner, *The Great Calming and Contempla-tion: A Study and Translation of the First Chapter of Chih-i's* Mo-ho chih-kuan (Honolulu: Kuroda Institute and the University of Hawaii Press, 1993), 241, 243, 258, 281, and 298.

67. Leon Hurvitz, trans., *Scripture of the Lotus Blossom of the Fine Dharma* (New York: Columbia University Press, 1976), 57; Sakamoto Yukio and Iwamoto Yutaka, *Hokke-kyō*, vol. 1 (Tokyo: Iwanami Bunko, 1989), 156.

68. Hurvitz, *Scripture of the Lotus Blossom*, 219; Sakamoto and Iwamoto, *Hokke-kyō*, vol. 2, 272.

69. In this case, "matter" refers to the first *skandha* (*rūpa*) while the remaining four *skandhas* are "mind." Yoshito S. Hakeda, trans., *The Awakening of Faith: Attributed to Aśvaghosha* (New York: Columbia University Press, 1967), 72.

are continually reproduced. This process is usually presented as habitual in a negative sense, and therefore something from which we need to extricate ourselves. Outside the teachings, however, writers often describe their attachments to the self and the world in positive terms. The desire for love and expressions of longing for beauty have been extolled throughout human history, not less so in Japan than elsewhere.

For example, the first two sentences of the Kana Preface to the *Kokinshū* are a particularly clear illustration of how one's attachment to a self and to desires is depicted as the source of inspiration for artistic creation. The author Ki no Tsurayuki certainly had no intention of describing the five *skandhas* in this text; rather, he is describing the artistic process as it was conceived at that moment in history. Tsurayuki compares Japanese court poets of his time to those of the past, when they were the attendants of sovereigns of old (*inishie*), and when they were summoned by those sovereigns to write poems on the morning blossoms of spring (*haru no hana no ashita*) or the evenings under an autumn moon (*aki no tsuki no yogoto*). At this time, he wrote, the poet would wander off far away from his home (*tayori naki tokoro ni madoi*) and tread into the darkness (*yami ni tadoreru*) in order to look into his heart (*kokorogokoro o mitamaite*) for inspiration. Concluding the *Kanajo*, Tsurayuki adds, "Those who know the *uta* and understand the heart of things (*koto no kokoro*) will venerate the past just as they gaze [longingly] at the moon in the great sky. How could they not be attached to the [auspicious] present era?"[70] In this passage, Tsurayuki calls on all poets to revere the Japanese poetic tradition and to exemplify that tradition in their own poetry. The way in which Tsurayuki makes that connection to the past is explained in the first two sentences of the *Kanajo*, where he writes about the creative source for all poetry: the heart itself.

The Rodd-Henkenius translation of both sentences reads, "The seeds of Japanese poetry lie in the human heart and grow into leaves of ten thousand words. Many things happen to the people of this world, and all that they think and feel is given expression description

---

70. Kojima and Arai, *Kokinwakashū*, 17–18.

of things they see and hear."[71] The first sentence contains a description of the first four *skandhas*.[72] The seed, or *tane*, of this sentence is the first *skandha* of form. We have neither good nor bad nor neutral reactions to this seed, which is matter without affect. When the seed produces feelings in the human heart (the second *skandha*), what occurs there is still provisional. These are not fully developed psychological feelings, but preliminary neural reactions coming from the initial contact one has had with some object. The production of a feeling then gives rise to (*narerikeru*) a perception, the third *skandha*, which is characterized here as a process. What we perceive, according to the *Kanajo* is the phenomenal (*dharmic*) world (*yorozu no koto*). Our perceptions (pleasure, displeasure, or neutrality) then are translated into the "mental formations" of language or words, one of the principal vehicles by which the fourth *skandha* (our thoughts, our attitudes) is expressed. Stated more simply: the Yamato song (comes forth) when the **form** (the seed) is changed by the **feelings** (in the human heart) and **transforms** (perceives) the myriad *dharmas* of the world into (as) **formations** of leaves of words.

The second sentence of the *Kanajo* expresses the final *skandha*—consciousness—as a kind of collective summation of the first four *skandhas*.[73] "Many things happen to the people of this world, and all that they think and feel is given expression in description of things they see and hear." Here we see that people experience actions (*koto*) and deeds (*waza*) with their senses (*miru mono, kiku mono*) that are then processed (*omou*) in the heart or mind (*kokoro*) and generated in language (*iidaseru*). Since each of the *skandhas* is dependent upon the one before it, the expression of all four in a single sentence represents the consciousness that is created by putting each into motion simultaneously. In the first sentence, the author tells us that the Japanese poem arises out of the factors of form, feelings, perceptions,

71. Rodd, *Kokinshū*, 35.

72. In Japanese, this sentence reads: *Yamatouta wa, hito no kokoro o tane to shite, yorozu no koto no ha to zo narerikeru.* Kojima and Arai, *Kokinwakashū*, 4.

73. In Japanese, this sentence reads: *Yo no naka ni aru hito, koto, waza, shigeki mono nareba, kokoro ni omou koto o, miru mono, kiku mono ni tsukete, iidaseru nari.* Ibid.

and formations, but when these steps are understood as a process (*kokoro ni omou koto o*), this understanding creates a consciousness (about poetry) within people in the world (*yo no naka ni aru hito*).

It is not surprising that the teachings of the five *skandhas* align so well with Tsurayuki's description of the artistic process because Tsurayuki's point of view is grounded in the sentiments of the human heart, sentiments that are subject to the vicissitudes of *samsāra*. For Tsurayuki, feelings, emotions, and sensitivity produced great poetry. A literary life that was void of such sentiment would have been counterintuitive to the kind of life that he and his fellow court poets wished to live. When poets began to realize that the goal of composing "worldly letters," including poetry, was antithetical to the goal of achieving bodhisattvahood—if the process of literary composition meant strengthening and supporting the unenlightened self—then a new, enlightened basis for literary endeavors would have to be developed, if these endeavors were to continue in an increasingly Buddhist court culture.[74]

THE FIVE *SKANDHAS* AND BUDDHIST *WAKA*

If we understand the opening two sentences of the *Kanajo* as a description of the *skandha* process as it is demonstrated in the poet's self toward the activity of writing poetry, then we see a reinterpretation of that activity in the Preface to the *Hosshin wakashū*. Here the author, Princess Senshi, describes a new use for the *waka* form that is not grounded in our attachments, but instead grounded in the enlightened words of the Buddha. In the same way that unwholesome perceptions (third *skandha*) can be replaced with wholesome perceptions, and thereby derail the seemingly unending circularity of the unenlightened self, Senshi believes that replacing the ordinary topics of *waka* with topics that come directly from the Buddhist texts will accomplish the same goal.

---

74. Hurvitz, *Scripture of the Lotus Blossom*, 208; Sakamoto and Iwamoto, *Hokke-kyō*, vol. 2, 244.

This new use for *waka* came to Senshi, she explains, after she comprehended the "virtue of song and realized that writing verse is a service to the Buddha."[75] Senshi realized this, she reports, when she understood serendipitously that the written words of the Buddha were also in verse form. This is not the only argument with which Senshi defends her verse, however. She also defends it by virtue of the fact that she has been "imbued with the sentiments of [her] country/ home [*sōshi*]" where she learned to compose the thirty-one-syllable *waka*. Her purpose for compiling the *Hosshin wakashū* was, as the title says, to "awaken the heart" (*kokoro o hossu*). What hearts will awaken to is the possibility of "rebirth [enlightenment]," when one will ascend to the Pure Land and sit "atop the ninth [and highest] level lotus pedestal." So she clearly believed that *waka* can awaken human beings to enlightenment—a belief that had never before found expression in Japan. Senshi also refers to various chapters of the Lotus Sutra to strengthen her case about what her collection can do and what it might do: first, as we might expect, she recognizes that the Buddha taught the truth of the One Vehicle of the Dharma Blossom (Chapter 2); second, she pronounces her veneration of the Buddha Many-Jewels (Prabhūtaratna, Chapter 11) to save all beings; and third, she vows to serve all beings just as the Bodhisattva Never-Disparaging (Sadāparibhūta, Chapter 20) did. By means of the first reference, she recognizes the direct link between what the Buddha taught and how he taught it (in *verse*); with the second reference, she expresses her hope that, *by reading or hearing her poems*, people may join her in venerating the vow of the Buddha Many-Jewels; and with the third reference, she declares her desire to create a bond *even with those who would criticize her collection* and to serve them in the same way that Bodhisattva Never-Disparaging served all who criticized him. Finally, Senshi calls the writing of verse "the path of *waka*" (*waka no michi*), a phrase that was not in common use until the Kamakura period or later. Clearly, she is referring to *waka* composition as a disciplinary practice since she locates her

---

75. Translation by author. For the original text, see Ishihara Kiyoshi, *Hosshin wakashū no kenkyū* (Osaka: Izumi Shoin, 1983), 71–72.

training in this path as having occurred before she entered the gate of Buddhism (*aji no mon*). Despite that, she says, both paths can be reconciled by writing verse on passages from various sūtras.

With a remarkable combination of logic and emotion, Princess Senshi reinterprets Tsurayuki's positive claim that humans use *waka* to declare their sensual reactions (or attachments) to the world's various forms. In her view, those forms—whether they are blossoms, moon, dew, or a loved one—are indeed extraordinary, but they remind her also of the unavoidable suffering such attractions arouse in those who crave their pleasures. If one can derail the constant circularity inherent in reconfirming the unenlightened self by replacing unwholesome perceptions with wholesome perceptions, Senshi also believes that the potentially negative consequences derived from composing worldly *waka* can also be circumvented if the poet replaces unwholesome topics with wholesome ones. In short, while she does not exactly equate Buddhism and the writing of *waka,* as the later phrase *kadō soku butsudō* would come to do, she comes very close to this kind of formulation. The only word her Preface lacks is the word *soku,* a Chinese graph signifying identity and meaning "is none other than" or "is equal to."

The implication of Senshi's argument is that one can use A in order to accomplish B. This would appear to put the composition of *waka* and the awakening of the heart to enlightenment on the same ontological plane, but in fact it is only through maintaining the bifurcation—a duality—between secular art and Buddhist practice that art can *become* a discipline as rigorous as Buddhist meditative disciplines. As Kamens says in his study on the *Hosshin wakashū,* the art of *waka* for Princess Senshi is "comparably transformative" to the practices of Buddhism, but still there is a significant semantic difference between this and A equals B.[76] Princess Senshi herself was certainly aware of the duality inherent in her writings since her gender, according to the teachings, presented a similar obstacle: as a woman, she could not either *be* or *become* enlightened. She needed to transform

76. Kamens, *The Buddhist Poetry of the Great Kamo Priestess,* 73.

into the body of a man to *be* enlightened. In turn, this also implied that her *waka* could not *be* either enlightened or enlightening. We cannot know if Senshi took this argument to its logical conclusion, but since she specifically mentions in her Preface that being born a woman is a hindrance, certainly she was aware of it.

The influence of Senshi's collection or her Preface on court poets living at the time or in the decades to come is unknown. However, Senshi's place at (or at least near) the court, her salon of *waka* poets, and her own recognition as a poet, indicate how extensive that influence probably was. The ideas expressed in her Preface were possibly not controversial at the time; they may have been part of a developing zeitgeist. This could help to explain the inclusion of *waka* on Buddhist themes in the *Shūishū* (presented to the sovereign five years before the *Hosshin wakashū* was written and compiled) as well as the inclusion of a subcategory of *shakkyō-ka* in the *Goshūishū* compiled in 1086.

CATEGORIES AND TERMINOLOGY

As stated earlier, terminology is a central focus of this study. Buddhist *waka* in the *Shūishū*, *Kin'yōshū*, and *Shikashū* are not compiled separately from the other *waka* with which they are included. Instead, the Buddhist *waka* in the *Shūishū* are compiled in the "Aishō-ka" (Laments) book (and thus, strictly speaking, are *aishō-ka*), while the Buddhist *waka* in the *Kin'yōshū* and the *Shikashū* are compiled in a "Zōka" (Miscellaneous) book (and thus, are *zōka*). One might argue that these poems should be referred to as "Buddhist *aishō-ka*" or "Buddhist *zōka*," but, since the rationale for discussing these *waka* is predicated on the basis of theme first and rubric second, I will refer to them simply as "Buddhist *waka*" or "*waka* on Buddhist themes." When, in the *Goshūishū* and the *Senzaishū*, Buddhist *waka* are designated as *shakkyō-ka,* I will use the latter term for them. Any discussion of *waka* on Buddhist themes that is inclusive of all these *waka* wherever they are found will refer to them to as "Buddhist *waka*." One final caveat is that the *waka* on Buddhist subjects (not themes) found in the *Man'yōshū, Kokinshū,* and *Gosenshū* will be referred to by the phrase "Buddhistic *waka*" following the lead of Muraishi Esho.[77]

One might ask whether there are differences between "Buddhist *waka*" (or "*waka* on Buddhist themes") and *shakkyō-ka.* There are some differences between the Buddhist *waka* in the *Shūishū* and the *shakkyō-ka* in the *Goshūishū,* but there are far fewer differences between the *shakkyō-ka* in the *Goshūishū* and the Buddhist *waka* in the *Kin'yōshū* and the *Shikashū.* In other words, because the thematic of the lament (*aishō-ka*) was more clearly defined than the thematic of a miscellaneous poem (*zōka*), the Buddhist *waka* in the *Shūishū* assume some of the thematic overtones of the lament. By the time the lament was dissociated from Buddhist *waka,* starting with the *Goshūishū,* a more clearly Buddhist thematic slowly evolved. During the twelfth century, this evolution finally resulted in an independent kind of *waka* that could be compiled within a separate book called "Shakkyō-ka."

Running parallel with the problem of terminology, and of equal importance, is the matter of categorization. Okazaki Kazuko has called the appearance of a separate, though not independent, section of *shakkyō-ka* in the *Goshūishū* "epoch-making" (*kakkiteki*) in the history of the imperial poetry anthology. While this may seem to be an exaggerated description of nineteen poems on Buddhist topics, it does suggest the significance of an act that brought a foreign religious tradition under the official purview of the imperial court.[78] More importantly, however, the inclusion and classification of poems on Buddhist topics in the *Goshūishū* also suggest a developmental change in the function of *waka* from a poetic form that is primarily lyric (and partially narrative) in its modes to one that retains lyrical and narrative aspects but increasingly utilizes the meditative mode as well. This developmental change in function parallels an increasing concern among writers of *waka* about their personal attachments to

---

77. Muraishi Esho, "Buddhism and Literature in Japan," *Understanding Japanese Buddhism,* Hanayama Shōyū, ed. (Tokyo: Japan Buddhist Federation, 1978), 185–186.

78. Okazaki, "Shakkyō-ka kō," 89.

the sensual, secular world of the court and the possible soteriological value of writing *waka* on themes that negate those personal attachments. Unlike the Buddhist *waka* collected in the Lament book of the *Shūishū*, these poems—at least according to their headnotes—deal directly with the texts and occasions of Buddhism whether or not they attempt to express any kind of truth about those texts or occasions.

It is possible to support Okazaki's claim that the category of *shakkyō-ka* in the *Goshūishū* was "epoch-making" using a relatively new set of scholarly tools drawn from the field of cognitive science. Edward Slingerland defined cognitive science in *What Science Offers the Humanities: Integrating Body and Culture* as "[a] blanket term for a set of disciplines—artificial intelligence (AI), philosophy of consciousness, and various branches of neuroscience, psychology, and linguistics—concerned with the empirical investigation of the human mind ..."[79] These disciplines may seem removed from the study of religion and literature, but an increasing number of scholars are applying cognitive science research to fields of study in the arts and humanities. In *Cognitive Science, Literature, and the Arts*, Patrick Colm Hogan says "... the arts are not marginal for understanding the human mind. They are not even one significant area. They are absolutely central."[80]

Cognitive linguist George Lakoff, in *Women, Fire and Dangerous Things: What Categories Reveal About the Mind*, supports this in his discussion about categorization: "Categorization is not a matter to be taken lightly. There is nothing more basic than categorization to our thought, perception, action, and speech."[81] Lakoff, in fact,

---

79. Edward Slingerland, *What Science Offers the Humanities: Integrating Body and Culture* (Cambridge: Cambridge University Press, 2008), 10.

80. Patrick Colm Hogan, *Cognitive Science, Literature, and the Arts: A Guide for Humanists* (New York and London: Routledge, 2003), 3. Recent works that have dealt with the cognitive foundations in literature are Mary Thomas Crane, *Shakespeare's Brain: Reading with Cognitive Theory* (Princeton and Oxford: Princeton University Press, 2001), Mark Turner, *Reading Minds: The Study of English in the Age of Cognitive Science* (Princeton: Princeton University Press, 1991), and Lisa Zunshine, *Why We Read Fiction: Theory of Mind and the Novel* (Columbus: Ohio State University Press, 2006).

81. George Lakoff, *Women, Fire and Dangerous Things: What Categories Reveal About*

elevates the study of categories to the level of a reassessment of how we perceive and conceive of our world: "To change the very concept of a category is to change not only our concept of the mind, but also our understanding of the world."[82] In light of this last statement, it is possible, even necessary, to view the development of *shakkyō-ka*—a new category of *waka*—as a re-visioning of the Heian world.

From where does the human desire to categorize arise, and why is understanding the human penchant for categorizing important to understanding the mind itself? In *The Oxford American Dictionary*, "category" is defined as "a class or division of people or things regarded as having particular shared characteristics."[83] In philosophy, the word's meaning is extended only slightly, "... one of a possibly exhaustive set of classes among which all things might be distributed."[84] But the sub-sense of this second definition is the most important for this study: "one of the a priori conceptions applied by the mind to sense impressions."[85] This aspect of the definition demonstrates a fundamentally dualistic view of the mind and the body. In this view, the mind applies itself *to* the sense impressions one feels in the body, as if the mind had a mind of its own and work to do *on* the body, that is, to make sense of or derive meaning from what the body is feeling. This concept is referred to as a disembodied theory of mind, and its source is objectivist philosophy which claims that the "structure [of reality] exists, independent of any human understanding."[86]

In a disembodied analysis of the mind, the body receives data input through its sensory motor structure. This data is then re-cognized by the mind—that is, analyzed through reason or imagination—and then re-presented in the world through language or other kinds of symbols. This three-step process assumes that our representational modes—writing, debating, speaking, ritualizing, drawing, casting—re-present

---

the Mind (Chicago and London: The University of Chicago Press, 1987), 5.

82. Ibid., 9
83. *The Oxford American Dictionary* (Oxford University Press, 2001), 271.
84. Ibid.
85. Ibid.
86. Lakoff, *Women, Fire, and Dangerous Things*, 159.

the true nature of the world. However, Mark Johnson in *The Meaning of the Body: Aesthetics of Human Understanding* warns us about the limitations of this view, claiming that the mind is embodied rather than disembodied: "An embodied cognition must avoid one of the most dangerous dualistic traps of Western philosophy, namely, asking how something inside the 'mind' (i.e., ideas, thoughts, mathematical symbols) can represent the outside (i.e., the world.)"[87]

Embodied cognition—the theory that we cognize with the brain *and* the body (that is, the mind) as we interact with our natural or social environment—is a relatively new view of mind and consciousness.[88] It uproots the disembodied theory of cognition with what Lakoff and Mark Johnson claim in *Philosophy in the Flesh: The Embodied Mind and Its Challenge to Western Thought* are "two kinds of evidence: (1) a strong dependence of concepts and reason upon the body and (2) the centrality to conceptualization and reason of imaginative processes, especially metaphor, imagery, metonymy, prototypes, frames, mental spaces, and radial categories."[89] While some of this terminology may not be familiar to literary critics and religion scholars, not all of it is necessary for understanding two basic points: that concepts and reason are dependent upon the body and that they are grounded in imagination and creativity. Earlier in this same book, Lakoff and Johnson are even more direct about the importance of the body to the mind, "Our claim is ... that the very properties of concepts are created as a result of the way the brain and the body are structured and the way they function in interpersonal relations and in the physical world."[90]

---

87. Mark Johnson, *The Meaning of the Body: Aesthetics of Human Understanding* (Chicago and London: The University of Chicago Press, 2007), 113.

88. Researchers and scholars do not all understand embodied cognition the same way, but there seems to be a general consensus that is fundamental to what is called second-generation cognitive science. Gibbs says, "... there is an ever-growing literature to support a view of imagery, memory, and reasoning as intimately tied to bodily activity, such that higher-order cognitive processes are situated, embedded, and embodied." Raymond W. Gibbs, Jr., *Embodiment and Cognitive Science* (Cambridge: Cambridge University Press, 2006), 157.

89. George Lakoff and Mark Johnson, *Philosophy in the Flesh: The Embodied Mind and Its Challenge to Western Thought* (New York: Basic Books, 1999), 77.

90. Ibid., 37.

It should be apparent at this point that I do not regard categories as a kind of filing cabinet in the mind. Categories are conceptual, and concepts belong as much to the body as to the mind. The formation of a category like *shakkyō-ka* did not come about by mental acrobatics alone. A category of this sort that involves two different domains of knowledge—poetic and Buddhist—had to come about through the actual felt experiences of Heian literati who found sufficient similarities between the worlds of *waka* composition and Buddhism that a category of "*waka* on the teachings of the Buddha" became viable within the world of the imperial poetry anthology.

The fact that we can identify the first effort to categorize Buddhist *waka* as *shakkyō-ka* in the *Goshūishū* does not mean, however, that the poets of the court were not experiencing and being affected by Buddhism before that time. Since there are *waka* that contain Buddhist words (*butsugo*) as far back as the *Man'yōshū*, it is clear that certain aspects of Buddhist culture were being tracked within the poetic vision at least as early as the eighth century and probably before. The same can be said for aspects of Buddhism—again mostly through individual *butsugo*—found in the poems in the *Kokinshū* (905) and the *Gosenshū* (951). But at this time between the mid-eighth through mid-tenth centuries, poets and anthologizers had not yet experienced the practices, rituals, doctrines, and teachings of Buddhism sufficiently to imagine creatively any parallels between the composition of *waka* and the Buddhadharma.

In the same way that terminology is central to our understanding of Buddhist *waka,* so too is the matter of categorizing those poems in each of the imperial anthologies under discussion in this study.

TRANSLATION STRATEGY

The poems in this study have been translated in what could be called a "literary" style.[91] As Gideon Toury has said, the term "literary

---

91. All of the *waka* for this study were translated by Stephen D. Miller and Patrick Donnelly.

translation" has been "afflicted by *systematic ambiguity*," because it can refer either to the literary nature of the source text where the "retention of … [an] internal web of relationships" is the focus, or the resultant target text "in such a way that the product be acceptable as literary to the *recipient* culture."[92] Toury understands that both senses of the term can sometimes "concur," but the attempt to retain "[an] internal web of relationships" in the source text often threatens its reception by the culture of the target language text.

While a *waka*'s inclusion within an imperial poetry anthology is an indicator of its acceptability as a literary artifact, this in no way helps to clarify how its literariness might be rendered in English. And, of course, the differences between Western-style poems and Japanese *waka* are as numerous as they are substantial. As poems that were originally written in one or two vertical lines and in a calligraphic style unknown in the west, its very shape is one of the most immediately obvious differences. When one adds to this other formal aspects of *waka* such as syllabics (rather than stress) and the *ku* (rather than the line) that are essential to its form, the impossibility of retaining the *waka*'s written character in an English translation seems to be a foregone conclusion. It goes without saying that other defining factors of the *waka* such as rhetorical devices and diction are also extremely difficult to render into English.

One aspect that can be retained, however, is the poem *as* poetry. Any translator makes choices according to a hierarchy of values, whether consciously or unconsciously. Some translation values are mutually exclusive, so we have tried to travel a middle way, aesthetically speaking, between Scylla and Charybdis. We were aware that because of differences in the two languages, which had determined from antiquity the poetics of each, any translation of a *waka* into English could only have some sort of "family relationship" to the original at best. It was our limited goal—difficult enough—to convey in our translations the emotional and spiritual arguments of these poems in accurate versions that are also excellent poems in idiomatic, musical, contemporary English.

---

92. Gideon Toury, *Descriptive Translation Studies* (Amsterdam and Philadelphia: The John Benjamins Publishing Company, 1995), 168.

CONCLUSION

This study's argument—that the gradual formation of a new subgenre of Buddhist *waka* (that becomes *shakkyō-ka*) contributed to the formation of the medieval concept of *waka*-as-*michi*—will be based upon a close reading of five poetic sequences in the *Shūishū, Goshūishū, Kin'yōshū, Shikashū,* and *Senzaishū.* The presence of Buddhist *waka* starting in the third imperial poetry anthology was not only the introduction of a new subgenre, but also the beginning of a social, cultural, and religious endeavor to unite court practices with Buddhist goals. Specifically, this endeavor focused on the Buddhist goal of salvation (in various senses of this word) through poetic composition.

Fundamental to the Buddhist goal of salvation was the *path* (*michi*) of practice that led one to it. The men and women of the Heian court were not, for the most part, engaged in meditative discipline, but they did have a *michi* to follow: this path consisted of their knowledge of the Buddhist texts and teachings gained through an attendance at the Buddhist ceremonies, lectures, and rituals that were prevalent at the time. Their awareness of this path is more apparent in some poems than others, but the schematic constructions of the *Shūishū* Buddhist *waka* sequence and the *Senzaishū shakkyō-ka* sequence in particular prove the relevance of such schemas to Heian court culture.

Finally, using conceptual tools such as the five *skandhas*, the modes (lyric, narrative, meditative), and the modalities (heavenly/courtly, soteriological/courtly, soteriological/monastic) we can connect the goal of Buddhist salvation to the actual (religious) practice of writing *waka.* Describing how the modes were deployed in particular poems will demonstrate how Buddhist *waka* remained tethered to a literary practice rooted in the traditions of the imperial court, while reference to the five *skandhas* and the modalities will demonstrate the philosophical framework and manner in which pathways were created between that traditional literary practice and the medieval concept of writing *waka* as a path to salvation. ✿

2 "BUDDHISTIC" *WAKA* AND BUDDHIST *KANSHI*
—*MAN'YŌSHŪ* TO *GOSENSHŪ*

INTRODUCTION

The issues of religiosity in relation to Japanese *waka* that are covered at some length in the previous chapter are of less concern in this chapter than in those to follow. Problems of terminology, venue, and genre, however, are already evident in the *Man'yōshū*, *Kokinshū*, and *Gosenshū*, and not only in relation to Buddhist poems in Japanese. Buddhist *kanshi* (poems in Chinese) appear in the *Man'yōshū*, in the imperial *kanshi* (*chokusenshishū*) anthologies of the early ninth century, and in private *kanshi* anthologies of the tenth century. Okazaki Kazuko has referred to these latter poems as *shakkyō-shi* (Chinese poems on the teachings of the Buddha) and claims they are precursors to *shakkyō-ka*, but there is no evidence that this is a widely used term for such poems.[93] While some Buddhist *kanshi*—like those by Yamanoue no Okura—are deeply religious, many of those found in other anthologies are only superficially so.

Examples of *waka* that incorporate some aspect of Buddhist culture from the *Man'yōshū*, *Kokinshū*, or *Gosenshū*—*waka* that I will call

---

93. Okazaki, "Shakkyō-ka kō," 80. Though Okazaki uses this term, it does not appear as a separate entry in any of the standard reference works on premodern Japanese literature, Japanese Buddhism, or *Bukkyō bungaku*.

"Buddhistic," following Muraishi Esho—are clearly distinguishable from the *waka* on Buddhist themes in the third, fifth, and sixth anthologies as well as the *shakkyō-ka* in the fourth and seventh anthologies in three ways.[94] First, in the early anthologies there are no extended sequences of *waka* that express Buddhist themes, concepts, or narratives. Second, the relationship of the Buddhist scripture or religious event contained in the poem or its headnote in these early poems is only tangentially related to the theme of the poem. Third, there is no Buddhist sentiment, other than the emotions surrounding the idea of impermanence (*mujō*), which I will discuss in more detail later in this chapter, in any of these poems.

"BUDDHISTIC" *WAKA* AND BUDDHIST *KANSHI* BEFORE THE *SHŪISHŪ*

Man'yōshū

The history of the encounter between Buddhism and the composition of *waka* begins long before the *Shūishū*. There are foreshadowings of a Buddhist poetic tradition in the imperial *kanshi* anthologies of the early ninth century, as well as in the first and second imperial *waka* anthologies, *Kokinshū* and the *Gosenshū*, but the earliest examples are found in the *Man'yōshū*. The interaction of Buddhist culture and poetry in the *Man'yōshū* is evident in every poetic form represented in the anthology: *waka, chōka* (long poem), *sedōka* (head-repeated *waka*), *bussokuseki-ka* (Buddha's stone footprint poems), *kanshi* (Chinese *shih*), and Chinese prose passages. However, in this chapter, the focus will be primarily on the *waka* genre. The *Man'yōshū* is not an imperial anthology—the topic of this study—but examples from it prove that poets were not silent about the culture and teachings that had come from the continent.

Those *waka* from the Man'yō era regarded by Japanese scholars

---

94. For Muraishi Esho, see footnote 77 in Chapter 1.

as having some connection to Buddhism are based primarily upon authorship, vocabulary and, occasionally, theme. These "Buddhistic" poems are different from both later *waka* on Buddhist themes and *shakkyō-ka* in that they are not so much an interaction with, but a reaction to, aspects of Buddhist culture, including the teachings. Their stance is observational rather than contextual; their major concern is with the utilization of some aspect of Buddhism (reference to a temple or a priest) for reasons that have nothing to do with the Buddhist teachings. The reason for this, according to Arita Shizuaki, is that "Buddhism did not have much influence over the general populace (*minshū*)."[95] Lack of influence alone does not necessarily explain the lack of depth in the few poems that are included in the *Man'yōshū*, but other factors, such as the relative scarcity of Buddhist priest-poets represented (only slightly more than ten), the inclination to associate Buddhism with humor (especially in book sixteen), and the emphasis on "sorrow" or "grief" (*hiai*) in the *banka*, or elegies, rather than impermanence (*mujō*), help to demonstrate the "introductory" negotiation between poetry and Buddhism during this period.[96]

Referring to *waka* with marginal Buddhist meaning as "Buddhistic"—that is, of or relating to Buddhism *in some capacity*—is helpful and even necessary to distinguish them from *waka* that are "Buddhist"—that is, *directly* engaged with the teachings and culture of Buddhism.[97] Buddhistic *waka* are not limited to the period of the

---

95. Arita Shizuaki, "*Man'yōshū* ni arawareta mujōkan," *Bukkyō bungaku* (Tokyo and Kyoto: Bukkyō bungaku kenkyū kai, 1978), 3.

96. Ibid., 8.

97. Japanese scholars identify the following *Man'yōshū waka* (or *hanka*, envoy to a *chōka*), *chōka* and *sedōka* as having some relationship to Buddhism. Unless otherwise specified, the numbers refer to *waka*: #327, 348, 349, 351, 353, 412, 442, 462, 465, 608, 794 (*chōka*), 795 (*hanka*), 796–799, 802 (*chōka*), 803 (*hanka*), 804 (*chōka*), 805 (*hanka*), 885, 897 (*chōka*), 898 (*hanka*), 899–903, 1018 (*sedōka*), 1045, 1151, 1264, 1268–1270, 1594, 3822, 3823, 3840, 3841, 3846, 3847, 3849–3851, 3852 (*sedōka*), 3856, 4160 (*chōka*), 4161 (*hanka*), 4162, 4216, 4468, and 4469. Some of these poems are clearly based on Buddhist teachings, while others are either marginally related (by authorship, for example) or fall under the category of *banka* (elegy). This information has been culled from the following sources: Ishihara Kiyoshi, "Jōdai Nihon bungaku ni tōei shita Bukkyō," unpublished manuscript; Nishida Masayoshi, *Mujō no bungaku* (Tokyo: Hanawa Shobō, 1975), 19–49;

Man'yōshū; there are many poems (especially those on *mujō* or temples) from the Heian period that one might call Buddhistic as well. But by the period of the *Shūishū* and the *Goshūishū*, as we will see in Chapters 3 and 4, other factors lessen the usefulness of this terminology.

Buddhistic *waka* in the *Man'yōshū* identified by author's name and by vocabulary seldom display little more than the most superficial relationship with Buddhist culture. The fact that a *waka* is attributed to a Buddhist priest does not necessarily mean that the poem will have Buddhist content. The same can be said for *waka* that contain a term or word identified with Buddhism. For the most part, these poets utilize such terminology more for its contrast with the secular rather than for its religious value. In other words, the words of Buddhism are used to enhance, through contrast, the secularity of the poem.

The following three Buddhistic *waka* are exemplary of the kinds of poems Japanese scholars point to when they identify the intersection of Buddhism and *waka* according to criteria such as authorship or vocabulary. The first is by Shaku Tsūkan (dates unknown), a poet/priest who is thought to have had some contact with Ōtomo no Tabito (665–731) and others.[98] The poem has no Buddhist content; it is merely attributed to a Buddhist priest.

Manaka Fujiko, *Kokunbungaku ni sesshu sareta Bukkyō* (Tokyo: Bun'ichi Shuppan, 1972), 10–22; Okazaki, "Shakkyō-ka kō," 79–80 and 113; Ishida Mizumaro, *Nihon koten bungaku to Bukkyō* (Tokyo: Chikuma Shobō, 1975), 22–26; Kikuchi Ryōichi, *Kodai chūsei Nihon Bukkyō bungaku ron* (Tokyo: Ōfūsha, 1976), 109–119; Fukaura Masafumi, "Kokubungaku ni oyoboseru Bukkyō shisō no eikyō—toku ni *Man'yōshū* ni tsuite," *Bukkyōgaku kenkyū* (The Studies in Buddhism), vol. 18–19 (January 1967): 138–147; Aso Mizue, "*Man'yōshū* to Bukkyō," *Kokubungaku: kaishaku to kanshō*, vol. 48, no. 15 (December 1983): 120–122, and Arita Shizuaki, "*Man'yōshū* ni arawareta mujōkan," *Bukkyō bungaku*, 3–8.

98. WDJ, 686. "Shaku" in this attribution means one who has entered the Buddhist path. It is the same *kanji* used in the name of the historical Buddha *Shakamuni* (Śākyamuni).

[*Man'yōshū* 353]

み吉野の高城のやまに白雲は行きはばかりてたなびけり見ゆ
miyoshino no / takaki no yama ni / shirakumo wa / yukihabakarite / tanabikeri miyu

A POEM BY SHAKU TSŪKAN

> above Takaki Mountain
>   of beautiful Yoshino—
>
> white clouds unsure whether
>
> to move or not move
>   appear
>   hang
>   and trail—
>
>   — Shaku Tsūkan[99]

An earlier poem (327) in the *Man'yōshū* also by Tsūkan refers more directly to Buddhism: when some girls sent Tsūkan some dried abalone and playfully asked him to offer prayers (*shugan*) for them, he replied: "Even if you took these out into the vast sea and released them, how could they come to life again?" But in this poem, Tsūkan's word for "come to life" is *yomigaeri* (to resuscitate), a play on the word *yomi* (the underworld, the world of death) rather than the Buddhist concept of rebirth.

Poems by, respectively, Prince Ichihara and Lady Kasa—love poems in the form of similes based on religious terms—demonstrate some level of familiarity with those terms on the part of listeners or readers.

---

99. Original poem in Kojima Noriyuki, Kinoshita Masatoshi, Satake Akihiro, eds., *Man'yōshū*, vol. 1, *Nihon koten bungaku zenshū* [hereafter NKBZ] (Tokyo: Shōgakkan, 1989), 237.

[*Man'yōshū* 412]

いなだきにきすめる玉はふたつなしかにもかくにも君がまにまに
*inadaki ni / kisumeru tama wa / futatsu nashi / ka ni mo kaku ni mo /
kimi ga manimani*

A POEM BY PRINCE ICHIHARA

> as with that jewel
> hidden in the topknot
>
> > —there are not two—
>
> in all things, my lord,
> whatever your will ...
>
> > > — Prince Ichihara[100]

[*Man'yōshū* 608]

相思はぬ人を思ふは大寺の餓鬼の後に額つくごとし
*aiomowanu / hito o omou wa / ōtera no / gaki no shirie ni / nuka tsuku
gotoshi*

A POEM BY LADY KASA

> longing for a person
> > who doesn't long for you—
>
> is like kowtowing in a great temple
> > behind a hungry ghost
>
> > > — Lady Kasa[101]

---

100. *Man'yōshū*, NKBZ I, 257.
101. *Man'yōshū*, NKBZ I, 341.

Japanese commentators claim that the "jewel" (*tama*) in Prince Ichihara's poem is a reference to the jewel in Chapter 8 of the Lotus Sutra (Receipt of Prophecy by Five Hundred Disciples),[102] but the jewel in the Sutra is found in a man's coat and not "a crown of hair." Understanding the significance of the jewel in the Lotus Sutra—a common trope found in Buddhist poetry of all kinds—yields no deeper comprehension of Prince Ichihara's poem. He describes the jewel as "unique" ("there are not two"), but any jewel may be described as precious, and nothing about this *tama* definitively indicates that it is the same that appears in the Lotus Sutra, which carries the quite specific meaning of hidden enlightenment.

The organizing metaphor of Lady Kasa's poem, set in the "great temple" (*ōtera*), compares unrequited love to the humiliating act of kowtowing behind (or, to the behind of) a *gaki* (a hungry ghost, representative of the *preta* realm, one of the six realms of rebirth to which all unenlightened beings are subjected). The metaphor is more complex than may at first appear: the woman gives reverence to a hungry ghost, a being driven by a desire to consume which can never be satisfied. Thus the woman's own desire is unlikely ever to be fulfilled: in the scene the poem describes, the *gaki* is not even facing her, and is in any case, unsatisfiable by his very nature. The metaphor expresses the intensity of unrequited love, and the tragi-comical figure of the *gaki* lends the poem a satirical tone. Lady Kasa may have come to her knowledge of the *gaki* and the Buddhist six realms from priest Mansei (about whom see below), to whose family she belonged. But the point for our purposes is that this Buddhist image is incorporated into the poem to intensify, or perhaps denigrate, the speaker's despair, not as a point of departure for understanding desire, in terms of the second of the Four Noble Truths.

Later poems in the *Man'yōshū* also exhibit a similar superficial relationship to Buddhism. Though anonymous, the following two poems are purportedly by an unnamed priest and his benefactor. The

---

102. Throughout this study, I will, for the most part, use the chapter titles from the Leon Hurvitz translation of the Lotus Sutra: *Scripture of the Dharma Blossom of the Fine Dharma.*

headnote to the poem says that these poems deride priests. The only vocabulary related to Buddhism are in the attributions: *hōshi* (priest) and *dan'ochi* (benefactor). The humorous intent of the poems is what the reader primarily notices, rather than their Buddhist elements.

[*Man'yōshū* 3846]

法師らがひげの剃り杭馬繋ぎいたくな引きそ僧は泣かむ
hōshira ga / hige no sorikui / umatsunagi / itaku na hiki so / hōshi wa nakamu

POEM POKING FUN AT A PRIEST

>   if you tie your horse
>   to priests' stubbly beards—
>   don't pull so hard!
>   or the priest will surely cry

>   — Anonymous

[*Man'yōshū* 3847]

壇越や然もな言ひそ里長が課役徴らば汝も泣かむ
dan'ochi ya / shikamo na ii so / satoosa ga / edachi hataraba / imashi mo nakamu

THE PRIEST'S REPLY

>   hey, patron!
>   don't talk like that:
>   if the mayor raised your taxes
>   you too sir would surely cry

>   — Hōshi (Priest)[103]

---

103. *Man'yōshū*, NKBZ 4, 137–138.

The conversational nature of these two *waka* is appropriate to the implied narrative. Since the sight of a nonbearded priest (when most men were bearded) with a two to three-day stubble was unusual, it provoked laughter if not ridicule—especially when it is suggested that one might tether a horse to the whiskers. The priest, however, does not take this mockery lying down. His retort—*no, dear benefactor, you'll be the one in trouble*—is almost worthy of a punch line cymbal crash. We do learn something from these poems about the material nature of Buddhist culture during this period—the grooming habits of priests and the responsibilities that those who donated to the priesthood had to the tax system. But the Buddhist teachings are not the concern of these *waka*.

Waka on the theme of evanescence (*mujō*) are the most cited examples for claims about the influx of Buddhist thought into the world of Japanese poetry during this early stage in Japanese literary history. The problem with identifying *waka* on *mujō* as Buddhist, however, is that they are not always identified as such in the anthology. As well, it must be acknowledged that Buddhism is not the only source for regarding evanescence as integral to human life. However, if we compare the concept of evanescence to both the sense of eternalism and sentiments of grief more commonly found in the *Man'yōshū*, then it is accurate to say that Buddhism was at least partly responsible for inflecting the outlook of poets toward a Buddhist view of impermanence later in Japanese literary history.

Nishida Masayoshi, who has written extensively about the relationship between literature and *mujō*, has shown that the concept of impermanence did not exist in early literary documents such as the *Kojiki* (710).[104] There we see the frequent appearance of words like *tokoyo*, eternal world, used to describe not only the world of the gods but also the world governed by the gods. This worldview is based on an ontological continuity in which death does not necessarily disrupt life. As Gary Ebersole puts it in *Ritual Poetry and the Politics of Death in Early Japan*, "For the early Japanese, death was not an immediate, complete, and permanent break with the world of the living. Rather,

---

104. Nishida, *Mujō no bungaku*, 6–18.

communication between the living and the dead was assumed to be possible through various ritual practices—divination, oracles, possession—as well as through dreams."[105]

It is not surprising that this worldview—what Nishida calls an "ideology of immortality" (*fushi no shisō*)—lingers in the *Man'yōshū*. Evidence for this lies in those poems that imply a belief in *tokoyo* (50 and 261, for example) as well as those poems that emphasize the everlastingness of life (22). Such poems seem to demonstrate that the concepts of the inevitability of death and the transience of life had not yet saturated the literary consciousness of the anthology's poets, as they were to do.[106]

Yet, there are at least three poems in the *Man'yōshū* that offer another view. One of the earliest poems cited as proof of Buddhist influence is by the Novice (*Shami*) Mansei (early eighth century), a poem which is reanthologized later by both Minamoto no Shitagō (911–983) in the *Kokinrokujō* (finished in 987) and by the compiler(s) of the *Shūishū* in a slightly different form.

[*Man'yōshū* 351]

世の中を何に喩へむ朝開き漕ぎ去にし舟の跡なきごとし
yo no naka o / nani ni tatoemu / asabiraki / kogiinishi fune no / ato naki gotoshi

> to what shall I liken
>
> this world?
> > a boat
>
> rows out in the morning
>
> leaving no trace
>
> > — Shami Mansei[107]

105. Ebersole, *Ritual Poetry*, 83.
106. Ibid, 19.
107. *Man'yōshū*, NKBZ I, 237.

Claims about this poem having been influenced by Buddhism are neither deniable nor provable, but three factors indicate that Buddhist influence is likely. First, the poem is attributed to a Buddhist priest. Second is its suggestive location in the third imperial anthology, *Shūishū*, when it was reanthologized in the late tenth to early eleventh centuries. That it was located near the Buddhist *waka* sequence in book twenty does not prove its Buddhist origins, but it does suggest how the poem might have been interpreted from the early eighth to the early eleventh century. Third, the poem's central metaphor is similar to two of the ten metaphors in the Vimalakīrti Sūtra (J: Yuima-kyō). Of course, similar to does not mean the poem was based upon this Sūtra, but we know that this Sūtra and, presumably, its famous metaphors were known in Japan as early as the beginning of the seventh century.[108] Though Mansei does not borrow either of these two metaphors exactly, their similarities and the poem's interrogative opening ("To what shall I compare/this world?") suggest a familiarity with the metaphors of impermanence in the Vimalakīrti Sūtra.

Even later in the *Man'yōshū* collection, there are two *waka* without attribution, whose topics are designated as *mujō*. The afterword to the poems relates that they were written onto the front of a Japanese-style *koto* found behind the Buddha Hall at Kawaradera in present-day Nara. The headnote to poems 3849 and 3850 states: *yo no naka no mujō o itou uta nishu:* Two poems about reviling *mujō* in the world. The first poem reads: *ikishini no / futatsu no umi o / itowashimi / shiohi no yama o / shinoitsuru kamo* (despising the two seas of life and death, I long for the mountain where the waves don't reach [enlightenment]). The second is: *yo no naka no / shigeki kariho ni / sumi sumite / itaramu kuni no / tazuki shirazu mo* (residing in this temporary world confounded by endless suffering, I know nothing of the Pure Land where I shall go).[109]

---

108. Daigan and Alicia Matsunaga, *Foundation of Japanese Buddhism*, vol. 1 (Tokyo: Buddhist Books International, 1974), 14. The two metaphors in question are "[This body] is like a water bubble, not remaining very long" and "[This body] is like a mirage, born from the appetites of the passions." See Robert A. F. Thurman, trans., *The Holy Teaching of Vimalakīrti* (University Park and London: The Pennsylvania State University Press, 1976), 22.

109. *Man'yōshū*, NKBZ 4, 138–139.

We also find in the *Man'yōshū* some evidence of efforts to coordinate artistic elements with religious ceremony, as in poem 1594 by Empress Kōmyō (consort to Emperor Shōmu, r. 724–749), a poem purportedly composed at the time of a lecture (Yuima-kō) on the Vimalakīrti Sūtra (Yuima-kyō) during a Yuima-e ceremony that took place at Kōfuku-ji, the Fujiwara family temple in Nara.[110]

[*Man'yōshū* 1594]

しぐれの雨間なくな降りそ紅ににほへる山の散らまく惜しも

shigure no ame / manaku na furi so / kurenai ni / nioeru yama no /
chiramaku oshi mo

SONG-POEM BEFORE THE BUDDHA IMAGE

> stop,
> > endless
> sleet and cold drizzle—
>
> regrettable, how on
> the mountain dyed crimson
>
> a scattering
> > is at hand

— Empress Kōmyō[111]

The postscript to this poem tells us that Empress Kōmyō sponsored a lavish service at which was performed both Korean and Chinese

---

110. According to Mikoshiba Daisuke, it was Kōmyō's father, Fujiwara no Fuhito (659–720) who revived the Yuima Ceremony after it had been neglected by Empress Jitō (r. 690–697). Fuhito declared that the ceremony be held on the tenth day of the tenth month of each year, the anniversary of the death of Fuhito's father (Fujiwara no Kamatari, 614–669). "Empress Kōmyō's Buddhist Faith: Her Role in the Founding of the State Temple and Convent System," *Engendering Faith: Women and Buddhism in Premodern Japan* (Ann Arbor: The Center for Japanese Studies, 2002), 27.

111. *Man'yōshū*, NKBZ 2, 351–352.

music in addition to Japanese music: the aforementioned Prince Ichihara (author of poem 412) played the *koto*. In conjunction with instrumental music, offerings were made and songs were sung. This information suggests that, at Buddhist services sponsored by the imperial family, integration of artistic elements had already begun.[112]

The fifty-three *waka* that are said to have some relationship to Buddhism in the *Man'yōshū* cannot be dismissed entirely as superficial, but neither can they be characterized as deep, in either religious or poetic terms.[113] Clearly, though the concept of *mujō* began to engage Japanese poets during this era, it had not yet become a central topic of concern.

Buddhist *Kanshi* by Japanese Poets

Though this study is primarily focused on *waka* on Buddhist themes and *shakkyō-ka*, particularly those compiled in the imperial poetry anthologies during the second half of the Heian period, it is important to note the composition of poetry in Chinese (*kanshi*) by Japanese authors, especially those *kanshi* on Buddhist topics. As we

---

112. For more on Kōmyō's Buddhist faith, see Mikoshiba, "Empress Kōmyō's Buddhist Faith," *Engendering Faith*, 21–40 and Hongō Masatsugu, "State Buddhism and Court Buddhism: The Role of Court Women in the Development of Buddhism from the Seventh to the Ninth Centuries," *Engendering Faith: Woman and Buddhism in Premodern Japan* (Ann Arbor: The Center for Japanese Studies, 2002), 41–61.

113. Some scholars have tried to push the influence of Buddhism on Japanese poets back to the late seventh and early eighth centuries, especially to Kakinomoto no Hitomaro. Gary Ebersole, apparently concurring with the arguments of Watase Masatada, is one such scholar. He says, "No individual in the capital in the late seventh century could have remained completely immune to Buddhist influence or ignorant of Buddhist beliefs or practices. More specifically, Watase argues that Hitomaro's poetry was affected by the heavy presence of Buddhism in the court and by its ritual expressions. Indeed, he goes so far as to suggest that some of Hitomaro's poetry may have been performed in a Buddhist ritual context." Ebersole, *Ritual Poetry*, 163–164. Sueki Fumihiko also locates the first consciousness of Buddhism (as an awareness of *mujō*) in the poetry of Hitomaro, but he qualifies his claim by saying that it is impossible to know to what extent Hitomaro was influenced by Buddhist ideas in works of Chinese literature with which he was quite familiar and to what extent that he was influenced by the Buddhist teachings themselves. See "*Man'yōshū* ni okeru mujōkan no keisei," *Tōyō gakujutsu kenkyū*, vol. 21, no. 1 (Tōyō tetsugaku kenkyūjo, 1982): 62–63.

have seen, Okazaki called *kanshi* on Buddhist topics *shakkyō-shi*, or *shi* (C: *shih*) on the teachings of the Buddha. Unlike the term *shakkyō-ka*, however, *shakkyō-shi* is not a formal poetic term: it does not appear as either a book or section title in any of the *kanshi* collections preceding the appearance of the term "Shakkyō" in the *Goshūishū* in the late eleventh century. A few scholars besides Okazaki, such as Manaka Fujiko and Takagi Yutaka, have also used the term *shakkyō-shi*, but it is not found in either literary or Buddhist reference works. For these reasons, though there is little difference between "Buddhist *kanshi*" and "*shakkyō-shi*," I will use the former term to refer to Chinese poems on Buddhist topics that have been attributed to Japanese authors.

The earliest extant collection of *shih* in Japan was the *Kaifūsō* (751). Compiled eight years prior to the *Man'yōshū* during the Nara period, the *Kaifūsō* contains 120 poems, none overtly about matters pertaining to the Buddhist teachings. Four of the sixty-five poets in the anthology are priests (Chizō, Benshō, Dōji, and Dōyū), but among their poems only two by Dōyū could be interpreted as marginally connected to Nara Buddhist culture.[114]

Yamanoue Okura (660?–733), one of the most famous of the Man'yō era poets, incorporated the Buddhist teachings more explicitly into his Chinese poetry and prose than did the priests of the *Kaifūsō*. Compiled only in the *Man'yōshū*, Okura's poetry is regarded by some Japanese scholars as "individual"[115] and "original."[116] Konishi says about one poem that it is "the first poem in Yamato made of the stuff of philosophical thought" and "the first poem to deal with [the doctrines of Buddhism] in terms of the poet's own experience."[117] Yet, these factors have not been enough to exempt his Chinese writings from criticism: Konishi goes on to say that they are

---

114. For a translation of these two poems by Dōyū, see Judith N. Rabinovitch & Timothy R. Bradstock, *Dance of the Butterflies: Chinese Poetry from the Japanese Court Tradition* (Ithaca: Cornell East Asia Series, 2005), 46–47.

115. Konishi, *A History of Japanese Literature Volume*, vol. 1:384.

116. Edwin Cranston, *A Waka Anthology*, vol. 1 (Palo Alto: Stanford University Press, 1993), 344.

117. Konishi, *A History of Japanese Literature*, vol. 1:388.

"utterly lacking in beauty."[118] This sort of negative criticism about Buddhist poetry (and prose) occurs frequently in modern scholarship, but for now it is sufficient to recognize that Okura frequently incorporated the names of Buddhas and bodhisattvas (Śākyamuni, Maitreya), Buddhist ideas and doctrines (impermanence, taking refuge in the three jewels), and terminology or lines of text from the sūtras (Vimalakīrti Sūtra) into his poetry. Interestingly, this liberal use of Buddhism did not lead Okura to do the same in his *chōka* and *waka*, but his poetic efforts in Chinese reveal a strong inclination to attempt to reconcile religious experience (Confucian as well as Buddhist) with poetic practice.[119]

In 814, thirty years after the start of the Heian period, Emperor Saga (r. 809–823) ordered the first of what would become three imperial *kanshi* anthologies (*chokusenshishū*), *Ryōunshū*. Compiled by Ono no Minemori (d. 830) this anthology contains, unlike the *Kaifūsō*, no poems by Buddhist priests and only a few poems with Buddhist themes. The following by Ono no Nagami (fl. ca. 800), the father of Ono no Minemori, is an example:

> Long weary of the miseries of the bird cage,
> I've come to find the crossing that leads to release.
> I've calmed my heart, returned to the Six Pāramitās;
> Changed my ways and look now to the Three Wheels.
> The moon in the water is not the true moon of dawn;
> The flowers in the sky from a springtime that is not real.
> Now that I've started my journey to
> Enlightenment this morning,
> How could I ever go astray in the mundane world?[120]

---

118. Ibid., 386 and 388.

119. It may not be entirely appropriate to think of Confucianism as "religious" at this point in Japanese history, but it was certainly regarded as a system of thought equal to (if not more important than) Buddhism.

120. Konishi, *A History of Japanese Literature*, vol. 1:50 and 57.

As attested by the Buddhist terms such as *haramitsu* ("Pāramitās") and *sanrin* ("Three Wheels") as well as by the sentiment "my journey to Enlightenment," Nagami's poem does not treat the teachings lightly; in fact, we could say that it exhibits great certainty about the direction in which the teachings will lead and how they will affect him. The question of whether, or how deeply, Nagami actually understood the meaning of the words he used will have to be set aside, since no proof exists as to whether his poem is a mere intellectual exercise or is based on practical instruction in the Buddhist teachings.

The second and third imperial *kanshi* anthologies—*Bunkashū-reishū* (818) and *Keikokushū* (827)—were different from the *Ryōunshū* in that they were no longer compiled according to author or by rank. Instead, they were organized by category (*bu*). The *Bunkashūreishū*, in three *maki*, contained about sixty more poems than the *Ryōunshū*, but considerably less than the nine hundred plus poems in the *Keikokushū* in 827.[121] There was a category of Buddhist *kanshi* in both called *Bonmon no bu* ([poems pertaining to] the gate of Sanskrit), a category that was absent from their Chinese model, the *Wen hsüan*.[122]

The *Nihon koten bungaku daijiten* proposes two possible reasons for the inclusion of Buddhist poems in the *Bunkashūreishū* and the *Keikokushū*. One is the religious activity of Kūkai (774–835) and Saichō (767–822), the founders of the Shingon and Tendai sects of Buddhism, especially during the first decades of the ninth century. Their interactions with the Emperor (first Saga and later Junna [r. 823–833]) during these periods increased as they sought recognition from the court apart from the Nara schools. Second is the importation of Chinese anthologies (other than the *Wen hsüan*) that contained Buddhist poems.[123] Whatever the reason, the creation of a category or

---

121. The *Keikokushū* was originally compiled in twenty *maki*, but only exists in a truncated form now.

122. In "Early Buddhist Kanshi: Court, Country, and Kūkai," Paul Rouzer notes that there was a category of poems in the *Wenyuan yinghua* of 987 called *shimen* (J: *sha-kumon*). But this appears to have been more the exception than the rule. *Monumenta Nipponica*, vol. 59, no. 4 (Winter 2004): 434.

123. *Nihon koten bungaku daijiten (kan'yaku ban)*, 1st edition (Tokyo: Iwanami Sho-ten, 1986), 1625–1626.

book of Buddhist poems in these two *shih* anthologies was the first of its kind in the history of extant Japanese literary anthologies.

In "Early Buddhist *Kanshi*: Court, Country, and Kūkai," Paul Rouzer claims that after the *Kaifūsō*, Buddhist priests were rarely included in the three imperial *kanshi* anthologies; he claims that this absence signifies a distancing of court from clergy in terms of their "symbolic realms."[124] Rouzer says, "The Heian anthologies that emerged from the composition circles of Emperors Saga and Junna portray monks and their world in a way more typical of Tang literature, where literati address their comments to the monk who is 'out there,' at the periphery, potentially marginalized and away from public power."[125] This is confirmed in a poem found in the *Ryōunshū*. The poem states that Emperor Saga sent a poem entitled "Written Upon Presenting a Gift of Silk to Priest Kūkai." Kūkai was apparently practicing on Mount Takao at the time, while Saga was probably in the capital: "From afar, I can guess that deep in the hills the spring must still be cold." and "In recent days, there's been in news from your temple in the hills."[126] The fact that there is no poetic reply in the *Ryōunshū* by Kūkai to the gift seems to reinforce the distance between the author and the recipient of the poem. However, the lack of a response may reflect an effect created by the compiler, because in Kūkai's personal poetry anthology, *Seireishū*, compiled by his disciple Shinzei (800–860), we find Kūkai's response to Saga in a poem entitled "A Poem Expressing Appreciation for the Emperor's Kind Gift of a Hundred Bolts of Silk and a Poem in Heptasyllabic Lines."[127]

This same phenomenon of presenting only one half of a poetry exchange occurs also in the *Bunkashūreishū*, which contains poems by Saga, Prince Nakao, and Kose no Shikihito to Saichō while he was sick on Mount Hiei. Again, the poetic responses by Saichō are not recorded in the anthology, just as Kūkai's were not in the *Ryōunshū*.

---

124. Rouzer, "Early Buddhist Kanshi," 441.
125. Ibid., 442.
126. Rabinovitch & Bradstock, *Dance of the Butterflies*, 54.
127. Ibid.

Kokinshū and *Gosenshū*

Almost a hundred years passed between the compilation of the three imperial *kanshi* anthologies in the early ninth century and the compilation of Japan's first imperial *waka* collection in 905. Konishi says the Chinese compositions found in the three *kanshi* anthologies represent the "zenith" of the *ga* (elegant, refined) tradition of *shih* poetry.[128] Whether this is true is beyond the scope of this study, but the presence of Buddhist *shih* in these anthologies is important. Since Buddhist *shih* were not a feature of either mainstream Six Dynasties poetry or early T'ang poetry in China (though exceptions do exist), one can only assume that interaction between the literati and the monastic community or between literature and the Buddhist teachings were viewed differently in China and Japan. While one might point to factors such as the importance of poetry and poetics to Kūkai's view of the world (and the dissemination of that knowledge to the court) or the attendance by members of the court at Buddhist ceremonies such as the Yuima-e (readings and lectures on the Vimalakīrti Sūtra, beginning eighth century) or Butsumyō-e (reading and intoning of Butsumyō-kyō, beginning ninth century), there is, in fact, no way to know what the literary motivation was.

Whatever factors led some writers of *shih* to write poems on Buddhist topics in the early part of the ninth century did not lead to the same result for *waka* poets during the ninth or tenth centuries. In fact, most Japanese literary scholars claim outright that there are no Buddhist *waka* or *shakkyō-ka* during the era of the *Kokinshū* and the *Gosenshū*. Although the reasons for this absence are unknown, one can speculate that it was not as easy for *waka* poets to weave aspects of Buddhist philosophy into such a short poetic form. *Waka* were an artifact of social exchange between members of the court by the beginning of the tenth century, but at that point it remained to be seen whether that same poetic form could be used to express any ideas or feelings about the Buddhist teachings or Buddhist ceremonies, rituals, lectures, and teachings. It required another century or so for poets in the court tradition to answer this question.

---

128. Konishi, *A History of Japanese Literature*, 2:55–56.

Okazaki Kazuko and Sakaguchi Genshō, however, agree that the *Kokinshū* in particular is not completely free of Buddhist influence.[129] They point to poems by Buddhist priests such as Bishop Henjō (815–890) and a set of poems in the second book of *zōka* on the topics of impermanence (*mujō*) and reviling the world (*ensei*). The opinions of Okazaki and Sakaguchi rest solely on their readings of the poems since almost none of them have *kotobagaki*. Poem 947 by the priest Sosei (dates unknown) is representative of this group:

[*Kokinshū* 947]

いづくにか世をば厭はむ心こそ野にも山にも迷べらなれ
izuku ni ka / yo oba itowamu / kokoro koso / no ni mo yama ni mo / madou beranare

> my heart resolves
> to hate the world—but
> from where? it seems
> lost in fields and
> mountains both

> — Priest Sosei[130]

More than a quarter of the poems in this second book of *zōka* contain some version of the adjectives *ushi* (sad, melancholy—usually about the *yo* or "world") and *tsurashi* (bitter), and several, as with the poem above, contain some form of the verb *itou* (revile), which we have translated in this case as "hate." Clearly, evidence for the need to, or the fear of, turning one's back on the secular world—whether sad or bitter—was expressed in some of the *waka* compositions of this time, but Okazaki thinks they are of the "lineage" (*keitō*) of *waka* found in the *Man'yōshū* rather than indicators of a shift in poetic conception.[131]

---

129. Okazaki, "Shakkyō-ka kō," 84–85. Sakaguchi, *Nihon Bukkyō bungaku josetsu*, 236.
130. Kojima and Arai, *Kokinwakashū*, 4.
131. Watanabe Yasuaki has written on the use of a group of words in a set of *Kokinshū*

Okazaki and Sakaguchi also agree that, as in the *Kokinshū*, there are a few such *waka* on similar topics—impermanence, reviling the world—in the second imperial anthology, *Gosenshū*.[132] There are in a number of these poems (or in their headnotes) words derived from Buddhist culture. Terms such as *rakushoku* (taking the tonsure, usually reserved for the imperial family in the Heian period), *jukai* (receiving the precepts), *yamadera sankei* (view of the mountain temple), *nyodan'ochi* (benefactress), and *juzu* (rosary beads) appear in this anthology, along with poems by a greater number of Buddhist priests than are found in the *Kokinshū*: Shinsei (b. 825), Shōhō (active late ninth century), Zōki (priest under Emperor Uda, r. 887–897), Shin'en (dates unknown), Kaisen (d. 931–946), Yuisei (dates unknown), Ninkyō (d. 949), Gachō (dates unknown), and Yamada Hōshi (dates unknown).

An examination of poetry on Buddhist themes before the *Shūishū* does not reveal on the part of court poets a concerted effort to interact with the Buddhist teachings in a focused, systematic, or complex way, but it does show a willingness on the part of some poets to include certain limited aspects of Buddhist culture and thought into the realm of court poetry. The interaction of the poetic and religious worlds would change, however, during the second half of the tenth century as the court became even more familiar with the teachings, ceremonies, and rituals of Buddhism thanks, in part, to the efforts of the abbot Ryōgen on Mount Hiei. However, the growing Buddhification of court life was not the only source of influence. The world of *waka*—and of literature in general—was changing at the same time. Interest among court women in the *nikki* (diary) and *monogatari* (tale) genres, the flexibility of authors to write both *waka* and *shih* and to compile

---

poems that he feels indicate the sentiment of *mujōkan*, in this case, the feelings (*kan*) attached to the experience of transience rather than the Buddhist concept or view (*kan*) of *mujō* itself. To give just one example is poem 933: "in this world of ours / what is there that does not change / Tomorrow River— / the deep pools of yesterday / have become today's shallows." (Rodd, *Kokinshū*, 318) The words Watanabe discusses involve contrasts in quantity or time: *fuchi* (deep pools) and *se* (shallows), as well as words for tomorrow (found in "Asukagawa"), yesterday (*kinō*), and today (*kyō*). "*Kokinshū* to shinkō: Mujōkan o megutte," *Kokubungaku: kaishaku to kanshō*, vol. 65, no. 10 (October 2000): 33–39.

132. Okazaki, "Shakkyō-ka kō," 85. Sakaguchi, *Nihon Bukkyō bungaku josetsu*, 237.

them in the same anthology (*Wakan rōeishū*), and the interest in collecting Buddhist tales in *setsuwashū* (*Sambō ekotoba*) all spoke to a new self-awareness and self-consciousness about what literature was and could be. The members of the aristocracy were not free to write about just anything; their lives and their poetry were circumscribed by the proscriptions of the court. But within the limits of form and content, Japanese writers gradually—work by work, poem by poem—expanded their horizon of appropriate topics and communicated this spirit of expansion to others in their world. Between alternating periods of stasis and dynamism, Japanese poets discovered a possible road to reconciliation between the limitations of their thirty-one syllable *waka* and the colorful, rich, and philosophical culture of Buddhism.

ORGANIZATION OF THE *CHOKUSENSHŪ*

For all intents and purposes, it is the imperial poetry anthologies from the second half of the Heian period that represent the first efforts to introduce *waka* on Buddhist themes into a public venue. There were of course other venues for the compilation of *waka* such as private anthologies (*shikashū*) and personal anthologies (*shisenshū*), but the imperial poetry anthology superseded both in official importance and prestige, because the source of the commissions (*choku*) was the sovereign himself.

The topical format of the imperial anthologies was also determined, more or less, by the structure of *Kokinshū*.[133] They begin with several books of seasonal poems ordered temporally from the first of the year starting with the *haru no uta*, or spring poems. There are between four to eight books of seasonal poems—books of summer, fall, and winter poems follow the *haru no uta*—in each anthology, leaving anywhere from two to six books (which I will discuss below) to fill out the first

---

133. The fifth anthology, *Kin'yōshū* (1124–1127), and the sixth, *Shikashū* (1151–1154) were the only two to be comprised of only ten books, so the number of books of seasonal and love poems is significantly reduced.

half. For all but the second of the imperial anthologies (*Gosenshū*, 951), the second ten books begin with *koi no uta*, or love poems, of which there are between four to six books in each anthology (except for the fifth and sixth anthologies, in which there are two each). In the twenty-book format, this left four to six books to fill out the ten books in the second half.

Various books occupied the remaining sections of the *Kokinshū*, some of which were reproduced in subsequent anthologies and others of which were eliminated. In addition to two books of Miscellaneous Poems, there were also "Aishō-ka" (Laments), "Ga no uta" (Celebratory poems), "Ribetsu no uta" (Poems of Parting), "Kiryo no uta" (Poems of Travel), and "Mono no na," or "Butsumei" (Names of Things).[134]

Each of these books and the placement of their poems within are crucial to the imperial worldview the sovereign and his compilers wished to display. Therefore, it is of some literary significance that a separate book (as opposed to a separate subsection) of *shakkyō-ka* does not appear until the seventh anthology, *Senzaishū*, despite the fact that Buddhism had migrated to Japan in various doctrinal and ritual forms since the sixth century. The question arises: why did it take so long?

Perhaps this question about a book whose poems are relatively few may seem unimportant when considering the enormous imperial poetry project as a whole. Are not the meaning of individual poems and the accumulated meaning of entire anthologies worthy of more attention than the question of when a book title or category of poems begins? I would argue it is not: the occasion of a new book and category of *waka*—Buddhist *waka*—in the imperial poetry project is actually a momentous event when we consider the source of the project—that is, the sovereign—and what the sovereign is said to represent—the *kami* lineage dating from the age of the gods. One might expect the *kami* lineage of the Emperor to preclude the elevation of *shakkyō-*

---

134. The book titles I have left out are "Zattei," or "Zattai" (Poems in Miscellaneous Forms), "Ōutadokoro no onuta" (Ceremonial Poems of the Court), "Kamiasobi no uta" (God-playing Songs), and "Azumauta" (Songs of the Eastern Provinces). The last two are included within the "Ōutadokoro no onuta;" all these titles are limited to the *Kokinshū* alone.

ka and of Buddhism itself (indeed, during some later periods, the imperial family *did* distance itself from Buddhism); instead, during this period, the *chokusenshū* project adopted Buddhism as one of its topics to represent the imperial world. Moreover, if we consider the way in which the writing of *waka* was regarded in the medieval period—as a form of Buddhist practice—the appearance of a separate category of Buddhist *waka* would seem to signal a change in how the composition of *waka* was understood. Of course, the appearance of a new category does not mean that *waka* were immediately regarded as acts of Buddhist practice. The Buddhification of *waka* occurred over a period of time, through the efforts not only of poets but also compilers, and is reflected in the various sequences of poems examined in this study.

Buddhist *waka* and *shakkyō-ka* evolved more slowly in the imperial poetry anthologies than in more private venues. For example, the Buddhist poems in the *Hosshin wakashū* (1012) reveal a level and range of development not reflected in an imperial poetry anthology at that time. The *Sanboku kikashū* (1127), the *Hōmon hyakushu* (ca. 1156) and the *Chōshū eisō* (1178) contain *shakkyō-ka* with a much broader range in topic than anything we find before the seventh anthology, *Senzaishū* (1188). I will discuss these private anthologies and their *shakkyō-ka* in further detail in the chapters ahead.

CONCEPTUAL DEVELOPMENTS BEFORE THE *SHŪISHŪ*

There were at least three obstacles inherent in court *waka* that needed to be addressed before poems on Buddhist themes could be written or integrated with the court poetry tradition. The first obstacle was structural: the thirty-one syllable form of a *waka*. The second was the range of topics acceptable for *waka* compositions. Finally, there were the Buddhist admonitions about writing secular poetry. Conversely, it is possible to identify certain historical factors from the tenth century that probably contributed to the inclusion of Buddhist *waka* in the *Shūishū*.

The brevity of the *waka* might seem as if it would preclude any poeticization of Buddhism: how could the complex philosophical doctrines of Buddhism be addressed in thirty-one syllables? But brief or not, *waka* was primarily what the aristocracy wrote, and by the time it became entrenched in court culture during the late Nara and early Heian periods (through the frequency of composition and the attention to poetic skill), other poetic forms with which poets could have experimented had already lost their cultural capital—the Chinese *shih* and the Japanese *chōka*, for example. Therefore, if poets were moved (even encouraged or obligated) to write about Buddhist topics (as, for example, at a memorial service for a loved one), their sensibilities would be confined to *waka*, the poetic form with which they were most familiar and could be the most creative.

That the topics of *waka* poetry were limited by precedent—the second obstacle—was, as we will see, similar in kind to the third obstacle, but originated from the literary rather than the religious realm. *Waka* topics had already been established in the first imperial poetry anthology (if not before), and *waka* on Buddhist themes were not included among them.

It has long been recognized that Japanese court *waka* are affective—that is, emotionally evocative. The Japanese were able to evoke these emotions in *waka* because they relied upon a complex system of verbal implication and allusion, a library of images and vocabulary that each poet drew upon in making a new poem. When they began to wrestle with the possibility of addressing Buddhist topics in poetry, they had to confront the fact that the brevity of the *waka* form precluded any explication of the teachings themselves; that explication would have to be accomplished by other means. The anthologizers would come to rely, as they had done previously, on the *kotobagaki*, or headnote, to provide the narrative, scriptural/occasional, or lyric situation that had prompted the poem. The *waka* that followed might repeat the information given in the headnote or veer off in a different direction. Thus, understanding the teachings, and making a poetic response to them, called upon both the intellectual and emotional faculties of the practitioner-poet. To the extent that this is true, the reader of Buddhist *waka* and *shakkyō-ka* must also come to the poem with an understanding of the teachings, as the poem will not explicate them *per se*.

The third obstacle—the admonitions of Buddhist texts against what we would now call "creative writing"—came from the religious realm. The challenge to *waka* from the Buddhist teachings did not concern the nature of poetic topics so much as it addressed the *act* of writing secular literature (on any topic) and the effect such activities would have on one's personal salvation. For example, one of the most well known admonitions came from the Lotus Sutra, of which all members of the Heian aristocracy were aware from their attendance at lectures, sermons, eight-day religious services (Hokke hakkō), and thirty-day religious services (Hokke sanjikkō) held in and around the capital. This warning taught that the "… [bodhisattva-mahasattva] does not approach with familiarity … those who compose worldly letters."[135] As Japanese poets became increasingly aware of the implications of statements such as these (in part through the Kangaku-e services to be discussed in the next paragraph), it may have seemed that the attainment of salvation would be forever out of reach as long as they were engaged in composing secular verse, to the extent that they took the proscriptions seriously.

A compromise between the secular and the religious realms was initiated in 964 during the reign of Emperor Murakami (r. 946–967). Almost sixty years after the compilation of the *Kokinshū*, a group of twenty literature students from the Daigaku (University) in the capital and twenty monks from Mount Hiei organized a service at a temple or temple building near the mountain's base close to the present-day city of Sakamoto. They met, according to the earliest account in the *Sanbō ekotoba* (984), to profess their beliefs in and encourage one

---

135. Hurvitz, *Scripture of the Lotus Blossom*, 208; Sakamoto and Iwamoto, *Hokke-kyō*, vol. 2, 244. In the Vimalakīrti Sūtra as well there is a reference to proper speech ("When [the bodhisattva] attains enlightenment, living beings…are enhanced by true speech, soft-spoken, [and] free of divisive intrigues …"), though the intention of this particular passage pertains to nondualistic speech. Thurman, *The Holy Teaching of Vimalakīrti*, 17.

another about "the way of the Law and the Way of Literature."[136] This twice-yearly event (on the fifteenth day of the third and ninth months) continued with some interruptions until 1122, which would suggest that it was well known to the people of the capital for more than 150 years. The attendees called their group the Kangaku-e (Assembly for the Encouragement of Learning).[137]

The name of their group does not evoke images of religious sacrality, but according to the description in the *Sanbō ekotoba*, the first day was devoted to discussing the Lotus Sutra while in the "evening they meditate[d] on Amida Buddha."[138] The religious service was completed the next day when, "… until dawn … they compose[d] Chinese verses [*shih*] in praise of the Buddha and of his teachings. …"[139] We do not know what kinds of verses were actually written at the time; they might have been inspired by phrases in the Lotus Sutra that could have been incorporated into the poem or they might have been more secular verses written in a *spirit* of "joy" (*zuiki*) to the Buddha, which is what the *Kangaku-e ki* says.[140] Although the *Kangaku-e ki* was written almost two hundred years after the first Kangaku-e meeting, its author, Fujiwara no Tadamichi (1097–1164), who became Regent (*kanpaku*) in 1121, fills out our knowledge about what occurred at the inaugural meeting.[141] He too writes that verses were composed, but he

---

136. Edward Kamens, trans., *The Three Jewels: A Study and Translation of Minamoto Tamenori's* "Sambōe" (Ann Arbor: Center for Japanese Studies, 1988), 295.

137. It is interesting to speculate whether the enthusiasm generated by the Ōwa debates (961–964) between Hossō and Tendai monks on Mount Hiei that "attracted considerable attention from lay Buddhists" from the capital might also have led to the occasion of the first Kangaku-e assembly at which there was a similar commingling of attendees. Paul Groner, *Ryōgen and Mount Hiei: Japanese Tendai in the Tenth Century* (Honolulu: University of Hawai'i Press, 2002), 7.

138. Kamens, *The Three Jewels*, 295

139. Ibid. According to Komatsu Shigemi, the *Fusō ryakki* (completed between 1094-1107) claims that the participants of the assembly composed *waka* as well as *shih*. Komatsu Shigemi, *Fujiwara no Tadamichi hitsu Kangaku-e ki kaisetsu* (Tokyo: Kodansha Publishing, 1984), 23.

140. Ibid., 34.

141. By the time Tadamichi wrote the *Kangaku-e ki*, it is possible that the events had been embellished, but since they were written by a man of high social stature who had attended the later Kangaku-e meetings, it is also possible that this additional information

adds they were written "for the sake of the Buddha, for the sake of the Dharma, for the sake of *kangaku* (advancement of [secular?] learning), and for the sake of actuating a connection [with the teachings/Buddha] (*kechien*)."[142] He adds that they were not composed on the "wind and moon" (*fūgetsu*)—a metonymical word referring to the natural world to which the Japanese were deeply attached. Interestingly, we also know from the *Kangaku-e ki* that saké was offered during the service.[143]

A critical aspect of the Kangaku-e assembly was the recitation of a verse by the Chinese poet Po Chü-i (772–846). The poem is found among Po's works that were presented to the Hsiang-shan Monastery, and it represents his desire to find conciliation between his secular profession and his devotion to Buddhism. The verse reads, "May my worldly works conceived in error in this life— / All the wild words and fanciful phrases— / Be transformed in the next into hymns of praise / That will glorify Buddhism through age after age / And turn the Wheel of the Law forever and ever."[144] The crucial part of this verse is the phrase translated as "wild words and fanciful phrases" (J: *kyōgen kigo*; C: *k'uang-yen i-yu*), a metaphor for the composition of worldly literature.[145]

As both William LaFleur and Rajyashree Pandey have indicated, the phrase *kyōgen kigo* was critical to the Heian aristocracy because its efficacy (to transform the secular into the religious) provided a rationalization for the ever-present need to compose *waka* at the court.[146] One might surmise, however, that if the aristocracy were to write *waka* on Buddhist topics, then their compositions would require no rationalization even if they eventually came to include both "the wind and the moon." In other words, *waka* verse as well could be based on the teachings and serve as a kind of intermediary

---

was excluded from Minamoto no Tamenori's version, a more concise, and perhaps more temperate, account for Princess Sonshi.

142. Komatsu, *Kangaku-e ki*, 33.

143. Ibid.

144. Kamens, *The Three Jewels*, 296.

145. The word *kigo* alone appears in the *Kangaku-e ki*. It is possible that this is shorthand for the entire phrase. Komatsu, *Kangaku-e ki*, 34.

146. LaFleur, *The Karma of Words*, 8–9; Rajyashree Pandey, *Writing and Renunciation*, 17–21.

between them and the composition of nonreligious *waka*. Despite some doubt about its authenticity, the Preface to Princess Senshi's *Hosshin wakashū* (*Waka* Collection for Awakening the Heart, 1012) provides the logic for writing poems based upon the Buddhist sūtras:

> The Buddha preached the teachings of the One Vehicle of the Dharma Flower [Hokke-kyō] and composed hymns on the goodness of the various Tathāgathas. Knowing this, I realized the virtue of hymns and came to understand that writing verse is [the same as] a [religious] service for the Buddha.[147]

Later in the same Preface Princess Senshi explains the title of her anthology: "… [the *Hosshin wakashū*] will plant the seed of karma to awaken the desire for enlightenment [in the western Paradise], and … [lead people to] rebirth on the uppermost level of the Lotus blossom in the Pure Land." Assuming that Senshi's Preface is her own, it provides the only critical work to explain why composing *waka* on Buddhist topics would be seen as beneficial by a Heian-period poet.

There are examples of Buddhist *waka* that predate both the *Hosshin wakashū* and the compilation of the *Shūishū*. For example, there are Buddhist *waka* in the *Shūishū* that are attributed to Gyōki (668–749), Empress Kōmyō (701–760), and Shōtoku Taishi (574–622), though the attributions for some, such as Gyōki's poem, are apparently dubious.[148] There are also examples of *waka* on the chapters of the Lotus Sutra attributed to Saichō (767–822), Ennin (794–864), and Ryōgen (912–985) in the "Shakkyō-ka" book of the eleventh imperial poetry anthology, *Shokukokinshū* (1265).[149] While

---

147. Translation by author. Based on the text in Ishihara Kiyoshi, *Hosshin wakashū no kenkyū* (Osaka: Izumi Shoin, 1983), 71–87. Suspicions about the author of the Preface are addressed in Kamens, *The Buddhist Poetry of the Great Kamo Priestess*, 66.

148. See Jonathan Morris Augustine, *Buddhist Hagiography in Early Japan: Images of Compassion in the Gyōki Tradition* (London and New York: Routledge Curzon, 2005), 107–108.

149. Takagi Yutaka, *Heian jidai Hokke-kyō Bukkyō-shi kenkyū* (Kyoto: Heiraku-ji Shoten, 1973), 260 and 315.

it is possible that these attributions are accurate, there is no indication that the practice of writing *waka* on the chapters of the Lotus Sutra was a widespread custom during these eras.

This practice became more common during Emperor Ichijō's reign, however. In 1002, Fujiwara no Michinaga (966–1027) held a memorial service for his elder sister Higashi Sanjō-in Senshi (961–1002), the mother of Emperor Ichijō (980–1011).[150] At the service Michinaga asked attendees such as Fujiwara no Kintō, Fujiwara no Tadanobu (957–1035), Fujiwara no Yukinari (971–1027), and Minamoto no Toshikata (960–1027) to compose *waka* on the twenty-eight chapters of the Lotus Sutra. Poems on such topics are referred to as *Hokke-kyō nijūhappon-ka* by Fujiwara no Arikuni (943–1011) who wrote the Preface to them.[151] All of Kintō's twenty-eight poems produced for this occasion can be found in his private anthology *Kintōshū*, and a similar group of twenty-eight poems in the private anthology of Akazome Emon (?–1041), but we cannot be sure that they are derived from the same event.[152] *Hokke-kyō-ka* by the other participants mentioned above are scattered about in other anthologies.[153]

Important as well to the background of the Buddhist *waka* in the *Shūishū* was the dissemination of the Tendai teachings during the tenth century. As the teachings that had the most influence on the aristocracy who, along with some priests, wrote court *waka*, Tendai was certain to affect the struggle between writing secular verse and

---

150. A description of Senshi's death and the memorial service *sans* poetry contributions can be found in *Eiga monogatari*. William H. and Helen Craig McCullough, trans., *A Tale of Flowering Fortunes* (Stanford: Stanford University Press, 1980), vol. 1, 247–248.

151. The Preface ("San Hokke-kyō nijūhappon wakajo") is all that remains of that particular document. It can be found in *kanbun* form in Ōsone Shōsuke, et. al, *Honchō monzui* in SNKBT, vol. 27 (Tokyo: Iwanami Shoten, 2007), 323. *Waka* on the Lotus Sutra are considered to be a variety of *shakkyō-ka*, and they are usually designated as they are in the Preface, that is, *Hokke-kyō nijūhappon-ka* or *nijūhappon-kyō-ka*. See also Takagi, *Heian jidai Hokke-kyō Bukkyō-shi kenkyū*, 260–261.

152. Takagi, *Heian jidai Hokke-kyō Bukkyōshi kenkyū*, 261.

153. Private anthologies by Kintō and Akazome Emon also contain a number of poems based on the Yuima-kyō (Vimalakīrti Sūtra). For the *Kintōshū*, *Akazome Emon shū*, and the Yuima-kyō poems, see *Shin kokka taikan* [hereafter SKT], vol. 3, *Shikashū hen* (Tokyo: Kadokawa Shoten, 1987), 306, 323.

abiding by the doctrines of Buddhism. One of the ways in which we see the increasing power of the Tendai sect is in the overall membership of the Sōgō, the Office of Monastic Affairs. Between 925 and 995, the number of Tendai monks increased from two to eighteen while Shingon only increased their numbers from three to four.[154] Another factor was the massive fire on Mount Hiei in 966 that forced Ryōgen, Tendai's abbot at the time, to spend the next twenty years seeking resources from potential contributors (many of whom came from the imperial court and the nobility) to rebuild its temple buildings.[155] Finally, Ryōgen's close ties with the Fujiwara family—especially Tadahira (880–949) and Morosuke (908–960)—secured the place of Tendai within its most important branch, the Northern house.[156]

CONCLUSION

Buddhist *waka* of the late Heian period did not spring fully developed from nothing. In the poetic tradition, there was a history of engagement with the culture of Buddhism and even occasionally with Buddhist thought before Buddhist *waka* ever appeared in the *Shūishū*. However, for a time this engagement was isolated and infrequent. The precise reasons for this are unknown, but we can conjecture that the brevity of the *waka* form, the limited range of topics deemed acceptable, and limited involvement with the occasions and ceremonies held at the Buddhist temples inhibited the creativity needed to overcome these obstructions.

In the mid-tenth century, however, a confluence of historical factors came together so that these obstructions weakened. The formation of an assembly of monks and students devoted to studying the sūtras and writing poetry about them affirmed the association of the religious and literary spheres and emphasized their compatibility rather than their differences. The strengthening of ties between the

---

154. Groner, *Ryōgen*, 126.
155. Ibid., 219.
156. Ibid., 93.

Tendai institutions on Mount Hiei and the imperial court increased the influence one had on the other and brought the religious and literary spheres closer together. The compilation of certain *setsuwa* collections and *ōjōden* relating the rebirth of men and women in the Pure Land also hastened the acceptability of these two spheres. Other more specific events such as Michinaga's command to compose *waka* on the twenty-eight chapters of the Lotus Sutra turned what was previously the purview of *kanshi* into an acceptable topic for *waka*. By the beginning of the eleventh century, *waka* on various Buddhist themes, occasions, and texts could be found in the private collections of Fujiwara no Kintō, Akazome Emon, and Princess Senshi while the construction of a Buddhist *waka* sequence was completed and compiled in the third imperial poetry anthology, the *Shūishū*. It is to the *waka* in this collection that we now turn our attention. ✿

3   BUDDHIST *WAKA* IN THE *SHŪISHŪ* (1005–1007)

Issues of terminology, Buddhist religiosity and concepts, and the courtliness of Japanese Buddhist *waka* discussed in Chapter 1 take center stage in the *Shūishū*. For example, the Buddhist *waka* in the *Shūishū* are the first poems referred to as "*shakkyō-ka*" by Japanese scholars, yet these poems appear in the "Lament" book of the anthology. Because these poems were not yet designated as *shakkyō-ka* by the compiler(s), however, but are ideologically dissimilar to the *aishō-ka*, we will refer to them with the more generic term "Buddhist *waka*" or "*waka* on Buddhist themes." While these *waka* individually reflect a deepening awareness of Buddhist ideas, texts, and events, they are compiled together within an organizational framework that reflects the path (*michi*) of the Buddhist devotee. Of equal importance is how—that is, through what combination of the modes and modalities in particular—these *waka* retained their courtliness while they were exhibiting their roots in the sphere of Buddhist ideas. None of these poems represents the actual experience of enlightenment like poems we will see in later sequences, but their arrangement as a group acknowledges an awareness of the chronological path one must walk to become enlightened. Finally, we also find poems in this sequence that create an imagined history of Buddhist *waka* dating back to Shōtoku Taishi.

INTRODUCTION

The first mention of the *Shūishū* in a public document after its completion occurs in the Preface to the fourth imperial poetry anthology, *Goshūishū* (1086).[157] In it, the compiler, Fujiwara no Michitoshi (1047–1009), wrote that it was ex-Emperor Kazan (968–1008) who "gathered and picked" (*torihiroite*) those *waka* that had not been included in the first and second anthologies and who compiled them in the third which he called the *Shūishū* (Collection of Gleanings).[158] This is significant not only because of the *Shūishū*'s unusual compilation process but also because of how interchangeable the titles, *Shūishū* and *Shūishō* (Selections of Gleanings), were during the Heian period.

In his commentary to the SNKBT version of the *Shūishū*, Komachiya Teruhiko admits that we know very little about the compilation process of the third imperial anthology.[159] What we do know is that there was a shorter, previous version of it called the *Shūishō* (in ten books), and that this personal collection was compiled by Fujiwara no Kintō (966–1041) in the middle of the last decade of the tenth century.[160] It is to the *Shūishō* that Fujiwara no Yukinari (972–1027) refers in his diary *Gonki* for the entry of the fourteenth day of the twelfth month of 999: "[I returned] to Higashinoin the *Shūishō* which I had borrowed ..."[161] The person living at Higashinoin at this time was a woman called Kyū no Onkata, the aunt of ex-Emperor

---

157. Hashimoto Fumio, "Shūishū," *Man'yōshū to chokusenwakashū* (Tokyo: Ōfūsha, 1972), 103.

158. Kubota Jun and Hirota Yoshinobu eds., *Goshūiwakashū*, vol. 8 SNKBT (Tokyo: Iwanami Shoten, 1994), 8.

159. Komachiya Teruhiko, ed., *Shūiwakashū*, vol. 7 SNKBT (Tokyo: Iwanami Shoten, 1990), 477. For this chapter, the SNKBT version of the *Shūishū* as well as Ishihara's version in *Shakkyō-ka no kenkyū* were consulted. SNKBT, 371–397; *Shakkyō-ka no kenkyū*, 27–62.

160. Most of our information about the *Shūishō* comes from Fujiwara no Yukinari's diary, *Gonki* (spanning the years 991-1017). Komachiya, *Shūiwakashū*, 476. WDJ (463) surmises that Kintō's *Shūishō* was most likely an extraction of an earlier collection by Kintō called the *Nyoihōshū*. Only fifty poems of the latter are extant, but originally it was thought to have consisted of 775 poems in eight books. See SKT, vol. 6, 20–22 for the extant text of *Nyoihōshū*.

161. Hashimoto, "Shūishū," 105.

Kazan and Yukinari. We find another reference to the *Shūishō* in an entry to Murasaki Shikibu's diary for the eighteenth day of the eleventh month of 1008: "The next morning Her Majesty held a close inspection of the gifts she had received the night before ... In the top tray of one of them were some booklets made of white patterned paper: the *Kokinshū*, *Gosenshū*, and *Shūishō*, each in five volumes, four sections to a volume, copied by Middle Counselor Yukinari and the priest Enkan."[162] And contradicting how he had referred to it in his Preface to the *Goshūishū* in 1086, Fujiwara no Michitoshi referred to the *Shūishū* as the *Shūishō* in a document called the *Goshūishū mokuroku-jo* (1087). All of this indicates that there was considerable confusion about what the two works were and what they were called. It is quite possible that contemporaries were referring to the twenty-book *Shūishū* when they used the designation *Shūishō*.

Between the time of the compilation of the ten-book *Shūishō* and the completion of the twenty-book *Shūishū*, ex-Emperor Kazan presumably added several hundred additional poems, but whether he did this work alone or with help from others is not known.[163] It is important to note, however, that the work was carried out at a critical juncture in the history of Japanese literature. Under Emperor Ichijo's reign (986–1011), Michinaga consolidated the Fujiwara-family hold on the sovereign, while ushering in a period of "flowering fortunes" (*eiga*) during which Murasaki Shikibu (exact dates unknown) and Sei Shōnagon (d. 1021–1028) composed *The Tale of Genji* (*Genji monogatari*) and the *The Pillow Book* (*Makura no sōshi*), respectively.

In the following section, we will examine the differences between the laments and the Buddhist *waka* in the "Aishō-ka" book.

---

162. Richard Bowring, trans., *The Diary of Lady Murasaki* (London: Penguin Books, 1996), 37. Bowring translates *Shūishō* as *Shūishū*, but I have modified the translation here.

163. Included within the *Shūishō*, according to the SKT version, are three of the Buddhist *waka* that appear in the final version of the twenty-volume *Shūishū*, but this number is only accurate if you agree with Ishihara's account of how many Buddhist *waka* there are. Ishihara refers to all Buddhist *waka* in the *Shūishū* as *shakkyō-ka* regardless of the name of the book in which they are compiled. For the *Shūishō*, see SKT, vol. 6 *Chokusenshū hen*, 94–108.

FROM LAMENT (*AISHŌ-KA*) TO BUDDHIST *WAKA* IN THE *SHŪISHŪ*

Depending on which Japanese scholar you consult, you will find a different opinion about how many Buddhist *waka* are in the *Shūishū*. Okazaki claimed there are fifteen, while more recent scholars such as Takusu Yōko, Kubota Jun, and Ishihara Kiyoshi claimed there are thirteen, twenty, and twenty-three, respectively.[164] This wide spectrum of numbers represents an obvious disagreement about which poems are "Buddhist" and which poems are not, and this, in turn, points to issues of terminology: are these poems *aishō-ka* with a Buddhist sentiment, Buddhist *waka* related to *aishō-ka* by association, or *shakkyō-ka*, as most scholars refer to them?

It is clear that the compiler(s) of the *Shūishū* did not call the poems in this sequence *shakkyō-ka*, since the word appears nowhere in the anthology itself. So why do modern scholars of *shakkyō-ka* refer to them as that? The most cynical answer would be that by doing so, scholars broaden, simplify, and homogenize the academic territory within which Buddhist *waka* can be discussed. But in truth these scholars are not unjustified to have found within these poems characteristics that are comparable to the *shakkyō-ka* in the *Goshūishū* and, perhaps even the *Senzaishū*.

One possible explanation for the appearance of Buddhist *waka* in the "Aishō-ka" book is the memorial service for Michinaga's elder sister, Senshi (961–1001), a service that was held in 1002 just before the *Shūishū* was completed. As the most powerful person in the government at the turn of the eleventh century, Michinaga (966– 1027) certainly had the influence to initiate a new poetic trend. His relationship to Fujiwara no Kintō, the compiler of the *Shūishō* and other collections and poetic treatises that incorporated Buddhist ideas in them, is well documented.[165]

---

164. Okazaki, "Shakkyō-ka kō," 82; Takusu Yōko, "Shakkyō-ka o meguru kōsatsu," *Kokubun* 37 (June 1972): 12; Kubota Jun, "Hōmon-ka to shakkyō-ka," 264; Ishihara, *Shakkyō-ka no kenkyū*, 27–30.

165. According to WDJ, 249, one of the texts Kintō authored is called *Daihannya-kyō jishō*, (Selections on Characters in the Great Prajñāpāramitā Sūtra).

Still, it is more likely that *waka* presented at this service were part of a more widespread turn of affairs at which Buddhist practices, connected initially to mourning, were affecting other social practices such as the writing of poetry.

There are seventy-seven poems in the "Aishō-ka" book in the *Shūishū*.[166] While even a cursory reading would immediately reveal the Buddhist tone of the final sequence of poems, it is hard to determine where exactly the *aishō-ka* end and the Buddhist *waka* begin. We may speculate whether the anthologizer deliberately made a gradual shift from one kind of theme into another that he saw as closely related.

That *waka* on themes of grief and death are predominant within the first fifty poems in the "Aishō-ka" book should not, of course, come as much surprise given the book's title. Through vocabulary alone—*namida* (tears), *naki hito* (one who is not here), *nakunarishi* (is gone/has died), *Toribeyama* (cremation fields), *shi* (death) as well as *kakuru*, *makaru*, and *usu* (euphemisms for death)—the reader experiences the emotional, lyrical tone of the Japanese lament. On the other hand, references to grief in the last third of the book are limited to the word *naku* (cry). Similarly, vocabulary used to evoke the Buddhist teachings or the culture of those teachings in the first fifty poems are confined to *Hie* (referring to Mount Hiei) and Onyonjūkyū nichi no hōji (the Forty-ninth Day Buddhist Memorial Service). In the last twenty-seven poems, however, we encounter numerous Buddhist words (*butsugo*) such as *Gokuraku* (Western paradise), *Namu Amida Bu(tsu)* (the *nenbutsu*), *Shaka* (the Buddha Śākyamuni), *Hokke-kyō* (Lotus Sutra), *shinnyo* (suchness), and *Monju* (Mañjuśrī).

Of course, a change in vocabulary alone is not the whole story. There comes a point during a sequence of three poems, 1324–1326, at which the reader's attention begins to shift from lamenting death to the teachings of Buddhism. While symbols of grief and death are obvious in poems 1324 and 1325—the cremation grounds (*Toribeyama*), the smoke (*keburi*) that rises (*moetatsu*) from those grounds, and illness (*yamai*)—this gives way in poems 1325 and

---

166. "Poem," in this case, includes the *kotobagaki* or *dai*, the attribution, and the thirty-one syllable *waka*.

1326 to comparing our lives to dew (*inochi o tsuyu ni tatouru*) and lamenting the impermanence of the world (*yo no hakanaki koto*). Yet there is still little in the rhetorical argument of these *waka* to indicate that the Buddhist teachings are the reference point. When we come to the phrase *yo no hakanaki koto* in the headnote to poem 1326, it may *appear* that the poems in the book are leaning in the direction of the Buddhist concept of *mujō* (impermanence), but *hakanashi* and *mujō* are not always interchangeable. *Hakanashi* also has the meaning of "aimless" and "pointless," which is the meaning in this particular case. In this particular poem the author is focused upon a traveler who has fallen (died) on the side of the road making his "grass pillow" (*kusamakura*) in the hills and fields (*noyama*) his "final resting place" (*tsui no sumika*). The sudden and often unexpected nature of death is surely a reminder of life's impermanence to everyone at some time, but the sadness of death is made even more poignant by a traveler who has no home in which to die.

The poem that follows 1326, on the other hand, is a somewhat different case. It is a variant of a well-known poem from the *Man'yōshū* by the priest Mansei. The following are the two versions of this poem in the *Man'yōshū* and the *Shūishū*:

Man'yōshū version

世の中を何にたとえむ朝開き漕ぎ去にし舟の跡なきごとし

yo no naka o / nani ni tatoemu / asabiraki / kogiinishi fune no / ato naki gotoshi

> to what shall I liken
> this world?
>   a boat
> rows out in the morning
> leaving no trace[167]

Shūishū version

世の中を何にたとえむ朝ぼらけ漕ぎ行く舟の跡の白波

yo no naka o / nani ni tatoemu / asaborake / kogiyuku fune no / ato no shiranami

> to what shall I liken
> this world?
>   dawn half-light—
> white wavewake
> of a boat that rowed out

---

167. For previous discussion of this poem in the *Man'yōshū*, see Chapter 2, pp. 58–60.

While the differences between these two variants are minor, the aspect that concerns us and to which Japanese scholars point is the sense of impermanence created by the image of the boat rowing through the water. Writing primarily in the meditative mode (building an argument by means of question and answer), the author, who was a Buddhist priest, is explicit about making this comparison to our human existence in the world. Whether the poem is consciously expressing the concept of Buddhist *mujō* or some less Buddhist-focused sensibility seems beside the point. There is at least at this point in the "Aishō-ka" book a *sense* that the teachings are for the first time being communicated.

The poem that follows Mansei's—1328—takes the reader back to the theme of grief and death, however:

契あれば屍なれども逢ひぬるを我をば誰か訪はんとすらん
chigiri areba / kabane naredomo / ainuru o / ware oba tare ka / towan to suran

NOTICING A PAINTING IN THE MONKS' HALL IN WHICH THE PRIEST CHŪREN WEEPS OVER A CORPSE, THE AUTHOR SPEAKS AS THE PRIEST

> my fate
>> brought me
>>> to this corpse—
>
>> who will
> visit me
when I'm in this shape?

> — Minamoto no Sukekata

The speaker of the *waka*, written by Minamoto no Sukekata (dates unknown) on the occasion of seeing a painting or drawing of Priest Chūren crying over a dead person (*shinin*), inquires "who will / visit me / when I'm in this shape" (shape = *kabane*). It might be possible to make a case for this poem as Buddhist since there is a priest in the painting, and since the speaker of the poem is looking at the painting inside temple grounds, but this evidence seems hardly enough to render it a Buddhist poem. The poem's central question—a cry for reassurance of some kind—concerns one's mortality in the world, a question more suitable for a lament.

Ishihara claims, and I concur, that the Buddhist *waka* sequence in the *Shūishū* begins with poem 1329. Mansei's poem (1327) is metaphorical, meditative, conceptual and certainly Buddhist in tone. Sukekata's poem (1328), on the other hand, written in a strong lyric mode is only superficially Buddhist, but does move the reader's attention from the sea to the temple. This location (and the lyric mode) is retained in poem 1329, but the speaker's recognition of impermanence *through the Buddhist temple bells* indicates a thematic shift in which the impermanence of Mansei's poem and the temple setting of Sukekata's poem cohere in a single poem.

山寺の入相の鐘の声ごとに今日も暮れぬと聞くぞ悲しき
yamadera no / iriai no kane no / koegoto ni / kyō mo kurenu to / kiku zo kanashiki

> with each call
> > of the mountain temple bell
> > > as darkness falls
> > I hear today too
> is gone:
>
> > > sad, knowing that—
>
> > > > — Anonymous

The author's central image—the *yamadera* (mountain temple)—may actually be one that the speaker or poet is *not* actually seeing. The speaker is, however, aware of its presence through the ringing temple bells. These aural and possibly visual images are placed within the time of day most commonly associated with—in a metaphorical sense—old age and death: the sunset. Hearing the bells and watching (presumably) the sunset evokes sadness that "today too is gone" (*kyō mo kurenu*). The emphatic particle "mo" in this phrase as well as the fact that she is hearing "each call" (*koegoto ni*) of the temple's bell suggests the inexorable passage of time—a narrative element—that in turn points to the theme of impermanence. Finally, the metaphor "voice" (*koe*) for the ringing of the bell strengthens and humanizes the sadness at the end of the poem, while serving as a call to embrace the Buddhist teachings at the same time. The voice of the teachings is also the voice of salvation, so it is here that a new modality of religious poetry—soteriological/courtly—first appears.

THE PATH OF THE SEEKER

The most notable characteristic of the Buddhist *waka* in the *Shūishū* is their schematic arrangement. Compiled to simulate the paradigmatic journey a seeker would make on the Buddhist path (J: *michi*, S: *mārga*) to enlightenment, the sequence can be read as a metaphorical representation of that path. In broad outline, the Buddhist path is comprised of three general parts: (1) awakening to and setting out on the journey, (2) devoting oneself to certain practices, and (3) salvation, or enlightenment.[168] Although the historical Buddha is the most common reference, this story appears in different

---

168. In her article "'*Shūishū*' maki dai-nijū aishō no shakkyō-ka gun e no isshiten: '*Makashikan*' to hairetsu kōsei," Imano Atsuko tries to fit the broad outline of the journey paradigm into the structure of the *Makashikan* text known as *goryaku jikkō* (five abbreviated and ten wide). I think that this structure *is* superimposable on the *shakkyō-ka* sequence in the *Senzaishū* (see Chapter 6) where the fifty-four-poem sequence allows for more intricate divisions, but Imano's efforts are unconvincing when she tries to illuminate which poems match which of the final three abbreviated categories. The five categories are *hosshin* (awakening to the teachings), *shugyō* (practice), *kanka* (summon the rewards), *retsumō* (rend the net), and *kisho* (return to the abode). *Waka bungaku kenkyū*, vol. 81 (December 2000): 11–20.

forms in the biographies and hagiographies of many other Buddhist masters from Chih-i (538–597) in China to Shōtoku Taishi (574–622) in Japan.[169] The story of the Buddha's journey is summarized in a single sentence in Tamenori's *Sanbō ekotoba* (984) where we find the same three elements listed above: "... [H]e was born in the palace of a king and, while still in his youth, rejected the Five Cravings and left his father's house, and when he sat under the Tree of Enlightenment, he subdued the Four Forces of Evil and became a Buddha."[170] The *Shūishū* sequence refers only once to the Buddha's life story directly. However, it presents the journey of a seeker in the same three steps as the *Sanbō ekotoba*: "he ... left his father's house," "he sat [meditated]," and "he ... became a Buddha."

Even though a Śākyamuni cult did not develop in East Asia the same way that it did in South and Southeast Asia, this does not mean that the life of the Buddha was not revered. Texts like the *Nihon ryōiki* (completed ca. 810–824) and *Sanbō ekotoba* contain legends and stories about the historical Buddha, making it clear he was present to the Japanese even in his physical absence.[171] The *waka* that best expresses the Buddha's absence/presence and underscores his religious journey in this *Shūishū* sequence is Empress Kōmyō's poem (1345) composed on the footprints of the Buddha at Yamashinadera, the significance of which I will discuss more fully in the section of this chapter entitled "The Final Seven Poems: Introduction."

The implied narrative of a seeker on the path to enlightenment comes only partially from the individual *waka*. The continuity of the story was created by the compiler(s) who not only arranged the poems in a certain order, but also wrote the prose *kotobagaki*, or headnotes, that provide the "historical" contexts for each poem.

---

169. For Chih-i, see Kenneth Ch'en, *Buddhism in China: A Historical Survey* (Princeton: Princeton University Press, 1964), 303–304. For Shōtoku Taishi, see Michael Como, *Shōtoku: Ethnicity, Ritual, and Violence in the Japanese Buddhist Tradition* (Oxford: Oxford University Press, 2008), 151.

170. Kamens, *The Three Jewels*, 101.

171. For the subject of the Buddha's presence and absence, see Malcolm David Eckel, *To See the Buddha: A Philosopher's Quest for the Meaning of Emptiness* (New York: Harper Collins, 1992), 73–94.

The veracity, or lack thereof, of a headnote is only important in a scholarly sense. In a literary or religious sense, it is the continuity of the story—derived by reading the poems carefully in sequence—that takes precedence.

As a poetic device for enriching and integrating *waka* in an imperial anthology, the headnote began to lose some of its power in the imperial anthologies following the *Shūishū*, as the *dai*, or topic, gained a foothold. Writing poems on fixed topics (the moon, the autumn leaves etc.) reflected the professionalization of *waka* that accompanied the increased frequency of poetry competitions (*utaawase*) at the court in the second half of the Heian period, but the rise of Buddhist *waka* on fixed topics—scriptural *waka*—probably reflected the familiarity of sacred texts and sūtras among the aristocracy. Buddhist *waka* based upon texts and sūtras are not unknown in the *Shūishū* as we will see, but the distinction between occasional and scriptural *waka* will become more prominent with the compilation of the *Goshūishū* in 1086.

A second and related characteristic of the Buddhist *waka* in the *Shūishū* is the fact that the final seven poems of this sequence (ending as well the book and the anthology) are all attributed to notable historical figures from the distant past, figures known more for their role in Buddhist history than for their status as poets: Kōmyō Kōgō (701–760), consort to Emperor Shōmu (r. 724–749, d. 756), Gyōki (668–749), the Indian dharma master Bodhisena (J: Baramon Sōjō, 704–760), and Shōtoku Taishi. This inversion of the historical timeline from newer (poems/poets) to older (poems/poets) can be understood from a number of different angles, but what is important here in terms of the creation of a poetic path, or *michi,* is that the older figures represent the path's conclusion: that is, enlightenment.

Before we discuss the final seven poems in more detail, however, we must read the sequence from the beginning—that is, from the anonymous *yamadera* poem discussed previously.

MICHI: LEAVING ONE'S HOME

[1330]

憂き世をばそむかば今日もそむきなん明日もありとは頼む
べき身か

*ukiyo oba / somukaba kyō mo / somukinan / asu mo ari to wa / tanomu
beki mi ka*

WRITTEN AND LEFT AT HOME WHEN HE DEPARTED TO
BECOME A PRIEST

> if I'm going to turn my back
> on this terrible world
>
> it ought to be today—
>
> can this body
> count on any tomorrow?

— Yoshishige no Yasutane

[1331, no headnote]

世中に牛の車のなかりせば思ひの家をいかで出でまし

*yo no naka ni / ushi no kuruma no / nakariseba / omoi no ie o / ikade
idemashi*

> if there were in the world
> > no jeweled chariot
> > > drawn by a lovely white ox
>
> > what would coax us out
> of the burning house
>
> of our mind?[172]

> > > — Anonymous

---

172. Our translation of this poem includes a few words not found in the original
poem—"jeweled," "lovely," "white"—because "ox cart" does not convey what Heian
readers would have understood by this allusion. "Jeweled," "lovely," and "white" are from
the parable in the Lotus Sutra, and in this instance we felt justified in importing them.

[1332]

世中にふるぞはかなき白雪のかつは消えぬる物と知る／＼
*yo no naka ni / furu zo hakanaki / shirayuki no / katsu wa kienuru /
mono to shirushiru*

WRITTEN ON A FOLDED PIECE OF PAPER DURING A
SNOWFALL AS THE AUTHOR WAS ABOUT TO ENTER THE
PRIESTHOOD

    my days in the world
          —are vanishing!—

we know about snow:

    falls

    white

    disappears

                   — Fujiwara no Takamitsu

[1333]

墨染の色は我のみと思しを憂き世をそむく人もあるとか

sumizome no / iro wa ware nomi to / omoishi o / ukiyo o somuku / hito mo aru to ka

SENT TO A CERTAIN WOMAN THE POET KNEW WHEN HE WAS IN MOURNING AND HEARD SHE HAD BECOME A NUN

> the "I" who grieves
>   thought I was the only one
>   to put on black—
>
>   but did you too
>   give your back
> to a world of hurt?

— Ōnakatomi no Yoshinobu

[1334]

墨染の衣と見ればよそながらもろともに着る色にぞ有りける
sumizome no / koromo to mireba / yosonagara / morotomo ni kiru / iro ni zo arikeru

A REPLY TO THE PREVIOUS POEM

> my reason
> "to put on black"
> may seem different—
>
> but believe me:
> we wear that color
> together

> — Anonymous

[1335]

思知る人も有ける世中をいつをいつとて過すなるらん

omoishiru / hito mo arikeru / yo no naka o / itsu o itsu tote / sugusu naruran

SENT TO THE MAJOR CONTROLLER OF THE LEFT
YUKINARI WHEN NARINOBU AND SHIGEIE TOOK THE
TONSURE

> shall I
> while away this world
> thinking "when oh when?"—
>
> when there are people
> already long since
> awake?

— Fujiwara no Kintō

[1336]

さゞなみや志賀の浦風いか許心の内の涼かるらん
sazanami ya / shiga no urakaze / ika bakari / kokoro no uchi no /
suzushikaruran

SENT TO LESSER COUNSELOR FUJIWARA MUNEMASA
WHEN THE POET HEARD HE HAD TAKEN THE
TONSURE, AS THEY HAD BOTH LONG VOWED TO DO

if a breeze
ripples off the shingle
across the lake at Shiga

how much freshness
must rest
in your heart?

— Fujiwara no Kintō

The seven *waka* after the anonymous *yamadera* poem (1329) are all related in some way to the act of leaving one's home (*shukke*) in order to take the tonsure. The word *shukke* does not always mean becoming a full-time monk or nun, but the phrase "leaving one's home" does capture the finality of withdrawing from coveted public life in the court and the capital. These conflicting choices—remaining part of secular life or withdrawing from it—comprise one of the central tensions of the Heian court.

Despite the monastic destination implied in the act of *shukke*, most of these poems—except for one—still express a soteriological/courtly (rather than soteriological/monastic) modality, with an emphasis on the lyric mode and the emotions that these predicaments inspire. However, the contextual prose headnotes that preface the poems and the manner in which the poems are ordered provide a narrative element that pulls the sequence forward.

The anonymous *yamadera* poem (1329) already pointed the reader in the direction of the narrative about *shukke* to follow. The realization signaled by the tolling temple bells is one of the most important realizations in the Buddhist teachings: the impermanence (S: *anitya*; J: *mujō*) of life. The teachings say that without the realization of impermanence we would be mired in the misguided comfort of immortality derived from a mistaken belief in a permanent self. So the lyric sentiment that it is sad (*kanashiki*) to truly understand the passing of time is mitigated by the source of this knowledge: the Buddhist temple. In other words, the sadness of impermanence is tempered by religious practice in the Buddhist temple, and is also a motivating force toward such practice.

In the *waka* that follow 1329, the temple continues to play a role, albeit a silent one. The word *temple* (*tera*) does not appear in either the headnotes or the poems, but it is the place imagined by those in the aristocracy who chose to cast the worldly aside and lead a life of introspection and reclusion. However, before entering the temple must come the act of renouncing the world—an act fraught, at least at this time in Japanese history, with great social significance. For those who performed the act before an age that was deemed appropriate by others, there was sadness and consternation. Those who wanted to perform the act but could not bring themselves to make the decision had to live with this internal conflict.

The theme of this sub-sequence (1330–1336) may be the act of *shukke*, but this does not mean that it aligns perfectly with the paradigmatic story of the Buddha who gave up his home (and wife and child) decisively after he encountered the suffering of the sick, the old, the dying, and the deprived. In the original sources we are told little about the emotional turmoil that undoubtedly preceded the Buddha's decision. But the poems of this sub-sequence emphasize precisely the range of emotions that accompanied such a decision in the Japanese court, compiled not according to a linear temporal order, but ordered to reflect the authors' vacillating states of mind, some of which express feelings of decisiveness (like the Buddha) while others express feelings of hesitation, or envy of those whose time of decision is past.

In this section, most of the narrative elements are provided by the compiler's headnotes: for example, "Written and left at the home when he departed to become a priest," and "Sent to the Lesser Counselor Fujiwara no Munemasa when the poet heard he had taken the tonsure, as they had both long vowed to do." These headnotes provide the minimum narrative information needed to ground the *waka* in a particular situation. Later in the second sub-sequence we will encounter longer headnotes that approach the early Heian ideal of the *utamonogatari* (poem tale).

The second poem (1331, Anonymous) is based upon a story in which the characters literally have to "leave the house" (*shukke*) to discover the road to salvation. The parable of the burning house from the third chapter of the Lotus Sutra was one of the most commonly alluded to in premodern Japanese literature, which explains why this *waka* did not seem to require a headnote to alert the reader to its meaning. However, since it is the first such Buddhist *waka* in this study to use the parable, for modern readers a quick review of the story and its meaning is likely necessary.

In the parable, children (the Buddha's disciples) are so consumed by the attractiveness of their toys (attachments to the things of this world) that they do not notice the house they are in is on fire. The children's father (the Buddha) tries to coax them out with promises of a deer-drawn, a horse-drawn and an ox-drawn cart (representing the three vehicles of Buddhism—the *pratyekabuddha, śrāvaka,* and the *bodhisattva*). Once the children are finally persuaded to leave the house (*shukke*), they find only one large bejeweled cart pulled by a great white ox. According to the parable, this cart, representing the One Buddha Vehicle (S: *ekayāna*; J: *ichijō*) of the Lotus Sutra, is all one needs to be freed from the neurotic mental states that encourage attachment (S: *kleśas*; J: *bonnō*) and to reach the state of *anuttara samyak sambodhi* (true perfect enlightenment). The means and the end are conflated in this story through the use of skillful means (*hōben*, the subject and title of the previous chapter in the Lotus Sutra) employed by the father. The father's promise is a well-intentioned lie; there are no deer-drawn or horse-drawn carriages. In the parable, however, the father's lie is necessary and is transformed, through *hōben,* into enlightened words, because it leads his children to safety and to realization.

The critical relationship of this story to *shukke* in the *waka* under consideration comes to life in the words *house* (*uchi*) and *leave* (*idemashi*)—*uchi o deru* in its modern Japanese reading, *shukke* in its modern Sinitic reading. The image of the burning house is created through the use of the pivot word (*kakekotoba*) in the phrase *omo[h]i no uchi,* in which the word *omo[h]i* can be read *hi no uchi* (house of fire). A person's mental state (*the burning house / of our mind* in our translation) is indicated by the word *omoi.* The Japanese sense of *shukke* might not be implied in the original Sutra text, but whether one is leaving one's house to discover the One Vehicle of the Lotus Sutra or leaving one's to take the tonsure, the result is the same.

Among the six other *waka* in this sub-sequence, two—by Yoshishige no Yasutane (?–1002) and Fujiwara no Takamitsu (?–994)—represent *shukke* as a foregone conclusion. Yoshishige's poem is an intellectual argument (thus in the meditative mode) that pivots on the following proposition: "if A is the case, then B is probably the case." This proposition is the answer to the rhetorical question that follows ("can this body / count on any tomorrow?"), inverting the usual question and answer order. The word *mi* (body) in the final *ku* personalizes the poem since it often indicates the first person singular "I." However, the lyric sentiment that one might find in a personal *waka* such as this is strongly deemphasized or only implied. Instead, the poem favors the spiritual argument: since one cannot depend on the future, one must turn one's back on the world *now.*

Takamitsu's *waka* (1332) has, like Yoshishige's poem, a meditative aspect, in that his comparison of the vanishing snow to the quickly passing years of his life only hints at the emotional toll it might have taken on him. The result, however, is the same as Yoshishige's poem: his understanding of how the world works (expressed by the metaphor of the snow) has led to the decision to leave it for the contemplative life. The use of the adjective *hakanashi* (vanishing) is especially appropriate in this case, because it carries the additional meaning of time spent in vain.

Takamitsu's poem resonated strongly in the hearts of other members of the court because of events in the poet's life: at the very young age of twenty-three he retired from the court for a life in the priesthood. Takamitsu's age alone would have been sufficient to move the members of court, but as the son of the regent Fujiwara no Morosuke (908–960) and Princess Masako (910–954), a daughter of Daigo Tennō (880–949), Takamitsu's prospects for a career at the court were excellent.[173] After he left the court and his family in 961 to study on Mount Hiei, he moved to Myōraku-ji on Mount Tōnomine in the area of Yoshino. It was sometime during his stay on Mount Tōnomine that someone (the author is unknown) penned the tale known variously as *Tōnomine shōshō monogatari* (*The Tale of the Tōnomine Lesser Counsellor*) or *Takamitsu nikki* (*The Diary of Takamitsu*). Aileen Gatten says that this work "is one of the earliest extant attempts to tell a unified story in Japanese; it is the first surviving vernacular prose narrative to depict realistic characters in place of folk or courtly

---

173. Aileen Gatten, "Fact, Fiction, and Heian Literary Prose: Epistolary Narration in Tōnomine Shōshō Monogatari," *Monumenta Nipponica,* vol. 53, no. 2 (Summer, 1998): 167–169.

stereotypes ..."[174] The fact that one of the earliest extant prose works in Japanese literature concerns the effect of *shukke* on family members is clearly indicative of the narrative power such an act held for the aristocracy at this time. As Gatten puts it, "His influential family and the aristocratic world at large were shocked by his action, which became the talk of society."[175] We see confirmation of this in later works of literature such as *Eiga monogatari* (*The Tale of Flowering Fortunes*, ca. 1092) and *Ōkagami* (The Great Mirror, ca. 1119) in which the event is called "sad," "poignant," and "deeply moving."[176] *The Tale of Flowering Fortunes* encapsulates these emotions thus: "Someone is sure to mention Takamitsu whenever people speak of sad things."[177]

Fujiwara no Kintō's two poems (1335–1336) later in this seven-poem sub-sequence emphasize the lyric mode far more than the two poems just discussed, though Kintō's poems also address similar kinds of events. The first was composed at the time two young men, Minamoto no Narinobu (b. 979) and Fujiwara no Shigeie (dates unknown), abandoned their positions at court for the rigors of a priestly life on Mount Hiei. Minamoto no Narinobu and Fujiwara no Shigeie took the tonsure at Miidera on the fourth day of the second month of 1001.[178] If these two men had not been, respectively, the adopted son of Fujiwara no Michinaga, the Minister of the Left, and the only natural son of Fujiwara no Akimitsu (944–1021), the Minister of the Right, the impact might have been less shocking. Considering their youth, backgrounds, family lineages, potential for rank and power, and the benefits that inevitably accrued to such status, it is not surprising that their elders at the imperial court were perplexed by such acts.

---

174. Ibid.

175. Ibid.

176. McCullough and McCullough, *A Tale of Flowering Fortunes*, vol. 1, 91; Helen Craig McCullough, *Ōkagami: The Great Mirror* (Princeton: Princeton University Press, 1980), 135.

177. McCullough and McCullough, *A Tale of Flowering Fortunes*, vol. 1, 92.

178. For further information on this incident, see Komachiya Teruhiko, *Fujiwara Kintō* (Tokyo: Shūeisha, 1985), 172–175.

The question in Kintō's poem does not lead to the same predetermined conclusion that the previous rhetorical questions did. In both Yoshishige's *waka* and the *waka* on the parable of the burning house, the answer to the rhetorical question is provided in the first three *ku*: *if I'm going to turn my back / on this terrible world / it ought to be today* and *if there were in the world / no jeweled chariot / drawn by a lovely white ox.* In Kintō's poem (1336), however, the answer could either lead to *shukke* or to further indecision.

The second Kintō poem was sent to the Lesser Counselor Fujiwara no Munemasa (dates unknown) on the occasion of his taking vows in 999.[179] There is nothing in the headnote to Kintō's second poem that hints at the reason for Munemasa's act of renunciation, but some have conjectured that it occurred at a time of great personal loss, perhaps the death of a close loved one. Leaving the world due to this kind of loss was perhaps more comprehensible to the court, and maybe even to Kintō himself, than Narinobu and Shigeie's sudden departure in their prime.

Some commentators have noted a self-derogatory (*jichōteki*)[180] tone in the first of Kintō's poems, but I would agree with Ishihara in this case who considers it self-admonitory (*jikai*) and self-reflective (*jisei*) instead.[181] This tone contrasts with that of the second poem, in which Kintō expresses some envy for the spiritual comfort Munemasa must have found in his temple in Shiga—a resolution of the painful indecision Kintō felt. Kintō would not take the tonsure for another thirty years after this poem was written, but clearly the roots of his desire to do so can be seen much earlier.

Two poems, 1333 and 1334, in this subsection about departure from one's home, are a *zōtōka* between Ōnakatomi no Yoshinobu, one of the compilers of the *Gosenshū,* and an anonymous woman.

---

179. Historically, the event upon which the second poem is based took place before the event recounted in Kintō's first poem, but their order in the *Shūishū* takes precedence over historical accuracy.

180. Kubota Jun, *Chūsei,* Volume 3 in *Nihon bungaku zenshi* (Tokyo: Gakutōsha, 1990), 391.

181. Ishihara, *Shakkyō-ka no kenkyū,* 38.

As a poetic exchange, *zōtōka* are always more social, and thus, more grounded in a narrative mode than individual poems, but in this case there are also strong lyric and meditative elements. The conceit of this exchange revolves around the phrases *sumizome no / iro* and *sumizome no / koromo* (color of black dye, black-dyed robes). Despite the different purposes for which they wear the robes, the nun says that they "wear that color / together" (*morotomo ni kiru / iro ni zo arikeru*), implying, as she reasons, that they have both experienced "a world of hurt" (*ukiyo*), as Yoshinobu's poem says. On his part, Yoshinobu understands that turning one's back (*somuku*) on this world of hurt is the only proper response, but there is no indication that he will follow the same path as the nun. In the end, the motivation for his inquiry seems to derive equally from a desire to contact the anonymous nun and to explore a common grief as it does from a desire to understand the act of renunciation she undertook.

The second sub-sequence of poems (1337–1342) in the Buddhist *waka* sequence in the *Shūishū* concerns the theme of attending certain ceremonies (i.e., performing religious practices)—the midpoint on the path—and the devotion that is derived from those acts.

MICHI: PRACTICE AND DEVOTION

[1337]

業尽す御手洗河の亀なれば法の浮木に逢はぬなりけり

*gō tsukusu / mitarashigawa no / kame nareba / nori no ukigi ni / awanu
narikeri*

SENT TO THE EMPRESS WITH A GOLDEN TURTLE AT
THE TIME OF THE EIGHT LECTURES ON THE LOTUS
SUTRA

> for my sins
> I'm the turtle
> in this hand-bath of the gods—
>
> the raft of truth
> will never drift
> *my* way!

— Saiin

[1338]

いつしかと君にと思し若菜をば法の道にぞ今日は摘みつる
itsu shika to / kimi ni to omoishi / wakana o ba / nori no michi ni zo /
kyō wa tsumitsuru

WRITTEN WHEN THE TENRYAKU EMPEROR'S PLANS
FOR A CELEBRATION IN HIS MOTHER'S HONOR WERE
CUT SHORT BY HER DEATH, AND A CEREMONY TO
RECITE THE SŪTRAS WAS HELD INSTEAD

> the tender
> shoots of spring
> I picked today—
>
> I wanted to hurry them
> to you
> for your journey

— Gyosei

[1339]

たき木こる事は昨日に尽きにしをいざおのの柄はこゝに朽
さん

*takigi koru / koto wa kinō ni / tsukinishi o / iza ono no e wa / koko ni
kutasan*

WRITTEN A DAY AFTER A SŪTRA MEMORIAL AT
FUMON-JI, WHEN THE AUTHOR WITH TAMEMASA
ASON AND A COMPANY OF OTHERS WERE DRAWN BY
THE CHERRY BLOSSOMS AT ONO

> because yesterday
> we finished "gathering
> our firewood"—
>
> today let's let
> our axe handle rot,
> shall we?

— Tōgū Tayū Michitsuna no Haha

[1340]

今日よりは露の命も惜しからず蓮の上の玉と契れば
kyō yori wa / tsuyu no inochi mo / oshikarazu / hachisu no ue no / tama to chigireba

AFTER HEARING A SERMON AT THE SHIRAKAWA VILLA
OF THE MAJOR CAPTAIN OF THE LEFT NARITOKI

I don't regret
a life as dew—

because as of today

I've vowed to bejewel
the lotus leaf

— Sanekata Ason

[1341]

朝ごとに払ふ塵だにある物を今幾世とてたゆむなるらん

asagoto ni / harau chiri dani / aru mono o / ima ikuyo to te / tayumu naruran

ON THE SURPRISING APPEARANCE OF A STRANGE
PRIEST IN THE AUTHOR'S DREAM DURING A TIME OF
ARDUOUS PRACTICE

> though every morning
> the same dust of suffering
> must be swept away—
>   I ask myself
> *how many lives do you expect,*
> *that you might loiter*
>   *through this one?*

— Anonymous

[1342]

暗きより暗道にぞ入ぬべき遥に照せ山の端の月
*kuraki yori / kuraki michi ni zo / irinu beki / haruka ni terase / yama no
ha no tsuki*

SENT TO HER TEACHER SHŌKŪ SHŌNIN

the path I have to take
    will lead from dark
        to darker—

                O moon

    on your mountain edge
   shine across
  the vast emptiness

          — Masamune no Musume
            Shikibu[182]

---

182. For a long time it was thought that this poem was written at the end of Izumi's life, perhaps even on her deathbed, but more recent scholarship has shown that it was composed much earlier, a fact supported by the name or title used to refer to the author in the *Shūishū*. (Robert Brower and Earl Miner, *Japanese Court Poetry* [Stanford: Stanford University Press, 1961], 218; Roy Andrew Miller, *Footprints of the Buddha*, [New Haven: American Oriental Society, 1975], 86) The name "Masamune" is Izumi's father's name, and links the author more closely to him than to a spouse. The word "Izumi" in her name (as it appeared after her marriage) refers to the province in which her first husband, Tachibana no Michisada (dates unknown), served as governor. Masuda Shigeo, *Kuraki michi* (Kyoto: Sekai Shisōsha, 1987), 3–10; Kikuchi Hitoshi, "Setsuwa: Denshō to Izumi Shikibu," *Kokubungaku* vol. 35, no. 12 (October 1990): 114.

[1343]

極楽は遥けきほどと聞きしかどつとめて至る所なりけり
gokuraku wa / harukeki hodo to / kikishikado / tsutomete itaru / tokoro narikeri

HE WROTE THIS LONGING FOR THE PARADISE IN THE WEST

> though I've heard
> > the distance to supreme delight
> > > is vast
> > > > with practice
> > I can reach that place
> by morning

— Priest Senkei

[1344]

一度も南無阿弥陀仏と言ふ人の蓮の上にのぼらぬはなし

hitotabi mo / namu amida bu to / iu hito no / hachisu no ue ni / noboranu wa nashi[183]

LEFT ON THE MARKETPLACE GATE

>   among those who call
>   the Name
>   even one time
>
>   there are none
>   who won't reach
>   the top of the lotus leaf[184]

> — Kūya Shōnin

---

183. According to Ishihara, *Shakkyō-ka no kenkyū*, 59, this poem also appears in the *setsuwa* collection *Kokonchomonjū*.

184. Kūya's poem is reminiscent of Sanekata's (1340) in that the fourth *ku* in both are almost identical: *hachisu no ue no* and *hachisu no ue ni*.

After a seeker starts on the path, the next step is usually to strengthen commitment and devotion through spiritual practice and to cultivate associations with other seekers in the spiritual community (*sangha*). In modern times, we view devotion and practice as concomitant—one does not practice a religion until one has made a commitment (devoted oneself) to its principles and teachings. At the same time, however, one's commitment to a religion will not be strengthened unless one puts its teachings into practice. Buddhist tradition views practice and devotion somewhat differently. The Theravādin Buddhist teachings are inseparable from the experience of meditation: the Buddha's devotion to meditation is presented as the means by which he practiced the teachings into existence.

Meditation was not the only practice, though, that survived as Buddhism developed in the centuries after the Buddha's death. Theravādin Buddhists believe that most of the Buddha's teachings survive in the *tripitaka*, the three "baskets" that contain the discourses, the monastic rules, and the scholastic treatises. These teachings, or at least a proximate form of these teachings, are believed to have spread throughout South and Southeast Asia to countries like Sri Lanka, Myanmar, Thailand, Cambodia, and Laos. Many centuries after the Buddha's birth, however, a different form of Buddhist teachings arose gradually, not from the monastic centers, but from religious practices and teachings (what became Mahāyāna literature) that flourished around the *stūpas,* a more social rather than reclusive location. As Paul Williams explains about this phenomenon, early Mahāyāna monks and nuns were probably no different from other Buddhist monks and nuns. But eventually "the monks, nuns, and perhaps a small number of lay practitioners who accepted this new [Mahāyāna] literature formed a series of cults, probably based on different *sūtras* and their attendant practices. It is likely that they had little or no direct and regular connection with each other."[185] Williams's point is that different practices were based on different sūtras, and many of these

---

185. Paul Williams, *Mahāyāna Buddhism: The Doctrinal Foundations* (London: Routledge, 1989), 32–33.

practices (with their sūtras) were transmitted out of India and into Tibet and Central Asia, China, Korea, and Japan where the Mahāyāna teachings—rather than the Theravādin teachings—flourished.

Therefore, when we speak about practice in the mid-Heian court context, we must keep in mind that it was not confined to meditation alone, but encompassed many other forms of religious expression, all under the umbrella term of "practice" (shugyō). First and foremost were practices that pertained to sūtras and other religious texts. For example, copying, reading (chanting), lecturing on, and presenting Buddhist texts at temples were religious occasions at which participants accrued merit for themselves and others. Writing waka based upon a Buddhist text can also be included in this category. Second were practices that pertained to the occasions of ceremonies and services at which the sūtra or text may be secondary to some larger purpose, such as a memorial service for a loved one or the consecration of a building. Third were practices performed at ceremonies and services that focused on actuating a connection between an attendee and her or his devotion (Kechien-kō, Bodai-kō), or that focused on worshipping relics (shari) of the Buddha. And fourth, pilgrimages to Buddhist temples or other sacred sites were another form of practice open to the lay believer. While all of these Mahayanic Japanese practices were different in form from the Buddha's meditation practices (expressed now in the Theravādin tradition), essentially they served the same purpose: as a vehicle for salvation from suffering and samsāra. As William LaFleur has said about these practices in the context of Japan, "… it is … important to note that the extensive rituals of Tendai and Shingon Buddhism in the Heian period were actually modes through which the people of that time participated fully in the received Buddhist tradition and its teachings. These rituals should not be dismissed as some kind of excrescence or superfluity."[186]

Like the seven waka in the first sub-sequence, the poems in the second sub-sequence display a range of modes and two modalities. Some, like those by Princess Senshi (Saiin, 1337), Emperor Murakami (Gyosei, 1338), Michitsuna no Haha (1339), and Izumi Shikibu

---

186. LaFleur, The Karma of Words, 16.

(Masamune no Onna Shikibu, 1342), are primarily written in a lyric mode and communicate in a courtly modality. Sanekata's poem (1340) is primarily meditative, but still courtly in its modality. The poem attributed to anonymous (1341), is in the lyric mode and the monastic modality. Two others, by Priest Senkei (1343) and Kūya Shōnin (1344), are meditative and monastic. Thus, the poems each respond to some aspect of Buddhist practice and devotion to the Buddhist teachings with a range of poetic resources.

The first three *waka* (1337–1339) in this eight-poem sub-sequence were composed on occasions when certain ceremonies were performed: an imperially sponsored eight-part ceremony based on the Lotus Sutra (Hokke hakkō), a sūtra memorial service (Kyō kuyō/*gofuju*), and an imperially sponsored reading/chanting of the Lotus Sutra. However, these poems do not offer facile benefits of practice and devotion. Instead, they reveal their authors as frustrated, grieving, and distracted. The second five poems (1340–1344), on the other hand, are more positive and confident about the rewards and benefits of practice and devotion.

In poem 1337, Princess Senshi (964–1035), personally committed to the path of the Buddha, expresses her frustration at not being able to practice openly because of her position at the court. As the chief priestess of the Kamo Shrine, where her duties required exclusive devotion to the *kami*, she is prevented from attending Buddhist ceremonies like the Eight Lectures on the Lotus Sutra. Thwarted in her efforts to "exhaust her karma" (*gō tsukusu*) by participating in the same practices as her contemporaries, Princess Senshi compares herself to the one-eyed tortoise in the twenty-seventh chapter of the Lotus Sutra for whom it is rare "to encounter a hole [the teachings, *nori*] in a floating piece of wood [*ukigi*]."[187]

While Senshi's poem draws on her knowledge of the Lotus Sutra, she asserts what she knows to be true for her personally: as long as she presides over the Kamo Shrine (her "hand-bath of the gods"), she will never encounter what she needs to set her free. An occasional *waka*

---

187. Hurvitz, *Scripture of the Lotus Blossom*, 328; Sakamoto and Iwamoto, *Hokke-kyō*, vol. 3, 298.

written in the lyrical-narrative mode (the narrative derived primarily from the headnote and supported by the poem), Senshi's poem speaks forthrightly to the recipient, the Empress, and bares her feelings of frustration.

The *waka* (1338) by Emperor Murakami (926–967) is written, like Senshi's poem, in a lyric-narrative mode, and also communicates in a soteriological/courtly modality. The sentiment of the poem is prompted by the ceremonial responsibility Murakami had to fulfill when his mother, Fujiwara no Onshi (885–954), died suddenly. Picking the spring herbs (*wakana*) usually signals renewal and hope for longevity, but in an ironic twist of fate, Murakami had to offer them at her funeral service where Buddhist sūtras were recited (*gofuju*) rather than present them to her on her birthday. The herbs and the sūtras were symbolic offerings meant to accompany Onshi as she set out on the "path of the Dharma" (*nori no michi*)—that is, toward her rebirth.

As the first *waka* in the *Shūishū* sequence that specifically mentions the path (*michi*) to Buddhist salvation, it contributes to the meta-narrative of the *michi* depicted by the whole sequence, and simultaneously refers to Onshi's individual journey. The visual image of the herbs and the aural image of the recitation create an atmosphere that is at once courtly and ritualistic. In addition, the theme of the poem recalls the "Aishō-ka" book of which this poem is a part, and it reminds us of the close relationship between the lament and Buddhism at this point in the history of Buddhist *waka*.

The practice referred to in the *kotobagaki* of Michitsuna no Haha's poem (1339) is also a Sūtra Memorial Service—in this case one that took place at Fumon-ji in the northern part of the capital. While Senshi's poem and Murakami's poem reflect the seriousness of the occasions upon which they were composed, Michitsuna no Haha's poem has only the slimmest connection to Buddhism. Having finished their religious practice in front of the Buddha the previous day, Michitsuna no Haha (?936–?995), the author of *Kagerō nikki* (after 975), and her fellow travelers were free to enjoy the beauty of the cherry blossoms at Ono the next. This is the courtly modality in its purest expression: the poem could just have easily been compiled in one of the seasonal books, and would have lost little of its religious significance. (It is possible, though, to read the poem, in the context of the sequence, as a humorous variation of the painful vacillation expressed by other poems.) The only way the reader knows a religious practice has been performed, other than the information provided in the headnote, is through the phrase "gathering the firewood" (*takigi koru*), a well-known expression from Chapter 12 of the Lotus Sutra in which Devadatta served (practiced his devotion to) the Buddha.

In the poems just discussed, Buddhist practice and the devotion it engendered were not contemplative at all. There is no doubt that the ceremonies alluded to were religious in nature, but they were also social activities that often resulted in a religio-literary artifact. Attendance at any kind of Buddhist ceremony or occasion brought merit to and expressed the devotion of both the attendee and other sentient beings, and it was most likely thought that writing a poem on that event could do the same.

The courtly aspect is less obvious in the next poem, and there is some indication that it might lean toward the monastic. The author, Sanekata Ason, attended a sermon (presumably on the Lotus Sutra) at the Shirakawa villa of his uncle, Naritoki (941–995), the Major Captain of the Left.[188] Such occasions at private residences were quite common at the time, so it is difficult to determine how much of the event was religious and how much social. The author's straightforward declaration of devotion—he has vowed "to bejewel / the lotus leaf" (*hachisu no ue no / tama to chigirireba*), that is, become enlightened— might have been nothing more than a thank-you poem to the priest who gave the lecture, or it might have been a serious vow in poetic form. The poet personifies the metaphoric image of the dew by giving it a "life" (*inochi*), as fleeting as that of the poet. If indeed the poet grasped the Buddhist idea of impermanence (*mujō*) at the sermon, the poem could be interpreted as a poetic vow of devotion expressing

---

188. In *dan* 32 of *The Pillow Book*, an event that is described as "a set of Salvation Lotus Discourses" is thought to be the *sekkyō* (sermon) that is being referred to here. McKinney dates this event to 986. Sanekata is named in this section. Meredith McKinney trans., *The Pillow Book* (New York: Penguin Books, 2006), 34–38.

kechien, one's just-realized connection to the teachings of Buddhism. This interpretation would categorize the poem under a more monastic modality. Rather than regretting (*oshikarazu*) life's brevity, he will embrace it; indeed, he will be the jewel (spiritualizing the drop of dew) that represents the very essence of an enlightened understanding of transience.[189] On the other hand, if Sanekata's declaration of devotion is nothing more than a social propriety, then the poem rests firmly in the tradition of after-event correspondence much like the morning-after letter to one's beloved.

If the overall tone of Sanekata's *waka* was indeed sincerely devotional (as its placement in the sequence suggests), then it fits well with the themes of the next four poems, all of which express the authors' personal determination to reach a state of attainment on the Buddhist path. The first two of the four poems, by an unknown author and Izumi Shikibu, are strongly emotional, expressing feelings of frustration at the same time that they express determination. In the first of these four—a *takusen-ka*, or an oracle poem—the speaker is visited in his dream by a priest (some commentators say the Buddha) who questions him about his doubts. Aware that after all his efforts he has not rid himself of the samsaric impurities (*chiri/jin*) that lead to further rebirth, the author questions his own capabilities to persevere in his practice.

---

189. The modern commentary to the SNKBT version of the *Shūishū* suggests that the sermon may have been the same Kechien hakkō (Eight Lectures to Actuate Belief) that Sei Shōnagon wrote about in *The Pillow Book* (see previous footnote), an event which did take place at Naritoki's villa. However, Takagi says this Hakkō occurred in 1018, well after Naritoki and Sanekata were dead and the *Shūishū* had been compiled. Takagi Yutaka, *Heian jidai Hokke Bukkyō-shi kenkyū*, 244. Rhetorically speaking, the three poems just discussed by Emperor Murakami, Michitsuna no Haha, and Sanekata each include either the word for "today" (*kyō/kefu*) or "yesterday" (*kinō*). In the order that they are compiled, the *waka* read: "today" (*the tender / shoots of spring / I picked today*), "yesterday" (*because yesterday / we finished "gathering / our firewood"*), "today" (*because as of today / I've vowed to bejewel / the lotus leaf*). One should probably not overemphasize the importance of these compilation gestures, but the temporal progression and regression from today (someone died), to yesterday (we fulfilled our religious duties) and back again to today (I've made a vow) increase the tension between what one has done and what one is doing. A listener or a reader of this sequence in the Heian period would surely not have missed the temporal dimensions of such an arrangement.

The *chiri* (dust) that one clears away is a Buddhist word (*jin* in its Sinitic pronunciation) that refers to *bonnō* (S: *kleśas*) that persist in causing suffering and rebirth. Any mental or physical attachments about the world or about ourselves are referred to as *jin*.[190] Thus, that the poet would use a word like *chiri/jin* indicates a familiarity with the Buddhist teachings of suffering and attachment. While the poem reflects some of the characteristic ambivalence about commitment to the Buddhist path that we saw in earlier poems, the difference here is that the author is already committed to some form of contemplative practice. The anonymous poet has already entered into a life in which awareness of suffering and commitment to removing its cause are intrinsic.

If there is a sense of lingering self-doubt in *waka* 1341, this is amplified in the next poem by Izumi Shikibu (late tenth–early eleventh c.). Here the poet's devotion is not in doubt, but her ability to continue on the path is. The speaker asks (actually, demands) that the moon—a symbol of the Holy Priest Shōkū (917–1007) of Mount Shosha—"shine across" to her, to "en*light*en" her, as it were.[191]

Izumi's *kuraki yori* poem may be one of the most cited *waka* from the Heian period, and is certainly one of her most famous poems. As Masuda Shigeo has shown, there are various theories about when the poem was composed, but he places its composition in the third month of 1002 when Retired Emperor Kazan and his retinue traveled to Shōkū's temple, Enkyō-ji, on Mount Shosha.[192]

---

190. *Bukkyōgo daijiten (shukusatsuban)*, 5th edition (Tokyo: Iwanami Shoten, 2006), 799.

191 For biographical information on Shōkū Shōnin, see Masuda, *Kuraki michi*, 10–18. Legends about Shōkū abound, but some of his extraordinary abilities are recounted in the *Dainihonkoku Hokekyōgenki*, translated by Yoshiko Dykstra as *Miraculous Tales of the Lotus Sutra from Ancient Japan* (Honolulu: University of Hawaii Press, 1983), 71–72.

192. Masuda also speculates that since Izumi was familiar with Sei Shōnagon (966? –1017?), and Sei Shōnagon's husband was part of that retinue, it is not unreasonable to conclude that the poem was written just before Kazan's imperial visit, and entrusted to him to deliver to the priest. Masuda continues that this scenario is even more likely because Izumi's husband and Sei's husband were both part of the Tachibana clan. If this were the case, however, then the attribution—Masamune no Musume Shikibu—to the poem would mean that the poem was written before her marriage to Michitaka or before 999, by which time she was already married. Masuda, *Kuraki michi*, 97–100.

The most important aspect of Izumi's poem, and what renders it a Buddhist *waka,* is the section borrowed from a short passage in Chapter 7 (Parable of the Conjured City) of the Lotus Sutra: "Throughout the long night of time they gain in evil destinies / And reduce the ranks of the gods. / From darkness proceeding to darkness / They never hear the Buddha's name."[193] The parable from which these lines come concerns a group of travelers being led by a guide to a cache of jewels (the Buddha's teachings). Along their treacherous journey, they become tired and disillusioned and want to turn back. Their guide, however, who is wise, possesses supernatural abilities. Understanding their frustration, he conjures a beautiful city in which the travelers can rest. In the final *gāthā,* or verse, of this parable, we are told that the Buddha teaches the truth of the "One Buddha Vehicle," by resorting to the "power of expedient devices" (*hōben riki*).[194] The conjured city where the travelers rest is merely a means to an end: "… to provide a resting place [so] that the other two [vehicles] are preached."[195] This, then, is the journey to which Izumi alludes in her poem. But how are we to align the journey in the Lotus Sutra with Izumi's journey in the poem? Is the speaker imagined as a member of the group in the Lotus Sutra traveling to reach the truth of the One Buddha Vehicle, or as isolated and alone far from any source of enlightenment? While it is clear that both the actual moon and the metaphorical moon of enlightenment, the Tendai priest Shōkū Shōnin, are in the distance (*haruka ni*), does she request that her path be lit so she can make her way to enlightenment/Shōkū or does she request enlightenment in this very body at this very moment in time? Furthermore, why does Izumi use the imperative form of the verb (*terase*) to a figure as exalted as Shōkū (a representative of the Buddha himself)? Whether "dark / to darker" indicates actual despair in Izumi's life or not is unknown,

---

193. Hurvitz, *Scripture of the Lotus Blossom of the Fine Dharma,* 133; Sakamoto and Iwamoto, *Hokke-kyō* vol. 2, 20.

194. Ibid., 155; Ibid., 90.

195. The other two vehicles are *śrāvakayāna* (the attainment of *arhat* status by hearing the teachings) and the *pratyekabuddhayāna* (the attainment of buddhahood by personal striving and ascetic practice).

but the combination of the image of darkness coupled with the plea for light implies someone in need. The tone of the speaker's plea is intensified by the repetitive use of syllables from the *ka*-line of the Japanese syllabary, the *k* sound of each mora lending the poem a sonic element of sharpness.

Following Izumi's poem are two poems attributed to priests—Senkei (dates unknown) and Kūya. Senkei's poem is, like Sanekata's, a declaration of determination. In this case, Senkei has concluded that he can be reborn in the Pure Land, if he persists in his practice (*tsutomete*). There is a lyric element to this poem insofar as Senkei expresses both his determination and longing, but the meditative aspect of his argument predominates. His intellectual reasoning is reflected in the grammar: "although A is the case, I can accomplish it."

Historically, the Pure Land teachings had been present in Japan for two or more centuries, but had found an increasingly eager audience in the aristocracy in the mid-Heian period, since it was commonly believed that the period in which the Buddhist teachings could no longer be understood (*mappō*, Latter Days of the Law) would begin in 1052. For those at court not able to engage in the various sitting and walking *samadhi* common to priests on Mount Hiei and Mount Kōya, chanting the *nenbutsu* would have provided a convenient substitute with tempting rewards. If, as *mappō* claimed, the written word of the Buddha's teachings were no longer accessible or comprehensible to the laymen and laywomen of the court, the *nenbutsu* would at least assure rebirth in a land where it would be easier to comprehend those teachings.

Priest Senkei's poem expands upon the journey metaphor used in Izumi Shikibu's poem in several ways. For the speaker of Senkei's poem, where he will arrive at the end of his journey is, in fact, a "place" (*tokoro*) which can be "reached" (*itaru*) with the proper effort or practice (*tsutomete*). The spatial indicator in both poems (*haruka ni/ harukeki hodo*) underscores that an effort must be made to get where one is going, but there is a difference in emphasis. While Izumi's poem forcefully pleads (*terase*) for assistance, Senkei's poem confirms the poet's devotion to Amida's Western Paradise. (Interestingly, the grouping of *ka*-line sounds in Izumi's *waka* is repeated in the first three *ku* of Senkei's poem continuing the tone of her poem phonologically and perhaps hinting at the subtle reasons the compilers chose the order of the poems.)

Kūya's poem continues the theme of devotion to the Pure Land that we saw in Senkei's poem, but does so in a more didactic way. Didacticism is not particularly surprising in Kūya's case since he wandered the countryside and the towns promoting the practice of chanting the *nenbutsu* (which is adopted into the poem). Known as the *ichihijiri*, the holy man of the marketplace, Kūya makes a religious call to practice: repeat the Name (*Namu Amida Bu*) just once (*hitotabi mo*), he says, and you will be reborn in Paradise. In addition to the thematic similarities between Kūya's and Senkei's poems, there is similarity as well in terms of the manner by which understanding and salvation occurs, which is through the senses. Aurality (*kikishika[do]*) guides the reader to the practice in Senkei's poem while orality (*iu*) is the means by which the practice is conducted in Kūya's.[196]

Common to most of the poems in this sub-sequence is movement, which is expressed in terms of actual travel (such as the journey Michitsuna no Haha and her party made to Fumon-ji) or making progress on a metaphorical journey (such as the journey the mother of Emperor Murakami made after her death). Both kinds of journeys are paths of practice in this life and the next: the anonymous author of poem 1341 asks how many lifetimes of rebirth it will take before she sees the benefits of practice come to fruition. In Izumi's *kuraki yori* poem, she requests light for her spiritual journey to enlightenment. Senkei's poem affirms the possibility of arriving at a place of salvation (Amida's Paradise), while Kūya's reveals the practice one needs to arrive at that place: intoning the name of Amida just once.[197]

---

196. It should be noted that Kūya was extremely popular during his life. On the third day of the famous Ōwa debates held in 962 on Mount Hiei between Tendai and Hossō monks and attended by lay Buddhists as well, there was a simultaneous ceremony being held on the banks of the Kamo River at which Kūya dedicated a copy of Prajñāpāramitā Sūtra. As Paul Groner tells us, though the Ōwa debates were well attended, it is likely that attendance at Kūya's ceremony was even larger, including at least six hundred monks and an unknown number of lay people. Paul Groner, *Ryōgen*, 116–117.

197. It is possible that Senkei and Kūya are linked by more than religious ideology.

Kūya's poem is also linked historically to the poems in the next sub-sequence, in that Kūya was, like most of the authors in the final seven poems, well known in Japanese Buddhist history. Having died thirty or forty years before the compilation of the *Shūishū*, Kūya was, like Gyōki, possibly more infamous than he was famous. As he wandered through Japan, he flouted the government regulations that controlled monks' activities, unconcerned about obeying the rules of a single temple or tradition. Paul Groner tells us that "[Kūya's] movement was primarily for the masses and for both men and women."[198]

THE FINAL SEVEN POEMS: INTRODUCTION

In the final sub-sequence of seven poems, the compiler(s) link the past with the present. According to the attributions, all the poems in this final sub-sequence predate mid-Heian court society by as many as three to four hundred years. Moreover, the poets to whom they are attributed are regarded as influential in Japanese Buddhist history: the consort of Emperor Shōmu (r. 724–749), ex-Empress Kōmyō (701–760), the monk Gyōki (668–749), Bodhisena (J: Baramon Sōjō, 704–760), and Shōtoku Taishi (574–622). What might it mean to conclude the sequence, the "Aishō-ka" book, and the *Shūishū* anthology with these poems?

In the twelfth-century poetic treatise *Fukurozōshi*, Senkei's poem is attributed to Sen-kan (914–969), one of Kūya's disciples. (See Tsuji Zennosuke, *Nihon Bukkyō-shi*, vol. 1 [Tokyo: Iwanami Shoten, 1944], 576 and Groner, *Ryōgen*, 110–111, for more information about Senkan.) If, as the *Fukurozōshi* claims, Senkan was the author of the *gokuraku wa* poem, the two poems would be linked by religious lineage as well as ideology. More-over, the poem that is attributed to Senkei in the *Shūishū* is attributed to Kūya in the last poem of "Miscellaneous" book 18 (the book that immediately precedes the "Shakkyō-ka" book) in the *Senzaishū*. Komachiya, *Shūiwakashū*, 394–395 and Katano Tatsurō and Matsuno Yōichi, *Senzaiwakashū*, SNKBT vol. 10 (Tokyo: Iwanami Sho-ten, 1993), 364. Even though the principal Tokugawa commentary to the *hachidaishū*, the *Hachidaishūshō*, does not suggest that Senkei's poem was mistakenly attributed, it seems likely that there was some uncertainty surrounding the authorship. Ishihara, *Shakkyō-ka no kenkyū*, 58–59.

198. Groner, *Ryōgen*, 117.

First, it should be noted that all but one of the poems (Kōmyō's *waka*) are also found in the *Sanbō ekotoba*, written and compiled by Minamoto no Tamenori in 984. Explanations for this are not hard to find, since the work was composed for Princess Sonshi (d. 985), sister of Emperor Kazan (r. 984–986). If as most scholars believe Kazan was the final compiler of the *Shūishū*, he probably had access to the *Sanbō ekotoba* and most likely used it as the source for the final six *waka*. Since none of these *waka* occurs in the *Shūishō* compiled by Kintō, Kazan would be the likely candidate for these additions.

Second, including poems from the distant past at the end of the sequence imbues the entire Buddhist *waka* sequence with a sense of religious authority by connecting the earlier contemporaneous poems with a more ancient history known to all Japanese at the time. One of the most important aspects of this history was the building and consecration of Tōdai-ji in 752 in the capital of Heijō-kyō (Nara). Three of the four poets (Gyōki, Bodhisena, Kōmyō) in the final sequence participated in the consecration ceremony, an event of great historical consequence, considering the fund-raising efforts that preceded its construction, the immense size of the finished building, and the influence of the temple on late Nara and early Heian Buddhism.

Third, Gyōki, Bodhisena, and Shōtoku Taishi were all regarded as bodhisattvas either during or soon after their lifetimes. While the term *bosatsu* (bodhisattva) did not carry the same meaning in the sixth and seventh centuries that it would acquire in the mid-Heian period, by the time of the *Sanbō ekotoba* and the *Shūishū*, the term came to be associated with the other-worldly bodhisattvas such as Mañjuśrī. Jonathan Augustine, in his study of the hagiography of Gyōki, says that the author of *Nihon ryōiki*, Kyōkai (late seventh to eighth centuries), "explicitly states that it was the local believers who called certain extraordinary monks 'bodhisattva' or 'bodhisattva monks'. In tale I.5, Kyōkai explains that Gyōki was an incarnation of the Bodhisattva Mañjuśrī, but even earlier sources ... explicitly state that the local people, rather than the imperial court, called him *bosatsu*."[199] In her study of early Japanese kingship, Joan Piggott concurs: "[E]ven as

---

199. Augustine, *Buddhist Hagiography in Early Japan*, 37.

Gyōki was being castigated by officials, he was being called 'Bosatsu,' meaning bodhisattva, by his followers."[200] Bringing us closer to the time of the *Shūishū*, a tale in the third volume of the *Sanbō ekotoba* also refers to Gyōki as Gyōki Bosatsu, but refers to other monks including Bodhisena, "the Brahman Abbot" from India, "all of whom were said to be reincarnations of Buddhas."[201]

As for the status of Prince Shōtoku, Michael Como has shown that the cult and legends that accrued around the Prince also served to elevate his status first to that of a bodhisattva, and later to a "World Savior":

> ... [T]he legend of Shōtoku as the incarnation of Hui-ssu [a Chinese Buddhist patriarch] was far more than a simple illustration of Shōtoku's superhuman powers. Rather, the legend built upon a long tradition of hagiography concerning Hui-ssu in order to create an image of Shōtoku as a millennial savior. Shōtoku's previous lives were now shown to be those of a monk who had declared both that he would transmigrate to a land without the Buddhist law and that with the advent of Maitreya at the end of the Latter Days he, and not Maitreya, would save all sentient beings ... [202]

The tale about Shōtoku in the *Sanbō ekotoba* also refers to his salvific qualities. As the son of Emperor Yōmei (r. 585–587), Shōtoku appeared to his mother in a dream as a "golden monk" who said, "I intend to save the world ... I am the World-Saving Bodhisattva, and my home is in the West."[203] Clearly, in the case of Shōtoku Taishi, Gyōki, and Bodhisena, we are dealing with iconic figures regarded not so much as poets but as sacred figures in the history of Japanese Buddhism.

---

200. Joan Piggott, *The Emergence of Japanese Kingship* (Stanford: Stanford University Press, 1997), 225.

201. Kamens, *The Three Jewels*, 328.

202. Michael I. Como, *Shōtoku: Ethnicity, Ritual, and Violence in the Japanese Buddhist Tradition* (Oxford and New York: Oxford University Press, 2005), 149–150.

203. Kamens, *The Three Jewels*, 174.

The two sets of exchange poems (*zōtōka*) between Gyōki and Bodhisena and between Shōtoku Taishi and the starving man were concerned events that were mythic by the time of the mid-Heian period. They appear in many *setsuwa* collections and were sometimes blended into fictional tales (*monogatari*) as well. The story of the exchange between Gyōki and Bodhisena supposedly took place at Naniwa when the Brahman abbot came for the consecration of Tōdai-ji. The tale as it is usually recounted says that Gyōki was ordered by the Emperor (Shōmu) to greet the abbot, but as Augustine points out the story must be apocryphal since Gyōki was not on good terms with the imperial court at this time in his life.[204] And as Michael Como has shown, the Shōtoku legend was tied to the Buddhist teachings through literature so that "by creating the image of Shōtoku as a paradigmatic lay Buddhist prince, ancestor, and sage scholar, the immigrant lineages at the forefront of the early Shōtoku cult thus played a major role in establishing the parameters of Buddhist discourse in Japan."[205] Whether the immigrant connection held much sway in the mid-Heian period is doubtful, but Shōtoku's Buddhist associations and accomplishments were clearly in place by then.

Kōmyō is a different case because she was a woman, and, as Ōsumi Kazuo puts it, "Fundamental to Buddhism was the concept that women were barred from salvation. A passage in *The Nirvana Sutra* ... claims that the sinful obstacles of one woman equal the sum of harmful attachments of all men in the world."[206] Despite this, however, Kōmyō was elevated in terms of her Buddhist status. According to the contemporary accounts in the *Shoku Nihongi* (*Sequel to the Chronicles of Japan,* 797), Kōmyō was a devout Buddhist. She is said to have been "benevolent and did her utmost to help other beings. The building of Tōdai-ji temple and the establishment of official state temples through-

---

204. Augustine, *Buddhist Hagiography in Early Japan,* 107–108.
205. Como, *Shōtoku,* 156.
206. Ōsumi Kazuo, "Historical Notes on Women and the Japanization of Buddhism," in *Engendering Faith: Women and Buddhism in Premodern Japan* (Ann Arbor: Center for Japanese Studies, 2002), xxvii.

out the land were initiated by the empress."[207] Mikoshiba Daisuke has corroborated these statements through his examination of court and government documents, and shown that Kōmyō was a significant force in the promulgation of the Buddhist sūtras, the building of separate temples and convents (*kokubunji* and *kokubun niji*) for monks and nuns in the provinces, and the raising of funds for the completion of Tōdai-ji.[208] As a representative of the state through Emperor Shōmu, Kōmyō consolidated national interests and concerns around the teachings of Buddhism by focusing on their practical applications within the monastic community.

We find further corroboration of Kōmyō's status in Japan in a tale from the third volume of the *Sanbō ekotoba*. The opening paragraph restates much of the information from the *Shoku Nihongi* about her family lineage as the granddaughter and daughter of Fujiwara no Kamatari (614–669) and Fujiwara no Fuhito (659–720), respectively, and about her devotion to Buddhism, her role in the construction of provincial temples and convents, as well as the fact that she "established the Hokke-ji as the official convent of the province of Yamato."[209] This particular tale goes on to recount how Kōmyō initiated the first Kegon Service at Hokke-ji where lectures about the Kegon-kyō (Avatamsaka Sūtra) were delivered.[210] In an unrelated section of this same tale, Kōmyō is compared to an Indian nun from the Sūtra on the Life of the Nun Utpalavarṇā. Here the nun Utpalavarṇā urged women to also become nuns whether they believed they could uphold their vows or not. She tells them that she was reborn into "this world of the Tathāgatha Śākyamuni ... and ... attained the status of an arhat" after having suffered through previous lives in hell because she broke her vows.[211] The *Sanbō ekotoba* story concludes: "The merit generated by [Kōmyō's] introduction of this [Hokke] service is equal to that generated by Utpalavarṇā's encouraging words to the nuns of long ago.

---

207. Mikoshiba, "Empress Kōmyō's Buddhist Faith," 22.
208. Ibid.
209. Kamens, *The Three Jewels*, 291.
210. Ibid.
211. Ibid., 292.

A meeting with a worthy teacher is a repetition of the experience of Sudhana [from the Kegon-kyō] in former times."[212] It is not difficult to imagine that the aristocracy of the late tenth century might have conflated the holiness of Utpalavarnā—who became an arhat—with the beneficence of Kōmyō.

Related to the religious status of the poets in the final seven poems of the Buddhist *waka* sequence is their placement at the end. The poems serve, as I have noted, to imbue the entire sequence with a sense of historical authority, an authority derived in part from beliefs about the salvific powers of the authors. By placing the "enlightened" authors at the end of the sequence, the compiler of the *Shūishū* created a schema of the Buddhist practitioner on the path, or *michi*, from the point of awakening to enlightenment.

---

212. Ibid.

MICHI: ENLIGHTENMENT

[1345]

三十あまり二つの姿そなへたる昔の人の踏める跡ぞこれ
misoji amari / futatsu no sugata / sonaetaru / mukashi no hito no / fumeru ato zo kore

LEFT BY EMPRESS KŌMYŌ AT THE STONES OF THE
BUDDHA'S FOOTPRINTS AT YAMASHINADERA

possessor of
the thirty plus two marks—that man
of long ago—
is this
where he put his foot?
these his prints?

— Empress Kōmyō

[1346]

法華経を我が得し事はたき木こり菜摘み水汲み仕へてぞ得し

hokekyō o / waga eshi koto wa / takigi kori / na tsumi mizu kumi / tsukaete zo eshi

WRITTEN BY ARCHBISHOP GYŌKI

> to discover the teaching
> of the dharma flower
>
> I cut wood, carried water,
> gathered the tender shoots—it was
>
> as a servant
> I came Awake

— Grand Archbishop Gyōki

[1347, no headnote]

百くさに八十くさ添へて賜ひてし乳房の報今日ぞ我がする
momokusa ni / yasokusa soete / tamaiteshi / chibusa no mukui / kyō zo waga suru

> the debt
> > I owe the breasts
> > > my mother in tender mercy gave—
>
> > to one hundred stones
> > add eighty—
>
> I repay today

> — Gyōki

[1348]

霊山の釈迦の御前に契りてし真如朽ちせずあひ見つる哉
ryōsen no / shaka no mimae ni / chigiriteshi / shinnyo kuchisezu /
aimitsuru kana

WRITTEN WHEN BODAI REACHED THE SHORE TO
ATTEND THE CONSECRATION AT TŌDAI-JI

        to Shakyamuni on Vulture Peak
     I made a vow of reunion—

never having let
    that promise rot—

      I greet your face again

          — Gyōki

[1349]

迦毘羅衛に共に契りしかひありて文殊の御顔あひみつるかな
kabirae ni / tomo ni chigirishi / kai arite / monju no mikao / aimitsuru kana

A REPLY

in the promise
    we made to one another
        in Kapilavastu

    there was power—

Mañjuśrī I greet again
your noble face

            — Baramon Sōjō

[1350]

しなてるや片岡山に飯に餓へて臥せる旅人あはれ親なし

shinateru ya / kataokayama ni / ii ni uete / fuseru tabibito / aware oya nashi[213]

WHEN PRINCE SHŌTOKU, LEAVING THE HOME OF A
MOUNTAIN ASCETIC, CAME UPON A STARVING MAN
LYING IN THE ROAD

> His horse stopped and would not proceed;
> even when he struck the horse with his whip,
> it stepped backwards and froze. Dismounting,
> the Prince went to the starving man, and covering him
> with his purple cloak, composed this poem, saying:

> *on the mountain road*
> *a starving traveler*
> *lying face down—*
>
> *oh for pity*
> *to have no parents*

> Can it be you have no parents? No master?
> This is a poem of sadness for the starving traveler
> lying face down in the road.

> — Shōtoku Taishi

213. In both editions of the *Shūishū*, the place names are "Takaokayama" in the *koto-bagaki* and "Kataokayama" in the poem itself. We have deleted the first reference in the *kotobagaki* that is thought to be a mistake. Komachiya, *Shūiwakashū*, 397; Ishihara, *Shakkyō-ka no kenkyū*, 41.

[1351]

いかるがや富緒河の絶えばこそ我が大君の御名を忘れめ
ikaruga ya / tominoogawa no / taeba koso / waga ōkimi no / mina o wasureme

RAISING HIS HEAD, THE STARVING MAN COMPOSED
THIS REPLY

> not even if the river Tomino-o
>> at Ikaruga should cease to flow

>>> could I forget
>> your grace

> your name

>>>> — Anonymous

The theme of the final sub-sequence of poems in the Lament book of the *Shūishū* revolves around two related issues: the historical importance of the authors as well as their religious attainments on the Buddhist path. Each of the authors lived during either the pre-Nara or Nara periods, was instrumental in shaping Buddhism in Japan, and as we see in various literary collections was regarded by the populace as having attained a high—if not the highest—level of spiritual accomplishment.

The poems in this sub-sequence are not court *waka* in the usual sense. In fact, it is doubtful that court poets of the mid-Heian period considered any of these authors poets at all. They were, however, famous personages from the early history of Japanese Buddhism. They had become inextricably entwined with the story of both the Buddha and Buddhism in Japan, and as ancestors of that tradition, occupied a place in the Buddhist pantheon similar to the enlightened teachers of India, China, and Korea. This assumption that the Buddhist teachers of other countries were enlightened is common to many of their biographies and hagiographies, so it is not surprising that the same assumptions were made in Japanese stories of its historical figures.

As noted earlier, Gyōki, Bodhisena (Baramon Sōjō), and Shōtoku Taishi were already recognized as bodhisattvas by the late Nara period, and Kōmyō was well on her way to that same designation. Being a bodhisattva in East Asia was no different than being an arhat in the Theravādin tradition. A bodhisattva according to the Mahāyāna teachings meant that one had reached the highest stage of enlightenment, but had foregone the final stage of nirvāna in order to relieve the suffering of all sentient beings. Keeping the religious attainments of these four personages in mind, it seems logical to consider these final seven *waka* as representing the last stage of the Buddha's journey according to the Mahāyāna teachings: that is, bodhisattvahood. Interestingly, this sub-sequence is noticeably less emotional as a group, more characterized by the meditative mode.

Empress Kōmyō's poem that opens this sub-sequence is a kind of invocation that calls the Buddha to a particular place (*kore*) that Kōmyō can see with her own eyes. After she has invoked him in his physical form (*misoji amari / futatsu no sugata*), she calls our attention to his footsteps (*fumeru ato*) into which the invoked physical form can step. In a sense, she seems to try to materialize the Buddha in her poem. Kōmyō refers in her poem to the thirty-two physiognomic marks (*sanjūnisō*) of a realized Buddha.[214] It was by these features in combination that a person could be identified as a Buddha who had reached the highest stage of enlightenment. The associations of this reference may not be clear unless the reader is familiar with the final part of the *gāthā* upon which Izumi Shikibu's poem (1342) was based. Izumi's poem concerns the conjuring of a magical city for the repose of travelers on their journey to a cache of jewels (the One Vehicle of the Mahāyāna). After the Buddha declares that he has created this city as an expedient teaching—*hōben*—for the travelers, he proceeds to tell them that they will recognize a Buddha who has attained final "extinction" (nirvāna) in the following way:

> Now for your sakes I preach the reality,
>> For what you have gained is not extinction.
> For the sake of Buddha-omniscience
>> You must put forth great and vigorous effort,
> For only when you are directly aware of All-Knowledge
>> And of the ten strengths, of the Buddhadharmas
>>> comprising these and other things,
> Only when you are in full possession of the thirty-two
> marks,
> Shall you have real extinction.[215]

With Kōmyō's poem, the internal progression of the previous sub-sequence of poems comes full circle. Sanekata's poem (1340) was a vow to "bejewel / the lotus leaf," a metaphor for attaining enlightenment. In anonymous poem 1341, we find a priest receiving encouragement in a dream (perhaps from the Buddha himself) to practice more diligently. In poem 1342, Izumi Shikibu pleads to be led out of the

---

214. For a list of the marks, see *Nihon Bukkyōgo jiten*, 330.
215. Hurvitz, *Scripture of the Lotus Blossom*, 155; Sakamoto and Iwamoto, *Hokke-kyō* vol. 2, 90.

dark world of suffering to en*light*enment. Both of the poems by Priest Senkei (1343) and Kūya (1344) are declarations about attaining enlightenment in Amida Buddha's Pure Land, while Kōmyō's poem completes the journey to the enlightened Buddha himself. As well, the poem subtly supports the theme of the seeker on the path: the Buddha's footprints are the literal relics of the path he took, as well as an encouragement and guide to anyone who wishes to follow in the same footsteps.

Kōmyō's poem is important in another way. It is almost identical to anonymous poem 2 in the *bussokuseki-ka* (poems on the footprints of the Buddha in stone) sequence on the stele at Yakushi-ji.[216] Although Kōmyō's poem is associated with the Buddha's footprints at Yamashinadera (Kōfuku-ji) and not Yakushi-ji, there can be no doubt that the *Shūishū* poem is most certainly a reworking of this older poem. The *bussokuseki-ka* on the stone stele has been transcribed (in Old Japanese romanization) and translated by Roy Andrew Miller. The original text written in phonograms appears in Ishihara:

---

216. *Bussokuseki-ka* are a kind of *tanka* with one extra *ku* of seven syllables at the end. The poems on the stone stele at Yakushi-ji are the only extant examples except for one other found in the *Man'yōshū*. For more information on the *Man'yōshū* poem see Miller, *Footprints of the Buddha*, 38. For Miller's analysis of poem 2 in the sequence, see 79–98.

彌蘇知阿麻利布多都乃加多知　夜蘇久佐等曽太礼留比止
乃　布美志阿止々己呂　麻礼爾母阿留可毛²¹⁷

*misoti amari / Futatu nö katati / yasokusa tö / södareru Fitö nö / Fumisi
atö tökörö / mare ni mo aru ka mo*²¹⁸

> The footprints trod by
> Him who is complete with
> the thirty-and-
> two marks and
> the eighty [lesser] signs:
> 　　How rare indeed they are!²¹⁹

The first four words of the *bussokuseki-ka* are identical to Kōmyō's
poem, and if we grant that *sugata* and *katati* (*katachi*) are synonyms,
then the first two *ku* in both are almost identical. Likewise, parts of
the fourth and fifth *ku* are identical if one allows for the difference
between the *ren'yōkei* and *izenkei* endings of the verb *fumu* and the
corresponding auxiliary verbs *ki* (a past tense marker in the *rentaikei*
form) and *ri* (a marker of result or perfected action also in the *rentaikei*
form): *Fitö nö / Fumisi atö* and *hito no / fumeru ato*.

What sets Miller's philological analysis of the Yakushi-ji
bussokuseki-ka apart is its insistence on reading the sequence as ordered,
integrated, and allusive. Miller does not believe that the thematic
qualities and aesthetic qualities of the sequence are separable, insisting
that, whether we find them satisfying by contemporary standards
or not, these poems were written with both aesthetic and religious
purposes in mind. Referring to the principles of integration Konishi
elaborated, Miller says:

---

217. Ishihara, *Shakkyō-ka no kenkyū*, 60.

218. Miller says that certain syllables that end and begin with vowels, such as the "i"
in *misoti* and the "a" in *amari* would conflate into the Old Japanese vowel "e," and this
would in essence eliminate one syllable from *amari* and reduce the overall number of syllables in the *ku* from 6 to 5. Similar sorts of conflations occur between syllables that end
with "o" and begin with "a" creating the Old Japanese vowel "ö." Miller, *Footprints of the
Buddha*, 90.

219. Ibid., 79

... [my] study will attempt ... to bring attention
to bear upon the unique structuring by means of
which the poems in this text are found arranged into
a unified poetic sequence. Moreover, the sequence
of the Yakushi-ji stele is a sequence in which the
constituent poems are ordered according to an early
version of the same principles of integration and
progression that later come into full development in
the arrangement of the imperial poetic anthologies.[220]

Miller also says that the sequence is structured religiously: it is based
upon a schemata from the Mahāyāna Bhaiśajya-guru (J: Yakushi
Nyorai) texts,[221] a schemata that constitutes what Miller calls a
"sacramental" metaphor.

Study of the Bhaisajya-guru texts reveals that the
Yakushi-ji poem-stele inscription is ... nothing
more or less than a lyrical paraphrase of a concept
that forms the nucleus of these texts, the "twelve
great vows of Bhaisajya-guru" [Yakushi Nyorai].
... [T]he Yakushi-ji poem-stele may be viewed as a
concrete manifestation of other important features
of these same texts. ... [W]e have in our [poem-
stele] text the great structural metaphor of the poetic
sequence. In each instance, the goal is the same:
the achievement of an outward, visible expression
for inner, invisible concepts; both are religious
metaphors of tremendous subtlety, and both may
... be termed "sacramental."[222]

Understanding all of the philological and thematic nuances of

---

220. Ibid., 6.
221. The Bhaisajya-guru texts are T 450, 451, and 452. 451 and 452 appear to be variants of T 450 that is called Yakushirurikō Nyorai hongankudoku-kyō. Ibid., 27.
222. Ibid.

poem 2 in the poem-stele sequence as outlined by Miller is ultimately not as important for our purposes as understanding the principles of association and integration in the *Shūishū* sequence. Even though these principles may not be as well developed in the early imperial anthologies as they are in the late Heian period anthologies, this is the first time we see them being used to create a religio-literary sequence of Buddhist *waka* in a public venue.

Following Kōmyō's poem in this sub-sequence are the three poems attributed to Gyōki Bosatsu (the Bodhisattva Gyōki). The *Sanbō ekotoba*, to which this sub-sequence of Buddhist *waka* is clearly indebted, tells us that Gyōki was associated with the same Yakushi-ji at which the stone stele of the Buddha's footprints was located.[223] If there were any doubt about the nature of Gyōki's religious attainments, his first poem in the sub-sequence is explicit about it: *as a servant / I came Awake*. Thus, the theme of enlightenment that began in Kōmyō's *waka* continues in Gyōki's. The poem borrows a section of text from the Devadatta chapter of the Lotus Sutra, the same (though larger) section used in Michitsuna no Haha's poem (1339). In this poem, however, the significance of the Lotus Sutra is more apparent.

Devadatta is a "seer" in the Sutra who brought the teachings of the Lotus Sutra to the king, actually the Buddha in a previous life. The king says, "At that time there was a seer (*rsi*) who came and reported to the king, saying, 'I have a great vehicle; its name is the Scripture of the Lotus Blossom of the Fine Dharma. If you can obey me, I will set it forth for you'."[224] Overjoyed, the king/Buddha devotes his life to Devadatta (for whom he "cut wood, carried water, gathered the tender shoots") out of gratitude for the opportunity to hear those teachings. In this way, the poem tells us, the king "came Awake." In the same way that Kōmyō's poem is an invocation of the Buddha, Gyōki's poem is a literary resurrection of the Buddha's enlightenment, in which the speaker (Gyōki presumably) is

---

223. Kamens, *The Three Jewels*, 197. For more on Gyōki, see the biography by Inoue Kaoru, *Gyōki* (Tokyo: Yoshikawa Kōbunkan, 1959).

224. Hurvitz, *Scripture of the Lotus Blossom of the Fine Dharma*, 195; Sakamoto and Iwamoto, *Hokke-kyō* vol. 2, 206.

transformed into the enlightened one by holding (*motsu/ji*) the teachings (*jikyōsha*), that is, the Lotus Sutra (Hokke-kyō).[225]

The *zōtoka* (1348 and 1349) exchanged between Gyōki and the Indian Dharma master Bodhisena is another expression of Gyōki's awakened nature.[226] These two poems comprise a short narrative about one of the most important events in the development of Japanese Buddhism: the dedication of Tōdai-ji in 752. The episode comes more fully to life in the prose of the *Sanbō ekotoba*, so I will quote from Kamens's translation, using our own translations for the poems:

---

225. This poem and the next have a relationship to the subgenre of hymns known as *santan*, a precursor to or type of *wasan*, or Buddhist hymn of praise. (WD, 1102) Also called *butsue kayō*, or Buddhist ceremonial song, the *santan* is virtually indistinguishable from the *waka* since it is written in a 5-7 syllablic meter count though occasionally there may be more than five *ku*. (*Bukkyō bungaku jiten*, 112) Early *wasan*, on the other hand, are written in an indeterminate number of *ku* with a syllable count of 7-5 or 8-5. The difference between *santan* and *shakkyō-ka* seems to be the provenance of the poem: *santan* would have arisen from, and then have been used in, a Buddhist ceremony, while a *shakkyō-ka* would be a Buddhist *waka* compiled in either an imperial collection or a private or personal anthology. (Takeishi Akio, *Wasan: Bukkyō no poejii* [Kyoto: Hōzōkan, 1986], 8.) The earliest *santan*, *Hokke santan*, appears in the second book of the *Sanbō ekotoba*, and is said to have been sung during the first Hokke hakkō [Eight Lectures on the Lotus Sutra] (Kamens, *The Three Jewels*, 236). *Sanbō ekotoba* says that the attribution of the poem could be either Gyōki or Kōmyō, but that the truth is unknown. *Bukkyō bungaku jiten* attributes the poem to Kōmyō even though there is no attribution in either Ishihara or the SNKBT version of the *Shūishū*. It is this very hymn that becomes Gyōki's *waka* in the *Shūishū*. Its transference by the compiler(s) of the *Shūishū* from the realm of the Buddhist ceremony (as a hymn) to an imperial collection (as a waka in the court tradition) signals the increasing overlap between the religious and literary worlds. As mentioned earlier, this is not dissimilar to how the compiler(s) of the *Shūishū* (or someone before the compiler[s] of the *Shūishū*) created Kōmyō's poem from a *bussokuseki-ka* sequence on the stone stele at Yakushi-ji.

226. 1347, the poem between the one just discussed and the *zōtōka* to follow, seems equally "out of place," to quote Kamens, as it does in the *Sanbō ekotoba* (Kamens, *The Three Jewels*, 314). But there are subtle associative threads that connect the poem to the rest of the sub-sequence. Poems 1345–1349 share the sense of reaching across time to connect with original persons and principles, to fulfill a vow, or to realize the potential of effort in previous lives. The mother in poem 1347 could be read as a metaphorical representation of the Dharma itself, or the Buddha, to which a debt is owed, acknowledged and paid by walking on the spiritual path. The word "stones" of 1347 echo the stone of the headnote to 1345: the weight of the debt. Therefore, one could connect the gratitude expressed by the king/Gyōki in poem 1346 and the gratitude expressed by the speaker of poem 1347 to his mother.

When the day of the dedication service drew near,
Gyōki went to the port of Naniwa in Tsu Province
to welcome the expected teacher. At his request, the
government sent one hundred monks to accompany
him. Gyōki took his place at the end of the
procession. Officials of the Civil Affairs Ministry's
Bureau of Religious Affairs and of the Bureau of
Court Musicians got into boats, and as the musicians
played, they all went out to meet the visitor. But
then they reached Naniwa, there was no one to be
seen. Gyōki prepared a welcoming bowl of perfumed
water and set it adrift. Rafts of flowers and burning
incense were also set afloat in the currents. They did
not scatter or dissolve but drifted far off toward the
west. After a while a small boat appeared bearing the
Brahman Abbot named Bodhi. The bowl of perfumed
water was floating in front of his boat, undisturbed.
This Bodhisattva had come from Southern India to be
present on the day of the dedication of Tōdai-ji. He
got out of the boat, came up on shore, grasped Gyōki
by the hand, smiling joyfully. Then Gyōki uttered this
verse. ...

> to Shakyamuni on Vulture Peak
> I made a vow of reunion—

never having let
> that promise rot—
> > I greet your face again

[To which Bodhisena replies:]

in the promise
> we made to one another
> > in Kapilavastu

> > there was power—

Mañjuśrī I greet again
your noble face

and then they went to court together. Thus it was
discovered that Gyōki was Mañjuśrī.[227]

This extraordinary passage paints an almost shimmering portrait
of an event that, if true, must have been spectacular to behold.[228]
The *kotobagaki* to the *Shūishū* poem tells us only that the poem was
composed "when Bodai [Bodhisena] reached the shore to attend the
consecration at Tōdai-ji" and leaves out the more descriptive elements
of the story as it is told in the *Sanbō ekotoba*. What was important to
the compiler(s) of the *Shūishū* apparently was not the drama that led
up to it, but the actual revelation of Gyōki as Mañjuśrī. Because of
the *setsuwa*-like nature of these two poems, it is possible that literary
elements played a lesser role than religious ones. As one would expect
in a *zōtōka*, words from the first poem appear in the reply poem as
well: *chigirishi* and *chigiriteshi* in the third and second *ku* of each
poem respectively as well as *aimitsuru kana* in the fifth *ku* of both.
But it is the revelation of Gyōki as a bodhisattva that takes center
stage. Significantly, this recognition, granted by an Indian monk to
a Japanese monk, is a situation that can be read allegorically as the
transference of the Buddha's teachings from India to Japan.

That the third sub-sequence of the Buddhist *waka* reaches deep
into Japanese Buddhist history is nowhere more explicit than in the
final two poems, also a *zōtōka*.

Even though a modern reader might feel it implausible that a dying
man would reply in *waka* form to a stranger's poem, there was actually
nothing unusual about it in the context of the Japanese court poetry
tradition: to reply to a *waka* with a *waka* was proper and appropriate,
whatever the circumstances.

---

227. Kamens, *The Three Jewels*, 198–199. The same story is told in the *Dainihonkoku Hokekyōgen-ki*, but in a less elegant fashion. See Dykstra, *Miraculous Tales of the Lotus Sutra*, 29. In this version, Gyōki boards a boat with the offerings rather than placing the offerings in a boat.

228. See *Buddhist Hagiography in Early Japan*, 108, for Augustine's claim that the story is apocryphal.

The legend of Shōtoku Taishi encountering a starving man on Mount Kataoka and showing him some kindness before he died became one of the most widely recounted stories in medieval Japan. It appears first in the *Nihon shoki* (720). Various other versions occur later in the *Nihon ryōiki* (ca. 823), the Chinese Preface (*Manajo*) of the *Kokinshū*, the *Sanbō ekotoba*, and the *Konjaku monogatari* (ca. 1120).[229] It also became a part of *waka* legend as it was retold in the *Fusō ryakki* (ca. 1107) and *Korai fūteishō* (1197).[230] The story as it appears in the *Nihon shoki* and the *Nihon ryōiki* is not particularly Buddhist in concept. By the time it is recorded in the *Sanbō ekotoba*, however, the legend begins to resemble the form it takes in the *Shūishū*. In the *Sanbō ekotoba* the prose part of the story is associated with the Prince's knowledge of his own impending death and to the mysterious disappearance of a copy of the Lotus Sutra he had brought home from Mount Heng in China.[231] Yet the poems appear in *Sanbō* in the same form as they do in the *Shūishū*. In works later than the *Sanbō ekotoba*, such as the *Shunrai zuinō* (1115?) and the *Genkō shakusho* (1132), the starving traveler appears as either a manifestation of Bodhidharma or the bodhisattva Mañjuśrī, while in the *Kokon chomonjū* (1254) and in the *Genkō shakusho*, Shōtoku Taishi is regarded as a manifestation of Avalokiteśvara (Kannon).[232] While many of these works are not contemporaneous with the *Shūishū*, it seems clear that the relationship between the tale—first in secular and then later in its Buddhist form—and the poems, was set by the late tenth century. The significance of the story was certainly not lost on the compiler(s) of the *Shūishū*: the paired sequences of poems between Gyōki and Bodhisena and then Shōtoku Taishi and the starving man on Mount Kataoka served to paint a picture of a Buddhist land in which the bodhisattvas reside, a Buddhist ethic in

---

229. Komachiya, *Shūiwakashū*, 398; Ishihara, *Shakkyō-ka no kenkyū*, 41–43.

230. Ibid.

231. W. G. Aston, *Nihongi: Chronicles of Japan from the Earliest Times to A.D. 697* (Rutland and Tokyo: Charles E. Tuttle Co., 1972), 144–145; *Bukkyōgo jiten*, 109–110; Kamens, *The Three Jewels*, 177–179.

232. Ishihara, *Shakkyō-ka no kenkyū*, 42–43.

which the political leaders believe, and a poetic consciousness of this world inspired by both bodhisattvas and leaders.

The Shōtoku *zōtōka* is also a fitting end to the "Aishō-ka" (Laments) book, where it resurrects the theme of death. Even though readers at the time of the *Shūishū* were most likely aware of the Buddhist connotations of the Shōtoku Taishi story, the absence of any Buddhist words or themes in the *Shūishū* version does not prohibit it from being considered an integral part of the Buddhist *waka* sequence. But as a lament on the death of a fellow human being, Shōtoku's poem also clearly resonates with the theme of the book, and as a lament on the starving man's lack of connection—as evidenced by his abandonment in the road—the poem subtly resonates with others in a sub-sequence exploring the concept of spiritual lineage and connectedness.

CONCLUSION: GATEWAY TO MEDIEVAL POETRY

The complex thematic, historical, authorial, and aesthetic construction of the Buddhist *waka* sequence in the *Shūishū* foreshadows future sequences in subsequent imperial poetry anthologies of the eleventh and twelfth centuries. In the *Goshūishū*, *Kin'yōshū*, and *Shikashū*, similar sequences were no longer compiled with the laments, but included within the "Miscellaneous" (Zō) books. The compiler of the *Goshūishū*, Fujiwara no Michitoshi (1047–1099) recognized the thematic and topical variation of Buddhist poetry and sub-headed his sequence, "Shakkyō." Neither Minamoto no Shunrai [Toshiyori] (1055–1129) nor Fujiwara no Akisuke (1090–1155) followed suit in the *Kin'yōshū* and the *Shikashū*, though they included uninterrupted Buddhist *waka* sequences such as we see in the *Shūishū*. At the same time in the twelfth century, sequences of Buddhist *waka* also appeared in private anthologies such as the *Sanboku kikashū* (ca. 1128) by Minamoto no Shunrai and later the *Chōshū eisō* (1178) by Fujiwara no Shunzei. By the time Shunzei finished the compilation of the *Senzaishū* in 1188, *shakkyō-ka* (along with the Shintō poems, *jingi-ka*) became independent books of poems and remained so through the twenty-first anthology in 1439.

In his article "The Medievalization of Poetic Practice," Robert Huey says, "If we were to look closely at [imperial] anthology *content* issues ... we would find even more evidence of creeping medievalism."[233] As support for his claim, he points to the creation of separate books of Shintō and Buddhist poems in the *Senzaishū*. If the categorization of Buddhist poetry is the requirement for medievalization, then we need to push the date back at least to the *Goshūishū* in 1086. If, on the other hand, it is Buddhist poetry itself (Huey's "content") that signals medievalization, then clearly the *Shūishū* would be an even earlier example of the medievalization process.

That the *Shūishū* sequence is an historical nexus foreshadowing the increasing belief that the path of poetry equaled the path of the Buddha is confirmed by a section of the *Kanbun* Preface to the *Hosshin wakashū*, the private *shakkyō-ka* anthology written and compiled by Princess Senshi in 1012. Finished just five to seven years after the compilation of the *Shūishū*, this Preface is the first extant example of critical theorizing about *waka* composition based on Buddhist sūtras. Any discussion of Buddhist poetry in the *Shūishū* (which, of course, contains one of Senshi's poems) must take into account her prescient words:

> For a long time I have turned my thoughts to the Buddha. The reason why I have devoted my heart to the Dharma is for the attainment of enlightenment. The Buddha preached the teachings of the One Vehicle of the Dharma Flower and composed hymns on the goodness of the many tathagatas. Because of this, I realized the virtue of hymns and came to know that writing verse is a service to the Buddha.[234]

---

233. Robert Huey, "The Medievalization of Poetic Practice," *Harvard Journal of Asiatic Studies* vol. 50, no. 2 (December 1990): 660. The emphasis is Huey's. Before this statement in his article, Huey provides substantial evidence for the medievalization of poetic practice.

234. Translation by the author.

As she states in the passage just following this, Senshi is aware that the texts of Buddhism have been written in a language other than her own, but she remains undeterred about the value of her own language for producing the same enlightening effects as the Buddhist sūtras. In a remarkable example of philosophical conflation, Senshi states that one need not forsake the "path" (*michi*) of the thirty-one-syllable *waka* to enter the "gate" (*mon*) of *aji* (Buddhism), presumably because, as she understands it, the results are the same. Her use of the word *aji* in this context should not be taken lightly; it refers to the Shingon practice of meditation on the Sanskrit letter *A*, transcribed as 阿 in Chinese. As Kūkai explains this in the *Hizō hōyaku*, one enters the "gate of the letter *A*" when "one realizes that this Mind is originally unborn," and the realization of the unborn mind is one and the same as the "absolute Middle Way."[235] In the *Unji gi*,[236] a work in which Abe says Kūkai "argued that language in general is the manifestation of the Buddhist philosophy of emptiness,"[237] Kūkai calls this single letter "the mantra of Mahāvairocana."[238] Whether Senshi had a deep knowledge of Kūkai's writings is unknown, but her usage of a phrase from the esoteric tradition indicates a familiarity with those Buddhist teachings upon which later poets such as Fujiwara no Shunzei would base their own arguments for conflating the path of the Buddha with the path of *waka*.[239]

The fact that Senshi could make such arguments proves that there was an awareness of the religious power of *waka* in the mid-Heian period. While this religious power was connected in earlier

---

235. Yoshito Hakeda, *Kūkai: Major Works* (New York: Columbia University Press, 1972), 203–204.

236. Hakeda spells this as *Ungi gi* in (Hakeda, 246), but spells it *Unji gi* other places in the book. Ryūichi Abe also romanizes this as *Unji gi*. Abe, *The Weaving of Mantra: Kūkai and the Construction of Esoteric Buddhist Discourse* (New York: Columbia University Press, 1999), 13.

237. Ibid., 14.

238. Hakeda, *Kūkai: Major Works*, 249.

239. As the sūtras upon which Senshi based some of fifty-five poems show, she was familiar with texts important to the Shingon tradition. Kamens, *The Buddhist Poetry of the Great Kamo Priestess*, 76–77.

times to the *kami* and *kotodama,* increasingly it came to manifest itself in *waka* on Buddhist topics. If *waka* could move the gods in the heavens, it could also bring forth the soteriological power of the Buddhas and bodhisattvas who preached the Buddhist sūtras (and whose personalities became increasingly conflated with those of the *kami* during the second half of the Heian period). What Senshi expressed clearly both in the Preface to and in the poems of her private anthology of 1012, we find achieved poetically for the first time in the elaborate construction of the Buddhist *waka* sequence in the public domain of the *Shūishū,* Japan's third imperial poetry anthology. ✿

4 SHAKKYŌ-KA IN THE *GOSHŪISHŪ* (1086)

The nineteen Buddhist *waka* that appear in the *Goshūishū* can for the first time be called *shakkyō(-ka)*, due to the name of the subsection of *waka* ("Shakkyō") in which they were compiled. This usage will not occur again until the late twelfth century. We will continue to use the generic "Buddhist *waka*" and "*waka* on Buddhist themes" to refer to all *waka* of this type, but we can point to the late eleventh century as the time when a compiler of an imperial poetry anthology applied a separate categorical term for poems based upon Buddhist texts and Buddhist occasions. The fact that this is so provides us with the opportunity to reflect more directly on the manner in which Buddhist ideas were formulated within or around Japanese *waka*. *Waka* composed at the time of the Nirvāna Ceremony or *waka* composed on a section of text from the Lotus Sutra or the Vimalakīrtī Sūtra as we see in this sequence show a more explicit connection between the creative literary arts and spiritual aspiration, an attempt to fuse the experience of Buddhist practice within the constraints of a proper court *waka*. Finally, there are examples in this sequence of poems that express (or perhaps imagine?) the instant of enlightenment, that is, the moment when the continual re-creation of the ego as characterized by the five *skandhas* stops so that the poet gains a full glimpse of egolessness and emptiness.

INTRODUCTION

Approximately eighty years after the *Shūishū* was completed at the beginning of the eleventh century, Fujiwara no Michitoshi (1047–1099) presented the fourth imperial poetry anthology, *Goshūishū* (1086) to Emperor Shirakawa (r. 1072–1086), the sovereign who commanded its compilation.[240] Unlike the compilation process of the *Shūishū*, we know much more about the circumstances that led to and accompanied the selection process of the fourth anthology. Both the Kana Preface to the anthology as well as the *Goshūishō mokurokujo* written by Michitoshi in 1087 give a detailed explanation about these events.[241]

Emperor Shirakawa issued the decree to compile the fourth imperial poetry anthology in 1075 when Michitoshi was twenty-nine years old. Due first to Michitoshi's bureaucratic obligations at court and later to the death of Shirakawa's consort in 1084, the collection of materials was postponed for ten years until 1085. Michitoshi began work on the anthology in the early part of 1085 but due to illness postponed its completion that year and resumed work in the autumn. Finally, in the tenth month of 1086—one month before Shirakawa abdicated the throne to Horikawa (r. 1086–1107)—Michitoshi finished an initial draft of the *Goshūishū* and presented it to the Emperor for inspection. Before it was shown to now ex-Emperor Shirakawa again in 1087, Michitoshi made some minor structural changes along with additions and deletions. For the most part, however, the inspection of 1086

---

240. Four editions of the *Goshūishū* were consulted for this study: (1) Ishihara, *Shakkyō-ka no kenkyū*, 63–96; (2) Kawamura Teruo, ed., *Goshūiwakashū*, vol. 5, *Izumi koten sōsho* (Osaka: Izumi Shoin, 1991), 297–301; (3) Kubota Jun and Hirata Yoshinobu, eds., SNKBT vol. 8, *Goshūiwakashū* (Tokyo: Iwanami Shoten, 1994), 384–389; and (4) Fujimoto Kazue, *Goshūiwakashū zen'yakuchū*, 4 vols (Tokyo: Kōdansha, 1983), 383–410.

241. According to the WDJ, 334, the *Goshūishō mokuroku* (also known as *Goshūishū mokuroku*) is lost, but its Preface or *Jo* survives. See Kawamura, *Goshūiwakashū*, 3–7; Kubota Jun et al., ed., *Waka*, vol. 6 *Kenkyū shiryō Nihon koten bungaku* (Tokyo: Meiji Shoin, 1983), 85–87; Suzuki Hideo, "Goshūishū," *Inseiki bungaku-shi no kōsō tokushu* in *Kokubungaku kaishaku to kanshō*, vol. 53, no. 3 (March 1988): 82–83; Ueno Osamu, "Goshūishū," in *Man'yōshū to chokusenwakashū* (vol. 4 of *Waka bungaku kōza*, ed. Hisamatsu Sen'ichi et al. (Tokyo: Ōfūsha, 1970), 127–128.

marked the end of the most substantial portion of the editing process.

The relatively uncomplicated history of the compilation of the *Goshūishū* belies the politico-literary machinations that preceded Michitoshi's appointment. Michitoshi was not the most likely candidate for the job of compiler. Instead, this honor should have fallen to his elder, Minamoto no Tsunenobu (1016–1097), who was, by most accounts, the most respected poet of his age and therefore an obvious choice.[242] He was a man of wealth and political power who rose to the position of Major Counselor (*Dainagon*) before being sent to Dazaifu in 1094 as Acting Governor-General (*Gon sochi*), where he died in 1097. Brower and Miner have characterized Tsunenobu as a "transitional poet" who experimented with a style of descriptive poetry not yet in vogue among all the court poets.[243] His power at the court and especially his connections to Michinaga's branch of the Fujiwara family put him at odds with the increasingly antiregency (*sekkansei*) and pro-imperial (*tennōsei*) sentiments of Emperors Go-Sanjō (r. 1068–1072) and Shirakawa. The youthful Michitoshi, on the other hand, is known to have had an intimate relationship with the imperial family through his father's service to Go-Sanjō. It was this relationship that led Shirakawa to favor Michitoshi as compiler of the *Goshūishū*. The favoritism the Emperor showed toward Michitoshi expresses one aspect of what G. Cameron Hurst in his work on the Insei period (1086–1185) has called a "[reassertion of] control [by the imperial family] over the rest of society, within the existing system."[244] In other words, the selection of Michitoshi was a deliberate assertion of imperial power rather than a reasoned selection made on the basis of poetic ability and renown.

Michitoshi is usually regarded as a conservative poet whose tastes ran more to the style of the first three imperial anthologies

242. Kawamura, *Goshūiwakashū*, 5; Ariyoshi Tamotsu, "Hachidaishū to kadan," *Kokubungaku*, vol. 32, no. 5 (April 1987): 51.

243. Brower and Miner, *Japanese Court Poetry*, 181.

244. G. Cameron Hurst, *Insei: Abdicated Sovereigns in the Politics of Late Heian Japan 1086-1185* (New York: Columbia University Press, 1976), 8.

than to the newer style practiced by Tsunenobu.[245] Confirmation of his preference for earlier styles is evident in the title he gave to the fourth anthology—Goshūishū, or the *Later* Collection of Gleanings, following in the literary footsteps or perhaps even suggesting an extension of the *Shūishū*, the Collection of Gleanings. This assessment of Michitoshi as a conservative poet may be accurate in terms of the style of poetry to which he was attracted, but his conservatism did not carry over into the way he categorized the poetry in the *Goshūishū*. Even though Michitoshi followed the standard twenty-book format set at the time of the compilation of the *Kokinshū*, he also made several significant changes.[246] First, he relocated the "Aishō-ka" book to the first half of the anthology, a move that served to emphasize the poems' public rather than private nature. Second, the *kami* poems were reclassified as "Jingi" (*Kami* Matters), after having been classified as "Kamiasobi no uta" (lit., *Kami*-Play Songs) in the *Kokinshū* and as "Kagura uta" (Sacred Songs) in the *Shūishū*. Third, within the final book of "Miscellaneous" (Zōka) *waka*, he subcategorized three types of poems: (1) the previously mentioned *waka* on matters pertaining to the *kami*, (2) Buddhist *waka* which he called "Shakkyō," and (3) irregular, indecorous, or humorous poems called "Haikai-ka."[247] It is the second subcategory that will concern us here.

As discussed in the Introduction to this study, Japanese scholars often call indiscriminately any poem on a Buddhist theme *shakkyō-ka*, but such anachronistic terminology is not precise enough or appropriate for the previous anthology, the *Shūishū*, in part because it obscures and diminishes the significance of the shift in terminology when it did occur. However, because Michitoshi created the "Shakkyō" rubric for *waka* on Buddhist themes in the *Goshūishū*, it is appropriate

---

245. Brower and Miner, *Japanese Court Poetry,* 236. Suzuki Hideo says that the majority of poems in the *Goshūishū* came from the period of the *Gosenshū,* the *Shūishū,* and the so-called blank period of imperial anthologies (*chokusen kūhaku jidai*) between the compilation of the *Shūishū* and the *Goshūishū.* Suzuki, "Goshūishū," 82–83.

246. Kawamura, *Goshūiwakashū,* 9–10. Unfortunately, there is no information in either of the Preface or the *Goshūishū mokurokujo* about the motivation behind the changes Michitoshi made.

247. Kawamura, *Goshūiwakashū,* 5; Ariyoshi, "Hachidaishū to kadan," 51.

to call these poems *shakkyō-ka*. The stance the present study takes is simple: not every Buddhist *waka* is a *shakkyō-ka*, though every *shakkyō-ka* is a Buddhist *waka*.

MAPPŌ AND THE WARRIOR-MONKS

There were six imperial reigns between the compilations of the *Shūishū* and the *Goshūishū*: those of sovereigns Sanjō (r. 1011–1016), Go-Ichijō (r. 1016–1036), Go-Suzaku (r. 1036–1045), Go-Reizei (r. 1045–1068), Go-Sanjō (r. 1068–1072), and Shirakawa (r. 1072–1086). Not only does this list bring us up to the year that the *Goshūishū* was completed, but it also leads to the start of what is called the *Inseiki*, or the period of the cloistered sovereign, of whom Shirakawa was the first.

There were at least two conditions in the eight decades after the compilation of the *Shūishū* that could have affected Michitoshi's decision to include a new category of Buddhist *waka* in the *Goshūishū*. One was the onset of *mappō* (the Latter Days of the Law) during the reign of Go-Reizei. The second was the increased violence perpetrated by warrior monks from Mount Hiei and in Nara, which was regarded by contemporaries as strong evidence of *mappō*.[248]

Many scholars have discussed the importance of *mappō* consciousness on Japanese society during the premodern era, but I think the historical immediacy of *mappō* (thought to have begun in 1052 just thirty-four years before the compilation of the *Goshūishū*) justifies readdressing the issue.[249] Jacqueline Stone provides an

---

248. While "warrior monks" are usually referred to as *sōhei*, Adolphson claims this is a misnomer since the word itself was not used until the Tokugawa period. For that reason, I will use "warrior monks" instead. Mikael Adolphson, *The Teeth and Claws of the Buddha: Monastic Monks and Sōhei in Japanese History* (Honolulu: University of Hawaii Press, 2007), 12–13.

249. In "The Archeology of Anxiety: An Underground History of Heian Religion," D. Max Moerman argues for a less one-sided view of *mappō* consciousness, saying that it "has not gone unchallenged" within the Japanese academic community. He says, "One simply does not see in the Heian period a populace paralyzed in the face of irreversible religious decline …" On the other hand, he does not deny it played an important role, claiming instead that it instigated religious action in Heian society, "… the Heian period

excellent definition and a partial description of its effects on the Japanese:

> By the latter part of the Heian Period (794–1185), a majority of Japanese believed that the world had entered a dark era known as *mappō*, the age of the Final Dharma. Buddhist tradition held that in this age, owing to human depravity, the teachings of the historical Buddha Shakyamuni would become obscured, and enlightenment all but impossible to attain. By the mid-eleventh century, natural disasters, social instability and widespread corruption among the Buddhist clergy lent seeming credence to scriptural predictions about the evil age of *mappō*— predictions which in turn gave form to popular anxieties, feeding the growing mood of terror, despair and anomie known as *mappō* consciousness.[250]

Michele Marra extends this description into the realm of the literary, "From the second half of the eleventh century the expression 'final age' (*masse*) occurs in many *nikki, monogatari*, and works of history, often bringing with it a connotation of fear and inevitability."[251] No evidence for an awareness of *mappō* exists in the Preface to the *Goshūishū;* in it Michitoshi is more concerned with the continuity between his anthology and the three earlier imperial anthologies (including the *Man'yōshū*). The fact that we do not find evidence

---

witnessed a great deal of individual effort aimed at both counteracting the effects of *mappō* and ensuring, in the face of such a threat, one's own heavenly rebirth." D. Max Moerman, "The Archaeology of Anxiety," *Heian Japan: Centers and Peripheries* (Honolulu: University of Hawai'i Press, 2007), 245 and 248.

250. Jackie Stone, "Seeking Enlightenment in the Last Age: Mappō Thought in Kamakura Buddhism," *The Eastern Buddhist*, vol. 18, no. 1 (Spring 1985): 28.

251. Michele Marra, "The Development of Mappō Thought in Japan," *Japanese Journal of Religious Studies*, vol. 15, no. 1 (March 1988): 51. Moerman counters this view when he considers whether "the discourse on *mappō* ... found in literary texts" might signify that "it was more of a rhetorical trope than a motivational concern." Moerman, "The Archeology of Anxiety," 245–246.

for the growing awareness of *mappō* in the Preface does not mean that the concept did not influence Michitoshi or other persons in aristocratic Japanese society, however. It only means that Michitoshi did not choose to introduce a matter with negative implications into the refined public venue of the imperial anthology, which sought to represent the imperial literary project in the most positive light. It is possible, though, to interpret Michitoshi's creation of the "Shakkyō" subcategory in the *Goshūishū* as an acknowledgement of his and others' feelings about *mappō*. This speculation can be supported by the opening five *waka* that all express the loss of the Buddha from the world, either through the Nehan-e (Ceremony for the Buddha's *Parinirvāna*) or through the traditional recognition of the Buddha's death on the fifteenth day of the second month.

Escalations of religious conflict in the decades preceding the compilation of the *Goshūishū* cannot have eased the anxieties the aristocracy felt about the year 1052. While the tensions on Mount Hiei between monks who were the religious descendants of Ennin (at Enryaku-ji) and the religious descendants of Enchin (at Onjō-ji) increased during the second half of the tenth century, these tensions escalated to armed conflict during the eleventh century. Mikael Adolphson in *The Teeth and Claws of the Buddha: Monastic Warriors and Sōhei in Japanese History* cites three incidents in particular, in 1013, 1035, and 1081. In the first, a preceptor named Kaiju led a group of monks to the grounds of another temple building on Mount Hiei where they destroyed religious objects and then the hall itself. In the second incident, a fight broke out at a festival at Onjō-ji that resulted in at least one death.[252] This led four years later to objections by large numbers of Enryaku-ji priests about the appointment of an Onjō-ji priest, Myōson (971–1063), as head abbot of the Tendai sect. In the final incident in 1081, animosities from the early part of the century erupted into the worst violence to this point. Adolphson again: "A combined force of armed monks and secular retainers from Enryaku-ji attacked and burned down parts of Onjō-ji, and this action launched

---

252. Mikael Adolphson, *The Teeth and Claws of the Buddha*, 34–35.

a series of destructive acts that fueled running disputes between the two Tendai centers."[253] Another clash between monks from Kōfuku-ji and Tōnomine occurred the same year, indicating that warrior tactics among the sangha were not only confined to Enryaku-ji and Onjō-ji.[254]

A glance at any chronology of Japanese history in the decades preceding the *Goshūishū* points to many other instances of monks taking up arms against other monks. Given the atmosphere of aggression this must have created around the monastic centers, the start of *mappō* must have seemed well underway by 1086. And while fires at the capital and at the imperial palace in particular were fairly common throughout the Heian period, there are almost ten instances of conflagrations in the capital between 1026 and 1055, and as many instances of flooding, drought, famine, and disease during this same period.[255] Contrary to how society was painted in *monogatari* like the *Genji*, life in eleventh century Japan was difficult as cracks in the veneer of governmental control began to appear.

Max Moerman's observation that there was "a great deal of individual effort aimed at ... counteracting the effects of *mappō*" is positive support for the assertion that writing *waka* on Buddhist topics can be included as one aspect of that effort. If, as Princess Senshi says in the Preface to the *Hosshin wakashū*, writing *waka* could lead to the same benefits as the Buddha's hymns did (see Chapter 2), then poets need not be constrained by the fear that Buddhism was not a courtly poetic topic. Indeed, in the century ahead the relationship between Buddhism and *waka* would come to seem not only complementary, but also an inseparable support to the imperial poetry anthology project.

---

253. Ibid., 36.

254. Ibid., 36–37.

255. Kawasaki Mochiyuki et al., *Yomeru nenpyō: Nihonshi* (Tokyo: Jiyū Kokuminsha, 1998), 233–269. Farris notes that there were ten famine years—some widespread and others local—between 1008 and 1082, and four of those were caused by drought. Still, he says, "famine played a ... secondary role to epidemic disease in boosting mortality..." William Wayne Farris, "Famine, Climate, and Farming in Japan, 670–1100," *Heian Japan: Centers and Peripheries* (Honolulu: University of Hawai'i Press, 2007), 283 and 298.

HOW ARE THE *SHAKKYŌ-KA*
IN THE *GOSHŪISHŪ* BUDDHIST?

The creation of a subcategory to accommodate the Buddhist *waka* in the *Goshūishū* also appears to have signified a reconsideration of what a suitable Buddhist *waka* was. In other words, the category "Shakkyō" provided an opportunity for Michitoshi to define and delimit the concept of a *waka* on Buddhist themes. In the case of the *Goshūishū*, this resulted in poems on renunciation (*shukke*) and pilgrimages (*sankei*) being—at least temporarily—edited out of the "Shakkyō" book and included in the third and fourth books of "Miscellaneous" poems.[256] It also meant that poems exclusively on the theme of *mujō*, or impermanence, were excluded.[257] This is not to say that the concept of *mujō* was entirely excised from *shakkyō-ka*. The origins of *shakkyō-ka* in Fujiwara no Michinaga's memorial service for his sister in 1002 and in the "Laments" book of the *Shūishū* would bind them and *mujō* together forever. But poems whose only primary thematic focus was the expression of impermanence were no longer included in this category.[258]

What are the characteristics of the poems that *are* included in the "Shakkyō" subsection of the *Goshūishū?* First, there are the obvious characteristics: (a) *waka* by Ise no Tayū and her daughter Yasusuke Ō no Haha make up almost one-third of the entire sequence; (b) if we add to these two the poets Fujiwara no Kintō and Akazome Emon (each with two poems), then those four poets comprise more than half of the overall number of poems; (c) four Buddhist priests are included in the sequence; and (d) of the ten poets represented, seven were active during the decades immediately preceding the *Goshūishū* and three—Kintō, Akazome Emon, and Former Preceptor Kōgen—

---

256. *Shakkyō-ka* related to pilgrimages are reinstated in the *Senzaishū*.

257. Ishida, *Nihon koten bungaku to Bukkyō*, 27.

258. We see this reflected in "song" (*rōei*) anthologies such as the *Wakan rōeishū* (1012), which makes a distinction between "Buddhist Matters," "Impermanence," and "Mountain Temples." J. Thomas Rimer and Jonathan Chaves, eds. and trans., *Japanese and Chinese Poems to Sing: The Wakan Rōeishū* (New York: Columbia University Press, 1997).

were active during the era of the *Shūishū*. Second, while the Buddhist *waka* in the *Shūishū* focused on the effects of the Buddhist teachings on the structure of the society (renunciation, the benefits of practice) with only minimal emphasis on the texts of Buddhism, the *shakkyō-ka* in the *Goshūishū* are thematically connected, through their headnotes, to certain sūtras or parts of sūtras (primarily the Lotus Sutra and the Vimalakīrti Sūtra), Buddhist practices (*gachirinkan*), and Buddhist ceremonies such as sūtra memorial services and recitations. Third, *shakkyō-ka* in the *Goshūishū* sequence are historically tied to the era immediately preceding it whereas the Buddhist *waka* sequence in the *Shūishū* was compiled and organized in such a way as to give the impression that *waka* on Buddhist themes dated back to the eras of Shōtoku Taishi and Gyōki in the sixth and seventh centuries. Fourth, the *Shūishū* sequence was constructed according to mid-Heian period conceptions of the Buddhist *michi*, while the *shakkyō-ka* in the *Goshūishū* were compiled according to scripture (including Buddhist practices and concepts) and occasion (ceremonies and rituals, for example). The *shakkyō-ka* in the *Goshūishū* reflect an attempt to fuse the specificities of Buddhist culture with the desired outcome of enlightenment. This emphasis on the business of practice does not mean that the lyric-narrative mode of court *waka* was abandoned in favor of a more purely didactic one. However, it does mean that we see an increase in the number of *waka* that were written in a meditative mode, emphasizing a more intellectual inflection.

Closely related to the foregoing discussion about characteristics is the question of purpose. The purpose of a poem can easily be mistaken for authorial intention, but I am not using it in that sense. I am using the word "purpose" here to signify how the poem either points the reader to or away from phenomena that correspond to the meaning of the word *shakkyō* (the teachings of the Buddha). Unlike *waka* on the seasons or love or grief that can often, though not always, be identified by the poem alone, *waka* on Buddhist topics are often less direct in their relationship to the topic. Moreover, "the teachings of the Buddha" is such a broad category that trying to identify what aspect of "the teachings" is being referred to by the poem is often difficult. Of course, a headnote or topic can be helpful, but identifying the exact relationship between either to the *waka* can still be challenging. The question that arises often when reading *shakkyō-ka* or Buddhist *waka* sequentially or individually in an imperial anthology is "what exactly is Buddhist about this?"

One hundred years after the compilation of the *Goshūishū*, Fujiwara no Shunzei completed the seventh imperial anthology, *Senzaishū*, the subject of the last two chapters of this study. Thanks to Shunzei's Preface to the *Senzaishū*, his poetic treatise *Korai fūteishō* (1197), and his private *waka* collection *Chōshū eisō* (1178), we have come to understand how Shunzei found correspondences between composing *waka* and the Tendai teachings of radical nonduality. As a result, we are better equipped to "read" the Buddhism in his poems, as well as in the *shakkyō-ka* he collected, more easily than the *shakkyō-ka* in the *Goshūishū*. This holds true for the two imperial anthologies of the twelfth century that follow the *Goshūishū* and precede the *Senzaishū*. Consider, for example, the following *waka* (without its topic and attribution) from the *Goshūishū*, to which I will return later in this chapter:

月の輪に心をかけしゆふべよりよろづのことを夢と見るかな
tsuki no wa ni / kokoro o kakeshi / yūbe yori / yorozu no koto o / yume to miru kana

> since the evening
> I surrendered my heart
>
> to the circle of the moon
>
> the myriad things
> I see as a dream

There are certainly hints here that the author is expressing something that might be identified as Buddhist. First, it is not necessary to refer to the wheel shape of the moon since rarely in *waka* is it represented as anything but full (though it is frequently represented as hidden).

Second, if "surrendered my heart" is a faithful translation of *kokoro o kakeshi* (as I believe it is), then that phrase too might be a hint. And third, while seeing the myriad things as a dream is reminiscent of the *utsutsu/yume* confusion used in some *waka* from the era of the *Kokinshū*, this too provides a hint, especially combined with the other two. But there is still nothing that explicitly identifies this poem as Buddhist per se. This changed when the anthologizer added the topic "On Contemplation of the Moon Disk" and the author's name "Bishop Kakuchō" to the *waka*. Now our speculations, if we had any, would be substantiated. Still, however, we might ask: How *precisely* does surrendering one's heart to the moon result in a realization about the world being a dream? Moreover, how would surrendering one's heart to the moon effect Buddhist enlightenment?

In the *Goshūishū shakkyō-ka* sequence, there are signs, especially in poems by Kakuchō (1188/1190), Koben (1190/1192), and Ise no Chūjō (1191/1193) that the Tendai teachings of radical nonduality have begun to appear in court *waka*. There are also numerous explicit and implicit references to the path (*michi*) that seem to indicate a deepening interest in the duties of a practitioner and devotee as well as a curiosity about where these duties will lead. We cannot say that the concept of *waka-as-michi* as discussed in Chapter 1 is fully apparent, but there is ample evidence among these poems of authors locating certain spiritual ideals in Buddhist texts they read, and in the various religious services, ceremonies, and lectures they attended.

The *Shakkyō-ka*

Kakuchō's Poem on the Moon Disk Practice

One gateway through which to enter the world of *shakkyō-ka* in the *Goshūishū* is the previously discussed poem by Bishop Kakuchō, a good example of the third—soteriological/monastic—modality: "since the evening / I surrendered my heart / to the circle of the moon / the myriad things / I see as a dream." The topic of the poem, "On

Contemplation of the Moon Disk," is a Shingon visualization practice known as *gachirinkan* in which enlightenment is realized through the meditative discipline of gazing at and then visualizing a replica of the full moon, often depicted with the Siddham script syllable "A" and a lotus blossom drawn within it.[259] It is the environment of meditative practice that characterizes this *shakkyō-ka* as belonging to the monastic modality. The poem combines both meditative and lyric aspects, in that it includes both an intellectual assessment of the value of a particular meditative practice, and hints at the emotional consequences of spiritual liberation as a result of that practice.

The Shingon practice of *gachirinkan* with its goal of enlightenment is the only Buddhist meditative discipline referred to in the *Goshūishū shakkyō-ka* sequence, and it requires further examination before we can fully understand it in Kakuchō's poem. Kūkai wrote about *gachirinkan* practice in his work *Hizō hōyaku* where he elucidates an explanation of it found in the Bodaishinron (The Aspiration to Enlightenment).

> The Buddhas of great compassion ... with the wisdom of skillful means, taught them this profound Esoteric Buddhist yoga and made each devotee visualize in his inner mind the bright moon. By means of this practice each devotee will perceive his original Mind, which is serene and pure like the full moon whose rays pervade space without any discrimination ... It [his original Mind] is just like the full moon, spotless and bright. Why? Because all sentient beings are endowed with the all-pervading Mind. We are to perceive our Mind in the form of the moon. The reason the image of the moon is used is that the body of the bright moon is analogous to that of the enlightened Mind. ...[260]

---

259. Taizō Yamasaki, *Shingon: Japanese Esoteric Buddhism* (Boston: Shambhala Publications, Inc., 1988), 197.

260. Hakeda, *Kūkai*, 218–219.

Kūkai does not explain how one can recognize this original Mind, but much later, the Shingon master, Rikan (1635–1693), wrote about both the practice and its realization in his work *Ajikan* (Meditation on the Letter *A*):

> In doing visualization, first face the painting [the object of meditation] and look at the A-syllable, lotus, and moon. Then, with the eyes neither open nor closed, visualize them within. If at this time they appear as the Dharma reality in Samadhi, it is a matter for congratulation. If they appear by your own thought, they are delusions.[261]

If we consider the antipodal statements "If ... they appear as the Dharma Reality in Samadhi, it is a matter for congratulation" and "If they appear by your own thought, they are delusions," we can see the emphasis in the first is upon the spontaneous arising of emptiness within a state of *samādhi*. Yamasaki explains the realization that arises from the *gachirinkan* meditative practice as follows, "At this depth of contemplation, the self unites with the object, so that the object no longer remains an object to the self. Samadhi ... unites the subject and object of practice; in the esoteric tradition, it is said to result in the union of self and Buddha."[262]

Looking at Kakuchō's poem from the perspective of Rikan's explanation of how the experience of spontaneous moon-disk awareness should occur if it is an experience of enlightenment, it would appear that this is what Kakuchō describes in his *waka*. Kakuchō connects the actual fact of the experience (the "narrative cell" of the poem, about which the speaker thinks and feels) to its result: "since the evening / I surrendered my heart" what I, Kakuchō, experienced was "the myriad things" as "a dream." "The myriad things" is the Japanese reading of the Buddhist word *banji* (*yorozu [no] koto*), the phenomenal world of attachment and delusion. The "dream" (*yume*) in Japanese *waka* always contained

261. Yamasaki, *Shingon*, 102.
262. Ibid., 100.

an hallucinatory element in it even when it was being compared to "reality" (*utsutsu*), but when it was combined with a poet's familiarity with the Buddhist teachings, this hallucination came to represent something more encompassing—the fact that the phenomenal world as we experience it is insubstantial when viewed from the perspective of surrendering one's "heart" and seeing the world as it is.[263]

The crux of Kakuchō's poem is the verb *kakeshi* (*kaku*+past tense *jodōshi ki* in the *rentaikei* form). In classical Japanese, *kaku* can mean a variety of things such as "hang," "suspend," "compare," and "cover," but the meanings that come closest in this case are either the modern Japanese word *takusu* (to entrust [one's heart/life]) or the phrase *omoi o mukeru* (turn one's thought to). Since Kakuchō seems to have had a genuine realization about the nature of the world, the word *takusu*—a word that implies "giving something up" or "giving something over to something else"—fits better in this context than *omoi o mukeru*. Visualizing the moon disk by entrusting one's mind to it and in such a way that "it is a matter for congratulation," to quote Rikan, resonates well with a state of mind that allows one to see the phenomenal world as a dream.

Though not without emotional implications, Kakuchō's poem is not a spontaneous lyric treatment of the enlightenment experience; instead, it is a report of such an experience by the poet (assisted by the narrative indicator "since the evening"). Whether or not the speaker of the poem—in this case, we may assume that it is Kakuchō—is still experiencing that state of mind—a state of mind in which, as Yamasaki says, "the object no longer remains an object to the self"—is, without more information, impossible to know. Nor is

---

263. As a Tendai monk who studied with Genshin, Kakuchō (d. 1034) founded the Kawa school of esoteric Buddhism on Mt. Hiei. Therefore, he was well versed in the practices of the esoteric tradition. Since Kakuchō has no other poems in the imperial anthologies, but was the author of several religious texts, we can presume that his skills were not honed on the *waka* form. Moreover, since he died a half-century before the compilation of the *Goshūishū*, we can also presume that writing such *waka* had gained some currency during the time between the compilation of the *Hosshin wakashū* and the *Goshūishū*, if in fact the poem was written between 1012 (the date of the *Hosshin wakashū*) and 1034 (Kakuchō's death). If it was written before 1012, then it is one of the earliest examples of a Buddhist *waka* that is specifically connected to enlightenment by theme.

it particularly relevant to our understanding of the poem. However, it is interesting to speculate about the limited emotional tone of the poem. The final exclamatory particle *kana* interjects the author's feeling (introducing a lyric element, which is enhanced by the image of the moon), suggesting that seeing the phenomenal world as a dream was a remarkable event certainly worth having and equally worth reporting. Whether this feeling expresses the joy, surprise, or wonder that would arise naturally from having such an experience of nonduality (the pleasure that comes from obstructing the ordinary development of the *skandhas*) or whether it is a reflective pat on the back for a job well done (a return to the five *skandhas* and duality), it is an example of the difficulty involved in exploring the depth of a poet's understanding of Buddhism and how to associate that understanding to a poet's *waka*.

In the *Goshūishū*, there are no other *shakkyō-ka* like Kakuchō's that express the same momentary disengagement with the *skandhas* and thus, the soteriological/monastic modality. However, there are other poems (1185/1187, by Ben no Menoto, 1196/1198, by Fujiwara no Kintō, and 1190/1192, by Koben for example) written in a meditative mode that suggest a notable comprehension of the concepts of Buddhism.

Most of the poems in this sequence, however, communicate through a soteriological/courtly modality. Their mere inclusion in an imperial poetry anthology connects them to their courtly roots, but how is it that they are also demonstrably soteriological? There is no historical evidence that can point to a particular moment or moments in Japanese literary history when court poets began to believe, as Senshi did, that *waka* can have the same transformative capabilities as Buddhist sūtras, ceremonies, and rituals. However, if we imagine that there was an increasing belief in what Senshi proposed in the *Hosshin wakashū*, an assumption substantiated by Shunzei's view of *waka* as path in the late twelfth century, certainly it is not a far stretch to also imagine a belief in the possible soteriological intentions of the remaining *shakkyō-ka* sequence in the *Goshūishū*.

Beyond Kakuchō

In his work *Shakkyō-ka no kenkyū,* Ishihara claims all the *shakkyō-ka* (he applies the term retroactively) in every anthology from the *Shūishū* can be divided into two categories: experiential (*taiken-ka*) and topical (*daiei-ka*). I refer to these as occasional and scriptural. It is obvious once you read the headnotes and topics that many of the poems were composed (if the headnotes and topics are accurate) on the occasion of a ceremony or other Buddhist event and also that many others were composed on the basis of a certain Buddhist sūtra, a chapter of a sūtra, a passage from a sūtra, or concept related to the sūtra. While this information is useful to a certain extent, it provides limited assistance in understanding these poems. In fact, we risk the danger of missing what is emphasized in the poems themselves. If, on the other hand, we use our understanding of the poetic modes in which the poems were written (lyric, narrative, and meditative) in conjunction with the headnote or topic of the poem, we have a better chance to understand a poem's project and its level of engagement with the Buddhist teachings.

Reading the headnotes alone, we can glean the following information about the remaining *shakkyō-ka* in the *Goshūishū* sequence. The first five poems (1179/1181–1183/1185) concern the death of the Buddha. The headnote to the first poem specifically mentions the Nehan-e, the yearly ceremony held to commemorate the Buddha's *parinirvāna,* while the other four refer somewhat more obliquely to the month and day (fifteenth day of the second month) the ceremony was held. Another group of five *waka* (1192/1194–1196/1198)—what many scholars call *kyōshi-ka,* or *shakkyō-ka* based upon the import of a Buddhist text—takes specific chapters from the Lotus Sutra as their topic. There are two poems (1189/1191–1190/1192) based upon the metaphors in the Yuima-kyō (S: Vimalakīrti Sūtra), and one poem (1191/1193) that is based upon a concept from the Kegon-kyō (S: Avatamsaka Sūtra). The remaining five poems are occasional and refer to various Buddhist ceremonies, occasions, or events. Among these is the recovery of Fujiwara no Yorimichi's fan by the Empress Dowager in the Buddhist sanctuary of the Higashi Sanjō Palace

(1186/1188) and a Penitence Ceremony (Senbō, 1185/1187) held at an undisclosed location. The presentation of the Lotus Sutra among the Five Great Mahāyāna sūtras (Gobu daijō kyō, 1186) that were being copied at a ceremony in the Empress Dowager's Palace is another. The final two poems were written on the occasion of the Enlightenment Lectures (Bodai-kō, 1187/1189)—location unknown, and an unnamed Sūtra Memorial Service (Kyō kuyō, 1196/1198) at which the poet, a female performer/prostitute, was in attendance. The association of these *waka* with a variety of Buddhist venues indicates to some degree the influence that Buddhist culture had on the *waka* tradition by the end of the eleventh century. The number and kinds of venues will continue to increase over the next century, but it seems apparent at this point in Japanese history that the poets at the court, as well as the monks from the monastic institutions who composed *shakkyō-ka*, were exploring the limits of what could be addressed and written about Buddhism in the courtly poetic form.

THE BUDDHA'S *PARINIRVĀNA*

[1179/1181]²⁶⁴

いにしへの別れの庭にあへりともけふのなみだぞなみだならまし

inishie no / wakare no niwa ni / aeritomo / kyō no namida zo / namida naramashi

A CEREMONY AT YAMASHINADERA COMMEMORATING THE BUDDHA'S DEATH²⁶⁵

today's tears

are the tears
of "if we had met"
in that long-gone garden

of goodbye

— Priest Kōgen

---

264. The SNKBT version and the Izumi Shoin version of the *Goshūishū* begin the "Shakkyō" section from #1179, while the texts used by Ishihara and Fujimoto begin with #1181. SKNBT, 384; Izumi Shoin, 297; Ishihara, 63; Fujimoto, 383.

265. The text of the *Goshūishū* upon which Fujimoto relied has Nehan-kō rather than Nehan-e in the headnote (383). In her notes to the poem, Fujimoto says that these two words indicate the same service.

[1180/1182, no headnote]

つねよりもけふの霞ぞあはれなるたきゞつきにしけぶりと思へば

tsune yori mo / kyō no kasumi zo / aware naru / takigi tsukinishi /
keburi to omoeba

> it hurts
> > that what I mistook
> > > for today's spring mist
>
> > > is just the smoke of wood
> > that has been
> consumed by the fire

> — Former Preceptor Keisen
> (or Kyōsen)

[1181/1183]

いかなればこよひの月のさ夜中に照しもはてで入りしなるらん
ikanareba / koyoi no tsuki no / sayonaka ni / terashi mo hatede / irishi naruran

SENT TO ISE NO TAYŪ ON THE FIFTEENTH OF THE
SECOND MONTH IN THE MIDDLE OF THE NIGHT

> why
>> instead of shining
>>> to the end
>
>>> did the moon of evening
>> go inside the veil
> during the night's small hours?

>>>> — Priest Keihan
>>>> (or Kyōhan)

[1182/1184]

よを照す月かくれにしさ夜中はあはれ闇にやみなまどひけん

yo o terasu / tsuki kakurenishi / sayonaka wa / aware yami ni ya / mina madoiken

AN ANSWER

> during the night's small hours
>> the moon
>>> that shone over the world
>
>>> has hidden—will everyone
>> have been lost
> in the dark?

—— Ise no Tayū

[1183/1185]

山のはに入りにし夜はの月なれどなごりはまだにさやけかりけり

yama no ha ni / irinishi yowa no / tsuki naredo / nagori wa mada ni /
sayakekarikeri

SENT TO ŌE NO SUKEKUNI WHEN THE MOON WAS
BRIGHT ON THE FIFTEENTH OF THE SECOND MONTH

    the moon of evening
        hid
        behind the mountain edge

    but the bright
        resonance—
        O, it leaves behind!

                — Anonymous

I have suggested that the placement of the five *waka* on the death of the Buddha at the beginning of the *shakkyō-ka* sequence could have been Michitoshi's way of acknowledging that Japan had entered the age of *mappō*. The fact that the first three of these five poems were written by Buddhist priests also suggests that the teachings of *mappō* came from the temple complexes. However, the range of emotions expressed in each is quite different. Some express longing, others hope, and regret.

The first poem by Priest Kōgen (alive in 1028) is the only one that specifically mentions the Nehan-e.[266] Subsequent poems only refer to the day of the ceremony: the fifteenth day of the second month. Priest Kōgen's *shakkyō-ka* is set imaginatively in the "garden" at Kuśinara where the Buddha died. Kōgen superimposes that setting onto the one where he is commemorating the Buddha's death at Yamashinadera (Kōfuku-ji) in Nara. Imagining the tears he would have shed in India, he compares them to the ones he shed at the ceremony.

Written primarily in the lyric mode, this poem emphasizes an expression of longing or regret, but its narrative elements (... " 'if we had met' / in that long-gone garden") also support the poem by alluding to the scene of the Buddha's actual death. But this narrative is not the primary focus: instead, it is the sentiment and, from that sentiment, the conclusion made in the poet's mind (the meditative element) that tears in India several centuries ago are no different from one's own tears being shed at this time and place—at Yamashinadera on the fifteenth day of the second month. The imaginative conflation of time and, thus, history, draws the poet closer to the Buddha, emphasizing that he too is the Buddha's student.

The *shakkyō-ka* that follows Kōgen's, by the Former Preceptor Keisen, refers to an unspecified location from where the author can see

---

266. According to Fujimoto, Kōgen, a Tendai priest, could have been alive during either the Chōgen era (1028–1037) or Chōkyū era (1040–1044), depending on which text is consulted. The Izumi Shoin version says there are two entries in the *kanbun* diary *Shōyūki* for the 21st and 22nd days of the seventh month of the fourth year of Chōwa, 1015, in which a priest by the name of Kōgen, a student of Abbot Keien, appears. Fujimoto, 384; Izumi Shoin version, 413.

smoke rising from the cremation grounds.[267] This narrative element is supplemented by the phrase *kyō no kasumi* (today's mist) and the verb *omoeba* (when I thought), what we translated as "what I mistook / for."[268] However, again the narrative component is not primary; it provides the platform for the disappointment or regret the poem expresses. Keisen's understanding that what at first seemed to be one phenomenon (the spring mist) is actually another (cremation smoke) creates a metaphor by which something new (spring) is associated with something thought to occur when one is old (death). Thinking he was gazing upon spring mist, Keisen realizes that what he sees is instead a plume of smoke from the place where bodies of the dead are burned. Of course, there is no indication that this poem refers specifically to the Buddha's death since there is no headnote, but the poem's content (and its narrative predicament) does support and continue the theme established by Kōgen's *waka*.

In the *zōtōka* by Priest Keihan and Ise no Tayū which follow the poem by Keisen, Keihan's *waka* expresses fear that the moon, a symbol/ metaphor for the Buddha, having gone behind some obstruction, indicates the inaccessibility of the Buddhist teachings for everyone.[269] This interpretation fits well with *mappō* consciousness in general, but the poem could also be an expression of the priest's personal fear that he does not have the spiritual capability to overcome whatever obstacle prevents him from attaining enlightenment. Whichever it is, Ise no Tayū's response in the form of a rhetorical question ("will everyone / have been lost / in the dark?") either confirms Keihan's expression of fear for the salvation of all or extends the personal sense of Keihan's fear to everyone who will be affected by *mappō*.

While longing, regret, and fear are the emotions expressed in the

---

267. Keisen (993–1064) was born in Ise and became Provisional Preceptor in 1040 on Mt. Hiei. He quit the following year. As a master of meditation, he is said to have been able to change a black-colored symbol for "A" to gold in the course of his practice. Jun and Hirata, *Goshūiwakashū*, 21.

268 The *kyō no* construction in Keisen's poem has grammatical, and therefore, musical resonance with Kōgen's poem: *kyō no namida.*

269 Keihan (dates unknown), a Hiei priest in the Yokawa section, was born into the Nakahara clan. Jun and Hirata, *Goshūiwakashū*, 17.

first four poems, the last poem, attributed to an anonymous author and sent to Ōe no Sukekuni (1012–1087?) on the fifteenth of the second month, expresses the hope that the Buddha's teachings will remain in this world for the benefit of everyone ("but the bright / resonance— / O, it leaves behind!").[270] Like the four poems that precede it, this one too is characterized primarily by the lyric mode (the headnote providing a limited narrative element), but its positive outlook suggests much more than just optimism. This poem is, in effect, a song of praise to the en*light*ening moon/the teachings of the Buddha, extolling the emotional and soteriological benefits brightness/spiritual illumination have left behind.

---

270. Ōe no Sukekuni was a student of Michitoshi's who aided his teacher in the selection process of the *Goshūishū*. Ibid., 54.

LOTUS SUTRA *SHAKKYŌ-KA*

[1192/1194]

こしらへて仮の宿りにやすめずはまことの道をいかで知らまし
*koshiraete / kari no yadori ni / yasumezu wa / makoto no michi o / ikade
shiramashi*

PARABLE OF THE CONJURED CITY

without a little coddling—

a momentary roof

under which to rest—

how could anyone

find the true path?

— Akazome Emon

[1193/1195]

道とほみなか空にてや帰らまし思へば仮の宿ぞうれしき

michi toomi / nakazora ni te ya / kaeramashi / omeba kari no / yado zo ureshiki

PARABLE OF THE CONJURED CITY

> go back? halfway there?

> > because the road is long?

> > > (though if I imagine
> > > there's a place I might
> > > rest for a moment

> > > > it does cheer me)

> > > > > — Mother of Yasusuke no Ō

[1194/1196]

ころもなる玉ともかけて知らざりき酔ひさめてこそうれしかり
けれ

koromo naru / tama to mo kakete / shirazariki / eisamete koso /
ureshikarikere

FIVE HUNDRED DISCIPLES RECEIVE THE PROPHECY
THAT THEY WILL ATTAIN BUDDHAHOOD

> of the jewel
> sewn in my coat
>
> > I had no inkling—
>
> what luck!
> to wake
>
> > from my long drunkenness
>
> > > — Akazome Emon

[1195/1197]

鷲の山へだつる雲や深からんつねに澄むなる月を見ぬか
な

washi no yama / hedatsuru kumo ya / fukakaran / tsune ni sumu naru /
tsuki o minu kana

LIFE-SPAN OF THE THUS COME ONE

> has some dark cloud
> come between me
> and Vulture Peak? because
>
> now that moon
> of ever-living brightness
> can't be seen

— Mother of Yasusuke no Ō

[1196/1198]

世をすくふうちにはたれか入らざらんあまねき門は人しさ
ゝねば

*yo o sukuu / uchi ni wa tare ka / irazaran / amaneki kado wa / hito shi
sasaneba*

THE GATE TO EVERYWHERE

the world is saved

because no one can shut
the gate to everywhere: O who

will not enter?

— Former Major Counselor Kintō

Poems based upon Buddhist religious texts, as well as the doctrine and practices derived from those texts, comprise about half of the Buddhist *waka* from the time of the *Shūishū* to the last imperial anthology of 1439. Moreover, about half of those are based upon the Lotus Sutra, poems which Japanese scholars call *Hokke-kyō no uta* or *Hokke-kyō-ka*.[271] *Waka* composed on single chapters of the Lotus Sutra and purportedly written by Buddhist luminaries such as Gyōki, Saichō, Ennin, Ryōgen, and Genshin can be found in various imperial anthologies, but it is likely that the attributions to these poems are traditional rather than actual.[272] It is more likely that the *Hokke-kyō-ka* tradition did not begin until 1002. Before addressing the *Hokke-kyō-ka* in this sub-sequence, it will be helpful to discuss *Hokke-kyō-ka* in general, because some understanding about their history and typology will help illuminate not only the poems in the *Goshūishū*, but also many of the Lotus Sutra-based *waka* in the anthologies to follow.

There are at least three kinds of *Hokke-kyō-ka* as indicated by headnotes or topics: (1) *waka* written about the "essence" (*kokoro*) of the Lotus Sutra as a whole, (2) *waka* written about the "essence" of a Lotus Sutra chapter (*daibon-ka*, poem on the chapter topic), and (3) *waka* written about a particular passage from the text. All three kinds are often referred to as *kyōshi-ka*, or sūtra *waka*. However, one might add a fourth kind to this list—*waka* that have no headnote or topic referring to the Lotus Sutra. Under this kind would fall the poems attributed to Gyōki and Izumi Shikibu from the previous anthology (see Chapter 3) that have clearly adopted a section of passage from the Sutra into the *waka* itself. In a general sense, *Hokke-kyō-ka* from the time of the *Goshūishū* forward are almost exclusively scriptural, but we do not know if the topics were created by the compilers based on their knowledge of the circumstances of the poems' composition or from

271. Yamada Shōzen, "Shakkyō-ka no seiritsu to tenkai," *Waka, Renga, Haikai* vol. 4 of *Bukkyō bungaku kōza* (Tokyo: Benseisha, 1995), 39. Unlike many other scholars of Buddhist *waka* such as Ishihara, for example, Yamada does not call the Buddhist *waka* of the *Shūishū*, *Kin'yōshū*, or *Shikashū* "*shakkyō-ka.*" See also Fukui Kyūzō, "Shakkyō waka ni tsukite," 318.

272. Takagi, *Heian jidai Hokke-kyō Bukkyō-shi kenkyū*, 260.

what the compilers deduced. In either case, the compilers are usually silent about the circumstances of composition and left only the topic (chapter name, in this case) to guide their readers. Sometimes *shakkyō-ka* written on the ceremonial occasion of presenting or copying the Lotus Sutra—without reference to its contents—are also referred to as *Hokke-kyō-ka,* but rather than calling these poems sūtra *waka* (*kyōshi-ka*), scholars—if they are using Okazaki's typology—are more likely to refer to them as *hōen-ka,* or covenant *waka.*

Many *Hokke-kyō-ka* are derived from sequences of *shakkyō-ka* written on each chapter of the Lotus Sutra. A full such sequence is referred to as a *nijūhappon-ka* (poems on the twenty-eight chapters), the first of which was probably written at the time of the memorial service for Fujiwara no Michinaga's elder sister, Higashi Sanjō-in Senshi, in 1002. It is believed that the twenty-eight-chapter sequence found in Fujiwara no Kintō's private anthology, *Kintō-shū,* was written on that occasion.[273] Some Japanese scholars also claim that poems by Michinaga himself from the same occasion can be found in the eighth imperial anthology, *Shinkokinshū* (1927), the ninth anthology, *Shinchokusenshū* (583), the tenth anthology, *Shokugosenshū* (595 and 596 [587 and 588]), the fourteenth anthology *Gyokuyōshū* (2650 [2637]), and the seventeenth anthology *Fūgashū* (2050 [2040].[274] Many sequences like the ones composed for Higashi Sanjō-in Senshi's memorial service were composed after 1002 as the result of ceremonies and readings held in conjunction with the Hokke hakkō, Eight Lectures on the Lotus Blossom, a religious event that was first held in the eighth century. The early Hokke hakkō from the eighth, ninth, and tenth centuries did not elicit *nijūhappon-ka,* but starting in the early eleventh century the occasion of a Hokke hakkō was

---

273. Japanese scholars are less certain about the twenty-eight-chapter *waka* sequence found in Akazome Emon's private anthology, but many think that it too may have come about as a result of the same occasion. The same is true for the twenty-eight-chapter sequence in the *Nagayoshi-shū* by Fujiwara Nagayoshi (ca. ?949–?1017). Kubota Jun, "Hōmon-ka to shakkyō-ka," 257–286.

274. Yamada, "Shakkyō-ka no seiritsu to tenkai," 47–48. The alternative numbers for the *shakkyō-ka* in the *Shokugosenshū, Gyokuyōshū,* and the *Fūgashū* are found in SKT, vol. 1, 300, 477, 595.

often accompanied by a complementary event at which the attendees would write a poem for each chapter. In this way, the association and proximity of *waka* composition with the religious activities of a Buddhist ceremony, ritual, or occasion sacralized the former, in much the same way that Princess Senshi's passages on various Buddhist sūtras sacralized her *waka* compositions in the *Hosshin wakashū*.

Returning now to the five *Hokke-kyō-ka* in the *Goshūishū*, we notice that they were written by three court poets: Akazome Emon, Yasusuke Ō no Haha, and Fujiwara no Kintō.[275] The first two of the five poems (1192/1194 and 1193/1195) on the Parable of the Conjured City chapter (7, *Kejōyu-bon*) utilize the parable's image of the path or road (*michi*) as an example of something that is both true (*makoto no*) and long (*tōmi*).[276] The parable concerns a group of travelers being led by a "guide [who is] perceptive and wise" to "a cache of precious jewels."[277] When the travelers express fear that their exhaustion will no longer allow them to travel, the guide conjures a great city (an expedient means) in which the travelers can rest. Once the travelers have regained their energy, the guide "dissolves the conjured city" so that they may continue their journey. References like these indicate how poets drew particular details of their understanding of the spiritual path from specific Buddhist scriptures.

These two particular Lotus Sutra poems complement each other in a number of ways. Other than the repetition of the word *michi* in both *waka*, another phrase with only a single syllable difference occurs as well in both poems (*kari no yadori; kari no / yado*). Moreover, there are also similarities between grammatical forms (*shira-mashi; kaera-mashi*) and verbal expressions (know: *shiru/ shiramashi;* think/feel:

---

275. The poem by Akazome Emon appears in a slightly different form in her private anthology: *koshiraete / kari no yadori wa / yasumezuba / saki no michi ni ya / nao madowamashi* (had we not rested here at this temporary home made just for us, wouldn't I have have lost my way on this path even more?). SKT, vol. 3, 322. Yasusuke Ō no Haha's poem does not appear in her private collection. SKT, vol. 3, 399–402.

276. Izumi Shikibu's poem in the *Shūishū* Buddhist *waka* sequence dealt with the same chapter of the Lotus Sutra, but not the parable.

277. Hurvitz, *Scripture of the Lotus Blossom of the Fine Dharma*, 148–149; Sakamoto and Iwamoto, *Hokke-kyō*, vol. 2, 72–74.

omou/omoeba). Given all these similarities, it is clear why Michitoshi placed them next to one another in the sequence. Written primarily in the lyric mode with a strong narrative element derived from the parable itself, both poems are expressions of relief, the same variety of relief expressed in the Sutra by the practitioners. The Japanese word *ureshiki* (happiness) in the second poem is the equivalent of the Chinese compound *kanki* (joy) in the Sutra: "At that time, the exhausted multitude, overjoyed at heart, sigh as at something they have never had before, saying, 'We have escaped that bad road, and shall quickly regain our composure.'"[278]

The *Hokke-kyō-ka* that immediately follow (1194/1196 and 1195/1197) are attributed to the same two poets. The first poem is based upon the Parable of the Hidden Jewel found in the chapter titled Receipt of Prophecy by Five Hundred Disciples (8, *Gobyakudeshi juki-bon*), and the second uses the chapter titled Life-Span of the Thus Come One (16, *Nyorai juryō-hon*). There are parables in both chapters, but the second poem by Yasusuke Ō no Haha does not utilize the parable from Chapter 16. Again, like the previous two poems, these are characterized by the lyric mode, and also rely upon the narrative from the chapters of the Sutra they represent.

The story of the hidden jewel concerns two men, one rich and the other poor.[279] The poor man visits the rich man's house, where he is served so much alcohol that he falls into a drunken sleep. While the poor man is asleep, the rich man (the Buddha) sews a priceless gem into the hem of his clothes. After the poor man awakens, he sets out on a difficult journey to another country where he struggles to support himself. Returning to his home sometime later, the poor man again meets the rich man who tells him about the priceless gem. Hereupon the poor man is able to realize his own inherent spiritual wealth, an obvious reference to one's own Buddha nature.

Akazome's poem on the hidden jewel, told from the point of view of the poor man, borrows words from the Sutra: *koromo* (clothes), *tama* (jewel), *kakete* (sewn), *shirazariki* (not known), *ei* (drunk). Like

---

278. Ibid.
279. Hurvitz, 164–167; Sakamoto and Iwamoto, vol. 2: 114–116, 118–120.

Princess Senshi, Akazome does not attempt to interpret the Lotus Sutra so much as to rewrite it in Japanese poetic form, thus reducing the epistemological distance between the teachings of the Sutra and the art of the *waka*. We may speculate that this kind of borrowing occurred within a perspective that believed that the *kyōgen kigo* of *waka* poetry could be transformed into sacred—and soteriological—words.

The verse in the Lotus Sutra upon which Yasusuke Ō no Haha's poem (1195/1197) is based reads: "I, ever dwelling here, / By the power of my supernatural penetrations, / Cause the topsy-turvy living beings, / Though they are near, not to see."[280] Vulture Peak (*washi no yama*) in the poem is the location in India where the Buddha supposedly preached the Lotus Sutra. The author/speaker cannot see the moon (the Buddha) shining above the peak because of thick clouds (*hedatsuru kumo ya / fukakaran*) hiding its glow. These intervening clouds—that which prevents the practitioner from experiencing her realization—are not the fault of the Buddha. The Buddha has skillfully made a "show of nirvāna" for all sentient beings for an incalculable number of kalpas. Yasusuke Ō no Haha's poem seems to point the reader back to ideas expressed in the opening *shakkyō-ka*: why indeed have the Buddha and his teachings become inaccessible? Have the teachings removed themselves from our grasp (obscuration=*mappō*), or are the clouds symbols of personal delusions that obscure the brilliance of the teachings?

Unlike the four poems just discussed, Fujiwara no Kintō's poem on The Gate to Everywhere chapter (25, *Kanzeon bosatsu fumon-bon*)—also known as the Kannon-kyō or the Avalokiteśvara Sūtra—is written primarily in the meditative mode with only minimal integration of lyric or narrative aspects. In this case, Kintō has removed himself, or any other subjective self, from the viewpoint of the poem. A speaker asks a rhetorical question, but the question does not pertain to the speaker except by inference.

The primary message of The Gate to Everywhere chapter is that all beings, regardless of position or status, good or bad, guilt or

---

280. Hurvitz, 242; Sakamoto and Iwamoto, vol. 2: 30.

innocence, are eligible for salvation "if [he] ... keeps the name of this bodhisattva He Who Observes the Sounds of the World ..."[281] What contributes to this poem's meditative quality is the element of causality and reasoning in its argument that "because no one can shut / the gate to everywhere," there are none "who / will not enter ..." The emphasis on salvation in this poem, as well as the lack of a first-person perspective, pushes the modality of this poem toward the soteriological and the monastic, but here, unlike Kakuchō's poem, the possibility of salvation is derived from the import of the Sutra, rather than from a religious discipline like the practice of *gachirinkan*.

---

281. Ibid., 311; ibid., vol. 3: 242.

OTHER SŪTRA-DERIVED *SHAKKYŌ-KA*

[1189/1191]

風吹けばまづやぶれぬる草の葉によそふるからに袖ぞつゆ
けき

*kaze fukeba / mazu yaburenuru / kusa no ha ni / yosouru kara ni / sode
zo tsuyukeki*

ON THE ESSENCE OF THE METAPHOR "THIS BODY IS
LIKE A BANANA TREE," from the Ten Metaphors of the Yuima-
kyō

> leaves of grass
>
> > that break at the first gust—
>
> no sooner do I make
>
> > that likening
>
> than my sleeves
>
> > are wet with tears

> — Former Major Counselor Kintō

[1190/1192]

つねならぬわが身は水の月なればよにすみとげんことも思
はず

*tsune naranu / waga mi wa mizu no / tsuki nareba / yo ni sumitogen /
koto mo omowazu*

ON THE ESSENCE OF THE METAPHOR "THIS BODY IS
LIKE THE MOON IN THE WATER," from the Ten Metaphors of
the Yuima-kyō

      to live in the world—
                I don't expect *that*
                          to last

      because my body
              is a mortal moon
                    of water

              — Koben

[1191/1193]

ちる花もをしまばとまれ世の中は心のほかの物とやは聞く
chiru hana mo / oshimaba tomare / yo no naka wa / kokoro no hoka no / mono to ya wa kiku

THE THREE WORLDS ARE NOTHING BUT ONE MIND

to regret

the falling blossoms

and command them: *stop!*

haven't I heard

the world is none other

than the heart?

— Ise no Chūjō

We find *shakkyō-ka* in the *Goshūishū* based upon sūtras other than the Lotus Sutra. Also popular among the aristocracy was the Yuima-kyō, or Vimalakīrti Sūtra. Ceremonies about or readings of the Vimalakīrti Sūtra (at Yuima-e) were the vehicle by which knowledge about the contents and meaning of the Sūtra were disseminated to the aristocracy. These ceremonies were said to have originated with, according to the *Sanbō ekotota*, Fujiwara no Kamatari (614–699) and later with his son Fuhito (659–720).[282] According to Mikael Adolphson, the ceremony was held annually at Kōfuku-ji, the Fujiwara clan temple, in Nara starting in 801.[283] There are only eight Buddhist *waka* on this Sūtra in the *hachidaishū* (the first eight imperial poetry anthologies), but poems based on the metaphors in the Yuima-kyō in private and personal anthologies and in imperial poetry anthologies after the *Shinkokinshū* are numerous.[284] In particular, the ten similes (often referred to as metaphors, *hiyu*) about the insubstantiality of the human body that appear in the second chapter of the Sūtra were the focus of most Vimalakīrti Sūtra *shakkyō-ka*.

Unlike the Lotus Sutra, upon which *shakkyō-ka* from most of the chapters were at one time or another composed, poems on the Vimalakīrti Sūtra were limited to Chapter 2, entitled in one of its English translations, "The Expedient Method of Teaching."[285] This chapter introduces the lay practitioner, Vimalakīrti, to the reader and establishes his skill practicing the "expedient method" (S: *upāya;* J: *hōben*). One of the reasons he engaged in this practice, according to the text, was in order "to [lead] others to the Mahāyāna. ..."[286] Vimalakīrti's principal technique for teaching people the truth of

---

282. Kamens, *The Three Jewels*, 353–354.

283. Adolphson, *The Gates of Power*, 24.

284. Yuima-kyō poems can be found in the private anthologies of Fujiwara no Kintō, Akazome Emon, Fujiwara no Kinshige (ca. 1118–1178), Fujiwara no Suketaka (ca. late twelfth century), Fujiwara no Masatsune (1170–1221), and Jakuren (b. ca. 1117–1123). See Kunieda Toshihisa, "Yuima-kyō jūyu to waka: Shakkyō-ka kenkyū no kisoteki sagyō (6)," *Bukkyō daigaku kenkyū kiyo*, vol. 64 (March 1980): 62–67.

285. Charles Luk, *The Vimalakīrti Nirdeśa Sūtra* (Boston and London: Shambhala Publications, Inc., 1972), 15–19.

286. Ibid., 16.

the Buddha's way was to manifest as a sick person. When people then came to inquire about his well-being, he used this opportunity to teach the Dharma, in particular the truth of impermanence.[287] The literary vehicle for this teaching was a series of ten similes (*jūyu*) in which the body is compared to phenomena whose existence is fundamentally insubstantial or fleeting, such as bubbles or dreams. The passage of the text to which the Heian poets referred reads in English as follows:

> Virtuous ones, all wise men do not rely on this body which is like a mass of foam, which is intangible. It is like a bubble and does not last for a long time. It is like a flame and is the product of thirst of love. It is like a banana tree, the center of which is hollow. It is like an illusion being produced by inverted thoughts. It is like a dream being formed by false views. It is like a shadow and is caused by karma. This body is like an echo for it results from causes and conditions. It is like a floating cloud which disperses any moment. It is like lightning for it does not stay for the time of a thought.[288]

Many of these images—foam, water, flames, illusions, dreams, shadows, floating clouds—were ready-made for Heian court poets who began to connect the art of *waka* to the Buddhist teachings. Writing about the human heart in terms of nature had been at the core of *waka* composition since the time of the *Man'yōshū* and is certainly one of the defining characteristics of Japanese poetry in general. The fact that such images occurred in both traditional Japanese *waka* and in the Buddhist sūtras was serendipitous for the court poet who sought Buddhist salvation without forfeiting the diction of the court tradition.[289]

---

287. For more on the connection between Vimalakīrti and impermanence, see LaFleur, *The Karma of Words*, 107–115.

288. Luk, *The Vimalakīrti Nirdeśa Sūtra*, 18.

289. There is only one problem concerning the images in the two *shakkyō-ka* in the *Goshūishū*. While one image—the banana tree—comes from the ten similes in Chapter 2, the other—the moon in the water—appears later in Chapter 7. This contradicts the

The two *shakkyō-ka* based upon the Vimalakīrti Sūtra in the *Goshūishū* are by Fujiwara no Kintō and Koben (dates unknown).[290] These poems are very similar to the *Hokke-kyō-ka* discussed previously, in so far as words from the Sūtra (i.e., the image, in this case) are repeated in the poem and a lyric response to the meaning of those words provides the *waka*'s primary gesture. Fujiwara no Kintō expresses his sadness about the impermanence of our bodies (compared to the hollow stalks of banana trees) by invoking the traditional image of his "sleeves / wet with tears" (*sode zo tsuyukeki*). Koben's poem takes a more direct approach, reaching the conclusion that because her "body / is a mortal moon / of water" (*mi wa mizu no tsuki nareba*) it cannot last in the world.

These two images/similes—the banana tree and the moon's reflection in the water—fit the courtly modality in which the *shakkyō-ka* sequence mostly communicates. However, the text that immediately follows the ten metaphors in the Vimalakīrti Sūtra is a graphic reminder of what insubstantiality actually means:

> [The body] is egoless for it is like fire (that kills itself).
> It is transient like the wind. It is not human for it
> is like water. It is unreal and depends on the four
> elements for existence. It is empty, being neither ego
> nor its object ... It is impure and full of filth. It is
> false, and though washed, bathed, clothed, and fed,
> it will decay and die in the end. It is a calamity being

headnote, which says the second poem is based upon the "same similes" (*dōyu*) as the previous poem. Ishihara takes a circuitous route to solve this problem, claiming that since the image of the moon in the water does not appear until a later chapter in the Sūtra, then it must not be part of the "ten similes" and must come from another text all together. Ishihara says that text is the Daichidoron (T. 1509), a commentary (S: śāstra) attributed to Nāgārjuna on the Larger Prajñāpāramitā Sūtra (S: Mahāprajñāpāramitā-sūtra) and translated by Kumārajīva in the early fifth century. However, due to the fact that the image of the moon in the water *does* appear in Chapter 7, it seems more logical to assume that either the poet or the compiler conflated the two, mistaking the moon-water image for one of the "ten similes."

290. This is the first appearance of Koben in an imperial poetry anthology. Twenty of her *waka* were chosen for this anthology through the eighth, the *Shinkokinshū*.

subject to all kinds of illnesses and sufferings. It is like a dry well for it is pursued by death. It is unsettled and will pass away. It is like a poisonous snake, a deadly enemy, a temporary assemblage (without underlying reality), being made of the five aggregates [*skandhas*], the twelve entrances (the six organs and their objects) and the eighteen realms of sense ... [291]

The original ten similes—dreams, shadows, bubbles—are not jarring or disturbing, despite their message. The images and comparisons that follow, however, are far less gentle, polite, and lyrical (which is almost certainly the reason court poets did not make use of them). The section of the text that explains that our bodies are "a temporary assemblage ... , being made of the five aggregates [*skandhas*] ... " speaks directly to the existential predicament that to insist on the permanence of the self, the ego, and the body— the perpetual re-creation of the five *skandhas*—leads to pain and suffering. However, one's reliance on the teachings, the words of the Buddha, and the truths they reveal (especially the truth of no-self) is the path to salvation. Therefore, writing a poem based on the teachings, the words of the Buddha, and the truths they reveal can also be—as Princess Senshi argued—equally salvational. I would argue that both of these poems by Kintō and Kōben were written with selflessness and the salvational power of recognizing selflessness in mind, a reiteration of the idea that the Buddhist teachings can be effective whether they are conveyed by the sūtras or re-created in poetry based on the sūtras.

The final sūtra-based *shakkyō-ka* in the *Goshūishū* sequence by Ise no Chūjō (dates unknown) is based on the topic *sangai yui isshin* (the three realms [worlds, spheres] are just one mind), traditionally attributed to the Avatamsaka Sūtra (J: Kegon-kyō), the foundation text for the Kegon School of Japanese Buddhism and an influential text in other sects of Buddhism as well.[292] According to the *Nihon Bukkyōgo*

---

291. Luk, *The Vimalakīrti Nirdeśa Sūtra*, 18.

292. Ishihara and Fujimoto attribute this poem to Ise no Tayū, while the SNKBT

jiten, however, this five-character topic phrase does not appear as it is in the Avatamsaka Sūtra.[293] *Bukkyōgo daijiten,* on the other hand, notes that a similar expression can be found in the "Jūchibon" (Ten Stages) chapter of the Sūtra (*sangai shou yuize isshin*), making this a potential source of the phrase.[294]

The "three realms" in the headnote to this poem refers to the realms of desire (*yoku*), form (*shiki*), and formlessness (*mushiki*) into which sentient beings can be born and some gods abide.[295] The realm of desire is composed of the *rokudō,* or six paths, into which any sentient being can be reborn, while the top two realms—form and formlessness—are primarily occupied by higher gods (*deva*). Humans can attain the upper levels of the realm of form, but the realm of formlessness is restricted to the deities who have "only pure mental existence."

In this system, the three realms are a reminder of the consequences of human actions. Functioning in the realm of desire (*yoku*)— wanting, as in Ise no Chūjō's poem, the falling cherry blossoms to stop their display of impermanence—can only lead to more desire and suffering. However, recognizing that all three realms are the "one mind" (*isshin*) means that even regretting the fall of the blossoms (*oshimaba*) in the realm of desire is coexistent with the single mind of nondiscrimination. The copenetration of desire, form, and

---

and Izumi Shoin versions attributes the author to Ise no Chūjō. Ishihara, *Shakkyō-ka no kenkyū,* 83–84; Fujimoto, 401; SKNBT, vol. 8, 387; Izumi Shoin, 300. Ise no Chūjō (dates unknown) was a lady-in-waiting at the court of Jōtōmon-in Akiko (988–1074). Jun and Hirata, *Goshūiwakashū,* 14.

293. *Nihon Bukkyōgo jiten,* 324. Ishihara claims that the headnote merely provides the gist (*yōshi*) of the Sūtra. *Shakkyō-ka no kenkyū,* 83

294. *Bukkyōgo daijiten,* 457. The *Bukkyōgo daijiten* actually says that this longer phrase is found in the "Daichibon" (Great Earth) chapter, but there is no such chapter in any of the editions of the Avatamsaka Sūtra. Instead, there is a "Jūjibon" (Ten Stages) chapter in which the longer phrase does appear. (T 279, 10.0194a14; for an English translation, see Thomas Cleary, *The Flower Ornament Scripture: A Translation of the Avatamsaka Sutra* [Boston and London: Shambhala Publications, 1993], 746]).

295. The following information about the three realms has been culled from Donald W. Mitchell, *Buddhism: Introducing the Buddhist Experience* (New York: Oxford University Press, 2002), 43–45.

formlessness highlighted in Ise no Chūjō's poem not only creates the single mind of nondiscrimination, but also unifies the Buddhist teachings of the Vimalakīrti Sūtra and the Lotus Sutra, the teachings that serve to ground the two poems that precede and the five poems that follow her *shakkyō-ka*.

FIVE OCCASIONAL *SHAKKYŌ-KA* IN THE *GOSHŪISHŪ*

[1184/1186]

つもるらん塵をもいかではらはまし法にあふぎの風のうれしさ
tsumoruran / chiri o mo ikade / harawamashi / nori ni ōgi no / kaze no ureshisa

WHEN THE EMPRESS DOWAGER FOUND HER FATHER'S FAN IN THE SANCTUARY OF HIGASHI SANJŌ PALACE

> the dust of suffering
> that must always gather—
> I wish I could whisk it away
>
> the way finding
> the Law fans
> a wind of happiness

> — Ise no Tayū

[1185/1187]

八重菊にはちすの露をおきそへてこゝのしなまでうつろはし
つる

*yaegiku ni / hachisu no tsuyu o / okisoete / kokonoshina made /
utsurowashitsuru*

A REPLY TO CHRYSANTHEMUMS SENT BY SUŌ NO
NAISHI, WHICH THE AUTHOR WISHED TO OFFER TO
THE BUDDHA IN A CEREMONY OF PENITENCE

> when the lotus shed
> its dew over the eight-
> petalled chrysanthemum

> that change

> lifted me
> to the ninth level

— Nursemaid Ben

[1186/1188]

咲きがたきみのりの花におく露ややがてころもの玉となる
らん

*sakigataki / minori no hana ni / oku tsuyu ya / yagate koromo no / tama
to naruran*

WRITTEN ON THE DAY THE LOTUS SUTRA WAS
OFFERED, among the Five Great Mahayana Sūtras copied and
presented at the Empress Dowager's Palace

> dew that seeded
> > the lotus of the Law
>
> > > (that rare bloom)
>
> must in a twinkling
> > have become
>
> > > a jewel in the seam
>
> > > > — Mother of Yasusuke no Ō

[1187/1189]

もろともに三の車に乗りしかど我は一味の雨にぬれにき

morotomo ni / mitsu no kuruma ni / norishikado / ware wa ichimi no / ame ni nureniki

WRITTEN WHEN LADIES-IN-WAITING OF THE LATE
TSUCHIMIKADO MINISTER OF THE RIGHT SET OUT TO
AN ENLIGHTENMENT LECTURE IN THREE CARRIAGES,
BUT RAIN TURNED TWO CARRIAGES BACK

(FROM THE PERSON WHO CONTINUED ON, TO ONE OF
THOSE WHO TURNED BACK)

> we climbed aboard
> the three vehicles
>
> in unison
>
> but that "One Taste"
> of rain
>
> soaked only me
>
> — Anonymous

[1197/1199]

津の国のなにはのことか法ならぬ遊び戯れまでとこそ聞け
tsu no kuni no / naniwa no koto ka / nori naranu / asobitawabure / made to koso kike

WHEN THE SAINT FROM SHOSHA, AFTER CONSIDER-
ATION, WOULD NOT ACCEPT THE AUTHOR'S ALMS AT A
SUTRA-OFFERING CEREMONY

I thought
the Law applied
to everyone, everywhere

here in Naniwa of Tsu?

—even to
gamblers, playboys,
servants of pleasure

— Courtesan Miyaki[296]

---

296. We took some liberties with the translation of this poem by interpolating vocabulary from the Sūtra upon which it is based, but we hoped to emphasize the Buddhist
restrictions that most likely applied to anyone who engaged in *asobi* or *tawabure*, though
Miyaki may only have been referring to herself.

These five occasional *shakkyō-ka* in the *Goshūishū* demonstrate the scope of sources Michitoshi drew upon to create the first *shakkyō-ka* sequence in an imperial poetry anthology.

The lengthy headnotes of these five occasional *shakkyō-ka* supply the primary narrative elements upon which, as they are presented in the anthology, the poems are grounded. Though there are narrative elements in the poems themselves, if the headnotes were deleted, their respective narrative predicaments would be much harder, if not impossible, to discern. As we will see, there is also a strong meditative element to some of these poems, indicating that a courtly consciousness of the concepts of the Buddhist teachings was never entirely excluded by the social nature of the occasions.

Like many court *waka*, the occasions upon which these poems were based usually involved two or more people who are either physically or imaginatively present, a characteristic that emphasizes their social nature as well. Since four of these five poems are sequential (1184/1186–1187/1189), their narrative elements create a short *utamonogatari* in which certain objects—fans, flowers, jewels, and carts—are foregrounded to remind us not only of their religious significance, but also for their importance at the court.

We do not have any critical guidelines from texts like Princess Senshi's *Hosshin wakashū* that illuminate how occasional *shakkyō-ka*, unlike scriptural *shakkyō-ka*, were supposed to ignite the soteriological power of the teachings. However, if religious occasions are conceived of as instances of Buddhist practice, then occasional *shakkyō-ka* that result from them would be no less powerful soteriologically than would scriptural *shakkyō-ka*. Members of the court—at least *while* they were members of the court—did not lead lives that were in any way separate from their beliefs. Separation from court social habits, for the purpose of singular devotion to Buddhist ascetic practices—came only after one left it and took the tonsure. But while one maintained a position at the court, Buddhist practice took the form of presenting oneself at such events as sūtra presentation ceremonies, sūtra memorial services, penitence services, and lectures on the nature and meaning of enlightenment. Buddhist practice even extended to reflecting on the meaning of a forgotten fan found at a residential sanctuary, or admonishing a holy man who refused alms from a female entertainer. Practicing Buddhism meant behaving as a Buddhist would behave and accruing the merit that was important to the salvation of every practitioner.

It should also be noted that many of the occasional *shakkyō-ka* are creatively linked to the teachings that were probably the topic of the ceremony, service, or event. Yasusuke Ō no Haha's poem that was written on the day the Lotus Sutra was presented at a time when the "Five Great Mahāyāna Sūtras [were] copied and presented at the Empress Dowager's Palace,"[297] deftly weaves two sections of the Lotus Sutra to create a *shakkyō-ka* that is, with its complex intellectual underpinning, primarily meditative in tone.

This poem not only corresponded temporally with the presentation of the Sutra, but also contextually in terms of its meaning. In the first three *ku* of the *waka*, the author makes reference to the udumbara flower that appears frequently in chapters such as Expedient Devices (2, *Hōbenbon*), the Parable of the Conjured City chapter (7, *Kejōyubon*), and the The Former Affairs of the King Fine Adornment chapter (27, *Myōshōgon'ō honjibon*). Said to bloom infrequently, the udumbara blossom is compared to the rarity of a Buddha who appears in the world to preach the Dharma. In the final two *ku*, the author transforms the dew that has fallen upon the udumbara blossom into the jewel from the Parable of the Jewel in the Receipt of Prophecy by Five Hundred Disciples chapter (8, *Gohyakudeshi jukibon*) extending the rarity of one blossom (a Buddha) to the rarity of another (the teachings)—the "Dharma flower," or the Lotus Sutra.[298]

---

297. The ceremony described in the headnote—Gobu daijō kyō kuyō—gained popularity during the Heian period. It took several days to copy and then present the five sūtras (Kegon-kyō, Daishū-kyō, Daibon hannya-kyō, Hokke-kyō, and Nehangyō) on behalf of the participants. The five sūtras upon which this ceremony was based were first delineated by Chih-i in his *Hokke gengi*. The Empress Dowager referred to in the headnote is Fujiwara no Kanshi (1036–1121), the wife of Emperor Go-Reizei (r. 1045–1068). She became Empress Dowager in 1069 after Go-Reizei died. See McCullough and McCullough, *A Tale of Flowering Fortunes*, vol.2, 780; Ueda Masaaki, et al., ed., *Nihon jinmei jiten* (Tokyo: Sanseidō, 1990), 1078; and *Nihon Bukkyōgo jiten*, 300.

298. Hurvitz, 164–165; Sakamoto and Iwamoto, vol. 2, 114–116.

The last poem in this sub-sequence is by an *asobi*, a female performer and (most likely) prostitute, called Miyaki. This *shakkyō-ka* is important for its unusual authorship (that is, someone outside the confines of the court), but also unusual for the criticism that is implied in the poem. The poem appears to critique both the hypocrisy of a Japanese Buddhist teacher and the inequitable treatment that befell those who were not blessed with more auspicious circumstances. The narrative the headnote describes involves the *hijiri*, Shōkū Shōnin (917–1007), who appears as a figure of salvation in Izumi Shikibu's poem in the Buddhist *waka* sequence in the *Shūishū*.[299] In Miyaki's poem, however, Shōkū appears as an obstacle to salvation rather than its conduit. The occasion of the poem is a *Kechien kuyō*, or Sūtra Memorial Service that provided a forum for listeners to discover their personal connections with the Buddhist teachings. According to the headnote, many people had gathered at this service to present their offerings. When Miyaki made her offering, Shōkū refused to accept it, apparently because of the reputation of *asobi*.

The traditional commentaries claim that the scriptural basis for this poem is the Expedient Devices (*Hōbenbon*) chapter of the Vimalakīrti Sūtra (J: Yuima-kyō), which states, "When entering a gambling house he always tried to teach and deliver people there. He received heretics but never strayed from the right faith."[300] It is true that this Sūtra was well known at this time (as poems in this sequence by Kintō and Koben attest), and it is possible that it was one of, if not the only, sūtra on which the Kechien kuyō focused on this occasion. The evidence for the poem's derivation from the Yuima-kyō is the two Chinese graphs for *asobitawabure* that appear in the second chapter, but which mean, in the context of Sūtra, gambling rather than sexual services. Whether this is the textual source of Miyaki's use of the word or merely the word used by female entertainers for the activities of their profession at this time in Japanese history, the meaning of the poem remains the same: if the teachings—and by extension salvation—are applicable to all sentient beings, then why are they being denied to me? Miyaki's skillful use of

---

299. See Chapter 3.
300. Ishihara, *Shakkyō-ka no kenkyū*, 78. Luk, *The Vimalakīrti Nirdeśa Sūtra*, 16.

the *kakekotoba naniwa* to mean both the place name Naniwa and the interrogative "where" evokes the narrative drama in the poem, while the final two *ku* provides the reasoning for her question.

If the commentaries are correct about the textual source of the words *asobi* and *tawabure*, then the poem might be understood in terms of Tendai and Shingon esoteric values, which would regard even the most despicable lifestyle as a path to enlightenment. Though Robert Thurman in his introduction to the translation admits that there is not sufficient proof of the Vajrayāna elements (*samsāra* is none other than *nirvāna*) in the Sūtra, Luk says, "The concept of the adept using paths generally considered evil for the attainment of enlightenment and the Buddha-qualities is basic in Tantric doctrine and practice."[301]

Another approach to reading Miyaki's poem may be suggested by its location after the last scriptural *shakkyō-ka*. The *shakkyō-ka* that precedes hers, by Kintō, asks rhetorically whether there is anyone who would be excluded from the saving grace of the bodhisattva Kannon. The answer, of course, should be in the negative, but Michitoshi injects a healthy dose of irony into the sequence by ending it with Miyaki's poem, which suggests that unfortunately people did not always behave as if universal grace were the case. This is another example of how anthology compilers could and did subtly inflect the reading of individual poems (and the message the reader would take away from the sequence as a whole) by strategies such as skillful ordering.

CONCLUSION

The *shakkyō-ka* in the *Goshūishū* represent a new direction for the interaction between the Buddhist teachings and the composition of *waka* in the late Heian period. There are precedents in the *Shūishū* and the *Hosshin wakashū* from the beginning of the eleventh century, but with the compilation of the *Goshūishū*, a shift occurred, which was made explicit by the compiler's use of the term "Shakkyō" as the rubric for these nineteen *waka*.

---

301. Luk, *The Vimalakīrti Nirdeśa Sūtra*, 7.

The designation *shakkyō* was not retained as a subcategory of poems in the fifth and sixth imperial anthologies, probably because of the reduced number of books in both. In those anthologies Buddhist *waka* were compiled in a "Miscellaneous" book, but unlike the *Goshūishū*, were not subcategorized. *Waka* classified as *jingi-ka* and the *haikai-ka* in the *Goshūishū* also did not retain their rubrics. However, a *shakkyō-ka* category was included soon after in venues other than the *chokusenshū*—in particular, the *Horikawa hyakushu* of 1105–1106 as well as in Shunrai's private anthology, *Sanboku kikashū*, compiled immediately after Shunrai finished the *Kin'yōshū*. In fact, the *shakkyō-ka* category in the *Sanboku kikashū* was the first of its kind in a *shikashū*.

As the chaos of life in the capital descended on the Heian aristocracy in the increasingly martial atmosphere of the twelfth century, the experiences expressed by the poets in the *Goshūishū* became more urgent. Eventually, the writing of *waka* would not just represent emotions and experiences, but would also become a path to salvation, as the road to the conjured city in the Lotus Sutra had been a path to absolute enlightenment. But at this point in Japanese history more time would be needed before writing (*waka*) and religious searching (for salvation) could integrate more fully.

There are more Buddhist *waka* in the *Kin'yōshū* (26) than we find in the *Shūishū* and the *Goshūishū*, but this number would drop precipitously to only six in the sixth imperial anthology, *Shikashū*. We will need to look for explanations for the changes in name and number of the Buddhist *waka* in the next two anthologies, but also for any corresponding changes in the depth of poetic expression about the Buddhist teachings. We will ask whether the compilers of the *Kin'yōshū* and the *Shikashū* (Minamoto no Shunrai [1055?–1129?] and Fujiwara no Akisuke [1090–1155]) had the kind of relationship with Buddhism that might in some way have affected their compilation of *waka* in their anthologies and to what extent the poems look back on or forward to previous and future developments of this new subgenre of Japanese court *waka*. ✿

5 THE ABBREVIATED IMPERIAL POETRY COLLECTIONS FROM THE *INSEI* ERA — *KINYŌSHŪ* (1127) AND *SHIKASHŪ* (CA. 1151)

Buddhist *waka* in the *Kin'yōshū* and the *Shikashū* each are located within a "Miscellaneous" book without separate designations. Since the word *shakkyō-ka* had already been applied to the Buddhist *waka* in the *Goshūishū*, it is possible that the significance of this change in placement and nomenclature lies in the fact that both anthologies were reduced in size from a twenty-book structure to a ten-book structure. However, it is also possible that the lack of designation indicates an unresolved tension within the world of court poetry about what to name *waka* on Buddhist themes. A further deepening of Buddhist sentiment and ideas is notable in both anthologies, due perhaps—in the case of the *Kin'yōshū* is at least—to the larger number of poems attributed to Buddhist priests. Another significant characteristic of the poems in the *Kin'yōshū* the emphasis on the Pure Land teachings. One or two poems on this topic appeared in earlier Buddhist *waka* sequences in the imperial poetry anthologies, but in the *Kin'yōshū*, we find eight such poems, nearly a third of the total. Associated with this influx of *waka* on the Pure Land are the religious beliefs of the *Kin'yōshū's* compiler, Minamoto no Shunrai, who envisioned within his own devotion to Amida a possible role for *waka* as *dhāranī*, an ascetic-literary development that highlighted the immediate soteriological capacities of *waka* through the religious practice of *mantra*.

The Buddhist *waka* in the *Shikashū* are so few—six—that one is tempted to overlook them as insignificant. To the contrary, though, these six Buddhist *waka* are arranged succinctly to reflect a path to enlightenment that begins with fear, regret, and sadness over one's separation from the teachings and develops into a belief in enlightenment in this very body (*sokushin jōbutsu*), and finally a belief that this experience can be shared with others so that they too may become enlightened. Also relevant to examining the Buddhist *waka* in these two anthologies is the evidence that we find in the history of the Rokujō family that played an important role in creating the religio-literary environment that pervaded the twelfth century.

INTRODUCTION

The fifth and sixth imperial poetry anthologies were, like the *Goshūishū*, compiled during the Insei (or Cloistered Government) period (1086–1185). Shirakawa (r. 1072–1086) dominated the Insei for the first forty-three years, and as its central figure, attempted to revive the authority of the imperial institution. Cameron Hurts says that, even after he abdicated the throne, Shirakawa was "the most powerful figure at the Heian court until his death in 1129."[302] Due in part to this power, he became the first sovereign to order the compilation of two anthologies. As the Retired Emperor in 1124, Shirakawa commanded the compilation of the fifth imperial poetry anthology, which came to be known as the *Kin'yōshū* (1127).[303] Twenty-years later in 1144,

---

302. G. Cameron Hurst, *Insei: Abdicated Sovereigns*, 125.

303. Two editions of the *Kin'yōshū* were consulted for this chapter. One is a variant text of the *nidohon* used by Ishihara in *Shakkyō-ka no kenkyū* and found originally in Yamagishi Tokuhei, ed., *Hachidaishū zenchū* (Tokyo: Yūseidō, 1960). The second text is Kawamura Teruo et al., *Kin'yōwakashū Shikawakashū*, SNKBT vol. 9 (Tokyo: Iwanami Shoten, 1989). The numbering system of the two texts is different. The Ishihara text begins with poem 666 while the SNKBT starts with poem 626. In the SNKBT version of the *Kin'yōshū*, the Buddhist *waka* sequence is comprised of twenty-two poems and four (707–710) that are included within a supplemental section (*Hoi-ka*). In Ishihara's text, these four supplemental poems are woven into the sequence as numbers 669 (corresponding to SKNBT 707), 675 (corresponding to SKNBT 708), 679 (corresponding to SKNBT 709), and 686 (corresponding to SKNBT 710). When discussing the Buddhist *waka* in the *Kin'yōshū* as a unified sequence, I will refer to the numbers in Ishihara's text

Retired Emperor Sutoku (r. 1123–1141)—also known as Shin'in or New Retired Emperor since Toba still occupied the same position—commanded the compilation of the sixth imperial anthology, *Shikashū* (completed 1151) while Konoe (r. 1141–1155) was the reigning sovereign. This fragmentation of the political situation in the first half of the twelfth century—with the Fujiwara in the background still vying for power against the retired sovereigns—had at least one undeniable effect on both anthologies: in order to protect political and cultural power (often the same thing), there was an unusual degree of imperial influence exerted upon the final product.[304]

The degree to which this political influence was exerted can be noted in at least two characteristics of both anthologies. First is the fact that for the first time in the history of the anthologies, they were composed of ten, rather than twenty, books.[305] This is a significant structural divergence from the first four anthologies, which would undoubtedly have required the approval of the Emperor. Second is the fact that there is an emphasis in both anthologies on contemporaneity, though in the *Shikashū*, many poets also date from just after the *Gosenshū* was compiled in 951. This second fact is reflected in the titles of the anthologies. As Konishi Jin'ichi says, "The fancy titles—*Kin'yōshū* (Collection of Golden Leaves) and *Shikashū* (Collection of Verbal Flowers)—must have been ... surprising for twelfth-century readers. The titles of the preceding anthologies—*Gosenshū* (Later Collection), *Shūishū* (Collection of Gleanings), and *Goshūishū* (Later Collection of Gleanings)—all signify the transmitting and supplementing of material bequeathed by earlier ages. This

---

in which the four supplemental poems in the SNKBT version are integrated with the other twenty-two poems.

304. The text used for the *Shikashū* is Kudō Shigenori et al., *Kin'yōwakashū Shikawakashū*, SNKBT vol. 9 (Tokyo: Iwanami Shoten, 1989).

305. The *Kin'yōshū* and the *Shikashū* were the only two *chokusenshū* comprised of ten books. Based upon what Fujiwara no Shunzei wrote in the *Korai fūteishō*, it is commonly presumed that the ten-book structure was based upon Fujiwara no Kintō's ten-book *Shūishō*, which was used later to compile the *Shūishū*. See Kawamura Teruo and Kashiwagi Yoshio, "Kin'yōwakashū kaisetsu," *Kin'yōwakashū Shikawakashū*, 432, and Takeshita Yutaka, "Shinpū e no taidō," in *Wakashi: Man'yō kara gendai tanka made* (Osaka: Izumi Shoin, 1996), 100.

was essentially true for the poems and their subjects."[306] Despite the fact that the title *Kin'yōshū* was undoubtedly meant to recall the *Man'yōshū* of the eighth century, this retrospection is not reflected in the poems included in the anthology.

There are at least four reasons for discussing these two anthologies in the same chapter. First, they are often considered contemporaneous since they were compiled within twenty-five years of each other, the shortest period of time between two anthologies. Second, their ten-book formats give them a structural affinity. Third, the "Shakkyō" subdivision that had been introduced in the *Goshūishū* was not included in either anthology. Fourth, there are so few Buddhist *waka* in the *Shikashū* that they can easily be considered along with the twenty-six Buddhist *waka* in the *Kin'yōshū*.

KIN'YŌSHŪ

Forty-nine years prior to his imperial decree to compile the *Kin'yōshū*, but in his capacity as reigning emperor, Shirakawa commanded the compilation of the fourth imperial poetry anthology, the *Goshūishū*, as we observed in the previous chapter. He approved the final version in 1086. Shirakawa's power to command the fifth anthology, our focus here, derived from the office of the *in-no-chō* that he created when he retired.[307] While the early political permutations of the *in-no-chō* were not as well formulated as they came to be in the first quarter of the twelfth century, there is no doubt that Shirakawa maintained supervisory control over the imperial throne until his death in 1129, two years after the *Kin'yōshū* received its official approval.[308]

---

306. Konishi Jin'ichi, *A History of Japanese Literature*, vol. 3 (Princeton: Princeton University Press, 1991), 25.

307. G. Cameron Hurst says, "A perusal of documents and diaries of the quarter century before Shirakawa's death in 1129 leaves no doubt that he was the political focus of the Heian court." "Insei," *The Cambridge History of Japan*, vol. 2, "Heian Japan" (Cambridge and New York: Cambridge University Press, 1999), 602.

308. Mikael S. Adolphson claims that there is a "dramatic increase in [Shirakawa's]

Shirakawa's command to compile the *Kin'yōshū* was directed to Minamoto no Shunrai (1055?–1129?), the son of Minamoto no Tsunenobu (1016–1097). Tsunenobu had been passed over for the position of compiler of the *Goshūishū* despite his distinguished literary status at the court. Some scholars think that Shirakawa may have appointed Shunrai as compensation for Tsunenobu's snub.[309] However, there is also the possibility that Shirakawa feared Tsunenobu's connections to the Fujiwara in power in the office of regent (*sekkan-ke*), because this was an office the Retired Emperor sought to render powerless when he created the *in-no-chō*.[310] Whichever is the case, this command marked the first time that a Minamoto became the sole compiler of an imperial poetry anthology.[311]

Shunrai had to present three different versions of his collection before Shirakawa would approve it.[312] Despite the fact that Shirakawa formally accepted only the third version (*sansōbon*) that Shunrai presented, the second version (*nidohon*) became the widely distributed text (*rufubon*) and the one that is read today.[313] The reason this is so seems to be due to historical serendipity: both Shunrai and Shirakawa died just two years after the third version was approved, giving it less time to be disseminated throughout the court. The first version (*shodohon*) apparently gained no traction with the court; it has been only partially preserved today.

These *Kin'yōshū* texts are quite different, producing, in effect, three separate texts that have all fallen under the umbrella title *Kin'yōshū*. The first version of the text included poets mostly from the period

---

power beginning in the Kōwa era (1099–1104)." *The Gates of Power*, 80.

309. See Brower and Miner, *Japanese Court Poetry*, 243.

310. Kawamura Teruo and Kashiwagi Yoshio, "Kin'yōwakashū kaisetsu," in *Kin'yōwakashū Shikawakashū*, 430.

311. Another Minamoto, Minamoto no Shitagō (911–983), was one of five members of the Nashitsubo no gonin (Five Men of the Pear Room) that compiled the *Gosenshū* (951).

312. The most thorough analyses of the different texts can be found in Ikeda Tomizō, *Minamoto Shunrai no kenkyū* (Tokyo: Ōfūsha, 1973), 86–201, and Matsuda Takeo, *Kin'yōshū no kenkyū* (Tokyo: Parutosu-sha, 1988), 185–271.

313. The *sansōbon* text is also found in its entirety in Kawamura, *Kin'yōwakashū Shikawakashū*, 353–388.

of the *sandaishū*—*Kokinshū, Gosenshū, Shūishū.* Thus the earliest version was also the most conservative. The poets included in the second version of the *Kin'yōshū*, however, came mostly from the era in which the anthology was compiled. As a result, the second version is the most contemporary.[314] In the third and final version, Shunrai restored the poems cut from the first version and added poems from the era between the *Shūishū* and the *Goshūishū*, thus striking a balance between the first and second versions. The differences between the versions are crucial for understanding why many current Japanese scholars refer to the *Kin'yōshū* as an innovative anthology.

The selection of Shunrai was auspicious for the potential it held to continue the lineage of Buddhist *waka* in the imperial anthology project. The reason for this was due to Shunrai's personal enthusiasm for such poems—especially those on themes concerning rebirth in the Pure Land (*Gokuraku ōjō*). However, the mere twenty-six Buddhist *waka* that Shunrai included in the *Kin'yōshū* does not reflect this religious enthusiasm. The paucity of poems on Buddhist topics was probably due more to the abbreviated nature of the anthology—comprised only of ten books rather than the usual twenty. In contrast, book six of Shunrai's private anthology, *Sanboku kikashū* (ca. 1128), finished after he compiled the *Kin'yōshū*, may give clearer confirmation than the *Kin'yōshū* of his interest in *shakkyō-ka*: here he collected 125 *shakkyō-ka*, as compared to only 67 laments (called *hitan* rather than *aishō*), and 20 *jingi-ka*.[315] The *Sanboku kikashū* is also the first example in Japanese literary history of a *shikashū* with a category called "Shakkyō."[316]

The *Kin'yōshū* is regarded as an innovative (*kakushinteki*) anthology for several reasons.[317] In addition to its abbreviated format, which may or may not have been an innovation for aesthetic reasons, and in

314. This is also the version upon which the editors of the SNKBT relied.

315. Sekine Yoshiko and Furuya Takako, ed., *Sanboku kikashū—shūchūhen gekan* (Tokyo: Kazama Shobō, 1999), 51–106.

316. There are groupings of *Hokke-kyō-ka* in the private anthologies of Akazome Emon and Fujiwara no Kintō, as well as other courtiers of the mid-Heian period, but other than being compiled together in sequences, they are not identified in any particular manner. See Chapter 3.

317. See Matsuda, *Kin'yōshū no kenkyū,* 48, and Ikeda, *Minamoto Shunrai no kenkyū,* 86.

addition to the fact that the title recalls the *Man'yōshū*, there are the eighteen (some texts have nineteen) *(tan)renga* included at the end of the anthology, immediately following the Buddhist *waka*.[318]

There is also the matter of an innovative style, a style that relied more on description. There are some descriptive *waka* in the *Goshūishū*, but with Shunrai, whose father, Tsunenobu, advocated for the descriptive style at court, we see a remarkable increase in such poems.[319] The real blossoming of this style still lies ahead with the poems in the *Senzaishū*, but there is a clear indication that writers are beginning to lean toward it in the *Kin'yōshū*.

Matsuda Takeo proposes three other distinctive features about these *chokusenshū* in general.[320] First, one must keep in mind that, in addition to being a poetry collection (*kashū*), a *chokusenshū* is also an imperial poetry collection, and as such is subject to the whims and strictures of the Emperor and the imperial household. Matsuda claims that the social and political power the Emperor held over the selection and approval process deeply affected the methods and strategies used by the compiler who is responsible for the finished product.[321] In such cases, the will of the compiler can be overridden by the commands of the sovereign. In the case of the *Kin'yōshū* and the relationship between Shirakawa and Shunrai, the sovereign's power was clearly exerted.

Matsuda's second point concerns the degree to which the compiler of an imperial poetry anthology had to subordinate his own personal tastes to the constraints of the *waka* tradition as a whole. No matter how much a compiler may have wished to assert his individuality over the compilation process and the final product, he or they were always forced to compromise in the face of the considerable pressure exerted by cultural and literary precedent.

The final point Matsuda makes concerns the creation of numer-

---

318. WDJ, 662–663.

319. This is substantiated in part by the increase in the number of nouns that occur in the *Kin'yōshū* Buddhist *waka* sequence (38) as compared to the number of nouns that occur in the "Shakkyō" sequence in the *Goshūishū* (19). Even if we take into consideration the addition of seven more poems in the *Kin'yōshū* sequence, this is still notable.

320. See Matsuda, *Kin'yōshū no kenkyū*, 46–47.

321. Matsuda says this applies to the *Shinkokinshū* as well. Ibid.

ous versions of the same anthology. It is only through the painstaking work of lining up the various texts and comparing them that one can discern certain aspects of the compilation process. In the case of the *Kin'yōshū* this is possible only in part since the extant text of the first version (*shodohon*) is incomplete.

Matsuda concludes that the *Kin'yōshū* text commonly read today—the second version (*nidohon*)—most certainly reflects the aesthetic concerns of both the sovereign and the compiler. Therefore, any discussion of the Buddhist *waka* in the *Kin'yōshū* must not assume that Shunrai is the only person who decided, finally, on what order or content the sequence would have. This could explain the tendency among Japanese scholars to base their comments about Shunrai's style and tastes on his private anthology, *Sanboku kikashū*, rather than on the imperial anthology he compiled.

CHARACTERISTICS OF THE BUDDHIST *WAKA* SEQUENCE IN THE *KIN'YŌSHŪ*

Like the Buddhist *waka* in the *Shūishū*, the Buddhist *waka* in the *Kin'yōshū* are located in a book of poems that is not designated as Buddhist. In the *Shūishū* the Buddhist *waka* were located in the book of "Laments," or Aishō-ka. In the *Kin'yōshū*, the sequence is located in the final book (book ten) of "Miscellaneous *Waka*" or Zōka.[322] While it might be tempting to think that poets and compilers had already dissociated Buddhist *waka* from the lament by the early twelfth century, the fact that the *aishō-ka* in the *Kin'yōshū* appear in the same book of "Miscellaneous *Waka*" as the Buddhist *waka* suggests a lingering connection. Except for one poem (614) regretting the loss of a person who had taken the tonsure, the other twenty *waka* that precede the Buddhist *waka* sequence in this book concern themselves with someone's death.

---

322. In a strict sense this was true with the *shakkyō-ka* in the *Goshūishū* as well, since the "Shakkyō" sequence was a titled subsection within a book of "Miscellaneous *Waka*."

We may observe two prominent characteristics of the Buddhist *waka* sequence in the *Kin'yōshū*. First is the number of poems (nine) based upon the teachings of the Pure Land (hereafter called *Jōdo-ka*).[323] Japanese scholars have recognized Shunrai as an innovator of *Jōdo-ka*. Manaka Fujiko says, "It was Shunrai who opened the gate of 'Jōdo literature' in the history of *shakkyō waka* by reading the *Ōjōyōshū* and composing poems on Amida and the Pure Land, as well as on the three foundational Jōdo sūtras, theoretical works and the like."[324] There are only two poems in the *Shūishū* sequence devoted to the Pure Land and none in the *Goshūishū;* the increase in poems that focus on this topic in the *Kin'yōshū* is significant in proportion to the overall number of poems.

The second prominent characteristic of the sequence is the large number of poems attributed to Buddhist priests and Shintō priestesses.[325] Well over half of the *Kin'yōshū* sequence is comprised of poets whose titles are *sōjō* (archbishop), *gon no sōjō* (acting archbishop), *shōnin* (holy person) and *hōshi* (priest) while one poet, Senshi Naishinnō, was the Grand Priestess of the Kamo Shrine. (Senshi has one poem in the *Shikashū* as well). This is the largest number of religious figures in such a sequence to date.

---

323. To my knowledge the word "Jōdo-ka" is my own creation and has not been used by scholars of *shakkyō-ka*.

324. Manaka, *Kokubungaku ni sesshu sareta Bukkyō*, 215.

325. A further striking characteristic of the sequence is the lack of female poets—only three. Two of these, Princess Senshi and Izumi Shikibu, date from the era of the *Shūishū*. As for Higo, although we do not know her exact dates, she served the household of Fujiwara no Morozane (d. 1101) for almost thirty years, so it is possible that she was alive when the *Kin'yōshū* was compiled.

THE PURE LAND TEACHINGS, *JŌDO-KA,* AND
THEIR RELATIONSHIP TO *HOKKE-KYŌ-KA*

According to Allan Andrews, the Pure Land teachings probably entered Japan along with "other forms of continental Buddhism during the late sixth and early seventh centuries."[326] He adds that these teachings were popular among the aristocracy during the Nara period for a fairly specific reason: "Pure Land devotionalism was chiefly concerned with assuring the peaceful repose of ancestors. In other words, it functioned as a funerary cult."[327]

During the Heian period, however, greater attention—in the form of *nenbutsu* practice—was devoted to obtaining salvation for oneself. Shigematsu Akihisa says that a more Japanized version of the Pure Land teachings emerged during the Insei period,[328] but Joseph Kitagawa has discounted the religiosity of the early Heian movement, saying, "Sincerity in seeking salvation was totally emasculated, so that the Pure Land of Amida was interpreted purely from aesthetic and sentimental viewpoints without any reference to its ethical, doctrinal, and philosophical content."[329] Confirmation of this viewpoint comes from different genres in Heian literature. Not surprisingly, *setsuwa* collections such as the *Nihon ryōiki,* the *Sanbō ekotoba,* and the *Konjaku monogatarishū* contain stories that refer to various aspects of the Pure Land, Amida Buddha, and the practice of the *nenbutsu,* but the faith on display in these stories seems to be more superficial than that expressed toward bodhisattvas such as Kannon and Miroku and in the efficacy of the Lotus Sutra.[330] In other literary genres such as the

---

326. Allan Andrews, "Genshin's 'Essentials of Pure Land Rebirth' and the Transmission of Pure Land Buddhism to Japan. Part 1. The First and Second Phases of Transmission of Pure Land Buddhism to Japan: The Nara Period and the Early Heian Period," *The Pacific World* 5 (Fall 1989): 21.

327. Ibid., 22.

328. Akihisa Shigematsu, "An Overview of Early Japanese Pure Land," in *The Pure Land Tradition: History and Development* (Berkeley Buddhist Studies Series, 1996), 267.

329. Joseph M. Kitagawa, *Religion in Japanese History* (New York: Columbia University Press, 1966), 80.

330. The one important exception to this are the various *ōjōden,* or tales of rebirth in

monogatari, there are numerous references to Amida and the Pure Land as early as the *Ochikubo monogatari* (ca. late tenth century), and in at least seventeen of the fifty-four chapters of *Genji monogatari*.[331] It is not until the eleventh century historical tale (*rekishi monogatari*) *Eiga monogatari* that the clearest literary evidence supporting Kitagawa's observation may be found. In Chapter 18 ("The Mansion of Jade"), we find an extended description of Fujiwara no Michinaga's construction of the Amida Hall at Hōjō-ji as well as some of the events Michinaga held there.[332] The opening sentence of this chapter reads, "As the number of halls at the Hōjō-ji increased, people began to feel that the Pure Land must present a very similar appearance."[333] William Deal comments as follows about the aestheticization of the Pure Land teachings exemplified in this chapter:

> One of the conspicuous elements of Michinaga's temple building project was the necessity to make it as lavish and opulent as possible. Michinaga felt that without proper attention to aesthetic detail, the entire enterprise would be compromised, and by extension, so would its ability to have an affective impact on those who would visit the sacred precincts. ...
>
> The cumulative impression that the *Eiga monogatari* makes with its detailed descriptions of the Hōjō-ji's magnificence is intended to leave no doubt about the reality of the Pure Land manifest in the human world. In fact, as the number of buildings at the Hōjō-ji multiply, the sense that there is a parallel between the Pure Land and the Hōjō-ji also expands. ... [334]

---

the Pure Land, especially the *Nihon ōjō gokuraku-ki* by Yoshishige no Yasutane. For an analysis of these tales in English, see Frederic J. Kotas, "Ōjōden: Accounts of Rebirth in the Pure Land" (Ph.D. dissertation, University of Washington, 1988).

331. Ishida, *Nihon koten bungaku to Bukkyō*, 249–251.

332. William H. and Helen Craig McCullough, *A Tale of Flowering Fortunes*, vol. 2, 564–580.

333. Ibid., 564.

334. William Edward Deal, "Ascetics, Aristocrats, and the Lotus Sutra: The Con-

Concurrent with an increasingly aestheticized version of the Pure Land teachings was the continued prominence and influence of the Lotus Sutra, about which Deal writes, in reference to the *Eiga monogatari*: "The *Lotus Sutra* lies at the core of their [the aristocrats'] thinking about reality, power, and proper behavior, indeed, about the workings of the entire universe."[335] This statement clarifies the hierarchy of textual and religious values when it came to the Tendai and Jōdo teachings. Even though, as Inoue Mitsusada has shown, the Jōdo teachings in the Heian period developed out of the Tendai teachings, it was still the Tendai teachings that retained primacy within the lives of Heian aristocrats, at least until the twelfth century.[336]

Most important to this study is the perspective of the poets— priestly or not—about the Buddhist teachings. We must assess to what extent and in what way this group of Buddhist *waka* contributes to the concept of *michi*, and whether there is a greater integration between the aims of Buddhist teachings and the ideals of court poetry. Evidence that there was in fact a deepening connection between the two projects at this historical moment can be found in Shunrai's *Sanboku kikashū*.

WAKA AS DHĀRANĪ

The relationship between court *waka* and the concept of Buddhist salvation is demonstrated in a series of sixteen poems in the *Sanboku kikashū* that each begin with a single syllable from the Amida *dhāranī* (J: *darani*), the last poem of which is especially relevant. As we proceed now to describe how the practice and concept of *dhāranī* became an important component of the gradual integration of the writing of *waka* with Buddhist practice, we must first examine the word *dhāranī* itself and its meanings in Japan.

The term is often conflated with *shingon* (*mantra*) and *ju* (C:

---

struction of the Buddhist Universe in Eleventh Century Japan" (Ph.D. diss., Harvard University, 1988), 223, 231–232.

335. Ibid., 22.

336. Inoue Mitsusada, *Nihon Jōdokyō seiritsushi no kenkyū* (Tokyo: Yamakawa Shuppan, rev. ed. 1989), 85–130.

chou), two words also used to refer to one another.[337] Ryūichi Abe says that *dhāranī* were used in the Nara and early Heian periods as verbal talismans against disease, and later as a means by which to repent one's sins.[338] *Dhāranī* were also components of exoteric texts such as the Lotus Sutra, Chapter 26 of which is titled Dhāranī.[339] In that chapter, *dhāranī* were given to the "preachers of Dharma" by the bodhisattva Bhaiśajyaguru, the bodhisattva of medicine, "for their protection."[340] Thus it is clear that in both exoteric and esoteric Buddhist teachings, *dhāranī* were used for their apotropaic, or talismanic, value.

Bowring focuses on epistemology when he explains that *dhāranī* were felt to contain the inherent meaning of the Dharma in that they are "the concentrated essence of the teachings; far from being nonsense syllables, they were the sound of the universe."[341] Abe confirms this sense of the word, quoting Kūkai's *Hizōki*: "… [the word] *shingon* suggests that dhāranī, as the speech of the Tathāgathas, contains only truth and no falsehood."[342] Such language is evidence that that *dhāranī* were felt to possess a salvific power, but what was the relationship or difference between the apotropaic meaning or application of a *dhāranī* and its soteriological capacities?

According to Ronald Davidson, *dhāranī* have not served any one purpose throughout history, but have been put to multidimensional and variously utilitarian uses. Davidson identifies five "parameters" that "satisfy the primary functional and ideological requirements of the class of items included in the category dhāranī …"

> Dhāranīs must be capable of being understood as vehicles (means and end) for the storage of previously experienced information, in a manner that could be interpreted as memory, whether this refers to memory of experiences in this life, in previous lives,

---

337. Abe, *The Weaving of Mantra*, 262–263.
338. Ibid., 159–167.
339. Hurvitz, *Scripture of the Lotus Blossom*, 320–324.
340. Ibid., 320.
341. Bowring, *The Religious Traditions of Japan 500–1600*, 142.
342. Abe, *The Weaving of Mantra*, 264.

or the "recollection" of items that had never in fact been memorized, such as mindfulness of the canon. Dhāraṇīs must be capable of functioning as the vehicle for the sonic power of mantras, whether these are for worldly purposes, as in the case of protection or other goals, or for soteriological purposes. Dhāraṇīs must be capable of storing and communicating scriptures, whether individual texts, or sections of the canon, or the entire canon itself, and whether this storage is understood as ontological compression or encryption or some other method. Dhāraṇīs must be able to speak to the deep structure of reality, so that they are events that have strong ontological claims, so much so that the universe is capable of being seen as a string of dhāraṇīs. These also have a soteriological component in the gnoseology of absolute reality. Finally, dhāraṇī must be ritually efficacious, for they play an important role in the rituals associated with the teaching of the Mahāyāna, the offerings to the Buddha, and other normative ritual enterprises of many Mahāyānist gatherings. This means that any value for dhāraṇī must be polysemic, for all of these functions must fall into the class of conditions exercised by dhāraṇīs, which can in turn have not a single purpose, but must be capable of exercising its functions in an environment-sensitive manner.[343]

Davidson's analysis amplifies the narrow sense of the term *dhāraṇī* as a kind of magical charm or mnemonic device by emphasizing its "polysemic" value in different religious environments. While Davidson allows that there are instances of *dhāraṇī* being used as a tool for memory, as an object of ritual, and as a container for "storing and communicating scriptures," he also recognizes their soteriological

343. Ronald M. Davidson, "Studies in Dhāraṇī Literature I: Revisiting the Meaning of the Term Dhāraṇī," *Journal of Indian Philosophy 37* (2009): 117–118.

potential when they act as a "vehicle" for the "sonic power of mantras," and when they are a component in the understanding of "absolute reality." In short, *dhāranī* were thought to be capable of providing salvation to a believer or practitioner of Mahāyāna Buddhism.

The "sonic power of mantras" which Davidson ascribes to *dhāranī* is not dissimilar to the Japanese concept of *kotodama* (word spirit). *Kotodama* also were attributed with spiritual power and efficacy through the activation of "tone and pronunciation."[344] The concept of the activation of *kotodama* through the proper articulation of Japanese words is closely connected to the syllabic structure of the language, in the sense that the power of *kotodama* is funneled through the precise utterance of each and every syllable. This was equally true for the intoning of both prose (*senmyō*, for example) and *waka*. *Kotodama* was, of course, not attributed with the power to effect Buddhist salvation, in part because the concept originated within the realm of *kami* belief. However, this autochthonous concept of magical power, in which verbal sound is held inseparable from the creation of meaning and the transformation of the world, persisted into the age of the Heian court where words—the thirty-one-syllables that comprise a *waka* in particular—were still felt to possess the power to move and shape the world, as Ki no Tsurayuki described in the *Kokinshū*. It was precisely in the similarity of the concepts of *kotodama* and *dhāranī* that Japanese poets discovered a useful metaphor for the gradual integration Buddhist practice with the writing of *waka*.

An integration of *kotodama* and *dhāranī* is at least partially in evidence in Princess Senshi's Preface to the *Hosshin wakashū*. Though the Kamo priestess mentions neither word in her Preface, by implication she does refer to the relationship between these concepts. *Kotodama* could not withstand the Sinicization of Japanese; it maintained its power only through intoning Japanese words. However, the belief that words have power and can be sacred was carried over into the reverence the Japanese had toward Buddhist texts. These texts promised salvation through the proper understanding,

---

344. Konishi, *A History of Japanese Literature*, vol. 2, 114.

reading, and recitation of their words—Chinese words. Princess Senshi argued that she was composing sacred poetry because it was based upon (the Chinese words in) Buddhist texts, even though the words in her poems clearly belonged to the Japanese language. The recognition of Japanese—particularly the Japanese used for *waka*—as a language equal in importance and potential spiritual power to Sanskrit and Chinese is an essential component of Senshi's argument. As she puts it, "Sanskrit is the language of India ... [a]nd *kanji* bear the imprint of China. Both are different from the customs of my land ... I have been born into the land of the imperial sun ... I have been thoroughly imbued with the sentiments of my country. For this reason, I studied the thirty-one-syllable *waka* of Susano-o. ..."[345] Senshi makes use of the concept of the sacrality of language by implying that all languages are equally sacred when used in service to the Buddha. Though Senshi does not mention *dhāraṇī* in her Preface, her poem on the Dhāraṇī chapter of the Lotus Sutra demonstrates her understanding of the concept:

なにといえど夢のなかにもあやまたじ法をたもてる人と成なば

nani to iedo / yume no naka ni mo / ayamataji / nori o tamoteru / hito to narinaba

"If in the form of a boy, or in the form of a girl, even in a dream: do no harm"[346]

> no matter what I speak—even in a dream—
>
> I cause no injury (make no mistake) if
>
> I've become one of those
>
> who has kept the Law[347]

---

345. Translation by author.

346. This is our translation of Princess Senshi's headnote, which in the context of the Sutra is spoken to the Buddha by the "ten daughters of *rākṣasas*, with the mother of the ghosts' children, as well as their own children and retinue ..." (Hurvitz, 322; Iwamoto and Sakamoto, vol. 3, 280) They proclaim that no one—even someone in the form of a boy or a girl—should do any harm to the "preachers of the Dharma."

347. Ishihara, *Hosshin wakashū*, 57, 211, and 243.

Here Senshi affirms, in unison with the disciples speaking to the Buddha, that she too wishes to protect "the preachers of the Dharma" from harm by couching that desire in the form of a Japanese *waka*. Not obvious from the poem or the headnote is that the retinue the Lotus Sutra describes has just "pronounced a [nineteen-syllable] charm [*dhāraṇī*]": "*itime itime itime atime itime nime nime nime nime nime ruhe ruhe ruhe ruhe tahe tahe tahe tuhe thuhe.*"[348] This *dhāraṇī* and the section of Lotus Sutra text that appears in Senshi's headnote highlight the apotropaic rather than soteriological value of Senshi's poem.

Though *dhāraṇī* were well known throughout the early part of the Heian period, especially through the Dhāraṇī chapter of the Lotus Sutra, it was not until the last half of the eleventh century that poets began closing the epistemological space between *dhāraṇī* and *waka*. A factor that may have assisted this connection is the fundamental importance of syllables to both enterprises. Davidson says, "… the elements of the [dhāraṇī] syllabary may be replaced easily by other syllables, by sounds, by words, by strings of syllables, or by entire texts, for encryption may be infinite. Such an interpenetration is possible, because of the Mahāyānist emphasis on interdependence, a doctrine common to all its schools."[349] What Davidson describes as "interpenetration" encapsulates the reasoning by which Japanese poets probably expanded this view to include the secular words used in *waka*. Through concepts such as interpenetration, or copenetration, the religious and the literary slowly achieved positive coexistence within the Buddhist *waka* sequences in the imperial poetry anthologies.

We have already encountered a poetic expression of interpenetration in the *waka* by Ise no Chūjō in the *Goshūishū shakkyō-ka* sequence. Here the poet takes up this concept from the Avatamsaka Sūtra:

---

348. Hurvitz, *Scripture of the Lotus Blossom*, 322–323; Iwamoto and Sakamoto, *Hokke-kyō*, vol. 3, 282.
349. Davidson, "Studies in Dhāraṇī Literature I: Revisiting the Meaning of the Term Dhāraṇī," 126.

THE THREE WORLDS ARE NOTHING BUT ONE MIND

to regret

the falling blossoms

and command them: *stop!*

haven't I heard

the world is none other

than the heart?

Ise no Chūjō interprets the world as a projection of her "heart" or *kokoro*. If her heart could penetrate—indeed, in essence, *was*—the world, in the same way that the world *was* her heart, then her heart should be able to assert control over that which she regrets: "the falling blossoms." Though this poem may be a partly ironic courtly interpretation of co-penetration, it does exhibit a familiarity with the concept.

Later authors and poets such as Mujū Ichien (1226–1312) and Shinkei (1406–1475) took the relationship between *waka* and *dhāranī* for granted. In *Shasekishū*, Mujū explains:

> Although *dhāranī* employ the ordinary language of India, when words are maintained *as dhāranī*, they have the capacity to destroy wickedness and remove suffering. Japanese poetry also uses the ordinary words of the world; and when we use *waka* to convey religious intent, there will necessarily be a favorable response. When they embody the spirit of the Buddha's Law, there can be no doubt that they are *dhāranī*.[350]

---

350. Robert Morrell, trans., *Sand and Pebbles* (*Shasekishū*) (Albany: State University of New York Press, 1985), 164.

Similarly, in *Sasamegoto*, Shinkei said, "The way of poetry has been from the very beginning the *dhāranī* of Japan. When a man dismisses poetry as an embroidery of delusions, even his study of the sūtras and commentaries and his practice of meditation amount to nothing but self-deception."[351]

As we have said, Minamoto no Shunrai also looked to *dhāranī* as one source of meaning for *waka*. The final sixteen poems of his *Sanboku kikashū* are devoted to the seventeen-syllable Amida *dhāranī* (*omuamiri-tateiseikara-umusohaka*). The headnote to the first of these poems (979) and to the group as a whole reads, "Composing a poem by placing a syllable from the short Amida *dhāranī* at the beginning of [each] poem."[352] (The first syllable of each poem corresponds to a syllable from the *dhāranī*.)[353] It is the final poem in this sequence (and in the *shakkyō-ka* sequence as a whole) that reveals Shunrai's particular understanding of the relationship between *waka* and salvation:

---

351. Dennis Hirota, trans., "In Practice of the Way: *Sasamegoto*, An Instruction Book in Linked Verse," *Chanoyu Quarterly* 19 (Kyoto: 1977): 41.

352. Sekine and Furuya, *Sanboku kikashū: shūchūhen gekan*, 98.

353. There is a lack of correspondence between the twelfth and thirteenth syllables "ra" and "u." There is no *waka* beginning with "u." The next poem begins with "mu," the fourteenth syllable. This accounts for the fact that there are only sixteen *waka* rather than seventeen. Ibid., 98–105.

かみにおけるもじはまことの法なれば歌もよみぢをたすけ
ざらめや

kami ni okeru / moji wa makoto no / nori nareba / uta mo yomiji o / tasukezarame ya[354]

WHEN I PLACED A LETTER OF THE TRUE WORD AT THE
BEGINNING AND COMPOSED,

                          although it was a game, I
composed with integrity

      when the true letter KA
      put at the start

      is the Law—

      won't that song

      save me
      on the dark path?

For the first time since Princess Senshi's Preface to the *Hosshin wakashū*, a poet has made a statement about the soteriological capacities of the *uta*. Shunrai argues (in the context of a rhetorical question to which the answer is *yes*) that by the deployment of a sacred syllable from a *dhāranī* at the head (*kami*) of a poem, a *waka* literally becomes capable of enlightening the poet on her path to salvation: both source (*dhāranī*) and act (*okeru*) of composition, he implies, ensure this result.

---

354. Ibid., 105.

THE ARRANGEMENT OF THE BUDDHIST *WAKA* IN THE *KIN'YŌSHŪ*

There appears to be no discernible comprehensive arrangement of the Buddhist sequence in the *Kin'yōshū*. The eight *Jōdo-ka* (630/671– 632/673 and 710/684 and 644/688–647/691) are located both before and after the eight *Hokke-kyō-ka* (634/676–640/683). Like the *Hokke-kyō-ka*, the *Jōdo-ka* are arranged, for the most part, in groups. We also find two groups of poems in the sequence based on other principles or texts: the first four poems (626/666–707/669) appear to be arranged according to the poets' relationship to Shirakawa or their relationship to each other. Finally, we find a group comprised of two poems (633/674 and 708/675) based upon belief in the salvational power of the bodhisattva Samantabhadra (J: Fugen), and a group of two miscellaneous scriptural poems (641/684 and 642/685) that follow the *Hokke-kyō-ka* sequence and precede the second sequence of *Jōdo-ka*.

THE FIRST FIVE POEMS (626/666–629/670)

Following perhaps the arrangement pattern of the *shakkyō-ka* in the *Goshūishū*, the *Kin'yōshū* sequence also begins with occasional poems. A common factor of the first four poems is the political and familial relationships of the authors.

[626/666]

色も香もむなしととける法なれど祈るしるしはありとこそ聞け
*iro mo ka mo / munashi to tokeru / nori naredo / inoru shirushi wa / ari
to koso kike*

AFTER A CEREMONY OFFERING THE HEART SUTRA,
THE AUTHOR ASKED EVERYONE TO COMPOSE A POEM
ON ITS ESSENCE

> the Law teaches
> "color and smell
>
> are empty"—
>
> but I've heard
> practice proves
>
> what's real
>
> — Sesshō Sadaijin
> [Fujiwara no Tadamichi]

[627/677]

見しままにわれは悟りを得てしかばしらせで取ると知らざ
らめやは

mishi mama ni / ware wa satori o / eteshikaba / shirasede toru to /
shirazarame yawa

WRITTEN WHEN THE PRINCE LEARNED THAT A
CERTAIN LADY-IN-WAITING HAD ASKED FOR SOME
PALACE SCRIPTURES TO BE SENT SECRETLY TO HER
WHILE SHE WAS VISITING HOME

if (as you found out)

those sutras were what

awakened me—

when you took them

without telling—

did you really expect me

not to know?

— Sannomiya [Sukehito Shinnō,
son of Emperor Go-Sanjō]

[628/668]

いさぎよき空の気色をたのむかな我まどはすな秋の夜の月

isagiyoki / sora no keshiki o / tanomu kana / ware madowasu na / aki no yo no tsuki

SENT TO SENSAI SHŌNIN ON A NIGHT WHEN THE
MOON WAS BRIGHT

> this brightness that fills
> the emptiness—

everything depends on it!

O moon of autumn eve

> don't let me
> wander bewildered

> — Bishop Gyōson

[707/669]

いかにせん憂き世の中にすみがまの果は煙となりぬべき身を
ika ni sen / ukiyo no naka ni / sumigama no / hate wa keburi to /
narinu beki mi o

DISCOURAGED BY ILLNESS, UNSURE HOW IT WOULD
TURN OUT

    live — and at the end
                become smoke
                         from the kiln—
what else
      in this sad world
             is a body to do?

          — Minamoto no Yukimune

[629/670]

心には厭ひはてつと思ふらんあはれいづくもおなじ憂世を
kokoro ni wa / itoihatetsu to / omouran / aware izuku mo / onaji ukiyo o

SENT TO THE MOUNTAIN TEMPLE WHERE I HEARD
JITSUHAN SHŌNIN HAD SECLUDED HIMSELF

how you must loathe
                  the world
                              to flee it—
but O—
        isn't the world
                still sad
there—
        here—
                everywhere?

                      — Priest Jōgon

As the reader may observe, these five poems have no unifying theme or topic. They are all occasional to some extent, but other than this, the only unifying connection is that the authors of the first four poems are related to Shirakawa or to one another. This association would have been obvious to readers at the time, but is obviously lost upon most modern-day readers.[355] Three of these five poems were composed as communications (*zōtōka*) between the author and a recipient. Sukehito's slightly humorous poem was addressed to an unnamed lady at the court who apparently absconded with Sukehito's collection of sūtras when she went home to visit her family. Gyōson's poem was addressed to another important poet-priest of this period, Sensai Shōnin (?–1127), author of a poem that appears later in this sequence.[356] Finally, Jōgon Hōshi's poem was sent to the priest Jitsuban (or Jippan, dates unknown), who it seems, from internal evidence of the poem and headnote, had cloistered himself.

The themes or topics of these five poems have only the most tangential connection: the teachings of emptiness that arose during the occasion of a ceremony copying the Heart Sutra, a playful poem on the value of the scriptures, the enlightened nature of a priest, the fear of death, and the impossibility of escape from the samsaric world. There is also no connection between the poems in terms of the mode of the author's response to his situational predicament: two poems take

---

355. Fujiwara no Tadamichi (1097–1164), regent from 1121–1158, whose poem takes the spot of honor at the top of the sequence (626/666), played an important role in imperial politics in the early part of the twelfth century. His role was enhanced after Shirakawa gave him full backing in 1122, and broke off an alliance with Tadamichi's father, Tadazane [1078–1162] (Adolphson, *The Gates of Power*, 127). A familial relationship connects the author of the next poem (627/667) to Shirakawa. Sukehito Shinnō (1073–1119) was Shirakawa's half brother and son of Go-Sanjō (r. 1068–1072). Gyōson (1057–1135), author of poem 628/668, continues an association with Shirakawa. Gyōson was Sukehito Shinnō's uncle through marriage, through Gyōson's sister Minamoto no Motoko (1049–1124), second consort of Emperor Go-Sanjō. The last poem (707/669) with an association with Shirakawa is attributed to Minamoto no Yukimune (1064–1193), Gyōson's younger brother. The author of the poem that follows, Jōgon Hōshi, has no obvious connection with either Yukimune or Shirakawa, but since very little is known about him, this cannot be known with any certainty.

356. The poem number is 635/677, appearing among the Lotus Sutra poems.

a meditative approach (Tadamichi's and Jōgon's), Gyōson's poem takes a lyric approach, and the focus of Sukehito Shinnō's poem is primarily narrative. They are each written in a soteriological/courtly modality, with some (626/666) emphasizing the soteriological more strongly than the courtly, and others (627/677) emphasizing the reverse.

Next in the sequence come three *Jōdo-ka*, the first of two such groups; the second group appears at the end. Though these two groups of poems do not occur sequentially, it is nevertheless useful to describe the two groups together and in relationship to one another.

THE *JŌDŌ-KA*
(630/671– 632/673 AND 710/686–647/691)

The eight *Jōdo-ka* in the *Kin'yōshū* are the first of their kind in a Buddhist *waka* sequence in an imperial anthology since the *Shūishū*, where only two such poems are to be found. This increasing number of *Jōdo-ka* in the *Kin'yōshū* would seem to support the view that the connection the nobility felt with Pure Land beliefs was strengthening during this period.

When it comes to adapting specific teachings for literary purposes, the Pure Land teachings would seem to be more suited for adaptation to a prose narrative genre than to a thirty-one-syllable poem, because the teachings contain a strong narrative component themselves. According to the Jōdo narrative, while on the earthly plane the Pure Land practitioner expressed faith in Amida by chanting the *nenbutsu*, focusing attention upon the West (especially at the moment of death), and other practices. Amida, for his part, would transport that person after death to the Western Paradise (sometimes, in pictorial representations, by means of a purple thread), which was variously understood as either a propitious venue for further education about the Buddhadharma, or a perfect paradisiacal end in itself. The Pure Land teachings enact in dramatic narrative fashion a reassuring vision of what death signifies and where one goes afterward, just one of a variety of approaches East Asian Buddhism made to this all-important concern. Therefore, it is not surprising that any poem attempting to address or allude to the Pure Land teachings on this topic would be more based in narrative than some of the other *waka*. This helps to explain why most of the *Jōdo-ka* in the *Kin'yōshū* are preceded by narrative-heavy *kotobagaki*.

FIRST GROUP OF *JŌDŌ-KA*

[630/671]

阿弥陀仏ととなふる声に夢さめて西へながるる月をこそみれ
amidabu to / tonauru koe ni / yume samete / nishi e nagaruru / tsuki o koso mire

SENT TO HER ATTENDANTS AT HOME WHEN THE MOON WAS BRIGHT IN THE EIGHTH MONTH, AFTER HEARING AN ASCETIC PASS CHANTING *NAMU AMIDA BUTSU*

> when I heard a voice
> call on the Name

> I woke from my dream
> to see — that moon! —

> on its journey
> to the West

— Senshi Naishinnō

[631/672]

教へをきて入りにし月のなかりせばいかで思ひを西にかけ
まし

*oshieokite / irinishi tsuki no / nakariseba / ikade omoi o / nishi ni
kakemashi*

ON CHANTING AMIDA'S NAME ACCORDING TO THE
BUDDHA'S TEACHINGS

without a reminder

that the moon would disappear

in the West

how could my longing

have turned

in that direction?

— Kōgōgū no Higo

[632/672]

かくばかり東風てふかぜの吹くを見て塵の疑ひをおこさずも
がな

kaku bakari / kochi chō kaze no / fuku o mite / chiri no utagai o /
okosazu mo gana

WHEN SHŌKAI SHŌNIN HAD BEEN FEARING THE
AFTERLIFE MORE AND MORE, HE FELL ASLEEP
PONDERING THIS MATTER:
                              IN HIS DREAM A PRIEST
APPEARED WHO STOOD AT HIS BEDSIDE AND
COMPOSED THIS POEM

                    behold: the wind
                    with a name

              that blows upon you thus

            from east to west: because

       I want you
       not to stir

    the worldly dirt of doubt

                         — Dream Oracle through Shōkai Shōnin

SECOND GROUP OF *JŌDO-KA*

[710/686]

よもの海の波にただよふ水屑をも七重の網に引きなもらしそ
yomo no umi no / nami ni tadayou / mikuzu o mo / nanae no ami ni / hiki na morashi so

THINKING OF PARADISE

> draw up in Your
>> seven-layered net
>
> this water trash
>> drifting
>
> west
>> east
>>> south
>>>> north
>
> on the waves
>> of a vast sea—
>
> don't let me slip
>> away

> — Minamoto Shunrai no Ason

[644/688]

あさましや剣の枝のたはむまでこは何の身のなれるなるらん
asamashi ya / tsurugi no eda no / tawamu made / ko wa nan no mi no /
nareru naruran

WHEN THE AUTHOR SAW ONE OF THOSE PAINTINGS
OF HELL IN WHICH A PERSON IS IMPALED ON A SWORD

> *terrible—*
>
>> until the sword
>>> has bent like a branch—
>>
>>> what kind of seed
>> could body forth
>
> such fruit?

> — Izumi Shikibu

[645/689]

くさの葉に門出はしたり時鳥しでの山路もかくやつゆけき
*kusa no ha ni / kadode wa shitari / hototogisu / shide no yamaji mo /
kaku ya tsuyukeki*

THE AUTHOR'S BREATHING STOPPED SUDDENLY during
a visit to the house of a certain person, and he was about to die.
When he was carried out to a main road on a wooden door, he heard
the cry of the cuckoo, as dew from the grass touched his leg. In a
weak voice, he composed this.

                    from these
               leaves of grass
          I am going
       out the gate—

          cuckoo—

               is the last
          mountain road
       this wet
    with dew?

                              — Taguchi no Shigeyuki

[646/690]

弛みなく心をかくる弥陀仏ひとやりならぬ誓たがふな

tayumi naku / kokoro o kakuru / mida hotoke / hitoyari naranu / chikai tagau na

AS THE AUTHOR BREATHED HIS LAST

I entrusted my

heart unceasingly to

you Amida Buddha:

your causeless vow—

don't break it

— Taguchi no Shigeyuki

[647/691]

阿弥陀仏ととなふる声をかぢにてや苦しき海をこぎ離るらん

amidabu to / tonauru koe o / kaji ni te ya / kurushiki umi o /
kogihanaruran

ON SEEING A SCREEN PAINTING OF A PRIEST SAILING
INTO THE WEST FROM THE WESTERN GATE OF TENNŌ-
JI

> your voice singing
>
> > *amida butsu*
> > > as your oar?
>
> to row away
>
> > across the sea
> > of sorrow?

— Minamoto no Shunrai no Ason

The strong linkage between a particular headnote narrative and the poem itself is one of the most prominent characteristics of these *Jōdo-ka*. Indeed several of the poems would be rendered largely incomprehensible without the link, which demonstrates just how essential the anthologizer's creative role was in providing this context. The headnote narratives of at least six of these poems are long enough that they resemble the *utamonogatari* genre, or perhaps the headnotes to poems in the second imperial anthology, *Gosenshū* (952), well known for its long, *monogatari*-like *kotobagaki*. The narrative aspect is particularly notable in poems 645/689 and 646/690, attributed to Taguchi Shigeyuki (dates unknown).[357]

A third characteristic of these *Jōdo-ka* is the presence of some form of the name Amida Butsu. In two poems by Senshi and Shunrai (630/671 and 645/689), we find a *ku* that reads "*Amidabu to*." The quotative particle "*to*" in both poems is followed in the next *ku* by the verb *tonau*, to intone. In another poem (710/686) by Shunrai, the author uses the word *ami*, a *kakekotoba* referring both to a "net" and Amida Buddha. Finally, in Shigeyuki's poem (646/690), the author supplicates Amida directly, using the words *Mida Hotoke*. In other poems, the Amida narrative is implied in language like "the moon would disappear / in the West" (*irinishi tsuki no*), hell (*jigoku* being the alternative to *gokuraku*, Paradise), and "the last / mountain road" (*shide no yamaji*), the road to death that many fervently believed would lead to Amida's Paradise. It is also possible that the presence of Amida's name in a *waka* was felt to lend it a religious stature comparable with the practice of intoning Amida's name. Moreover, when the poem was read aloud, it may have reminded the listener of the Pure Land *wasan*, popular since at least the time of Kūya and Genshin.[358] Religious songs (*Bukkyō kayō*) in general were a part of the Pure Land religious literary tradition, and were a reminder that salvation was close—in fact, might even be generated by the Buddhist *waka* of the court.

---

357. The editors of SNKBT version of the *Kin'yōshū* say, based upon *Kin'yōshū kanmotsu*, that Taguchi Shigeyuki is probably the same poet who is named Yamaguchi Shigeyuki and who has one poem in the Jingi section in the *Goshūishū*.

358. *Bukkyō bungaku jiten*, 321–322.

The presence of death, implicit or explicit, is characteristic of these *Jōdo-ka*, and of the Buddhist *waka* in general in the *Kin'yōshū*. Death was not generally regarded as a proper topic for *waka*, except, obviously, for laments (*aishō-ka*). When the topic made an appearance in Buddhist *waka*, even implicitly, it usually did so through the narrative in the headnote, as in the case of these *Jōdo-ka*. In the headnote to the dream oracle poem (632/673) as recited to Shōkai, we are told that he feared the afterlife. Likewise, in Shunrai's first poem (710/686), composed, it says, when the author was "thinking of paradise," the speaker pleads directly to Amida (unnamed except by implication of the pivot word): "don't let me slip away." Such "slipping" might occur at the time of death, when Amida came to save a devotee.

In other of these poems, death or its aftermath appear more explicitly and starkly. Izumi Shikibu's poem contemplates a frightening image of rebirth, a painting of hell in which a person was depicted as "impaled on a sword" ("*terrible*— / until the sword has bent like a branch—"), while Taguchi Shigeyuki's two poems, composed at the moment of his death, which in the first instance is referred to by the word *shide* and in the second by the words we have translated as "as the author breathed his last." Such Buddhist poems expanded the boundaries within which death became an acceptable topic beyond the lament category to which it had previously been confined.

Two Buddhist *Waka* on the Bodhisattva Samantabhadra

As we have said, all eleven scriptural *waka* in the *Kin'yōshū* sequence (634/676–642/685, plus 710/679), except the poem by Minamoto no Morotoki (636/678), are attributed to priests.[359] Moreover, the Lotus Sutra poems occur in a single continual sequence, arranged following sequentially according to the chapters of the Sutra. Only one poem,

---

359. Refer to footnote 303 for information about the numbering system of the *Kin'yōshū*.

640 by Yōen, could be called an occasional *waka,* in the sense that it is a reply to someone else's poem.[360] This organizational strategy seems to demonstrate that scriptural *waka* were becoming the core of a Buddhist *waka* sequence in the imperial poetry anthologies.[361]

This particular scriptural *waka* sequence begins with two poems on the bodhisattva Samantabhadra (J: Fugen). Both poems may be classified as *kyōshi-ka,* or sūtra-passage *waka.* The first (633/674), by the priest Kakuju (1081–1139), seems to be based upon a section of text spoken by the bodhisattva from the final chapter of the Avatamsaka Sūtra (J: Kegon-kyō, T 293). The second poem (708/675), by the priest Kakuyo (1068–1146), is based upon a passage from the Kanfugen-kyō (T 277) [Sūtra on the Meditation of the Bodhisattva Samantabhadra], the third part of the "Threefold Lotus Sutra," spoken by the Buddha.

---

360. In what appears to have become a pattern set by the Buddhist *waka* in the *Shūishū,* all of the Buddhist *waka* sequences up to but excluding the *Senzaishū* begin with several occasional poems. These are followed by what is ordinarily an unbroken sequence of scriptural poems. The final poems in the sequence return again to the occasional variety. After the *Senzaishū,* the *shakkyō-ka* sequence in the *Shinkokinshū* reverts to this same pattern. It is difficult to discern the exact significance of this pattern, and Japanese scholars—even Ishihara whose entire theoretical foundation is built on the dualistic premise of *shakkyō-ka* being divided into *taiken-ka* (experiential) and *daiei-ka* (topical)—are silent on the issue. My own explanation for this pattern is that occasional poems emphasized the courtly element, setting the stage for the rest of the sequence.

361. This is not the case for *shakkyō-ka* sequences in private anthologies where scriptural *waka* are usually the sole occupants.

[633/674]

命をも罪をも露にたとへけり消えばともにや消えんとすらん
inochi o mo / tsumi o mo tsuyu ni / tatoekeri / kieba tomo ni ya / kien to suran

ON THE PASSAGE "WHEN MY LIFE IS ABOUT TO END, I MAKE THIS WISH," FROM SAMANTABHADRA'S TEN VOWS[362]

> he likened both this life
> > and the sin
> > it carries
>
> to a dew
> > that perishes—
>
> might those disappearances
> > be close
> > at hand?

> — Priest Kakuju

---

362. The section of text from the Avatamsaka Sūtra quoted in the *kotobagaki* can be found in the Taishō Daizōkyō at T no. 293, 10:848a9.

[708/675]

罪はしも露も残らず消ぬらん長き夜すがらくゆる思ひに
*tsumi wa shimo / tsuyu mo nokorazu / kienuran / nagaki yo sugara /
kuyuru omoi ni*

ON THE PASSAGE "THE SINS OF SENTIENT BEINGS ARE
LIKE THE FROST AND DEW"[363]

like frost and dew
my sins will
surely vanish

as through the long night
remorse sets
me ablaze

— Priest Kakuyo

---

363. The section of text from the Kanfugen-kyō quoted in the *kotobagaki* can be
found in the Taishō Daizōkyō at T no. 277, 9:393b12.

Kakuju makes a meditative response to the Buddhist material, while Kakuyō's is a markedly lyric response. But the focus of both poems is more or less the same: repentance of and deliverance from sin (*tsumi*) [and in the case Kakuju's poem, repentance at the end of life], a concept that had not previously been addressed in the Buddhist *waka* in the imperial poetry anthologies. In the Avatamsaka Sūtra, Samantabhadra claims that sins must be confessed: "Whatever evil I may commit / Under the sway of passion, hatred, or folly, / Bodily, verbally, or mentally, / I confess it all."[364] In the Kanfugen-kyō, deliverance from sin is accomplished as a part of a contemplative practice in which "living beings ... salute the buddhas in all directions six times day and night, recite the Great-vehicle sūtras, and consider the profound Law of the Void [śūnyatā] of the first principle ... ."[365] Both poems use the courtly metaphor of the vanishing dew to convey how quickly one's sins can be erased if one applies Samantabhadra's teachings to them.[366]

The contrasting meditative and lyric modes of these two poems signal different approaches to the concept of sin. What emotional power Kakuju's poem has (strong feeling is not emphasized) arises from the implications of the rhetorical question "might those disappearances / be close / at hand?" The speaker of the poem anticipates the possibility that the attainment of a state of mind in which sins (*tsumi*) no longer produce karma—thus, the disappearance of the sin/dew signifying enlightenment itself—is about to occur. If one's sins have disappeared—presumably as a result of sufficient

---

364. Thomas Cleary, *The Flower Ornament Scripture: A Translation of the* Avatamsaka Sūtra (Boston and London: Shambhala Publishing, 1993), 1512.

365. Bunnō Katō et.al, ed. and trans., *The Threefold Lotus Sutra* (Tokyo: Kosei Publishing Co., 1988), 367.

366. The image of the dew does appear in the Kanfugen-kyō and therefore seems to arise naturally in Kakuyo's poem; that the image is not mentioned in the final chapter of the Avatamsaka Sūtra suggests that Kakuju drew it from elsewhere in the Sūtra, was working with a different version of the Sūtra, or simply interpolated it because it belonged to the courtly "library" of images and was useful in this instance. The section of text from which the headnote of Kakuyo's poem is taken reads: "All sins are just as frost and dew, / So wisdom's sun can disperse them." Ibid., 366.

religious practice—one's actions no longer cause *kleśas* (J: *bonnō*) to arise in others. This would be an extremely positive outcome: but the poem's emphasis is primarily on the "procedure" of salvation, an intellectual affirmation, rather than an emotional response.

Kakuyo's poem, though, emphasizes considerable emotional (lyric) force, arising from the sense of intense regret the speaker expresses about past sins. Through the device of the pivot word, the poet opens the poem to multiple layers of meaning and amplifies the lyric element. The headnote to the poem establishes that "the sins of sentient beings are like the frost [*shimo*] and dew [*tsuyu*]." The words "frost" and "dew" in the poem, however, both carry two meanings. *Shimo* is both the noun "frost" and a combined particle of emphasis (*shi* + *mo*). *Tsuyu*, on the other hand, means "dew" but also signals the adverbial phrase "at all" when used in combination with the negative auxiliary verb *–zu* in *nokorazu* ("not at all," or as our translation puts it, "will surely vanish").

The *Kokoro* of the Lotus Sutra

In the eight Lotus Sutra *waka*—*Hokke-kyō-ka*—that follow Kakuyo's poem, we find that the emphasis on the theme of repentance from the Samantabhadra poems continues, as well as the potential for transformation from unenlightened to enlightened. A significant characteristic of this group of poems is a shift in information that is provided by headnotes or *kotobagaki:* that is, a shift from narrative predicament to scriptural reference. The *kotobagaki* to six of the eight Lotus Sutra poems (those not in brackets below) introduce the poem with a chapter name (8, 12, [12], [12], 15, 20, 23, and 8) from the Lotus Sutra.

In all six *kotobagaki* of the poems just listed the name of the chapter is followed by the phrase *no kokoro o yomeru,* "composed on the heart/essence of [chapter title]."[367] If we look backward for

---

367. There is a seventh poem in the *Kin'yōshū* sequence (642/685) which uses a similar expression—*to ieru kokoro o yomeru.*

previous usage of this phrase in the imperial anthologies, no such expression appeared in the *kotobagaki* to any of the Buddhist *waka* in the *Shūishū*. In the *Goshūishū* we find an abbreviated form of the phrase (*to iu kokoro o*) as part of a *kotobagaki* to two poems on the Vimalakīrti Sūtra. In the *Kin'yōshū*, on the other hand, we find five usages of the word. Looking ahead to the *shakkyō-ka* of the *Senzaishū*, the word *kokoro* followed by some form of the verb *yomu* occurs in thirty-five of fifty-four *kotobagaki* and *dai*. Clearly, the use of the word and concept of *kokoro* was on the increase in the *kotobagaki* of Buddhist *waka* and *shakkyō-ka* during the early part of the twelfth century.

Konishi Jin'ichi says, "'[T]he kokoro of a topic' refers to the most characteristic aspect of a given topic—its hon'i, or essential nature."[368] When the expression *hon'i* came to be applied to *waka* is uncertain, but Konishi says it was not yet applicable during the era of Sei Shōnagon and the Ichijō Tennō court.[369] Support for this position—at least in terms of Buddhist *waka*—can be found in sequences of twenty-eight poems on the Lotus Sutra from the private collections of both Fujiwara no Kintō and Akazome Emon (poets roughly contemporaneous to Sei Shōnagon). In their *Hokke-kyō-ka*, the names of the Sutra chapters are the sole indication of the topic.

It is most likely the case that discussions about the *hon'i* of a *waka* topic came about as competitive matches became more popular during the late eleventh and early twelfth centuries, that is, when judges looked for criteria by which to evaluate the strengths and faults of competing poems. By the twelfth century, when "winning a waka match meant great glory for a poet, and ... conversely, defeat brought great shame," it was a strike against any poem if it was felt to inaccurately portray the essence of the assigned topic.[370]

The essence (or essential meaning) of a topic, however, could only be established by consensus, and consensus was established by reference to precedents. For seasonal *waka* and the love poems, this

---

368. Konishi, *A History of Japanese Literature*, vol. 3, 194.
369. Ibid., vol. 2, 392.
370. Ibid., vol. 3, 27.

was not difficult, since so many poems on those topics had been written by the time the *Kin'yōshū* was compiled. When it came to Buddhist *waka*, however, there were few precedents to consult. The one exception was poetry based upon the Lotus Sutra. It is quite possible that by the early twelfth century enough *Hokke-kyō-ka* had been written over the previous century that there was some consensus about what the "essence" of a given chapter might be.

In six of the following eight Buddhist *waka* the poetic *kokoro* of the Lotus Sutra chapters seems to have been established.

HOKKE-KYŌ-KA

[634/676]

吹きかへす鷲の山風なかりせば衣のうらの玉をみましや
fukikaesu | washi no yamakaze | nakariseba | koromo no ura no | tama o mimashi ya

ON THE ESSENCE OF THE FIVE HUNDRED DISCIPLES
CHAPTER

> if the wind
>> from Vulture Peak
>
> had not blown
>> my sleeves inside-out—
>
> would I have found
>> the jewel
>
> inside the reverse
>> of my coat?

> — Bishop Jōen

[635/677]

法のためになふ薪にことよせてやがて憂世をこりぞはてぬる
nori no tame / ninau takigi ni / kotoyosete / yagate ukiyo o / kori zo hatenuru

ON THE ESSENCE OF THE DEVADATTA CHAPTER

to all appearances
        I shouldered

  wood for the fire
        for the sake of the Law—

  the sorry world
        utterly weary

    I cut
        away in an instant

          — Sensai Shōnin

[636/678]

けふぞしる鷲の高嶺にてる月を谷川くみし人のかげとは

*kyō zo shiru / washi no takane ni / teru tsuki o / tanikawa kumishi /
hito no kage to wa*

[*Based upon the same chapter as the previous poem*]

today I understand:

the moon that shines

from high Vulture Peak

was the Buddha's reflection

in the valley water I carried

— Kōgōgū Gon no Tayū Morotoki

[709/679]

わたつ海の底のもくづと見し物をいかでか空の月と成らん
watatsumi no / soko no mokuzu to / mishi mono o / ikade ka sora no /
tsuki to naruran

ON THE DRAGON PRINCESS BECOMING A BUDDHA

> how could
>   what I regarded
>
>   as only weed-wrack
>   from the sea-deep
>
>   become the moon
>   in an empty sky?

> — Priest Shōchō

[637/680]

たらちねは黒髪ながらいかなればこの眉白き人となるらん
*tarachine wa / kurokami nagara / ikanareba / kono mayu shiroki / hito
to naruran*

ON THE ESSENCE OF THE WELLING UP OUT OF THE
EARTH CHAPTER

> the mother's hair
>> is black but
>
> the child's eyebrows
>> have turned white—
>
> how is it possible?

> — Provisional Bishop Yōen

[638/681]

あひがたき法を広めし聖こそうらみし人も導かれけれ
*aigataki / nori o hiromeshi / hijiri koso / uramishi hito mo /
michibikarekere*

ON THE ESSENCE OF THE BODHISATTVA NEVER
DISPARAGING CHAPTER

> even the people
> > who hated
> > > that rootless monk

> were led to the Law
> > — how hard to find! —
> > > he spread so far

> > — Provisional Bishop Yōen
> > in the SNKBT *Kin'yōwakashū*
> > *Shikawakashū* version
> > or
> > — Priest Kakuga
> > in the *Shakkyō-ka no Kenkyū* version

[639/682]

うき身をしわたすときけば海人小舟のりの心をかけぬ日ぞ
なき

*ukimi o shi / watasu to kikeba / amaobune / nori no kokoro o / kakenu
hi zo naki*

ON THE ESSENCE OF THE MEDICINE KING CHAPTER

    not one day
            my heart hasn't kept
                     the Law in sight

    since I heard
            the little fisher dory
                   will ferry

    this lonely body

                — Priest Kaijin

[640/683]

いかにして衣の玉をしるぬらん思ひもかけぬ人もある世に

ika ni shite / koromo no tama o / shirinuran / omoi mo kakenu / hito mo aru yo ni

IN REPLY TO THE DONOR OF A SŪTRA-OFFERING SERVICE, WHO SENT A GIFT
　　　　　　　　　　　　and, attached underneath, a poem on "The Reasons the Jewel in the Five Hundred Disciples Chapter of the Lotus Sutra Is Precious,"
　　　　　　　　　　after the author had preached on the essence of that chapter

　　　there are people
　　　　　for whom knowing

　　　　　　　never comes in the world—

　　how did you find
　　　　the jewel in the robe?

　　　　　　　　　　— Provisional Bishop Yōen

The Lotus Sutra sub-sequence is devoted to the various realizations of enlightenment that are recounted in the Sutra. This emphasis on enlightenment points to a strong soteriological modality at work in the sub-sequence, which still falls within the parameters of proper courtly *waka*. The poems by their very nature rely heavily for their narrative underpinnings on the Sutra itself: all derived from stories or parables in the Sutra, to varying degrees they require some understanding of those narratives to be comprehensible.

Many of these narratives emphasize the time, effort, and suffering required to attain realization. The speaker of Jōen's poem (634/676), for example, alludes to the Parable of the Hidden Jewel in the Receipt of Prophecy by Five Hundred Disciples chapter (8, *Gohyakudeshi jukibon*), a topic we saw in Akazome Emon's poem (1194) in the *Goshūishū*. The parable, it will be remembered, recounts the story of a poor man who has lived, unbeknownst to him, with a jewel that was sewn into the seam of his coat while he was intoxicated. When he is informed of his ownership of this possession by a "friend" (the Buddha), he discovers that he has long been rich without knowing it, or metaphorically speaking, spiritually rich. The speaker of Jōen's poem is the poor man of the parable, referring to the Buddha's teachings as "... the wind / from Vulture Peak," couching the poem's meditative argument in the rhetorical question "would I have found / the jewel / inside the reverse / of my coat?" The answer is obvious: without the Buddha's help, he would not. Jōen's response to the parable's material is more thoughtful than emotional, while Akazome's earlier response was the reverse. (She too wrote as the poor man in the parable, but emphasized, in a fairly one-dimensional way, the speaker's emotion of surprise and gratitude: "I had no inkling" the jewel had been "sewn in my coat" and "what luck! / to wake / from my long drunkenness.") Jōen's project is more intellectually complex, asking the reader to locate the hidden victory in the trial itself. On one level the poem proceeds logically: if A (hard thing) had not happened, would I ever have realized B (wonderful thing)? This argument seems to arise from a didactic impulse, but for all that, the poem does not neglect to skillfully interweave courtly images—

wind, sleeves, jewel, and coat—with a strictly Buddhist image: Vulture Peak (*washi no yama*), where the Lotus Sutra was believed to have been taught—that had never appeared in an imperial anthology up to this point.

The two poems that follow Jōen's, by Sensai Shōnin (d. 1127) and Minamoto no Morotoki (1077–1136), are based upon another narrative of realization from the Lotus Sutra: that of the Buddha (in one of his previous lives) while serving Devadatta (Chapter 12).[371] The speakers in the poems by Sensai Shōnin and Minamoto no Morotoki came to their realizations through acts of selfless service. In Sensai's poem, the cause of the Buddha's realization was that he "cut / away in an instant" from "the sorry world" of samsāra, the word "cut" (*kori*) serving as a pivot to signify both the spiritual action he has taken and the physical act of cutting wood. Morotoki's speaker says that now, today (*kyō*), he understands (*shiru*) that the bright "reflection / in the valley water I carried" was that of the Buddha himself. These are meditative responses to the scriptural material, and the arguments are "explanatory": *this is how realization occurred.* Moreover, Morotoki's moon shining from "high Vulture Peak" recalls "the wind / from Vulture Peak," in Jōen's poem, though the images differ slightly. Though sensual images tilt the poems slightly towards the lyric, and both share narrative elements from the Sutra itself, lyric and narrative elements are secondary to the arguments the authors make.

In the three poems (709/679, 637/680, 638/681) by Shōchō Hōshi and Gon no Sōjō Yōen that follow, the speakers have spiritual realizations that arise as the result of unfathomable circumstances. Shōchō's poem, on a different section of the Devadatta chapter than the previous two poems, is a response to the remarkable transformation of a dragon princess into a Buddha—that is, a miraculous solution to the ideological obstacle that, according to the Buddhist teachings, made it impossible for women to attain enlightenment in their

---

371. See the discussion in Chapter 3 of Devadatta as pertaining to Michitsuna no Haha's poem (1339) and Gyōki's poem (1346).

female bodies.[372] Shōchō's poem is a question expressing surprise or disbelief: "how could / what I regarded / as only weed-wrack / from the sea-deep / become the moon / in an empty sky?" As the poem makes a "how-did-this-happen" reaction to the narrative improbability of the dragon princess's enlightenment, it also enacts a moment of spiritual "enlargement," in which a student of the Buddha's teachings discovers that they extend to all sentient beings.

Like Shōchō's poem, Yōen's poem that follows also responds to an unfathomable circumstance, this time drawn from the Welling Up Out of the Earth chapter (15, *Jūjiyu jutsuhon*). The text upon which Yōen's poem is based reads: "It is as if there is a young man in the prime of life, / His years only just twenty-five, / Who points to men of a hundred years, / Their hair white, their faces wrinkled, / Saying, 'These are my begotten sons!'"[373] Yōen, like Shōchō, asks a rhetorical question that springs from disbelief: "how is it possible?" that "the mother's hair / is black but / the child's eyebrows / have turned white. …" Yōen changes the gender of the older person from male to female, but still the poem is clearly a reference to the Buddha's salvific powers, so remarkable that "[s]uch a thing as this the world finds hard to believe!"[374]

The third unfathomable circumstance, responded to by Yōen's second poem (638/681), occurs in the chapter The Bodhisattva Never Disparaging (20, *Jōfukyō bosatsuhon*), in which a monk "constantly subjected to abuse" by his fellow monks becomes a bodhisattva, then eventually leads "the people … / to the Law" that is so "hard to find."[375] After two poems that posed rhetorical questions, this one makes a simple declarative statement reflecting upon the lesson taught in the Sutra: "even the people / who hated / that rootless monk / were led to the Law … / he spread so far."

Questions like the ones posed in Shōchō's poem and in Yōen's

372. Hurvitz, *Scripture of the Lotus Blossom of the Fine Dharma*, 199 and 201; Iwamoto and Sakamoto, *Hokke-kyō*, vol. 2, 222.

373. Ibid., 236; ibid., 318–320.

374. Ibid., 234; ibid., vol. 2, 314.

375. Ibid., 280–281; ibid., vol. 3, 136.

first poem are subtly emotional—needing and requiring a response, a consent, even if only implied—and therefore, inflect these poems toward the lyric mode. This lyric aspect mixes with meditative argument, urging the reader to consider, to agree and finally to be transformed and comforted by the answer, as the speaker was. Shōchō's question is a recalculation of the speaker's point of view: "I was wrong to believe that the Buddha's salvific powers would exclude women." Though the poem leans heavily for its narrative upon the Sutra, the skillful weaving of sensually specific images like "weed-wrack," "sea-deep," and "moon" allows the reader to enjoy the lyric response the poet made to his material without absolutely requiring knowledge of the story behind it. Yōen's response to his material in the Welling Up out of the Earth chapter is likewise lyric. His question—"how is it possible?"—though one step removed from the first-person observation of Shōchō's question, expresses a variety of religious surprise and joy similar to that of the Sutra itself. Yōen's poem subordinates narrative (by excluding it) to emotional gesture, reinforcing this lyric aspect with sensually specific images of black hair and white eyebrows. The simple statement in Yōen's second poem is less emotional than the previous two poems, making a logical, meditative response to the narrative it summarizes.

The last scriptural *Hokke-kyō-ka* of this sub-sequence is attributed to Kaijin Hōshi, about whom we also have almost no biographical information.[376] The poem draws upon the last passage of a sentence in the The Former Affairs of the Bodhisattva Medicine King chapter (23, *Yakuōbosatsu honjihon*) of the Lotus Sutra, in which the Buddha entreated the bodhisattva "Beflowered by the King of Constellations" (Naksatrarājasamkusumitābhijña) to keep, hold, proclaim, and propagate his teachings. The Buddha told this bodhisattva to treat anyone else who behaves this way with respect and reverence. About such a man the Buddha says, "He shall blow the conch of the Dharma,

---

376. The biography of Kaijin Hōshi in the SNKBT version of the *Kin'yōshū* says only that he was born in 1059 and that he was forty-four years old when he became *rissha* (literally, one who determines the [correctness of] the Buddhist teachings; a candidate for debates, or *rongi*) in 1102. Kawamura, *Kin'yōwakashu Shikawakashū*, 15.

beat the drum of the Dharma, and ferry all beings over the sea of birth, old age, sickness, and death."[377] Kaijin makes a strongly lyric response to this passage, declaring that there has not been "one day / my heart hasn't kept / the Law in sight / since I heard / the little fisher dory / will ferry / this lonely body." The little boat ferrying the body across the water evokes this poignant visual tableau (a lyric gesture) while it establishes what is at stake in the poem. Precisely because the speaker has been reminded that his impermanent body (*ukimi*) will die, he realizes his only recourse is to keep "the Law in sight" (in his heart, *kokoro*). The poem simultaneously expresses religious devotion and answers the call to proclaim these teachings as the Sutra urged.

The last *Hokke-kyō-ka* in this sub-sequence is an occasional poem: the author, again the Buddhist priest Yōen, after he delivered teachings on the "Five Hundred Disciples" chapter (8), replies to a patron who has sent a gift. This poem recalls the first poem (634) by Jōen in the *Hokke-kyō-ka* sequence in which the poet asked "if the wind / from Vulture Peak / had not blown / my sleeves inside-out— / would I have found / the jewel / inside the reverse / of my coat?" and, moreover, it speaks to the same section of Lotus Sutra text. Here, though, it is in the context of flattering the patron, again in the form of a rhetorical question. The question presumes that the patron's enlightenment is a *fait accompli*, asking "how did you find / the jewel in the robe?," and amplifying this flattery by comparing the patron to lesser persons for whom enlightenment seems unlikely: "there are people / for whom knowing / never comes in the world—."

---

377. Hurvitz, *The Scripture of the Lotus Blossom*, 301; Iwamoto and Sakamoto, *Hokke-kyō* vol. 3, 208. In other English translations of the Lotus Sutra, the word "ferry" (*dodatsu*) has been interpreted as "free" [all living beings] and "deliver" [all living beings]. See Burton Watson, *The Lotus Sutra* (New York: Columbia University Press, 1993), 289, and Bunnō Katō et al., *The Threefold Lotus Sutra*, 311.

Three Miscellaneous Buddhist *Waka*

Following the *Hokke-kyō-ka* sequence, and preceding the second group of *Jōdo-ka* that conclude the sequence, are two scriptural and one occasional Buddhist poems, the topics and textual sources of which vary widely.

[641/684]

いつをいつと思ひたゆみて陽炎のかげろふほどの世をすぐ
すらん
*itsu o itsu to / omoitayumite / kagerō no / kagerō hodo no / yo o
sugusuran*

When people were composing poems on the Eight *Eta* Metaphors, the author wrote this
ON THE PASSAGE "THIS BODY IS LIKE AN
ILLUSION"

    ignoring the thought
        when will it end?

    do I while away
        my life in this world

    that is
    a shimmering

    mirage
        of a mirage?

            — Priest Kaijin

[642/685]

世とともに心のうちにすむ月をありと知るこそ晴るるなりけれ
yo to tomo ni / kokoro no uchi ni / sumu tsuki o / ari to shiru koso /
haruru narikere

IN MY HEART ALWAYS THE PERFECT INDWELLING
MOON

> in the night-world of my heart
> > a moon

> of ever-living brightness
> > *is*—

> to *know* that
> > is to come clear

> > > and free

— Priest Chōsei

[643/687]

今日もなを惜しみやせまし法のためちらす花ぞと思ひなさ
ずは

kyō mo nao / oshimi ya semashi / nori no tame / chirasu hana zo to / omoinasazu wa

ON SEEING THE BLOSSOMS FALL AT A SHARI-E
CEREMONY AT DAIGO

were I not quite certain

flowers are scattered

for the sake of the Law

today I'd regret them

yet again —

wouldn't I?

— Chinkai Hōshi no Haha

The first of these poems, by Kaijin Hōshi (also author of 639/682), is based upon a set of metaphors found in a Yuiishiki (Consciousness-Only; S: Vijñānavāda) text called Shōdaijōron (S: Mahāyānasamgraha, T 1593), attributed to Asanga (J: Mujaku, ca. 395–470), one of the principal proponents of the Yogācāra school of Buddhist teachings.[378] In Japan, the Hossō Sect (centered at Kōfuku-ji), which flourished primarily during the Nara period, regarded this scripture as significant.

Very similar metaphors can be found in the Yuima-kyō, or Vimalakīrti Sūtra. In fact, in the section of text about the impermanence of the body, the Sūtra reads, "[The body] is like a magical illusion ..."[379] While the metaphors in the Vimalakīrti Sūtra demonstrate the insubstantiality of one's physical body, the metaphors in the Shōdaijōron regard *any* phenomenon that arises as a result of dependence on other phenomena as insubstantial (an argument advanced by the Buddhist law of co-dependent origination.) The word *eta* in the headnote refers to the causes that create those phenomena (phenomena = "the other," the *ta* in *eta*). The metaphor Kaijin uses in the poem is *kagerō* (actually *kagerō no kagerō*), a "shimmering / mirage / of a mirage." By the early twelfth century this term had been used in many different literary genres; its presence here was not anything new to the court.

In addition to making use of a well-known court metaphor, the poem seems to allude, in part, to an almost identical Buddhist *waka* in the *Shūishū* (1335) by Fujiwara no Kintō, a poem undoubtedly well known by this time. The nearly equivalent sections of the Kintō and Kaijin poems read *omoishiru / ... yo no naka o / itsu o itsu tote / sugusu naruran* (Kintō), and *itsu o itsu to / omoitayumite / ... yo o sugusuran* (Kaijin). In his older poem, Kintō's poem bemoaned his lack of action to take the tonsure, but Kaijin's addresses the larger problem that that which is created from a cause can also be destroyed by a cause. Thus, he argues, ignoring the impermanence of that which comes about as a

---

378. There are both a set of eight metaphors and a set of ten. See the entry "eta jūyu" in *Bukkyōgo daijiten*, 101.

379. Robert A. F. Thurman, *The Holy Teaching of Vimalakīrti*, 22.

result of co-dependence causes suffering. Both poems employ rhetorical questions: Kaijin's, which makes both a meditative argument and engages an emotional response, is directed at the futility of living among mirages as though they had substance.

In the same way that Kaijin's poem recalls Kintō's, Chōsei Hōshi's poem on the esoteric practice of *gachirinkan* recalls Kakuchō's poem (1188) on the same practice in the *Goshūishū*.[380] Kakuchō's poem described what changed at the moment of his enlightenment ("the myriad things / I see as a dream"), but Chōsei's poem is an argument about what it is to live with the moon already in one's heart—that is, to hold enlightenment within: "to *know* that / is to come clear / and free." Kakuchō compared his new view of the world to awaking from a dream; Chōsei seeks to convince the reader that enlightenment (knowing) is already imminent within *samsāra* (the "night-world" of his heart). Chōsei's poem, in a soteriological/monastic modality, is expressed more abstractly and with fewer personal terms than Kakuchō's. As an eminent monk at the Shingon temple, Daigo-ji, Chōsei may have chosen this way to express himself because of his status.

The Mother of Chinkai Hōshi has only one poem in the *hachidaishū*, and there is little biographical information available about her.[381] We know that her son Chinkai (?–1152) was, like Chōsei, a resident of Daigo-ji.[382] Therefore, it is not surprising that Chinkai's mother's poem was composed upon the occasion of a ceremony at the same temple where her son lived.

The Shari-e mentioned in the headnote was a ceremony at which devotees worshipped the physical remains of the Buddha or the enlightened ones, the first recorded instance of which in the Heian period was held at Enryaku-ji in 860.[383] After that, the ceremony

---

380. Nothing is known about Chōsei Hōshi except that he attained the level of an *ajari*, a title for an eminent priest, at Daigo-ji, a Shingon temple in the capital.

381. In the *Shakkyō-ka no kenkyū* version of the *Kin'yōshū* Buddhist *waka* sequence, the poem by Chinkai Hōshi no Haha occurs after a poem by Minamoto no Shunrai that is a supplemental poem in the SNKBT version. Shunrai's poem is on the topic of Amida, so I included it in my discussion of *Jōdo-ka*.

382. Chinkai was a Sanron monk initially. *Nihon Bukkyō jinmei jiten*, 304.

383. Nakamura Hajime et al., *Bukkyō jiten* (Tokyo: Iwanami Shoten, 2006), 472.

gained in popularity and was held in various monastic venues. According to Minamoto no Tamenori's *Sanbō ekotoba*, the Shari-e at Enryaku-ji was "held when the cherry blossoms on the mountain were in their fullest bloom,"[384] likely the case at Daigo-ji as well.

The conceit of Chinkai Hōshi no Haha's poem hinges upon the image of blossoms, enacting a tension between the familiar courtly and lyric sentiment that laments falling blossoms and a contrasting Buddhist context in which falling blossoms is a *positive* image. Because it is recorded that miraculous blossoms fell in honor when the Buddha taught the Dharma (*nori*) at Vulture Peak—and because this ceremony at Daigo-ji has reminded the poet of this—she realizes she cannot fully participate in the courtly gesture of regretting the fall of the cherry blossoms. Thus the poem performs the skillful trick of having its courtly cake and eating it, expressing its lyric element but simultaneously critiquing it as an insufficient response in comparison to its meditative argument. As such, the poem is in a sense emblematic of how Buddhist *waka* served as a small stage on which to enact the tensions between the courtly worldview and the Buddhist teachings.

SHIKASHŪ

Just eighteen years after the *sansōbon* (third version) of the *Kin'yōshū* was approved by Retired Emperor Shirakawa in 1126 and fifteen years after both Shirakawa and Minamoto no Shunrai, the compiler of the *Kin'yōshū*, died in 1129, Retired Emperor Sutoku (1119–1164; r. 1123–1141) commanded the compilation of the sixth imperial poetry anthology, *Shikashū*, in 1144. This was the shortest interim between imperial poetry anthologies to date, and though the *Shikashū* was not completed until seven years later in 1151, it was highly unusual for two such public poetry projects to be undertaken in such a short period. It was not just the brief interval of time that was unusual; the fact that so few *utaawase* and *kakai* (poetry gatherings) had been held or *hyakushu-uta* compiled between 1126

---

384. Edward Kamens, *The Three Jewels*, 302.

and 1144 meant there was relatively little for Fujiwara no Akisuke (1090–1155), compiler of the *Shikashū*, to draw upon in order to create a poetic landmark that would represent the best *waka* of the new era.

A sense of tragedy later accompanied the *Shikashū*. Because Retired Emperor Sutoku was linked to the one-day military conflict known as the Hōgen Disturbance (*Hōgen no Ran*) of 1156, this resulted in his exile to Sanuki in Shikoku, where he died eight years later. While the Disturbance did not affect the compilation of the *Shikashū*, after the anthology was completed contemporary readers could not have engaged with it without remembering the escalating tensions that had developed within the imperial family since the establishment of the *in-no-chō* in 1086. After Retired Emperor Shirakawa died in 1129, the new Senior Retired Emperor, Toba (1103–1156; r. 1107–1123) insisted that his son, who would become Emperor Konoe (1139–1155; r. 1141–1155), succeed Sutoku who had been forced to abdicate in 1141. When Konoe died suddenly in 1155, Toba once again—being Senior Retired Emperor—picked his son, Go-Shirakawa (1127–1192; r. 1155–1158), to be emperor, rather than accede to Sutoku's wish that his (Sutoku's) son be selected. Toba's repeated rejections of Sutoku were the likely motivation for Sutoku's alleged attempt to "mobilize troops and overthrow the state."[385] The Hōgen Disturbance did not yet pit the Minamoto against the Taira (some Taira and Minamoto were involved on both sides of the conflict), but prefigured the Heiji Disturbance of 1159 and the eventual conflict that *did* set Minamoto and Taira against one another, the Genpei Wars of 1180–1185.

Shikashū compiler Fujiwara no Akisuke was a member of the Rokujō family of poets that began with Akisuke's father, Akisue (1055–1123) and continued through Akisuke's son and beyond;[386] father and

---

385. According to Takeuchi Rizō, this phrase comes from the *kanbun* diary of Taira no Nobunori, "an important source on the Hōgen clash." "The Rise of the Warriors," in Donald Shively and William McCullough, eds., *Cambridge History of Japan*, vol. 2 (Cambridge: Cambridge University Press, 1999), 689.

386. WDJ, 9.

son were both active poets during the late eleventh and early twelfth centuries. (As one of Shirakawa's closest retainers, Akisue's rank had risen steadily, peaking at the Senior Third Rank while he worked in the Office of Palace Repairs (Shurishiki) from 1094–1122. He died in 1123. The appellation "Rokujō" alluded to his residence at the intersection of Rokujō and Karasuma in the capital.) Higuchi Yoshimaro regards Akisuke as the most important *waka* poet at the court, after Fujiwara no Mototoshi's death in 1142,[387] but since Akisuke died in 1155, his preeminence was short-lived. After Akisuke died, the Rokujō lineage and its poetic ideals continued through his son, Fujiwara no Kiyosuke (1104–1177), a prolific author and compiler during the twelfth century.

THE ROKUJŌ POETS, THE *HITOMARO EIGU,* AND SENSAI SHŌNIN'S *WAKA MANDARA*

The Rokujō family is linked to the conception of *waka* as a path (*michi*) to enlightenment. One aspect of this link is the family's involvement in the *Hitomaro eigu,* a religio-literary service that Akisuke's father, Akisue, first held in 1118. Yamada Shōzen regards this yearly event as one of the significant factors leading to *waka* becoming more religious at the beginning of the twelfth century.[388] What we know about the service, which at first was not particularly Buddhist, is based upon the *Hitomaro eigu-ki* by Fujiwara no Atsumitsu (1063–1144).[389] According to this document, there were thirteen men present at the first service, among them Minamoto no Shunrai who compiled the previous imperial anthology.[390]

---

387. Higuchi Yoshimaro, "Shikashū," in *Man'yōshū to chokusenwakashū,* vol. 4 of *Waka bungaku kōza* (Tokyo: Ōfūsha, 1970), 185.

388. Yamada Shōzen, "Kakinomoto no Hitomaro eigu no seiritsu to tenkai: Bukkyō to bungaku to no sesshoku ni shiten o oite," *Taishō Daigaku kenkyū kiyō* (no. 51, 1966): 84–85. The information that follows is drawn from Yamada's article.

389. This can be found in vol. 16 of *Gunsho ruijū.* Ibid., 85 and 121.

390. In attendance were, in addition to Shunrai, Fujiwara no Nagazane (1075–1133), Akisue's first son, Akisuke, Fujiwara no Michitsune (dates unknown), a nephew of Akisue's named Fujiwara no Saneyuki (1080–1162), son of the poet Fujiwara no Kinzane

Since ten of the thirteen men who participated in the first *Hitomaro eigu* were from or related to the Rokujō clan, Yamada believes that the service was created initially to form a house (*ie*) of poets. Yamada describes the service—to the extent that he can—by reconstructing the sequence of events as explained in the *Hitomaru eigu-ki:* the service began when the host hung a portrait of Hitomaro, which the participants worshipped by making various offerings to it. Then everyone shared a meal and *saké*, listened to a lecture on Hitomaro and his poetry, composed *waka* on predetermined topics, and enjoyed one another's camaraderie by, among other things, singing (*rōei*) songs.[391] Initially, the service borrowed protocol and customs from another service, the ritual worship of an image of Confucius (*sekiten*), a practice that dates back to 701 in Japan. Others have proposed that the *Shōshi-kai* (literally a gathering to "respect the teeth," i.e., honoring those of advanced age) held first in Japan in 877, may have been another precedent for the *Hitomaro eigu*. In the case of the *Shōshi-kai*, the image Japanese participants worshipped was that of Po Chü-i, since he was known to have begun this service in China in 845.[392]

Hashimoto Fumio says that the primary rationale for the *Hitomaro eigu* was to regain cultural capital within the literary—*waka*—sphere. To accomplish this, two groups of poets were formed—one centered around Akisue and another around Tadamichi—to unite under Shunrai as head, and present a united aristocratic front within the palace. As this project progressed, it encouraged a de-emphasis of the recreational qualities of *waka* and a focus instead on *waka* as a literary art.[393]

(1053–1107) and son-in-law of Akisue, Fujiwara no Akinaka (1059–1129), Yukimori (family name and dates unknown), the aforementioned Atsumitsu, Fujiwara no Tsunetada (1075–1138), a relative of Akisue's through marriage, Fujiwara no Masazane (1059–1127), a second son-in-law of Akisue, Fujiwara no Munekane (dates unknown), and Fujiwara no Tametada (?–?1136), father to the three Jaku's of Tokiwa (Tokiwa sanjaku). The Tokiwa sanjaku—Jakunen, Jakuchō, and Jakuzen—figured prominently in both the *Senzaishū* and the *Shinkokinshū*.

391. Ibid., 87

392. Ibid., 92.

393. Ibid., 96–97.

The concept that composing *waka* was a religio-literary activity became much more important during the latter half of the twelfth century, but Yamada believes that the seeds of this idea can be traced not only to the *Hitomaro eigu* of 1118 but also to its precedent, the *Waka Mandara* (Waka mandala) of Sensai Shōnin (d. 1127). It will be remembered that Sensai Shōnin's Buddhist *waka* were included in the *Kin'yōshū*, and that he was deeply involved with the world of *waka* poetry, having held a famous *utaawase* at his temple Ungo-ji in 1116, two years before the first *Hitomaro eigu*. Sensai is also known to have created a poetic mandala based on the mandalas of the Tendai *mikkyō* tradition. Though this mandala is not extant and we do not know when it was drawn, what we do know about it is based upon a story in the *setsuwa* collection entitled *Kokonchomonjū*, compiled by Tachibana no Narisue in 1254. According to this story, the *Waka mandara* pictorialized thirty-six famous *waka* poets (perhaps the *sanjurokkasen*) along with seven Buddhas of the past. If Sensai's mandala was drawn to equate to a Buddhist mandala, we can speculate that it also functioned as a focus or apparatus of Buddhist practice.

Yamada is uncertain whether the *Waka mandara* was different from another pictorialization that Fujiwara no Mototoshi, Sensai's close acquaintance, described in *Ungo-ji shōnin zan kyōgen kigo wakajo* (A *Waka* Preface in which the Ungo-ji Holy Man repented the sin of *kyōgen kigo*).[394] From this Preface we learn that in 1106 Sensai pictorialized Kōki Tokuo Bosatsu (a bodhisattva who is the focus of an entire volume of the Nirvāna Sūtra), declaring him the *honji* (original form) of the *waka kami* at Sumiyoshi Shrine. The Preface claims that Sensai copied passages of the Sūtra onto the picture and worshipped it during lectures and sermons.[395] Though we cannot be certain that Mototoshi described the same *Waka mandara* as the one described in the *setsuwa* selection, the similarities between the pictorial and ritual aspects of the *Eigu* and the *Mandara* are clear.

---

394. This document can be found in the *Honchō bunshū* in the *Kokushi taikei*, vol. 30, 236. Yamada Shōzen, 101.

395. Ibid.

THE BUDDHIST *WAKA* IN THE *SHIKASHŪ*

As we have said, it is perhaps due to the brief time between the *Kin'yōshū* and the *Shikashū* (1126–1151) that the *Shikashū* is so short (415 *waka*). One suspects that Akisuke had less material to choose from to create an anthology worthy of the Rokujō house and Retired Emperor Sutoku.[396]

Likewise the number of Buddhist *waka* in the *Shikashū*—six—is small. Akisuke put these poems at the end of the last book of the anthology (the second "Miscellaneous *waka*" [Zōka] book). The compilers of the *Shūishū* and the *Kin'yōshū* both chose the last book for their Buddhist *waka*, which suggests that precedent was the main factor in the minds of successive compilers in deciding the most appropriate place for *waka* on such themes. That the *Shikashū*, like the *Shūishū* and *Kin'yōshū*, lacks any sort of categorical marker for these six *waka* suggests that the concept of an independent category of Buddhist *waka* or *shakkyō-ka* may have been in flux, a situation which would not permanently resolve itself until the *Senzaishū*.

---

396. There are multiple texts of the *Shikashū:* the SNKBT version has 415 poems while the Izumi Shoin version edited by Matsuno Yōichi has 413 or 420 poems. Kawamura Teruo et al., *Kin'yōwakashū Shikawakashū*, 217–350; Matsuno Yōichi, ed., *Shikawakashū*, in *Izumi Koten Sōsho*, vol. 7 (Osaka: Izumi Shoin, 1988), 1–120.

[410/406/410 and 404]³⁹⁷

思へども忌むとていはぬことなればそなたにむきて音をの
みぞ泣く

*omoedomo / imu tote iwanu / koto nareba / sonata ni mukite / ne o
nomi zo naku*

WHEN SHE HEARD SHE WOULD BECOME THE SAI-IN
PRIESTESS AT KAMO, SHE TURNED TO THE WEST AND
COMPOSED

> because what I wish
>
>   is forbidden
>
> (they tell me)
>
> I do not speak
>
>   I turn
>   in that direction
>
>   the only sound
>
>   my weeping
>   to myself

— Senshi Naishinnō

---

397. The numbering system of the *Shikashū* poems depends upon which text is used. The first number is from the SNKBT text; the second is from Ishihara's text in *Shakkyō-ka no kenkyū*; and the third (comprised of two numbers separated by the word "and") is from the Izumi Shoin text edited by Matsuno.

[411/407/411 and 405]

あくがるる身のはかなさは百年のなかばすぎてぞ思ひしらるる

akugaruru / mi no hakanasa wa / momotose no / nakaba sugite zo / omoishiraruru

ON THE ESSENCE OF THE PASSAGE "HE ROAMED IN
ANOTHER COUNTRY FOR MORE THAN FIFTY YEARS,"
from the Belief and Understanding chapter of the Lotus Sutra

   my body's impermanence?

      when half a hundred years

   of wandering were spent

         I understood

                  — Jingi Haku Akinaka

[412/408/412 and 406]

露の身のきえてほとけになることはつとめてのちぞ知るべ
かりける

tsuyu no mi no / kiete hotoke ni / naru koto wa / tsutomete nochi zo /
shirubekarikeru

ON THE ESSENCE OF THE IDEA "TO ATTAIN
BUDDHAHOOD IN THIS VERY BODY"

> a thing I understood only
> after morning practice—
>
> that this flesh of
> dew disappears
>
> to become
> Buddha
>
> — Anonymous

[413/409/413 and 407]

よそになど仏の道をたづぬらんわが心こそしるべなりけれ
yoso ni nado / hotoke no michi o / tazunuran / wagagokoro koso /
shirube narikere

COMPOSED WHEN THE AUTHOR HELD A CEREMONY
FOR THE BUDDHA'S RELICS, from among poems on the
passage "yearning for attainment on the path"

> why look
> some other place
>
>   for the Buddha way—
>
> the guide
> was my
>
>   own heart

>   — The Regent and Former
>   Chancellor (Tadamichi)

[414/410/414 and 408, no headnote]

いかで我こころの月をあらはして闇にまどへる人を照らさむ
*ikade ware / kokoro no tsuki o / arawashite / yami ni madoeru / hito o
terasamu*

> I will reveal
>   (somehow)
>
>   the moon
>   of my heart
>
>   to shine
>   for anyone
>
>   who wanders
>   lost in the dark

> — Senior Assistant Minister
> of the Left Ward Akisuke

[415/411/415 and 409]

世の中の人のこころのうき雲にそらがくれする有明の月
*yo no naka no / hito no kokoro no / ukigumo ni / soragakure suru /
ariake no tsuki*

ON THE PASSAGE "FOREVER I DWELL ON HOLY
VULTURE PEAK"

> of the world:
> of the people:
> of the heart:
>   grief—
>
> if floating clouds
> deprive the sky of
>   the dawn moon
>
>   — Priest Tōren

The *waka* that precede these six poems provide further evidence that the status of Buddhist *waka* was, in fact, still in flux. Reading through the second "Miscellaneous" book, there are a number of poems on the themes of impermanence (*mujō*) and grief (*aishō*) that have a distinct Buddhist inflection. The poem that immediately precedes the first Buddhist *waka* is based upon a dream of a priest secluded within the confines of Inari Shrine, praying for the equal distribution of an estate after the death of his parents. The poem uses metaphors and diction common to Buddhist *waka:* the long night (*nagaki yo*), a painful event (*kurushiki koto*), and a temporary lodging (that is, this life; *kari no yadori*).

This poem has two qualities in common with the first poem in the Buddhist *waka* sequence. The author of the first Buddhist *waka*, Princess Senshi of the Kamo Shrine, also composed her *waka* within the confines of a Shintō shrine. Both are poems of grief: the previous poem asks, "For what shall I grieve" (*nani nagekuramu*); Senshi's poem describes "the only sound / my weeping / to myself."

Explicating Senshi's poem in his study of the *Hosshin wakashū*,[398] Edward Kamens has shown how the narrative of the *kotobagaki* is key to understanding the poem: the speaker is a woman for whom the sadness of not being able to worship Amida Buddha (in the West) has rendered her essentially mute in terms of her true spiritual aspirations: "because what I wish / is forbidden / (they tell me) / I do not speak." The *waka* restates, in a compressed and oblique way, the narrative predicament of the *kotobagaki*, but places intense feeling, the lyric element, in the foreground. The *waka* enacts, as Kamens says, the painful, almost lifelong, dilemma Senshi had to wrestle with: obligated to serve at a *kami* shrine (for fifty-seven years) while desiring salvation in the Pure Land. As such, the poem represents yet another iteration of the discomfort Buddhist practitioners experienced trying to integrate the Dharma with the *kami*-centered parameters of courtly life and ritual.

As we will see, the six-poem sequence will end with the same

---

398. Kamens, *The Buddhist Poetry of the Great Kamo Priestess*, 16–23.

emotion of sadness with which it began. In between are a group of four poems that address the Dharma and its teachings in different ways. First is a poem by Akinaka that resolves separation through the long and arduous journey of the practitioner. Second are two poems—one anonymous and the other by Tadamichi—that emphasize the lack of separation between practitioners and enlightenment, that is, that it can be attained in this very body (*sokushin jōbutsu*). Third is a poem by Akisuke that promises to share the delight of enlightenment (discovered in this very body) with others.

In Akinaka's poem following Senshi's, the speaker warns about the dangers caused by separation from the Dharma. The narrative, as the *kotobagaki* indicates, is that of the prodigal son in the "Belief and Understanding" chapter (4, *Shingebon*) of the Lotus Sutra. The speaker's wandering (away from his father and the Buddhadharma) prevented him from penetrating to the truth of impermanence. Only "when half a hundred years / of wandering were spent," after he returned home, that he says, "*I understood*" (*omoishiraruru*) the impermanence of the body.

The following anonymous poem is a meditative-lyric hybrid that continues the theme of the body's impermanence found in the *ku* "this flesh / of dew" (*tsuyu no mi*). By placing this poem right after Akinaka's, the compiler has created another instance in which two poems speak to one another: this speaker contributes to the conversation of the sequence the consoling message that awareness and recognition does not have to take fifty years. The poem's *kotobagaki* points to the Buddhist concept (and source of the poem's meditative argument) that best embodied this belief: *sokushin jōbutsu*, Buddhahood in this very body. The speaker "understood" or awoke to (*shiru bekarikeru*) the potential for instantaneous Buddhahood "after morning practice" (*tsutomete nochi*)—a kind of *satori*, though it was connection with practice that made the difference.

That one can awaken to impermanence/Buddhahood "in this very body" is also the focus of the poem by Fujiwara no Tadamichi. Composed when the poet "held a ceremony [a lecture, perhaps] for the Buddha's relics" (Shari-kō), the poem again stresses how intimately available the Dharma already is. Senshi's poem expressed the pain of being separated from Dharmic guidance, but each poem since brought us closer to bridging the painful gap. In Tadamichi's poem the means and locus of practice are within one's own "heart" (*kokoro*); no one needs to "look / some other place / for the Buddha way." Like the two poems preceding and the one following, Tadamichi's message is not cast in strongly emotional terms, but in a calmly measured meditative mode: the implication perhaps being that intimacy with the Dharma releases one from the confusion of passion.

The penultimate poem by Akisuke, the *Shikashū*'s compiler, contains a narrative element that represents a variation on the theme of enlightenment that has characterized the sequence to this point. Previously, the focus was on the means by which one might attain enlightenment—through long and arduous practice and through the realization of enlightenment within oneself. In Akisuke's poem, the heart is the source from which enlightenment casts its guiding rays *outward*, while a strong component of the desire for enlightenment is to be of such assistance to others: "the moon / of my heart / to shine / for anyone / who wanders / lost in the dark." This message recalls Izumi Shikibu's *kuraki yori / kuraki michi ni* poem in the *Shūishū*, in part because it is based upon the same chapter of the Lotus Sutra. But Akisuke's poem enacts the reverse narrative to Izumi's: while she reached in near-desperation beyond herself to the moon (as symbol of both her teacher, Shōkū Shōnin, and the Buddha), in Akisuke's poem the speaker's own enlightenment will emanate, according to the Mahāyāna ideal of the bodhisattva, to guide all those who suffer "in the dark." In the poetic sense that courtly *waka* do allude to and enter into conversation with earlier *waka* with related themes, images or language, Akisuke's bodhisattva heart is the moon toward which Izumi directed her imploration.

The *kotobagaki* of Tōren's poem, last in the sequence, again emphasizes the eternally available nature of the Dharma. But the *waka* itself expresses the fear that although connection is possible, separation is also possible, "if floating clouds / deprive the sky of / the dawn moon." Coming full circle back to the tears of Senshi's poem,

Tōren emphasizes that when clouds of samsāra block the moon of enlightenment, grief (*uki*)—"of the world: / of the people: / of the heart"—is the inevitable result. Thus the sequence as a whole alternates consolation with warning, the implication being that effort, practice, and other-directed altruism are urgently required on the practitioner's part, to overcome the danger of separation from the Dharma.

CONCLUSION

The Buddhist *waka* in the *Kin'yōshū* and the *Shikashū* set the tone for the penetrating religiosity of the *shakkyō-ka* sequence in the *Senzaishū*. While there are examples in these two anthologies, as there were in the *Goshūishū*, of poems that express the immediateness of the enlightenment experience, there is no corresponding arrangement of poems in the *Kin'yōshū* that represents the path to enlightenment. In fact, there is no discernible arrangement of poems at all beyond organizing them according to religious occasion, Buddhist text, Pure Land teachings, and interpersonal relationships among the poets. This lack of narrative program changes in the Buddhist *waka* sequence in the *Shikashū*, where we see a shortened version of the Buddhist path (*michi*) that starts with the sadness experienced when one is isolated from the Buddhist teachings to the joy that comes with the realization of enlightenment in one's own body (*sokushin jōbutsu*), to the enhancement of that joy when one realizes such an experience can be shared with others. At the end of the sequence, we come full circle and return to sadness that isolation brings "if floating clouds / deprive the sky of / the dawn moon."

The "Shakkyō-ka" book in the *Senzaishū* was not only the product of the Buddhist *waka* sequences in the *Kin'yōshū* and the *Shikashū*, but also the culmination of numerous other kinds of religio-literary texts and events that occurred during the twelfth century. As we proceed I will examine some of those texts and events, as well as to note the influence certain poet-priests may have had upon Fujiwara no Shunzei, the compiler of the *Senzaishū*. ✿

6 THE "SHAKKYŌ-KA" BOOK IN THE *SENZAISHŪ*—THE CREATION OF A LITERARY *MĀRGA*

PART ONE: CONTEXT

INTRODUCTION

This study has thus far traced the evolution of Japanese Buddhist poetry from its inception as Buddhist *kanshi* (sometimes called *shakkyō-shi*), Chinese poems on the teachings of the Buddha, to its transformation into Buddhist *waka*, later called *shakkyō-ka*, starting with the fourth imperial poetry anthology (*Goshūishū*, 1086). Buddhism became an increasingly acceptable topic for *waka* during the twelfth century. Such topics were included in a wider variety of poetry events and compilations (private anthologies, personal anthologies, fixed-number sequences, and poetry competitions), and increasingly (after a hiatus during the *Kin'yōshū* and *Shikashū*) were classified as *shakkyō-ka*. By the end of the twelfth century, we also see the formal acceptance of Buddhist *waka* into the imperial poetry project with the creation of a separate and independent book comprised of fifty-four *shakkyō-ka* in the seventh imperial collection called the *Senzaishū* (1188).[399]

---

399. The principal text consulted for this and the next chapter was Katano and Matsuno, *Senzaiwakashū*, SNKBT vol. 10, 365–380. I also referred to Ishihara, *Shakkyō-ka no kenkyū*, 189–321, but used the numbering system of the SNKBT text.

As we have seen, by examining the Buddhist *waka* in the earlier imperial anthologies, the public repository for court *waka*, we make the discovery that it was not unusual for the compiler or compilers to arrange their poems in an expressive order. For example, the order and arrangement of the Buddhist *waka* in the *Shūishū* reflected a traditional conception of the Buddhist path divided into three parts: connection to the Buddhist teachings (*kechien*), putting those teachings into practice (*shugyō*), and then reaping the rewards (enlightenment) of one's practice (*nirvāna*). Other arrangements after the *Shūishū* have included grouping and arranging poems according to a particular sūtra, the order of a sūtra's chapters, or certain religious themes (hesitations about or the revelations that proceed from taking the tonsure, for example). We do not encounter a more sophisticated arrangement of poems until the "Shakkyō-ka" book in the *Senzaishū*, where Fujiwara no Shunzei (1114–1204) appears to have organized the poems to reflect religious typologies central to Tendai Buddhism.

One of the texts from which such a typology was drawn was the Chinese text *Mo-ho chih-kuan* (J: *Makashikan*), written in the sixth century by the greatest systematizer of T'ien-t'ai thought, Chih-i (538–597). Available to the Heian educated elite at the court, this text was regarded as one of the principle textual sources of support for the Lotus Sutra. As we have noted, the influence of the Lotus Sutra—the most important sūtra in continental Asia—was in no way diminished when it came to Japan. It was chanted (*tonau*), copied (*utsusu*), and held (*jikyō/kyō o motsu*), and was the source of Buddhist sermons, lectures, and ceremonies for the clerics of the monastic complexes. Due in large part to its emphasis on description rather than dogma, the Lotus Sutra was also accessible to writers of literature (who, in many cases, were themselves Buddhist priests). As we have described, composing *waka* on each of the twenty-eight (or thirty, including the opening and closing) chapters of the Lotus Sutra (*nijūhappon-kyō-ka*) became a common practice for the members of the court from at least the early eleventh century. It also became the springboard for other kinds of Buddhist poems based on a variety of religious experiences, knowledge of different religious texts, and reflections on both.

The Buddhist teachings became more personal with the advent of a widespread belief in the Latter Days of the Law (*mappō*), thought to have begun in 1052. The urgency of this belief generated a strong desire for a faster track than traditional meditation to salvation. One form of practice available to everyone was the chanting of the *nenbutsu* (*Namu Amida Butsu*), advocated by the increasingly important Pure Land teachings as a guarantee for rebirth in Paradise (*Gokuraku*). No longer was Buddhism something monks practiced only in the temples: in the face of increasingly threatening social predicaments, an individual devotee could chant this simple mantra.

At the same time, culture—territory governed and fostered by the court—was increasingly professionalized in the twelfth century, as the practitioners of various arts became masters, the holders of cultural tradition, with whom disciples studied. Court poets, for example, came to believe that the mysteries of the *Man'yōshū* and the *Kokinshū* could not really be understood unless an older, more accomplished poet led his students to their secrets. While the need for personal salvation increased and the art of composing *waka* became more professionalized, court poets also came to perceive the religious in poetic terms as poetry contests were held at Buddhist temples and fixed-number poetry sequences were offered to Shintō shrines. While the formal acceptance of this kind of *waka* into the *chokusenshū* tradition had to wait until the compilation of the *Senzaishū* in 1188, poets had already begun to use the term *shakkyō-ka* in the late eleventh and early twelfth centuries.

A parallel development was underway in the Buddhist temple complexes whereby a personal desire for salvation and a social desire for literary achievement intertwined. Some Buddhist monks came from aristocratic families, and therefore understood well the values of the court. When the monks sought patronage from the court, as they did increasingly during the mid-tenth to mid-eleventh century, they were drawn into participating in court culture. This also put members of the court into greater contact with the texts of Buddhism. They sought religious teachers for help in understanding sūtras and commentaries which, at first, must have seemed unapproachable. In this atmosphere of the Buddhist spiritualization of the court and the cultural aestheticization of the monastic institutions, it was not long until writing *waka* became imbued with the values of Buddhism and were written not only by secular poets but also by monks in Buddhist temples.

Fujiwara no Shunzei, the compiler of *Senzaishū*, grew up in this atmosphere of the interpenetration of the religious and literary, and came to believe that the writing of *waka* could be grounded in and deepened by the principles of Tendai Buddhism. Eventually, he viewed the act of composing *waka* as a path to Buddhist enlightenment, because he saw in poetry a capacity to engender meditative and contemplative expression. He recorded these ideas in prose in his Preface to the *Senzaishū,* and in his poetic treatise *Korai fūteishō* (Selections of Styles from the Old to the New) of 1197. Before that, however, he demonstrated the influence of Tendai ideology in the organizational structure of the poems in the "Shakkyō-ka" book in the *Senzaishū.* It is the purpose of this chapter to provide some context about the twelfth century before looking in more detail into Shunzei's life and the kinds of influences—personal, conceptual, and textual—that might have led him to express his Buddhist beliefs in the arrangement of these poems.

THE LATE TWELFTH CENTURY

During the thirty-plus years between the compilation of the *Shikashū* in 1151 and the *Senzaishū* in 1188, the Japanese court and the citizens of the capital Heian-kyō encountered political and religious unrest unlike anything they had ever experienced before. This was a period of conspiracies, military skirmishes (which later turned into Japan's first civil war), and violent temple rivalries. The ostensible head of the civil government, Go-Shirakawa (1127–1192), first as Emperor (1155–1158) and then as Retired Emperor (1158–1192), used diplomatic finesse and probably a fair amount of deceit to deal with the encroaching military families (first the Taira and later the Minamoto) and to juggle the increasing demands of the large monastic complexes on Mount Hiei (Enryaku-ji and Onjō-ji) and in Nara (Kōfuku-ji).

None of these events, however, seemed to have an obvious effect on the refined artistic activities of the aristocracy at court. In the field of *waka* poetry, in particular, attention to hundred-poem sequences (*hyakushuuta*), poetry competitions (*utaawase* and *jikaawase*), and poetry collections (both private—*shikashū*—and personal anthologies—*shisenshū*) continued unabated. In fact, it seems as if the instability of the culture at large only motivated poets to engage in even more poetry events.[400] The best poets of the era—Fujiwara no Kiyosuke (1104–1177) and Fujiwara no Shunzei (1114–1204)—wrote poetic treatises, judged poetry contests, and contributed poems to various poetry events without acknowledging (in their writings at least) the violent events around them. Shunzei's son Fujiwara no Teika (1162–1241), however, did mention the unrest of this era, only to insist that those affairs had nothing to do with him: "My ears are full of tales about the current uprisings and the campaigns to quell them, but I pay no attention to them. 'The chastisement of the red banner of the insurgents is no concern of mine.'"[401]

It would be foolish for us to take Teika at his word. Civil unrest, especially when it was violent, would have affected everyone in the capital. The Hōgen and Heiji Disturbances of 1156 and 1159—well before Teika was born in 1162—set the stage for further unrest to unfold twenty years later. The actual fighting in the Hōgen Disturbance of 1156, as the historian Takeuchi Rizō writes, may have been confined to the capital and lasted only a "few hours," but resulted in the exile of Emperor Sutoku, who had ordered the compilation of the sixth imperial poetry anthology, *Shikashū*. It also resulted in the horrifying acts of nephews executing uncles (Taira no Kiyomori and Taira no Tadamasa) and sons executing fathers

---

400. Kubota Jun provides a chart of the thirty-four documented *utaawase* held between 1166 and 1176, not including other kinds of poetry events. *Shinkokin kajin no kenkyū* (Tokyo: Tokyo Daigaku Shuppan Kai, 1978), 342–343.

401. Brower and Miner, *Japanese Court Poetry*, 237.

(Minamoto no Yoshitomo and Minamoto no Tameyoshi).[402] The Heiji Disturbance just three years after the Hōgen Disturbance must have had equally devastating effects. The Minamoto and Taira clans, which each fought on both sides of the previous conflict, were now mortal enemies who took their fighting into the imperial palace itself. The Minamoto warriors were driven from the capital at the end of the Heiji Disturbance, but those who survived retreated to the east where they consolidated their military power and secretly planned to avenge their previous defeat.

Go-Shirakawa's role as mediator between the Taira clan and the court continued throughout the 1160s and 1170s, until, with the Taira's imminent defeat, he switched his support to the Minamoto in 1183. However, it was not only in the realm of governmental politics that Go-Shirakawa played a major role. He also created suspicions among Tendai monks. Despite the prevailing power and predominance of the Enryaku-ji complex on Mount Hiei, Go-Shirakawa was, as Mikael Adolphson says, "more successful in creating a link with Onjō-ji than with its Tendai sibling."[403] In fact, he took Buddhist precepts with Onjō-ji (in 1169) before he did with Enryaku-ji (in 1176).[404] This angered the Enryaku-ji monks, who sought support from the Taira warriors in the capital, leading to more warfare on Mount Hiei in the late 1170s.

In spite of—perhaps because of—so many societal ruptures, Go-Shirakawa was also a patron of culture and religion. His first and foremost literary interest was a type of popular song called *imayō*. In 1179, he compiled a collection of *imayō* called *Ryōjin hishō*, which Yung-Hee Kim has analyzed in her study called *Songs to Make the*

402. Takeuchi, Rizō, "The Rise of the Warriors," in *The Cambridge History of Japan: Heian* (Cambridge: The Cambridge History of Japan, 1999), 690.

403. Adolphson, *The Gates of Power*, 138. Onjō-ji represented the *jimon* (temple-gate) branch of Tendai established by Enchin (814–891), while Enryaku-ji represented the *sanmon* (mountain gate) branch established by Ennin (794–864). Enchin and Ennin were both disciples of Saichō (767–822), the founder of the Tendai sect. Conflicts between the two branches had become increasingly violent from the time Onjō-ji declared its independence from Enryaku-ji in 993.

404. Ibid.

Dust Dance: The Ryōjin hishō *of Twelfth-Century Japan.* As Kim says, "Go-Shirakawa devoted himself to *imayō* with a fervor verging on fanaticism."[405] Unlike *waka,* the *imayō* genre was not an art of the aristocratic court, even though Go-Shirakawa invited its itinerant singers into his presence. We do not know the authors of the songs, but the people portrayed in them "cover a whole gamut of characters: learned, proselytizing priests; villagers and city dwellers ... ; courtesans ... ; pilgrim-seducing shamans; mountain ascetics; even fisherman on the shore,"[406] a fact that widens our view of Heian literary and performance culture substantially. But as Kim asserts, "Go-Shirakawa's patronage was not by any means limited to *imayō.*"[407] Other cultural events and practices to which Go-Shirakawa devoted himself were the *Senzaishū,* picture scrolls, and pilgrimages to Kumano.[408]

It is the *Senzaishū* that is of primary interest to us here, but Go-Shirakawa's religious pilgrimages also contribute to our understanding of this man. It is well known that, despite Go-Shirakawa's command to compile the seventh imperial poetry anthology, he had little interest in *waka.* His poetic passion, as noted above, lay elsewhere. Yet, Go-Shirakawa did commission Shunzei to compile the anthology in the second month of 1183 in order to reestablish, as Kim says, "his kingly position and its mandates."[409] Based on research by Taniyama Shigeru, Kim gives three reasons for this.

One reason was to "appease the soul of the late Emperor Sutoku," Go-Shirakawa's older brother. From the late 1170s, the Heian aristocracy began to believe that the resentment and anger Sutoku felt as a result of being exiled to Sanuki in 1156 after the Hōgen Disturbance, and his subsequent death there in 1164, resulted in an angry "soul" that was probably the cause many of the tragic events both natural and man-made in the capital.[410] The second reason was

---

405. Yung-Hee Kim, *Songs to Make the Dust Dance: The* Ryōjin hishō *of Twelfth-Century Japan* (Berkeley and Los Angeles: University of California Press, 1994), 18.
406. Ibid., xvi.
407. Ibid., 23.
408. Ibid., 23–26.
409. Ibid., 23.
410. Some of these events are recounted in Kamo no Chōmei's *Hōjōki* of 1212.

to "mitigate the Taira's growing aggressiveness." This reason fits well with the historical timeline, since the Taira were still wrecking havoc on the capital in the second month of 1183, when the anthology was commissioned, and were not expelled until the seventh month of the same year. The third reason for compiling the *Senzaishū* was "to give the aristocrats a much-needed moral uplift."[411] This may have been true, but it presumes that Go-Shirakawa was the kind of sovereign who wanted to bring such support to the aristocracy. Some people, including his father, Emperor Toba (1103–1156), Fujiwara no Michinori (1106–1159), Go-Shirakawa's retainer, and Kujō no Kanezane (1149–1207), the Minister of the Right felt he was "unfit for the emperorship owing to his indulgence in frivolous merrymaking" (Toba), and a "dull-witted man who was neither aware of the traitors around him nor heedful of truthful counsel" (Michinori and Kanezane).[412]

An aspect of Go-Shirakawa's involvement with *imayō* that is relevant to this chapter can also be found in, firstly, a book of *imayō* in the *Ryōjin hishō* called *hōmon no uta*, songs on the Dharma Gate, and secondly in the *Kudenshū* (Collection of Oral Transmissions), which is the final book of the *Ryōjin hishō*. The *hōmon no uta* are the most numerous of the songs extant to us now, based, like some *shakkyō-ka*, upon Buddhist scriptures such as the Lotus Sutra and religious concepts such as *nirvāna*, Paradise (*Gokuraku*), and the repentance of sins (*senbō*). The *Kudenshū*, on the other hand, was a memoir of Go-Shirakawa's involvement with the singers and the songs themselves. The latter work also expresses Go-Shirakawa's belief in the religious efficacy of secular writings, known as *kyōgen kigo*, an idea introduced into Heian court society at the time of the Kangaku-e meetings in the mid-tenth century and therefore not surprising to find in the *Kudenshū* in the

---

411. Ibid., 25–27.

412. Ibid., 1. George Sansom agrees, saying, "Go-Shirakawa was not a wise ruler. His was a rule of shifts and expedients and indeed, despite his enthusiasm for religious exercises and his favours to the Church, he was not a man of high principle." *A History of Japan to 1334* (Stanford: Stanford University Press, 1958), 331.

late twelfth century.[413] The relevant passage in Kim's translation reads:

> *Homon no uta* is no different from the words in the sutra. Each of the eight scrolls of the Lotus Sutra radiates light, and each character in the twenty-eight chapters is a golden Buddha. Why shouldn't secular words, too, transform themselves into praises of the Buddha and become a wheel for propagating the Dharma?[414]

Konishi Jin'ichi, one of the leading experts on the *Ryōjin hishō,* also cites part of this passage. However, he adds that what gave momentum to this belief was a "growing tendency in the twelfth century, to codify knowledge transmitted from the past." Furthermore, he says that it was the single-mindedness of the poet to codify knowledge and pursue his art—even if it was not a courtly art—which supported the idea that such efforts could produce effects similar to the single-minded meditation (*shikan*) that led to enlightenment.[415] The *Hosshin wakashū* of the early eleventh century is the first *waka* compilation to explicitly demonstrate this belief in the salvific value of secular verse, but we see examples of it in the late twelfth century as well in Jakuzen's *Hōmon hyakushu* (after 1156), a hundred-poem sequence on the "Gate of the Dharma" (the Buddhist teachings).[416] We cannot say with any degree of certainty that Go-Shirakawa's belief in the religious efficacy of secular verse led to him to suggest that a book of *shakkyō-ka* be

---

413. The *Ryōjin hishō* is thought to have originally been composed of twenty books (much like most of the imperial poetry anthologies); the *Kudenshū* is the name given to the second group of ten books. Kim, *Songs to Make the Dust Dance,* xiv.

414. Ibid., 42.

415. Konishi, *A History of Japanese Literature,* vol. 3, 154.

416. For the *Hōmon hyakushu,* see the following: Yamamoto Akihiro, *Jakuzen Hōmon hyakushu zen'yaku* (Kyoto: Kazama Shobō, 2010); Kawakami Shin'ichirō, "'Hōmon hyakushu' no kōsatsu," in *Ōchō no uta to monogatari* (Tokyo: Ōfūsha, 1980), 26–55; Kunieda Toshihisa, "Hōmon hyakushu shichū: Shakkyō-ka kenkyū no kisoteki sagyō (2)," *Shinwa kokubun* 8 (Feb. 1974): 75–88; Kunieda Toshihisa, "Hōmon hyakushu shichū (2)," *Shinwa kokubun* 9 (Feb. 1975): 36–45; and Ishihara Kiyoshi, "Hōmon hyakushu kō," *Ryūkokudaigaku ronshū* 419 (October 1981): 23–46.

included in the *Senzaishū,* but we can be certain that he would not have objected if Shunzei alone were responsible for its inclusion.

SHUNZEI[417]

The compilation of the *Senzaishū* was completed in 1188, three years after the defeat of the Taira and the end of the Heian period. The fact that the *Senzaishū* was being compiled just as the twelfth century and the Heian period came to a close provides a convenient demarcation line for the final two chapters of this study. But that is not the only factor, or even the most relevant one, suggesting a logical end-point. That point is indicated by the first instance in which an imperial anthology included a separate and independent book called "Shakkyō-ka." The *Senzaishū* is this moment, which not only marks the first time that Buddhism was integrated so assertively into the structure of an imperial poetry anthology, but also created a precedent whereby such books were included in each of the fourteen imperial anthologies to follow.

In addition to imperial poetry anthologies, another twelfth-century literary venue that provided an opportunity for composing and compiling *waka* on Buddhist topics was the *Kyūan hyakushu.* In 1150, when Shunzei was asked by Retired Emperor Sutoku to compile and categorize the one-hundred-poem sequences submitted by fourteen poets for the *Kyūan hyakushu,* Shunzei created a *shakkyō-ka* category (albeit within a book of "Miscellaneous *Waka*") for Buddhist poems.[418] This was the first such category for *shakkyō-ka*

---

417. The compiler of the *Senzaishū* was known by at least three given names during his life: he was given the name Akihiro when he was adopted after his father died; he was called Shunzei (in a Chinese reading of the characters of his name; Toshinari in the Japanese reading) during his middle years, and finally known as Shakua after he took the tonsure in 1176 until his death in 1204. For the sake of clarity, I will call him Shunzei consistently.

418. Matsuno Yōichi, *Fujiwara Shunzei no kenkyū* (Tokyo: Kasama Shoin, 1973), 167. All of the fourteen hundred submitted poems are included in Taniyama Shigeru, *Fujiwara Shunzei: Hito to sakuhin,* vol. 3 of *Taniyama Shigeru chosakushū* (Tokyo: Kadokawa Shoten, 1982), 160–251.

in any *hyakushu*, and Shunzei later drew upon it for the inclusion of three poems in the "Shakkyō-ka" book of the *Senzaishū*.

Also increasingly popular during the twelfth century were poetry competitions held at shrines and temples, at which often, though not always, *waka* on Buddhist topics were composed. Of the thirty-four *utaawase* held between 1166 and 1176, the year Shunzei took the tonsure, eight were held at Buddhist temples or Shinto shrines or were presided over by a Buddhist monk.[419] The fact that these poetry competitions were held at religious centers does not necessarily mean that poets regarded them as having more religious power than other poetry competitions, but it does indicate the increasing intimacy of religious and literary projects.

Finally, in the decades preceding the compilation of the seventh imperial poetry anthology, there were additional nonimperial poetry compilations that included a *shakkyō-ka* category. Shunzei's awareness of these must have provided some justification for his own inclusion of a "Shakkyō-ka" book, because they also became sources from which he selected poems for inclusion in the *Senzaishū*. Examples of such sources include the *Shokushikashū* (1165), the *Jishō ninen Kanezane no ie no hyakushu* (1178, also called *Udaijin no ie no hyakushu*), and the *Tsukimōdeshū* (1182).

The personal anthology *Shokushikashū* was compiled by Fujiwara no Kiyosuke as a contender for the seventh imperial poetry anthology, but the early demise of its supporter Emperor Nijō in the same year as its completion eliminated any chances that the anthology would attain imperial status. Book ten contained thirty-four *shakkyō-ka*. The second source, *Jishō ninen Kanezane no ie no hyakushu*, compiled by Kujō no Kanezane (1129–1207) contained five poems each on twenty topics, including *shakkyō-ka*. The third source from which Shunzei culled

---

419. The names of the eight *utaawase* are: *Kanchi hōgan utaawase* (facilitated by Priest Kanchi in 1169), *Sumiyoshi-sha no utaawase* (facilitated by Atsuyori—also known as Priest Dōin—in 1170), *Zengen hōin-bō utaawase* (facilitated by Priest Zengen in 1171), *Hōrin-ji utaawase* (facilitator unknown, in 1172), *Hirota-sha utaawase* (facilitated by Dōin in 1172), *Miidera no Shiragi no yashiro no utaawase* (facilitator unknown, in 1173), *Sanka utaawase* (facilitator unknown, in 1176), and *Inari-sha utaawase* (facilitator unknown, in 1176?). Kubota, *Shinkokin kajin no kenkyū*, 342–343.

shakkyō-ka was the *Tsukimōdeshū,* compiled by Kamo no Shigeyasu (1119–1191). It contained poems written on the occasion of monthly religious pilgrimages to the Kamo Wakeikazuchi Shrine. Included in this anthology was a book called "Shakkyō-ka" that contained sixty-five *waka.* The total number of *shakkyō-ka* that Shunzei culled from the *Kyūan hyakushu,* the *Shokushikashū,* the *Jishō ninen Kanezane no ie no hyakushu,* and the *Tsukimōdeshū* for inclusion in the *Senzaishū* "Shakkyō-ka" book accounted for almost one-third of the fifty-four poems.

Though the question of why Shunzei decided to include an independent book of *shakkyō-ka* in the *Senzaishū* is an intriguing one, we are lacking any written explanation from the compiler himself. Those contemporary Japanese scholars who have attempted an answer rely on various kinds of evidence like the personal anthologies compiled before the *Senzaishū* and the religious inclinations of Shunzei that can be discerned from his poetic treatise, *Korai fūteishō.* Taniyama Shigeru and Tsuda Sōkichi, for example, have tended to downplay the importance of this new independent book on the grounds that the composition of *shakkyō-ka* had a long and venerable history dating back to the late tenth century (presumably a reference to the *Shūishō*). During the second half of the twelfth century, they say, the cumulative effects of this history can easily be seen in the proliferation of *shakkyō-ka* sequences and independent "Shakkyō-ka" books in various personal and private anthologies as well as in the *hyakushu.*[420]

Scholars like Manaka Fujiko have made the claim that Shunzei's motivation for instituting this new book in the *Senzaishū* derived from his personal interest in and devotion to the Tendai doctrines espoused in the *Makashikan.* According to this line of reasoning, Shunzei is said to have utilized an otherwise intolerable social situation—the Genpei Wars—as an opportunity to consolidate his personal devotion to the meditative practices of calming (*shi*) and insight (*kan*)—known as śamatha-vipaśyanā in Sanskrit—with his

---

420. Taniyama Shigeru, *Senzaiwakashū to sono shūhen,* vol. 5 of *Taniyama Shigeru choshakushū* (Tokyo: Kadokawa Shoten, 1982), 206.

worldly devotion to the literary practice of composing *waka.*[421]

Takatsuka Zonkei does not contradict Manaka's thesis, but he assigns equal responsibility to both Go-Shirakawa and Shunzei.[422] He reasons that Go-Shirakawa's support (if, in fact, there was any) must have been derived from his devotion to Buddhism, which, Takatsuka says, is clearly confirmed by numerous anecdotes in Kujō no Kanezane's Chinese diary, *Gyokuyō.*[423] Moreover, we find further evidence of Go-Shirakawa's devotion, he says, in documents such as the *Kōya-san monjo* where, in entries for the 22nd day of the 4th month of the second year of Bunji (1186), it says Go-Shirakawa commanded the monks of Kongōbu-ji (on Mount Kōya) to pray not only for the repose of the souls of the Heike warriors recently killed in battle but also for the souls of every warrior killed since the Hōgen Disturbance of 1156.[424] Takatsuka's reasoning that Go-Shirakawa's general devotion to Buddhism must have led him to provide direct support for the "Shakkyō-ka" book is circumstantial, but his assertions about Shunzei's role in determining the creation of a new book is more firmly based on documents, such as the Preface to the *Senzaishū* and the poetic treatise *Korai fūteishō,* which Shunzei himself wrote. In short, like Manaka Fujiko, Takatsuka also believes it was influence from the Tendai teachings in general and from the *Makashikan* specifically that resulted in Shunzei's decision to include Buddhist poems in an independent book.[425]

Shunzei would elucidate his belief in the religious efficacy of poetry in the *Korai fūteishō,* finished eleven years after he compiled the *Senzaishū,* while Go-Shirakawa's belief in the religious efficacy of *imayō* had already been expressed, as we saw, in his poetic memoir *Kudenshū* in 1179. Before we examine Shunzei's Preface and poetic treatise, it will be helpful to look into other aspects of his life that may have played

---

421. Manaka, *Kobungaku ni sesshu sareta Bukkyō,* 225.

422. Takatsuka Zonkei, "*Senzaiwakashū* 'Shakkyō' bu ni tsuite," *Bukkyō bunka kenkyūjo kiyō* 8 (June 1969): 89–93.

423. Ibid., 89–90.

424. Ibid., 90.

425. Ibid., 91–92.

a role in his decision-making process while he was compiling the *Senzaishū*. The following abbreviated biography places Shunzei at the nexus of the religio-literary ethos of the twelfth century.

In 1140 or 1141, when Shunzei was twenty-seven or twenty-eight, he composed a one-hundred-poem sequence called the *Jukkai hyakushu*. According to Shunzei's private anthology *Chōshū eisō*, where all of these poems were compiled, this sequence was based on the same topics found in the *Horikawa hyakushu* when it was arranged in 1105 or 1106.[426] While there is nothing specifically religious about *jukkai-ka* (*waka* of reminiscence), they often included expressions of sadness about transience (*mujō*), lamenting one's public circumstances, and expressing regrets about the lost chances of life. In other words, *jukkai waka* were often the repository of feelings that were influenced by Buddhism (as well as native concepts), but were not poetic expressions *about* Buddhism or some particular aspect of Buddhism. After the Heian period, *jukkai-ka* became poetic complaints, but during Shunzei's life, they were still written as reflections on various topics.

According to Kubota, what is characteristic of Shunzei's *hyakushu* is the depth of despair (*zetsubōkan*) he expressed—the reasons for which were many.[427] Shunzei lost his father, Toshitada (1071 or 1073–1123), when he was either eight or ten, at which point he was adopted by Hamuro no Akiyori (d. 1148) and renamed Akihiro.[428] Shunzei's adopted grandfather, Akitaka, died in 1129 when Shunzei was sixteen, and his birth mother died when he was twenty-six in 1139. It is not

---

426. Kawamura Teruo and Kubota Jun, *Chōshū eisō Toshitada-shū* (Tokyo: Meiji Shoin, 1998), 21–38. The *kotobagaki* before the entire set reads, "*Horikawa-in no ontoki hyakushudai o jukkai ni yosete yomikeru uta, Hōen roku nana nen no koro no koto ni ya*" (Turning my attention to *jukkai*, these poems were composed [by me] most likely in Hōen 6 or 7 [1140 or 1141] on the one hundred topics [used] at the time of Retired Emperor Horikawa [1105].)

427. Kubota, *Shinkokin kajin no kenkyū*, 249–250. The following information is derived from both *Shinkokin kajin no kenkyū* and Kamijō Shōji, "Fujiwara no Shunzei," *Ōchō no waka*, vol. 5 of *Waka bungaku kōza* (Tokyo: Benseisha, 1993), 316–338.

428. Akiyori was a deeply devoted Buddhist, so Kubota suspects that Shunzei's first contacts with Buddhism came through him. Kubota, *Shinkokin kajin no kenkyū*, 247–257.

difficult to imagine Shunzei's sense of loneliness and isolation at this time.

By the time Shunzei was twenty-nine, he had received posts in the government, but his rank had not yet risen beyond junior fifth lower (*jūgoi no ge*), a rank that had its privileges, but as McCullough and McCullough write, left its holder with "less reason for optimism" that he would become *tenjōbito* who was allowed entrance into the Courtiers' Hall.[429] Shunzei's greatest fear seems to have been that the Mikohidari family would die out with his generation.[430] Many scholars, including Kubota, Kamijō, and Watanabe Yasuaki, are of opinion that this *Hyakushu* was a major turning point for Shunzei as a poet.[431] Kubota takes a leap into the poet's psychology to speculate that the sequence aroused Shunzei's self-confidence (*jishin*) and self-awareness (*jikaku*) about the art of *waka* composition, feelings Kubota believes he lacked before this time. But Kubota's praise for the *Jukkai hyakushu* does not end there: he expresses the opinion that the collection had "monumental" meaning for Shunzei, the Mikohidari family, and medieval *waka*.[432] There is strong evidence for this argument, since twenty-eight poems were chosen from this collection for later imperial anthologies, starting with the *Senzaishū* and ending with the *Fūgashū*.[433]

What stands out from reading the *Jukkai hyakushu* is Shunzei's willingness to take up his internal suffering as a topic, and with a more polished poetic technique than he had exhibited before he wrote and compiled it. Some scholars have expressed the opinion that, even at this early age, he wished to leave the secular world. As proof, they point to one poem—his representative poem in the *Hyakunin isshu*—that seems to suggest such a desire:

---

429. McCullough and McCullough, *A Tale of Flowering Fortunes,* vol. 2, 791.

430. Ibid., 249

431. Watanabe goes so far as to say that all of the *waka* produced by Shunzei up until this time were merely copies (*shūsaku*) of poems by others. Watanabe Yasuaki, *Chūsei waka no seisei* (Tokyo: Wakakusa Shobō, 1999), 34–35.

432. Kubota, *Shinkokin kajin no kenkyū,* 254.

433. Watanabe, *Chūsei waka no seisei,* 34; Kamijō, "Fujiwara no Shunzei," 318.

[*Senzaishū* 1151; *Hyakunin Isshu* 83]

世の中よ道こそなけれ思ひ入山の奥にも鹿ぞ鳴なる

yo no naka yo / michi koso nakere / omoiiru / yama no oku ni mo / shika zo nakunaru

ON THE TOPIC "DEER," from a hundred poems of recollection and regret

> no path out of this world:
>
> even in these deep mountains
>
> where I decide—
>   I hear
> the deer cry

> — Fujiwara no Shunzei

Watanabe and Yamamoto Hajime interpret this poem quite differently from one another. Yamamoto writes, "Shunzei's consciousness about his misfortunes in the world is part and parcel of his attachment to it. This means that his Buddhist faith is only expressed half-heartedly in terms of Buddhist morality (*Bukkyō rinri*); in the end the problem of whether Shunzei wants to leave the world is expressed rhetorically merely to emphasize his feelings of misfortune."[434] While this could be true, at the very least Shunzei does seem to have reflected on the uncertainty of public life and the inescapable transience of the material world. This realization would be expressed in more concrete terms within a year or two, when he had an opportunity to compose his first *shakkyō-ka,* a *waka* on the Lotus Sutra.

---

434. Ibid., 40.

Kubota says this opportunity came about when Shunzei (and also Saigyō) took part in a Kechien kuyō, a Service for Actuating a Connection to the Teachings, in 1142, when Taikenmon-in, empress to Emperor Toba and the mother of both Sutoku and Go-Shirakawa, took the tonsure (*rakushoku*).[435] Part of this service was to compose *waka* on the twenty-eight chapters of the Lotus Sutra (*Hokke-kyō nijūhappon-ka* or *nijūhappon-kyō-ka*), a practice common enough by this time. If, as Yamada Shōzen claims, the Lotus Sutra poems by Shunzei and Saigyō were not composed for the same event, then Kubota's discussion about the inferiority of Shunzei's poems to Saigyō's is probably irrelevant. However, Yamada's claim does not invalidate Kubota's point about Shunzei's Lotus Sutra poems in general, which is that even though these poems might reveal some of his personal feelings, ultimately they are more conceptual than based upon actual life experience.[436] Given the fact that Shunzei was only twenty-nine at the time and his exposure to writing poems on the Lotus Sutra may have been scant, Kubota says, perhaps we should not be surprised that there is a certain emotional immaturity about the poems.[437]

---

435. Kubota surmises that the twenty-eight poems Shunzei produced as a result of the Kechien kuyō for Taikenmon-in on the twenty-sixth day of the second month of 1142 may be the same event referred to in the entry for the fifteenth day of the third month of 1142 in Fujiwara no Yorinaga's *kanbun* diary *Taiki,* at which Saigyō requested support (*kanjin*) from Yorinaga for an Ippon-kyō (lit., "one chapter sūtra," but probably referring to an Ippon-kyō kuyō, a memorial service at which one poem for each chapter of the Lotus Sutra is composed and then presented). (These sequences are found in Shunzei's *Chōshū eisō* [poems 403–434, in Kubota and Kawamura, *Chōshū eisō Tadanori-shū,* 91–99] and in Saigyō's *Kikigakishū* [poems 1–34] and his *Sankashū* [poems 877–894 and 1536–1538], in Nishizawa Yoshihito, Utsugi Genkō, Kubota Jun, *Sankashū Kikigakishū Zanshū,* vol. 21 of *Waka bungaku taikei* [Tokyo: Meiji Shoin, 2003], Sks: 165–168 and 292–293, Kgs: 299–308). A similar group, but with only ten Lotus Sutra poems, are found in Yorinaga's private anthology *Hindō-shū* (SKT, vol. 3, *Shikashū,* poems 830–840, 861). Yamada Shōzen disputes that these two sequences were composed for the same event by pointing to internal poetic evidence and claiming that Saigyō, who was only twenty-five in 1142, did not yet have the skill to compose poems that are as theologically complex as those found in his *Sankashū* and *Kikigakishū*. Yamada Shōzen claims they were composed much later. *Saigyō no waka to Bukkyō* (Tokyo: Meiji Shoin, 1987), 120–121.

436. Kubota, *Shinkokin kajin no kenkyū,* 272–273 and 278.

437. This contradicts Kubota's opinion of Shunzei's emotional development as revealed in his *Jukkai hyakushu.* Yamada Shōzen agrees with Kubota's evaluation of Shun-

As we have said, approximately eight years after the Kechien kuyō for Taikenmon-in, Shunzei was commanded by Retired Emperor Sutoku to arrange and then categorize the *waka* that had been submitted for the *Kyūan hyakushu*. Since there were fourteen participants, this meant that Shunzei had to read and then organize 1,400 poems. One of the subcategories Shunzei chose for the *Hyakushu* was titled "Shakkyō-ka," the first usage of this term by him of which we are aware. Shunzei used only three *shakkyō-ka* from the *Hyakushu* for the "Shakkyō-ka" book in the *Senzaishū*. This fact does not, however, reflect its overall importance for the imperial anthology: in total, Shunzei selected 126 poems from the *Hyakushu* for inclusion in the *Senzaishū*.

Sometime before Bifukumon-in (Empress to Emperor Toba and mother to Emperor Konoe) died in 1160, she requested *waka* to accompany pictures of the various hours of the day as depicted in what is called *Gokuraku rokuji*, the six times of the day for performing services to Amida in the Pure Land (*Jōdo* or *Gokuraku*).[438] These poems—*shakkyō-ka*, actually—were eventually collected into a volume known as the *Gokuraku rokuji sanka*.[439] The poems were based upon sections of hymns (*wasan*) probably written by Genshin (942–1017). Though none of these poems was included in the *Senzaishū*, two were chosen for the "Shakkyō-ka" book in the *Shinkokinshū* (poems 1967 and 1968).[440]

Another religio-literary event in which Shunzei participated was the Higan nenbutsu-e held at Shirakawa's Oshikoji-dono. We do not know when this particular event occurred or who facilitated it, but it

---

zei's Lotus Sutra poems (that is, that they are weak). He also compares Shunzei's poems to Jien's *Hokke-kyō nijūhappon-ka*. See "Shakkyō-ka no seiritsu to tenkai," 74.

438. Though we do not know the exact date for the request, most probably it came at the time she took the tonsure in 1156. The pictures themselves are no longer extant. *Nihon jinmei jiten*, 1038.

439. The *Rokuji san* poems fall within a *shakkyō-ka* section in the third book of the *Chōshū eisō*. (There are separate sections of *shakkyō-ka* within the first and third books.) See Kawamura and Kubota, *Chōshū eisō Toshitada-shū*, 90 and 99.

440. Tanaka Yutaka and Akase Shingō, *Shinkokinwakashū*, SNKBT vol. 11 (Tokyo: Iwanami Shoten, 1992), 573.

is clear from the description of the service in the *kotobagaki* to poem 205 in the *Chōshū eisō* that Bifukumon-in was already dead (*ko join Bifukumon-in*), meaning it had to have taken place after 1160.[441] As the name of the ceremony suggests, it was held on the vernal and autumnal equinoxes,[442] and the act of intoning the *nenbutsu* for the seven days of the ceremony was an essential part of the service. Of the poems Shunzei composed, only ten are extant. Poem 205 from the *Chōshū eisō*, for example, was composed on the topic of "mist during travel" and contains within it one of the most commonly used words in literature during the Heian period: *mono[no]aware* (the pathos [felt on a certain occasion]). What inspired the particular pathos of this poem was the hazy mist that may hover over the landscape while one makes a journey alone. Scholars have long thought that the expression of *mono no aware* is related to the Japanese sensitivity about impermanence (derived perhaps from Buddhism). For our purposes, it is only necessary to note that these poems were composed at an event at which the religious and the literary interpenetrated.

Among the eight *utaawase* mentioned previously, held at or connected by name to a Shinto or Buddhist center, three were judged by Shunzei: *Sumiyoshi-sha* (or *Sumiyoshi no yashiro*) *no utaawase* of 1170, the *Hirota-sha* (or *Hirota no yashiro*) *no utaawase* of 1172, and the *Miidera no Shiragi no yashiro no utaawase* of 1173. None of the fifty participants in the *Sumiyoshi-sha no utaawase*, including Shunzei, were present at the shrine itself when the poems were composed or judged. However, because the *waka* from this contest were offered to the deity of *waka* at Sumiyoshi Shrine, it became known as the *Poetry Competition of the Sumiyoshi Shrine*.

Matsuno refers to the *waka* offered at the *Sumiyoshi-sha no utaawase*, as well as the *waka* offered to the deity of the Hirota Shrine at the *Hirota-sha no utaawase*, as *hōraku waka*.[443] The word *hōraku* ("Dharma pleasure") appears in the fourth chapter of the Vimalakīrti Sūtra: "You should devote yourselves to find joy in the pleasures of the

---

441. Ibid., 40.
442. Kubota, *Shinkokin kajin no kenkyū*, 305–310.
443. Matsuno, *Fujiwara Shunzei no kenkyū*, 417.

Dharma, and should take no pleasure in desires."[444] The "pleasure" of *hōraku waka*, then, is derived from *waka* written without desire (the subject of the second and third Noble Truths), as well as the pleasure the deity of *waka* will have receiving it.

Yamada Shōzen defines *hōraku waka* as *waka* offered to a Shinto shrine.[445] But this simple definition by itself does not elucidate the Buddhist implications of such an act.[446] The *kami* of Sumiyoshi was not only the *kami* of Japanese poetry (*waka*); this god was also a transformation, according to the ideology of *honji suijaku*, of the bodhisattva Kōki Tokuo, who was, in turn, one of the twenty-two manifestations of Kannon, the bodhisattva of compassion (S: Avalokiteśvara). The fusion of Buddhism and Shinto, a process described by the term *shinbutsu shūgō* (Shinto-Buddhist consolidation), had begun as early as the Nara period, and the concept of *honji suijaku*, whereby the native *kami* became the traces or manifestations (*suijaku*) of bodhisattvas (*honji*, or original ground), was just one aspect of this process. What stands out about the *Sumiyoshi-sha no utaawase* is the fact that the offering of *waka* was made by a Buddhist priest by the name of Dōin (secular name, Fujiwara no Atsuie, 1090– 1179) who was also the facilitator of the competition.

The implications of a Buddhist priest offering Japanese poems to the *kami* of *waka* are significant, according to Yamada. *Hōraku waka*, he says, promoted not only the fusion of bodhisattvas and *kami*, but also the fusion of Buddhism and *waka* whereby the composition of the latter eventually came to be regarded as a disciplinary path, or *michi*, of the former. That is, it was believed, as Princess Senshi had earlier asserted, that one could attain a similar level of Buddhist enlightenment through the art of *waka* composition. Later this idea was expressed in the phrase *waka soku darani* (*waka* are none other than Buddhist *darani*), an idea Shunzei explores in his poetic treatise

---

444. Thurman, *The Holy Teaching of Vimalakīrti*, 38.

445. Yamada Shōzen, "Mikkyō to waka bungaku," *Mikkyōgaku kenkyū* (March 1969), 151.

446. Yamada discusses the Buddhist implications in the aforementioned article. See previous footnote.

Korai fūteishō of 1197 and which becomes characteristic of medieval *waka* in general.

Some scholars, emphasizing the religious aspect of this *utaawase*, have said that, in fact, the Sumiyoshi *utaawase* marked another turning point in Shunzei's career as a poet. Clifton Royston, following Minegishi Yoshiaki, says, "... the Sumiyoshi contest, by virtue of its occasion, presages a deepening of ... religious and metaphysical significance ..."[447] Passing over Royston's use of the word "metaphysical" here which LaFleur criticized as "Platonic,"[448] it is helpful to focus instead upon a partial translation of the postscript to the *utaawase* that reads, "The Way that leads along Wakanoura, the Bay of Poetry, is as deep, and its aspects as difficult to plumb, as the thousand-fathomed sea; it is as far-reaching, and its limits unknowable, as the ocean waves that roll ten thousand leagues."[449] There is nothing specifically Buddhist about these words, but they do signify an awareness that *waka* could be more than just pretty poetry, a view Shunzei obviously shared.

At the *Hirota-sha no utaawase* held two years after the Sumiyoshi competition, a similar sequence of events occurred. The deity enshrined at the Hirota Shrine was also regarded during the Heian period as a deity of *waka*. Moreover, Dōin was again the facilitator of this competition, and he presented the poems to the deity after they were all submitted. The reason for another competition similar in theme and execution so close to the Sumiyoshi competition is recounted in Shunzei's *kotobagaki* to poem 471 in the *Chōshū eisō*. The poem Shunzei wrote clearly expresses his sentiment about *honji suijaku* ideology:

---

447. Clifton W. Royston, "The Poetics and Poetry Criticism of Fujiwara Shunzei (1114–1204)," Ph.D. dissertation, University of Michigan, 1974, 185.

448. LaFleur, *The Karma of Words*, 89.

449. Royston, 190.

いさぎよき光にまがふ塵なれやおまへの浜に積る白雪

isagiyoki / hikaru ni magau / chiri nare ya / omae no hama ni / tsumoru shirayuki

AFTER A DREAM ORACLE SAID THERE WAS ENVY AT HIROTA SHRINE BECAUSE A POETRY CONTEST HAD BEEN HELD AT ANOTHER SHRINE,

it was recommended that a similar contest be held there; this was among the three poems I composed and added to the others.

On the topic "the snow in front of the shrine."

> might the purest light
> have mixed with dust?—
>
> before You—the bay
> collects white snow[450]

— Fujiwara no Shunzei

In 1173, sixteen Buddhist monks from Onjō-ji on Mount Hiei took part in the *Miidera Shiragi-sha no utaawase* (the Shiragi Shrine is located on the Onjō-ji temple grounds), at which Shunzei was the judge. This event displayed the extent to which the Shintō and Buddhist spheres had become integrated and demonstrates that Tendai Buddhist priests engaged in the cultural practices of the court in much the same way that the members of the court engaged in the religious affairs of the monks. We gain insight into how this integration was represented in Shunzei's beliefs from an entry in Kujo no Kanezane's diary *Gyokuyō*:

> While near death, Shunzei was ordained into the priesthood. He had once been a devout worshipper

---

450. Translation by the author. Kubota and Kawamura, *Chōshū eisō Toshitada-shū*, 107.

at the Kasuga Shrine, and then had turned more recently to the worship of the Hie Shrine. For more than ten years now, he had not worshipped at Kasuga although he had repeatedly made religious retreats at Hie, I was told. We have entered the Latter Days of the Law, yet how powerful the gods are still, and how much we should stand in awe of them![451]

Soon after Shunzei judged this poetry competition his health began to decline, and in 1176 at the age of 63, he took the tonsure. Shunzei's illness in 1176 could easily have led to his death, but he survived and engaged in literary activities for another twenty-eight years, dying in 1204 at the age of ninety-one.

After Kiyosuke died in 1177, Shunzei became in effect the doyen of the *waka* sphere. The Rokujō poets who had prevailed during the decades following the compilation of the *Shikashū* did not disappear; they continued to hold poetry parties and competitions in the capital, but Kiyosuke was the last poet from their family of great renown.[452] As Kanezane (and Go-Shirakawa to a much lesser extent) turned to Shunzei for poetic guidance, cultural power began to shift away from the Rokujō clan to the Mikohidari family.

Many of Shunzei's closest relationships during his life were with influential poet-priests of the day. Though it is impossible to determine how exactly Shunzei's thinking changed as a result of these relationships, it is not too much to say that there must have been a cumulative effect of their religious views upon his own.

One of Shunzei's earliest influences was likely his adopted father, Akiyori, a devotee of Buddhism. More important than Akiyori's influence, though, was Shunzei's friendship with the poet-priest Saigyō, which lasted until Saigyō's death in 1190. As we have speculated, if Saigyō accompanied Shunzei when he composed *Hokke-kyō nijūhappon-ka* for Taikenmon-in in 1142, this could have

---

451. Royston, "The Poetics and Poetry Criticism of Fujiwara Shunzei (1114–1204)," 230.

452. Kamo no Chōmei and his son, Shun'e, had participated in many events of the Rokujō school, but they were not members of the Rokujō clan.

been one of the earliest events at which Shunzei and Saigyō shared poetic and religious aspirations. Later in the 1180s, when Saigyō heard that Shunzei was compiling the *Senzaishū*, he sent numerous poems for consideration. (Shunzei included eighteen, one of which appears in the "Shakkyō-ka" book.) At Saigyō's request, Shunzei also judged his *Mimosusogawa jikaawase* (personal poetry competition at Mimosusogawa) of 1187, which suggests that Saigyō placed great trust in Shunzei's skill as a poet.

Mezaki Tokue argues that it is important to keep in mind that Saigyō's early devotions were to the practice of *yūzu nenbutsu*, a belief that intoning the *nenbutsu* not only saved the intoner, but everyone else as well.[453] If this is true, Saigyō's religious orientation at the time of the *Hokke-kyō nijūhappn-ka* (if, in fact, he participated) would have leaned toward belief in the Pure Land, rather than the teachings of the Shingon sect, for which he is much better known. (Not irrelevantly, Saigyō's name means "going west," the location of Paradise).

Saigyō is often depicted as the quintessential *suki no tonseisha* (a recluse devoted to aesthetic beauty), who wrote *waka* while engaging in religious pilgrimages. For decades, he traveled to various locations around the country, many of them religious centers like Kōya, Yoshino, and Ise, and resided in huts (*sōan*).[454] Because Shunzei was a man of the capital, on the other hand, there is some doubt about how much time the two could have spent with one another. Even when Shunzei took the tonsure, it does not seem that he made any Buddhist pilgrimages or spent extended periods in Buddhist temples. (However, it should be noted that there are years of Shunzei's life for which there is no account).[455] In the end, it appears that what Saigyō and Shunzei perhaps shared more than anything else was a mutual love of *waka*. The fact that they practiced this art in a world thoroughly infused with Buddhist ideas does not necessarily mean that Saigyō influenced Shunzei in purely religious terms.

---

453. Mezaki Tokue, *Saigyō* (Tokyo: Yoshikawa Kōbunkan, 1989), 104.

454. Mezaki Tokue, *Suki to mujō* (Tokyo: Yoshikawa Kōbunkan, 1988).

455. The historical timeline (*nenpu*) of Shunzei's life in Taniyama's *Fujiwara Shunzei: Hito to sakuhin* reveals some of these gaps. See 282–436.

Shunzei and Saigyō were also intimates of the three brothers who came to be known as Ōhara sanjaku, the three "Jaku" of Ōhara. Sometime after these brothers took their precepts in the Tendai tradition, they moved to the area of Tokiwa near Ōhara. Shunzei came to know them through their father Fujiwara no Tametada (?–?1136), who held numerous poetry competitions and parties during the 1120s and 1130s to which Shunzei was invited, and in which Tametada's sons, Jakuchō (? 1113–1180), Jakuzen (?1117 to 1123–1182), and Jakunen (?1113–1181 or 1182) also took part. Jakuchō and Jakuzen were prolific writers, highly regarded within the court poetry tradition. Jakuzen, in particular, wrote Buddhist poems for a collection of *shakkyō-ka* called *Hōmon hyakushu.* As the title suggests, this was a collection of one hundred poems based on passages from various sūtras and other Buddhist texts (*hōmon*). Jakunen, on the other hand, while active in the world of *waka,* seems to have had a lesser reputation than his brothers.[456] As with Saigyō, however, we do not know to what extent Shunzei and the three "Jaku" discussed their religious beliefs, but if they exchanged ideas at poetry competitions and the like, it is at least possible their discussions turned to the teachings of Tendai Buddhism.

Another relationship of import for Shunzei was with his nephew the poet-priest Jakuren [1139–1202] (not one of the three "Jaku" just discussed). Shunzei adopted Jakuren from his older brother Shunkai (dates unknown), in all likelihood after Shunkai became a monk. Nurtured thereafter by Shunzei, Jakuren took part in many of the same *utaawase* and *hyakushu* as Shunzei, as well as numerous others in which Shunzei did not participate. It seems likely that the poetic influence in this relationship came from Shunzei and was directed toward Jakuren rather than vice versa, but it is equally possible that Jakuren's religious beliefs could have influenced Shunzei. Later, Jakuren was named one of the compilers of the *Shinkokinshū,* but he died before the selection process began. Jakuchō, Jakuzen, and Jakuren have one poem each in the "Shakkyō-ka book" of the *Senzaishū.*

---

456. WDJ, 458–459.

The priest Jien (1155–1225), another friend of Shunzei's, was the youngest of this group of poet-priests. Jien became abbot of Enryaku-ji in 1192 at the relatively young age of thirty-eight. His first term—there were four altogether—ended in 1197, just about the time Shunzei was writing the *Korai fūteishō*.

Jien was the author of over six thousand *waka*, which were compiled in the 14th century as the anthology *Shūgyokushū* (Collection of Jeweled Gleanings). Jien's relationship with Shunzei most likely began in the late 1170s, after Shunzei had taken the tonsure and become a poetry mentor to Kujō no Kanezane (at whose residence Shunzei and Jien probably met). Jien would have been in his twenties then, so it is unlikely that his religious influence on Shunzei was significant. However, Shunzei must have admired Jien's *waka*, because he selected nine for inclusion in the *Senzaishū*, one of which appears in the "Shakkyō-ka" book. After the *Senzaishū* was completed, Jien matured as a Tendai monk at Enryaku-ji, becoming its abbot in 1192. If there were a period of time during which Jien could have influenced Shunzei in terms of Tendai thought, it would have been during the 1190s, before Shunzei wrote his poetic treatise, the *Korai fūteishō*, in which he laid out his ideas about the relationship between *waka* and Buddhism.

Finally, another notable relationship in Shunzei's life was that with his older brother Kaishū (1100–1172), who like Jien became head abbot of Enryaku-ji, serving twice in this capacity, but for only short periods of time. In 1167 he was driven from the position by Go-Shirakawa who wanted to seat someone more amenable to his opinions.[457] Kaishū was only fourteen years older than Shunzei, so if they were close, a bond over Tendai philosophical ideas is certainly possible. The only documentation that would support this fact, however, is the appearance of one of Kaishū's poems in the "Shakkyō-ka" book in the *Senzaishū*.

The number of poems Shunzei included in the *Senzaishū* by each of these men is evidence of his respect for them as poets, and suggestive of some degree of discourse among them about Buddhist beliefs.

---

457. Adolphson, *The Gates of Power*, 137.

PART TWO: TENDAI CONCEPTIONS OF THE BUDDHIST PATH

How Poetry Enlightens

Go-Shirakawa's beliefs about the efficacy of *imayō* to effect enlightenment were explained in his personal memoir, the *Kudenshū.* But where in Shunzei's writings may we examine his thoughts concerning the salvific power of *waka?* There are three primary sources: judgments rendered at or for poetry competitions, his Preface to the *Senzaishū,* and his poetic treatise *Korai fūteishō.* (Some information can also be gleaned from Teika's remarks in his diary and his poetic treatises, but for this study we will only refer to Shunzei's writings).

Discussions about Shunzei's aesthetic often focus on *yūgen*, a word meaning "mystery and depth," according to Brower and Miner.[458] LaFleur, following Konishi's lead, says the word appears in Buddhist texts relating to emptiness, śūnyatā (J: *kū*).[459] Some Japanese scholars have seized upon the word *yūgen* to explain the general style of poetry Shunzei advocated. However, there are only fourteen instances in which Shunzei used this word in all of his extant writings, thirteen of which come from his work as a *hanja,* or judge, at various poetry competitions.[460] Moreover, the word *yūgen* does not appear in his poetic treatise at all, and, according to Ōe no Fumimaro, Shunzei employed numerous other poetic terms much more frequently.[461]

LaFleur makes a persuasive argument about *yūgen* and Buddhism based upon Shunzei's understanding of Tendai conceptions of radical

---

458. Brower and Miner, *Japanese Court Poetry,* 260.

459. LaFleur, *The Karma of Words,* 100.

460. Royston, "The Poetics and Poetry Criticism of Fujiwara Shunzei (1114–1204)," 213.

461. According to Royston, Ōe Fumiharu provided a quantitative breakdown of poetic terms Shunzei used in poetry contests; the top three in his list are *yū* (287 times), *en* (84 times), and *aware* (50 times). Ibid., 214.

nonduality. LaFleur's argument is not designed to define *yūgen* according to Shunzei, but to define how the term might be connected to Buddhist principles. Using his translation of a key section of Shunzei's treatise, LaFleur demonstrates that Shunzei regarded *waka* and Buddhism as interdependent and interpenetrating: "... there exists a reciprocal flow [*kore o en ni shite hotoke no michi ni mo kayowasan*] of meaning between such things [as poetry] and the way of Buddhism ..."[462]

The concept of a "reciprocal flow" is based upon the Tendai idea of the three truths (*santai*). *Kū*, the void; *ke*, the provisional; and *chū*, the middle, are philosophical (and religious) terms derived from the *Makashikan*, one of the three great Lotus texts (*Hokke sandaibu*) of the Tendai sect, and the only one that deals with contemplative practice.[463] The *Makashikan's* author, Chih-i, equates the provisional to the void through the mediation of the middle.[464] For Shunzei the poet, these three truths could be reformulated so that *waka* represented the provisional truth of *ke* and the Buddhist teachings (the writings, in particular) represented the absolute truth of *kū*. *Kū* and *ke* are equated ontologically through a process LaFleur describes as the "holding of both in a state of dynamic and equalized tension."[465] This "holding," *chū* (the middle), is a state of being, then, rather than a mental realization. *Chū* is not quantifiable, and is not realized by adding a little of the provisional to the absolute or subtracting some of the absolute from the provisional. *Chū* is that which is attained when one recognizes through *shikan* meditation (S: śamatha-vipaśyanā, "calming and insight")—the *shikan* of *Makashikan*—that, despite the apparent impossibility of two truths of equal and contradictory import being true at the same time, this is an accurate representation of the actual nature of the world.

Shunzei brings up the idea of "reciprocal flow" again later in his treatise, immediately after he discusses the numerous and varied *waka*

---

462. LaFleur, *The Karma of Words*, 90–91.

463. The other two texts—also written by Chih-i—are the *Fa-hua hsüan-i* (J: *Hokke gengi*) and the *Fa-hua wen-chü* (J: *Hokke mongu*).

464. Here I use LaFleur's translation of the three terms *kū*, *ke*, and *chū*.

465. LaFleur, *The Karma of Words*, 92.

styles that have existed throughout the ages: "Even if it is difficult to speak about the configuration and the sentiments (*sugata kokoro*) of the *uta* [due to the various styles that have appeared in anthologies up to the *Senzaishū*], we can discuss *sugata kokoro* skillfully by applying it in a reciprocal manner to the Buddhist path (*butsudō ni kayowashi*) in particular and by relying upon the teachings of Buddhism (*hōmon ni yosete*)."[466] Here, Shunzei reiterates his earlier statement about reciprocity, but applies it to two of the most important rhetorical terms in *waka* discourse: *sugata* and *kokoro*.

It is probably not an accident that subsequent to this passage about poetic configuration (*sugata*) and sentiment (*kokoro*), Shunzei discusses in succession three of the most well-known religious figures in Japanese history—Shōtoku Taishi, Gyōki, and Saichō—as well as a *waka* by each that appears in the imperial poetry anthologies. Shōtoku Taishi and Gyōki are familiar to us from poems attributed to them in the *Shūishū* Buddhist *waka* sequence, and it is to these same two poems that Shunzei draws our attention in the *Korai fūteishō*. The third figure, Saichō, the founder of Japanese Tendai, holds an equally important position in Japanese history. One of his Buddhist *waka*, if indeed he wrote it, was included in the "Shakkyō-ka" book of the *Shinkokinshū* (poem 1920).[467] The citation of Buddhist poems by these three religious figures allowed Shunzei to establish historical precedent for the application of configuration and sentiment to *waka* on Buddhist topics in his era.

Shunzei's suggestion that the "reciprocal flow" of *waka* and Buddhism is evident in these three Buddhist *waka* is a kind of endorsement—though perhaps a tautological one—for the existence of *shakkyō-ka*. But why did Shunzei feel any need to give such an endorsement? Buddhist *waka* and *shakkyō-ka* were, of course, court poems by virtue of who composed them and where they were compiled. But their topics and their sentiments were still relatively new in the

---

466. Translation by author. Hashimoto Fumio et al., *Karonshū*, vol. 87 of *Shin Nihon koten bungaku zenshū* (Tokyo: Shōgakkan, 2006), 253.

467. Saichō's poem begins with the Japanized Sanskrit phrase *anokutara-sammyaku-sambodai* (S: *anuttara-samyak-sambodhi*), which is an expression of perfect enlightenment.

court poetic tradition. The word "court" as it applies to Japan is used in historical and literary discourse to imply an institutional structure with a *kami* (the imperial sovereign) as its head. Poems based on Buddhism, a foreign religion from the continent, were not a part of the initial conception of court *waka* as imagined by Tsurayuki in the *Kokinshū*. It took someone of Shunzei's stature to certify once and for all the courtliness of Buddhist *waka*, though compilers had in effect been urging their certification by including them in anthologies since the beginning of the eleventh century.

Statements in Shunzei's *Korai fūteishō* clearly connect his thinking about poetry with the tenets of Buddhism. However, Shunzei had addressed the topic of *waka* and Buddhism eleven years before this, in his Preface to the *Senzaishū*. Here he argued that the exalted words of people like Shōtoku Taishi and Saichō allowed the tradition of *waka* composition to survive: "... there have been few occasions when those who were born into this world [of Japan] and those who came to my land, both the exalted and the lowly, did not compose these songs (*kono uta*). Shōtoku Taishi conveyed the words [he spoke] at Kataokayama, and Dengyō Daishi [Saichō] bestowed upon us his words 'where [Mount Hiei, that is] the timber that I cut' [*waga tatsu soma*] ... Due to the exalted nature of these poetic words, the emperors of our world could not bear to abandon this Path."[468] These words are not as striking an endorsement of Buddhism as we find in the *Korai fūteishō*, but a little later in the Preface, Shunzei reinforces this statement by criticizing *waka* poets for what they did *not* do to expand the limits of the thirty-one syllable poem:

> When we [Japanese poets] first spoke of studying the Path of the *uta*, we did not study the wide-ranging path of Chinese and Japanese letters, or awake to the profound teachings preached at the Deer Park and on Vulture Peak. Poets who composed *uta* by merely lining up thirty-one characters, none of which fell

---

468. Translation by author. Katano and Matsuno, *Senzaiwakashū*, 4.

beyond our forty-seven *kana* symbols, must have thought they penetrated the depths of the eight-layered clouds of Izumo [the *uta* as a literary art] and completely understood Mount Shikishi [Japan] and the implications of its poetic vocabulary.[469]

Shunzei's implication—though couched in terms of what court poets did *not* do—is that poets should in fact plumb the depths of *waka,* enlightening themselves by drawing upon the Chinese and Japanese literary tradition and the teachings of Buddhism. If they do not, he says, they will not understand the "lofty heights" (*takaki mono*) to which the Yamato *uta* could rise.

Shunzei utilizes vocabulary in the Preface to the *Senzaishū* that seem intended to convey to the reader the gravitas of the *waka* project: the word *michi* (path, journey) appears nine times and the verb *satoru* (awakening to, understanding) three times. *Michi* does not *always* refer to the Buddhist path, but it is fair to say that by this time in Japanese history it almost always implied a religious journey. Moreover, if, as Konishi told us, one devotes single-minded concentration to one's artistic path, the journey will lead to consequences (*satori*) as profound as Buddhist enlightenment.

The frequent uses of the word *michi* in the Preface are also a foreshadowing of what we find in the "Shakkyō-ka" book. Here Shunzei constructs a literary *mārga* (*michi*) by which the composition of *waka* is turned into religious praxis. The poems in this book are not only *used for* religious benefit (though that may have been their original intended purpose), they are also examples of poems *identified as* religious practice.

---

469. Translations by author. Ibid., 7.

THE COURTLY PATH TO ENLIGHTENMENT

Though similar to the arrangement of the Buddhist *waka* in the *Shūishū*, which reflected three principal stages of a practitioner's journey to enlightenment, the *shakkyō-ka* in the *Senzaishū* were arranged according to more complex Tendai conceptions of the Buddhist path. Like the *Shūishū* sequence when it is read from beginning to end as a unified whole, a similar pattern emerges whereby poems in the early part of the sequence evoke a sense of commencement while poems at the end evoke a sense of conclusion. However, it may also be demonstrated that this arrangement, obviously thought out with great care, may be seen to correspond in part to two kinds of arrangements of the Buddhist teachings: first, to the pseudo-historical claim that the sūtras were taught in chronological succession by the Buddha in "five periods," known as *goji* in Japanese (C: *wu-shih*); second, to the textual structure of the *Makashikan*, a structure referred to by Japanese scholars as *goryaku jikkō*, "five abbreviated [chapters] and ten expanded [chapters]."[470]

The Five Periods System (*Goji*)

The five periods organization of the sūtras is part of a larger doctrinal classification system known as *kyōhan*, a word made up of two characters meaning "teachings" and "judgment." (In China, the two characters are reversed: *p'an chiao*.) This system originated in China, and Kenneth Ch'en explains why a periodization system was considered necessary:

> The Chinese were beginning to be puzzled by [the] tremendous volume of literature, teaching so many diverse doctrines and ideas, and were asking how

---

470. The pseudohistorical order of the five periods, *goji*, is generally coupled with a word meaning "the eight teachings," *hakkyō*. But since I will only be concerned with the five periods in this chapter, I will use the abbreviation.

one could explain the numerous contradictions and doctrinal differences taught in the scriptures. One proposed solution at that time was to divide the Buddha's teachings into chronological periods.[471]

Buddhist sects in China often supported different temporal systems, usually asserting the primacy of the sūtra that buttressed their own teachings. Though scholars have long known that the *goji* system is an apocryphal arrangement with little or no relation to historical reality, there is a significant likelihood that it was accepted in both China and Japan.[472] In the opening paragraph of the Preface to the second volume ("The Teachings") of the *Sanbō ekotoba,* Minamoto no Tamenori writes: "Among all the teachings of the Śākyamuni—from the day he was enlightened to the night he entered Nirvāna—none are untrue." This statement is followed by Tamenori's own description of the five periods:

> First, like the sun rising at dawn and casting its light upon lofty peaks, he expounded the *Kegon* [Avatamsaka Sūtra] for the enlightenment of Bodhisattvas. Next, like the sun mounting high in the sky, casting its rays deep down into the valley, he delivered the Āgamas for the edification of his disciples. Then he propounded the diverse Mahāyāna scriptures in many different places, and though he spoke with one voice, all sentient beings responded in their own way and attained enlightenment ... At sixteen assemblies he taught the *Prajñā* doctrine of nonsubstantiality, and after more than forty years he opened up the marvelous Way of the *Lotus.*[473]

---

471. Ch'en, *Buddhism in China,* 305.

472. The *goji* system can be found in numerous Buddhist sects, but we will only be concerned with the Tendai *goji* system here.

473. Kamens, *The Three Jewels,* 165.

Tamenori omits the final Sūtra, the Nirvāna Sūtra that traditionally accompanied the Lotus Sutra in the fifth and final period. Though
he might have done so to emphasize the superiority of the Lotus Sutra,
this omission does not disrupt the basic division of the "five periods"
arrangement significantly.

The *Ōkagami* (The Great Mirror), a Heian pseudohistorical work
that Konishi dates to sometime between 1041 and 1151, also mentions
the "five periods" arrangement.[474] In the Preface to this work, the
author(s) write: "They tell us that the Buddha began by expounding
other sūtras when he wanted to explain the *Lotus,* which is why his
sermons are called the teachings of the five periods."[475] Kunieda
Toshihisa has analyzed this passage to show how the author(s) intended
to accentuate the importance of the Lotus Sutra in contrast to "other
sūtras" (*yokyō*) the Buddha preached.[476]

What is of utmost importance is whether or not Shunzei had
been introduced to the *goji* periodization system. Shunzei, as a
bunjin, or man of letters, probably knew both the *Sanbō ekotoba*
and the *Ōkagami.* Since some passages of the *Korai fūteishō* are
based upon doctrine presented in the *Makashikan,* it has long been
thought that it—and Chih-i—must be the source of Shunzei's
knowledge about the *goji* periodization system. There are examples
of this kind of thinking in older Japanese scholarship on the *goji*
system, but some modern scholars also still hold this view. Kunieda,
for example, says, "Shunzei learned about the *goji hakkyō hanjaku*
(classification of the five periods and eight teachings) from the
Makashikan," citing two passages from the *Makashikan* that provide
the basis for his argument.[477] The first passage—the weaker of
the two—is from Kuan-ting's "Introduction" to the *Makashikan*
and implies a developmental structure figuratively: the word *goji*

---

474. Konishi, *A History of Japanese Literature,* vol. 2, 374 n. 194.

475. McCullough, *Ōkagami,* 68.

476. Kunieda Toshihisa, "Tendai no goji hakkyō to Ōkagami," *Bukkyō bungaku,* vol.
8 (March 1984): 49–57.

477. Kunieda Toshihisa, "Tendai no goji hakkyō to waka: Shakkyō-ka kenkyū no
kisoteki sagyō (1), in *Kokugo kokubungaku ronshū: Taniyama Shigeru kyōju taishoku kinen*
(Tokyo: Hanawa Shobō, 1976), 106.

is not used. The relevant section reads: "It says in the *Avatamsaka Sūtra,* 'For example, it [calming and concentration meditation] resembles the rising of the sun: first at sunrise the peaks of the high mountains alone are illuminated, then their valleyed [slopes], and then plains'."[478] This passage is a metaphorical description of how the Buddha illuminated not only the high mountains—presumably those who could understand the teachings immediately—but also the "valleyed [slopes] ... and plains," where comprehending the Buddhist teachings took longer than in the mountains.

The second passage from the *Makashikan* that Kunieda cites comes from Chapter 7. It includes the words "Kegon," "Rokuon," "Hōdō hannya," "Hokke" and "Nehan"—terms found in the traditional Tendai arrangement of *goji*—but again the word *goji* does not appear.[479] This section of the *Makashikan* focuses on the sixth of ten ways to contemplate the mind (*kanjin*) in order to attain enlightenment, but is not concerned in any way with the historical structure of the sūtras. Sekiguchi Shindai, the great scholar of modern Tendai studies, says that what we find in the *Makashikan,* instead of the word *goji,* is the word *gomi* (five flavors), a term and concept from the Nirvāna Sūtra.[480] *Gomi,* as Chih-i used it, is also—like the sun's rays—a metaphor referring to the five flavors that arise as one is making clarified butter (*ghee*). The stages for making it were emblematic of the path one takes to enlightenment, but once again this was clearly not a systemization of the Theravadan and Mahāyāna scriptures.[481]

Western scholars have taken a similar view to Kunieda's about the *goji* system and Chih-i. In his biography of Chih-i, Leon Hurvitz translated the term *goji* when he wrote, "Chih-i spoke in terms of the Five Periods and the Eight Teachings. ..."[482] Hurvitz goes on to say:

---

478. Stevenson and Donner, *The Great Calming and Contemplation,* 122.

479. Kunieda, "Tendai no goji hakkyō to waka," 116. Sekiguchi Shindai, *Makashikan: Zen no shisō genri,* vol. 1 (Tokyo: Iwanami Shoten, 1989), 107.

480. David W. Chappell, *T'ien-t'ai Buddhism: An Outline of the Fourfold Teachings* (Tokyo: Daiichi Shobō, 1983), 36–37.

481. Kawamura Kōshō, *Tendaigaku jiten* (Tokyo: Kokusho kankōkai, 1990), 76–78.

482. Leon Hurvitz, *Chih-i (538–297): An Introduction to the Life and Ideas of a Chinese Buddhist Monk* (Brussels: Mélanges chinois et bouddhiques, vol. 12, 1962), 229.

> ... the idea or method of classifying the Buddhist
> scriptures ... played such a prominent part in [Chih-
> i's] thinking and in his total theological schema that
> not only his own movement, the T'ien-t'ai, but oth-
> ers as well ... came to be identified first and foremost
> by their peculiar systems of *p'an-chiao*.[483]

Sekiguchi has called into question these traditional assumptions
about the *goji* arrangement.[484] The term *goji*, he says, does not appear
in any of Chih-i's writings; nor does it appear in the texts of his chief
disciple Kuan-ting (561–632) or the texts of the founder of Japanese
Tendai, Saichō.[485] David Chappell provides a different explanation
for the source of the five periods system, pointing instead to Chan-jan
(711–782), the ninth patriarch of T'ien-t'ai Buddhism, and a text by
the Korean monk Chegwan (J: Taikan, d. 971) called *Tendai shikyōgi*
(Outline of the T'ien-t'ai Fourfold Teachings):

> If Chih-i did not emphasize the Five Periods but the
> Five Flavors ... then the question is raised as to who did
> devise the Five Periods and Eight Teachings classification
> ... [T]here are at least four occurrences of this scheme in
> the writings of Chan-jan. As far as we know, this is the
> first appearance of the phrase ... and it points to Chan-
> jan as the key figure in popularizing the idea, if not in
> fact the creator of it ... Thus, until further investigation
> is done, it seems reasonable to suggest that the *T'ien-
> t'ai ssu-chiao* [*Tendai shikyōgi*] ... is influenced ... by the
> formulation of Chan-jan of the eighth century.[486]

---

483. Chappell, *T'ien-t'ai Buddhism*, 40.

484. Ibid., 36–37.

485. Ibid. For another discussion of this, see Donner and Stevenson, *The Great Calming and Contemplation*, 4–6. Groner thinks that Sekiguchi's claim about Saichō not using the *goji hakkyō* system "must be questioned." Paul Groner, *Saichō: The Establishment of the Japanese Tendai School* (Honolulu: University of Hawai'i Press, 2000), 183. The term *goji* also does not appear in Shunzei's *Korai fūteishō*.

486. Chappell, *T'ien-t'ai Buddhism*, 40.

We know that Saichō brought back Chan-jan's texts to Japan, but if his writings about the *goji* system were included, one questions why Saichō did not use it.[487] If Groner is correct that the term does not occur in his texts, but that "... the various elements of this [*goji*] system do appear in close conjunction with each other," then it is possible that the five periods arrangement was introduced in some form by Saichō.

The *Tendai shikyōgi* hypothesis seems the most likely scenario, however.[488] In the Introduction to this work, Chegwan says, "The Great Master T'ien-t'ai Chih-che [Chih-i] [538–597] used the classification of the Five Periods and Eight Teachings to arrange and explain ... the sacred teachings of the Buddha that were flowing east."[489] Chegwan then introduced a system that he conceptualized as follows:

The Tendai "Five Periods" System

1. *Kegonji* (the Hua-yen period): the period during which the Avatamsaka Sūtra was taught. Taught in Buddhagayā after the Buddha attained enlightenment for a period of three weeks.

2. *Rokuonji* (the Deer Park period): the period during which the Āgama (Mainstream Buddhist) scriptures were taught. Lasted twelve years.

3. *Hōdōji* (the Vāipulya or Broad period): the period during which those who understood the Mainstream Buddhist teachings were given higher teachings in the form of various Mahāyāna sūtras such as the Vimalakīrti Sūtra, the Suvarnaprabhāsa Sūtra, and the Śrimālādevīsimhanāda Sūtra. Lasted eight years.

4. *Hannyaji* (the Wisdom period): the period during which the

---

487. Paul Groner, *Saichō,* 102–103.

488. Since Chegwan died in 971, the work must have been introduced to Japan quite soon after he wrote it for Tamenori to have referred to it in the *Sanbō ekotoba.*

489. Chappell, *T'ien-t'ai Buddhism,*, 53.

prajñāpāramitā (perfection of wisdom) sūtras were taught.
Lasted twenty-two years.

5. *Hokke-nehanji* (the Lotus and Nirvāna period): the period
during which the Buddha preached the Lotus Sutra and the
Nirvāna Sūtra. Lasted eight years.[490]

I will argue that the *shakkyō-ka* sequence in the *Senzaishū* was
compiled to correspond, with some minor differences, to the five
periods system above. Some of these correspondences accord with the
name of a particular sūtra or sūtras, while others accord with the type
of teachings preached during that period.

My reading of the poems in the *Senzaishū* "Shakkyō-ka" book
produces five topics that correspond closely to the five periods system.

Five Topics of the *Shakkyō-ka* in the *Senzaishū*

1. *waka* about actuating a connection to the teachings (*kechien*)
   and the subsequent practice (*shugyō*) that occurs as a result of
   having made this connection
2. *waka* about awakening (*satori*) due to one's practice, or the
   awakened heart that results from this *satori* (*bodaishin*)
3. *waka* about the concept of emptiness (*kū, śūnyatā*)
4. *waka* on the Lotus Sutra
5. *waka* on nirvāna (*nehan*)

The last three topics correspond well to the fourth and fifth
periods—*Hannyaji* and *Hokke-nehanji*—of the *goji* system, as long
as the reader recognizes a division between the *Hokkeji* and *Nehanji*
periods in the arrangement of the poems. Paul Williams explains the
reason Tendai needed to conflate the *Hokke* and *Nehan* periods, "For
Chih-i the final purpose of the Buddha coming into the world was to
preach the *Lotus Sūtra* ... One problem for those East Asian Buddhists

---

490. Adapted from Ch'en, *Buddhism in China*, 305–307, and Chappell, *T'ien-t'ai Buddhism*, 31.

who would treat [it] as the final teaching of the Buddha, however, was the enormous popularity of the Mahāparinirvāna Sūtra [J: Nehan-gyō]. ... The T'ien-t'ai tradition, therefore, classed the two sūtras together in its *p'an-chiao* schema of ranking."[491] Thus, the fourth and fifth topics—the Lotus Sutra and *nehan*—actually correspond quite well to the fifth period.

Minor discrepancies also occur between the *Kegonji, Rokuonji,* and *Hōdōji* periods and the first and second topics, but they can be accounted for without too much difficulty. The first discrepancy is with the *Kegonji* period. While a modern reader might expect Mainstream Buddhist texts (such as those in the *Rokuonji* period) to come before a Mahāyāna text, instead we find the Avatamsaka Sūtra that is central to the Japanese Kegon sect in the first position. Luis Gomez has characterized some of this text as "speculative mysticism," while Paul Williams has said that the world presented in the Sūtra is a "world of vision, of magic, of miracle."[492] The Tendai sect, however, criticized it as "insufficient because it made no allowances for the faculties of its listeners. It was thus considered an ineffective teaching for most people, leaving them as if they were 'deaf' and 'dumb'."[493] But if the Tendai sect criticized the Avatamsaka Sūtra, then why was it placed first in the chronology of periods? In the *Fa hua hsüan i* Chih-i explains that the Avatamsaka Sūtra can also be a gateway to the Buddhist teachings:

> Those who are originally transformed and have entered the Lotus Throne are one extreme. Those who have not yet entered are, like the skillful means ... without end. Those in the middle are also like this. Some [enter] by means of [the teachings of] the *Avatamsaka Sūtra,* the *Vaipulya,* or the *Prajñāparamitā Sūtras* ... These are no different from the original enlightenment [of the Lotus Throne by the Buddha.]

491. Williams, *Mahāyāna Buddhism,* 156.
492. Ibid., 121.
493. Groner, *Saichō,* 180.

... Those who have not yet entered [the Lotus Throne] should "brew" the four flavors [from milk to butter] and then all will achieve [the ghee of] entrance to the Lotus Throne by means of this *Lotus Sūtra*.[494]

Kūkai supports Chih-i's view when he explains in the *Hizō hōyaku* that Sudhana [an important character in one of the books of the Sūtra] "was caused by [Vairocana Buddha] to set his mind on enlightenment under the guidance of Mañjuśrī, and who finally attained enlightenment with the instruction of Samantabhadra [J: Fugen] by making efforts to improve himself all the time ..."[495] So while the Avatamsaka Sūtra was sometimes regarded as too expansive to elicit any connection to the teachings, others regarded it as a starting point. That some did regard the Sūtra this way perhaps helps to explain why it was placed at the beginning of the five periods system.

The second period of the *goji* system, the *Rokuon* (Deer Park) period, refers to the time when the Mainstream Buddhist teachings were expounded. Even in Mahāyāna Buddhism today, the teachings of the Deer Park are considered an entryway into the world of the Mahāyāna. In China, the Deer Park teachings—called the Āgamas— were not the same as what is found in the early Pāli texts that traveled south to southern India and Sri Lanka. The Āgamas—those northern Indian Buddhist texts translated into Chinese—are composed of the first four Pāli Nikāyas and part of the fifth, as well as the *Jātaka* tales. The teachings conveyed in these texts, according to Ch'en, "[were] not the full [truth], but accommodated truth, consisting of the four truths, the eightfold path, and dependent origination—doctrines which could be understood by beings of lower capacity."[496] Given that the *Kegon* (Avatamsaka) period could serve as an entryway into

---

494. Paul Swanson, *Foundations of T'ien-t'ai Philosophy* (Nagoya: Asian Humanities Press, 1989), 249. It is noteworthy that in this passage Chih-i uses the *gomi*, five flavors metaphor, rather than the *goji* system, to discuss the varying capabilities of those who heard the teachings.

495. Hakeda, *Kūkai*, 213.

496. Ch'en, *Buddhism in China*, 306.

the Buddhist teachings and that the Āgamas were introductory texts meant to inspire those who could not understand the Avatamsaka Sūtra, I think we can count both as corresponding to the first topic of the *shakkyō-ka* in the *Senzaishū*—*kechien* and *shugyō* (connection to the teachings and practice).

The third period, the *Hōdō* (Broad and Equal), or *Vaipulya*, occurred when the Buddha taught many other principal Mahāyāna sūtras, such as the Vimalakīrti Sūtra, the Suvarnaprabhāsa Sūtra, and the Śrīmālādevīsimhanāda Sūtra. As Ch'en says, the sūtras expounded during this time "did not preach the Mahāyāna truths in their fullness; [the Buddha] was mainly interested in comparing the Hīnayāna with the Mahāyāna."[497] Even though the Buddha purportedly did not reveal everything during this period, his teachings were profound enough to spark awakening (*satori*) and result in an awakened heart (*bodaishin*).

Though practitioners may have experienced *satori* and *bodaishin* upon hearing a Mahāyāna sūtra from the third period, this does not mean that the highest teachings of Buddhism had yet been conveyed. The Tendai sect believed that the highest teachings were contained in the Lotus Sutra, its principal text. The practitioner must encounter and understand these teachings as well as those in the Nirvāna Sūtra, the subject of the fourth and fifth periods and of the fourth and fifth topics.

The Organizational Structure of the *Makashikan: Goryaku jikkō*

A second schema upon which Shunzei may have drawn in arranging the *shakkyō-ka* in the *Senzaishū* was the internal textual structure of Chih-i's great work, *Mo-ho chih-kuan* (J: *Makashikan*). Nishizawa Makoto proposed this originally in a chapter called "Shakkyō bu no hairetsu kōsei" (The arrangement and structure of the *shakkyō[-ka]* category), but did not apply it in any detail other than to list those

---

497. Ibid.

poems he thought belonged to each chapter of Chih-i's text.[498] The *goryaku jikkō* structure can be itemized in the following manner:

Goryaku jikkō Schema

Ten Greater Chapter Titles	Five Lesser Chapter Titles
1. Dai-i (Synopsis)	*1. Hosshin* (Arouse the heart)
2. Shakumyō (Explanation of terms)	*Hosshin*
3. Taisō (Characteristics)	*Hosshin*
4. Seppō (Inclusion of dharmas)	*Hosshin*
5. Hen'en (Partial and complete)	*Hosshin*
6. Hōben (Expedient devices)	*2. Shugyō* (Practice)
7. Shōshu shikan (Right contemplation)	*Shugyō*
8. Kahō (Rewards)	*3. Kanka* (Summon the rewards)
9. Kikyō (Start to teach)	*4. Retsumō* (Rend the net)
10. Kishu (Return to purport)	*5. Kisho* (Return to the abode)[499]

498. Nishizawa Makoto, "Shakkyō bu no hairetsu kōsei," in Ariyoshi Tamotsu, ed., *Senzaiwakashū no kisoteki kenkyū* (Tokyo: Kasama Shoten, 1976), 251–264. The Five Lesser Chapter titles are from Donner and Stevenson, *The Great Calming and Contemplation*, 140, 219, 335, 338, 340.

499. Neal Donner, "The Great Calming and Contemplation of Chih-i, Chapter One: The Synopsis" (Ph.D. dissertation, University of British Columbia, 1976), 11–12. Sekiguchi Shindai, *Makashikan: Zen no shisō genri*, vol. 1, 15–16.

On the left are the titles of the Ten Greater Chapters (*jikkō*)—only seven of which were actually completed—and on the right are the names of the Five Lesser Chapters (*goryaku*). The content of the chapters on the right appears in Chapter 1 (Dai-i, or Synopsis) of the Ten Greater Chapters, and this content provides a summary of all the chapters. The five titles of the Lesser Chapters sometimes correspond to more than one chapter of the Ten Greater Chapters. For example, Chapter 1 of the Five Lesser Chapters—Hosshin (Arouse the heart)—is dealt with in Chapters 1–5 of the Ten Greater Chapters. Because the *Makashikan* is not a completed text, we will make use of the Five Lesser Chapters (*goryaku*) since they provide a summary of what the text could have been in its finished state.

The text of the *Makashikan* is an explication of the meditative or contemplative process through which the various stages of practice evolve. These practices are sometimes referred to as *chih-kuan* [*shikan*] (calming and contemplation; S: śamatha-vipaśyanā) while the practice of sitting mediation is called *zazen,* sitting in contemplation. As Donner and Stevenson put it:

> It is clearer from the list of lesser chapters than the list of greater chapters, yet true of them both, that their sequence contains an inner logic. That is to say, they trace the progress of the religious practitioner from (1) the first arousing of the thought of enlightenment (*bodhicitta,* J: *bodaishin*)—when he realizes the possibility of Buddhahood within himself and awakens the aspiration to achieve it—to (10) the full and final attainment of this indescribable goal, beyond all teaching, beyond all thought.[500]

Therefore, the *goji* system is organized according to the kind of scripture preached during a certain period of the Buddha's life, while the *goryaku jikkō* organization of the *Makashikan* is structured according

---

500. Stevenson and Donner, *The Great Calming and Contemplation,* 18.

to a contemplative or meditative path. The nature of the *goji* path and the nature of the *Makashikan* path are similar in that the level of understanding and capability of the listener (in the case of *goji*) or practitioner (in the case of the *Makashikan*) is crucial to instruction.

What arises after combining the various schemas just discussed— my five topics of the *Senzaishū shakkyō-ka* sequence, the *goji* system, and the structure of the *Makashikan*—is a pattern of correspondences that, though it does not match the *waka* sequence precisely at all points, matches sufficiently to suggest that Shunzei had these in mind when creating his literary *mārga*.

CONCLUSION

There is no doubt but that Fujiwara no Shunzei was raised in an environment rich with *waka* poets and *waka* poetry and deeply influenced by Buddhist ideas, texts, and religious services. Despite the social unrest that characterized the second half of the twelfth century, poets of the Rokujō and Mikohidari clans engaged in poetic activities with an enthusiasm and single-mindedness of purpose not seen since the late tenth and early eleventh centuries. In the Buddhist realm, the Tendai teachings, influenced by the teachings of esoteric Buddhism, pervaded aristocratic life, while the *kami* and bodhisattvas conflated into an ideology expressed as *honji-suijaku*. In short, the overlapping and interwoven nature of various realms of experience at this time in Japanese history was the norm rather than the exception.

As we know from the *Korai fūteishō*, Shunzei believed in the power of *waka* to create an experience of the world not at all unlike the world experienced through Buddhist practice. His arrangement of poems in the "Shakkyō-ka" book of the *Senzaishū* to mimic Tendai historical and contemplative conceptions of the Buddhist path indicated how thoroughly he understood the practices of Buddhism and *waka* to interpenetrate. ❀

TOPICS OF *SHAKKYŌ-KA* MATCHED WITH *MAKASHIKAN* AND *GOJI* SCHEMAS

1. a. kechien
(making a connection
with Buddhism)

Makashikan 1 & 2 (*Hosshin/shugyō*)

Arouse the heart/practice

b. shugyō
(practice)

: Poems 1202–1214

Five periods 1 & 2 (*Kegonji/Rokuonji*)
Avatamsaka Sūtra/Mainstream
Buddhist texts

2. satori/bodaishin
(awakening, the
heart of the bodhisattva)

: Poems 1215–1227

Makashikan 3 (*Kanka*)
Summon the rewards
Five periods 3 (*Hōdōji*)
Mahāyāna sūtras other than Avatamsaka

3. kū (śūnyatā)
(emptiness)

: Poems 1228–1238

Makashikan 3 (*Kanka*)
Summon the rewards
Five periods 4 (*Hannyaji*)
Prajñāpāramitā sūtras

4. Lotus Sutra

: Poems 1239–1248

Makashikan 4 (*Retsumō*)
Rend the net
Five periods 5 (*Hokke-nehanji*)
Lotus Sutra/Nirvāna Sūtra

5. nehan (nirvāna)
(extinction)

: Poems 1249–1255

Makashikan 5 (*Kisho*)
Return to the Abode
Five periods 5 (*Hokke-nehanji*)
Lotus Sutra/Nirvāna Sūtra

7 THE "SHAKKYŌ-KA" BOOK IN THE *SENZAISHŪ*

INTRODUCTION

Of several notable characteristics about the *shakkyō-ka* compiled in the *Senzaishū*,[501] first is that the ratio of scriptural *shakkyō-ka* to occasional *shakkyō-ka* is greater when compared to sequences in previous imperial poetry anthologies.[502] This suggests that what poets regarded as Buddhist poetry had changed over the course of the twelfth century, and that they came to regard scriptural *shakkyō-ka* as embodying and expressing the new religio-literary aesthetic more than occasional *shakkyō-ka* could.

A second characteristic is the appearance of six new Buddhist texts and sūtras upon which some of the *shakkyō-ka* are based: (1) the Amida-kyō or Muryōju-kyō (S: Sukhāvatīvyūha Sūtra, T 366), (2) the Daibon-hannya-kyō, Prajñāpāramitā Sūtra in 25,000 Verses (S: Pañcaviṃśatisāhasrikā-prajñāpāramitā-sūtra (T 223), (3) the Senju Darani-kyō (S: Nīlakanthaka Sūtra, T 1060), (4) the Daihatsu-nehan-gyō, or the Nirvāna Sūtra (S: Mahāparinirvāna Sūtra, T 364), (5) the Zaigō ōhō kyōke jigoku-kyō (no Sanskrit title, C: Tsui yeh ying pao chiao hua ti yü ching, T 724), and (6) the Bodaishinron (also known as

---

501. The principal text consulted for this chapter was Katano and Matsuno, *Senzaiwakashū*, 365–380. I also consulted Ishihara, *Shakkyō-ka no kenkyū*, 189–321, but I used the numbering system of the SNKBT text.

502. This is also true for the *shakkyō-ka* sequences in the eighth and ninth anthologies, *Shinkokinshū* and the *Shinchokusenshū*.

Kongōchō-kyō yuga chūhotsu anokutara sammyaku sanbodaishinron, T 1665). At least three of these texts—the Prajñāpāramita Sūtra, the Nirvāna Sūtra, and the Bodaishinron—were used in both Tendai and Shingon contexts specifically. The Amida Sūtra, of course, was one of the primary Pure Land texts, while the Thousand-Armed Kannon Sūtra (which included a *darani* that produced benefits granted by the bodhisattva Avalokiteśvara) was not specific to any one sect. The text of the Zaigō ōhō kyōke jigoku-kyō concerned those previous karmic factors that caused sentient beings to suffer in the hell, hungry ghost, and animal realms.[503]

The final notable characteristic of the *shakkyō-ka* in the *Senzaishū* is that, for the most part, the authors—all male except for Sei Shōnagon and Shikishi Naishinnō—are arranged chronologically. If we use the date of a poet's death as guide, poems 1202–1210 are mostly attributed to authors who died in the eleventh century, while poems 1211–1251 are attributed to poets who died in the twelfth or thirteenth centuries.[504] Since the stated intention of Shunzei in the Preface to the *Senzaishū* was to include poems by poets from the seventeen reigns of sovereigns that started with the era of Emperor Ichijō (r. 986–1011) and extended to and included the era of Emperor Go-Toba (r. 1183/84–1198), it is not surprising that he employed history as an ordering strategy, which served to highlight the development of the Buddhist *waka* tradition from the eleventh to the thirteenth centuries.

If the modes characterize a poet's handling of the poetic material, the modalities—heavenly/tribal, soteriological/courtly, and soteriological/monastic—primarily represent external realities about the social group toward which a poem is directed and the spiritual source from which it draws. The heavenly/tribal modality is not of principal concern to this study, because the spiritual source upon which *waka* in that modality draw is the world of the *kami*.

---

503. Itō Hiroyuki, et al., *Bukkyō bungaku no genten*, vol. 1 of *Bukkyō bungaku kōza* (Tokyo: Benseisha, 1994), 209–210.

504. In the first group of poems, there are two exceptions: Minamoto no Toshifusa (poem 1205) and Sensai Shōnin (poem 1206) both died during the 1120s.

The spiritual sustenance for *shakkyō-ka* in the soteriological/courtly modality was the written texts and religious occasions of Buddhism; these attained full courtly status in the context of their assignment to an independent book of poems within an imperial poetry anthology. Since salvation—rather than, for instance, philosophical discourse—was what clearly drew the members of the court to Buddhism, it is correct to say that *shakkyō-ka* of the soteriological/courtly modality express a soteriological impulse.

The social group to which the soteriological/monastic poems belong is, as the name suggests, the monastic community. This is the case not only because these poems were written by monastics (as most were), but because they address more directly the primary concerns of that community—the truth and efficacy of the teachings—rather than secular court concerns. This may seem to be a contradiction since both communities longed for salvation; the distinction is that *shakkyō-ka* in the monastic modality concerned themselves less with matters of the heart as commonly expressed in sense-specific images of the lyric mode. A member of the court might also have written poems in the monastic modality, but we do not find many instances of this.[505] Because the *shakkyō-ka* belonged first and foremost to the larger category of courtly *waka*, it is not surprising to find far more in a courtly than a monastic modality.[506]

If one were to make a chart of the relationship between narrative, lyric and meditative elements in the sequence, several characteristics would become apparent about Shunzei's disposition of each mode individually and in relation to one another. First, although narrative elements appear with some consistency in individual headnotes and/or poems, and though the sequence as a whole implies certain metanarratives and subnarratives, narrative elements are intermittent

---

505. Poems 1204, 1223, and 1229 are among the few examples of poems by courtly authors (or authors in transition from courtly to monastic) that belong to a soteriological/monastic modality.

506. The *shakkyō-ka* that most clearly belong to the monastic modality are 1204, 1205, 1223, 1225, 1228, and 1250.

and subordinate.[507] What we might call a "story cloud" arises on several levels from all the ordering and other aesthetic choices Shunzei has made, but of the three modes, narrative is least represented. In keeping with the court *waka* project as a whole, the *shakkyō-ka* sequence emphasizes feelings and thoughts rather than story.

Lyric and meditative elements are represented about equally in the fifty-four poems: it is possible to locate lyric elements in forty-five poems,[508] meditative elements in thirty-five poems,[509] and to find a layering of lyric and meditative elements in twenty-six poems.[510] Poems with meditative (intellectual) elements tend to appear in pairs or small-to-medium-sized groups (for instance, 1202–1215, 1207–1208, 1228–1231, 1240–1243), whereas an absence of lyric (emotional) elements never occurs for two poems in a row. What this suggests is that Shunzei caused a thread of feeling, ranging from subdued to strong, to run through the sequence, but that he subordinated emotion, periodically and briefly, to intellectual elements. This evolving alternation and layering of narrative, lyric and meditative elements creates for the reader a sense of continual variety; one response to the material does not dominate.

Further increasing our respect for Shunzei as poet and anthologizer, we find in the sequence an extremely skillful progression of interwoven images belonging primarily to two categories. Images of light and dark appear in fifteen poems; images of water (including water in the form of snow or ice) appear in fourteen poems; and images of water and

---

507. I locate some degree of narrative elements in 28 of the 54 poems in the sequence: 1202, 1203, 1206, 1207, 1207, 1209, 1210, 1211, 1212, 1213, 1215, 1216, 1219, 1220, 1222, 1225, 1227, 1231, 1232, 1236, 1238, 1239, 1241, 1244, 1246, 1247, 1248 and 1249.

508. Lyric elements appear in poems 1202, 1203, 1205, 1206, 1207, 1208, 1209, 1210, 1211, 1212, 1213, 1214, 1216, 1218, 1219, 1220, 1222, 1224, 1225, 1226, 1227, 1229, 1230, 1232, 1233, 1235, 1236, 1237, 1238, 1239, 1240, 1241, 1242, 1243, 1244, 1245, 1246, 1247, 1248, 1249, 1250, 1251, 1252, 1254 and 1255.

509. Meditative elements appear in poems 1202, 1203, 1204, 1205, 1207, 1208, 1211, 1213, 1214, 1215, 1216, 1217, 1218, 1220, 1221, 1223, 1224, 1226, 1227, 1228, 1229, 1230, 1231, 1233, 1234, 1237, 1240, 1241, 1242, 1243, 1250, 1252, 1253, 1254 and 1255.

510. Layered lyric and meditative elements appear in poems 1202, 1203, 1205, 1207, 1208, 1211, 1213, 1214, 1216, 1218, 1220, 1224, 1226, 1227, 1229, 1230, 1233, 1237, 1240, 1241, 1242, 1243, 1250, 1252, 1254 and 1255.

light/dark (in the form of reflected light or reflected image in or upon water) are combined in eight poems.

To fully appreciate the sophistication with which Shunzei deployed these images in a subtle evolution, it is helpful to list their iterations: 1202: foam on the water; 1205: rain falls over grass and trees; 1206: dew on the lotus; 1207: the moon obscured by clouds; 1208: moonset behind the mountain; 1210: the lamp of the Law, night, waiting for dawn; 1211: the Buddha as "a shining," the temple lamp; 1212: tears; 1213: a thousand years of ladled water contrasted with a single dewdrop; 1215: the Buddha of Wisdom Light *is* the light; 1216: a vast sea contrasted with a single dewdrop; 1218: the moon's light reflected upon the water of the heart; 1220: snow blocks the way out of the valley but the Buddha-sun still shines; 1221: the Buddha-sun melts both snow and sin; 1222: moonlight lights the path to the West; 1224: the body compared to moonlight reflected on water; 1225: worry that snow may hide the "tracks" of the teachings; 1226: such tracks will survive the snow; 1227: crossing the ocean of suffering; 1230: night of samsāra, dawn of enlightenment; 1231: apparent disappearance of the moon, the darkened heart; 1232: face reflected in temple pond; 1233: sleeves ruined with tears; 1236: night, waiting for the dawn moon; 1237: melting ice, nondifferentiation between ice and water; 1240: moon reflected upon water thick with weeds; 1241: a difficult-to-dig well contrasted with the imminent water of the Dharma; 1242: ladling the water, the speaker's reflected face; 1243: crossing (implied water) on a bridge; 1244: moonlight blesses Mount Obasuteyama; 1245: sun and moon enlighten the darkened heart; 1247: anticipating the moon's appearance; 1248: snow compared to flowers; 1249: the moon hidden by clouds; 1250: enlightenment compared to reflected light; 1252: the sound of waves; and finally in poem 1254: the dead of night.

As the preceding list makes obvious, it is not possible that such an expressive arrangement is accidental. Further, we notice that the two categories of images begin by alternating in small groups of poems, but there is a particular moment in the sequence at which occurs a deliberate integration of water images with light/dark images. Poem 1218, in which the moon's light is reflected upon the water of the heart, is the first time that water and light/dark images conflate. Five other such instances appear afterward at regular intervals.[511] Likewise, there are points in the sequence at which the image categories seem to expand conceptually: when snow appears in the 1220/1221 *zōtōka*, we may wonder if Shunzei considered snow a water image, poetically speaking, and thus whether poems 1220/1221 belong to those that combine water and light/dark imagery. That he in fact did consider snow a water image seems to be confirmed when the snow melts in poem 1221, and is confirmed even more strongly by poem 1237, in which nondifferentiation between ice and water is central to the argument.

In addition to light/dark and water images, we find that a smaller subcategory of imagery pertaining to growing things—grasses, trees, leaves, moss, weeds, blossoms and gardens—appears in ten poems, likewise often layered with water and light/dark imagery as the sequence progresses.[512] On a conceptual level, we notice that pairs of opposites such as assistance vs. obstruction (forty-one poems),[513] skillful equanimity vs. confusion (fourteen poems),[514] and reality versus illusion (eight poems)[515] also help to unify the sequence.

It draws upon one skill-set to write a poetic sequence in which the three poetic modes are layered, a system of imagery intricately interlinks, a diversity of modalities are represented, two separate historical constructs are expressed, and in which each of these aspects shift and evolve as the sequence progresses. It draws upon quite another

---

511. Combined water and light/dark imagery (as reflected light/image or sun melting snow): poems 1218, 1220, 1221, 1224, 1232, 1240, 1242 and 1250.

512. Imagery of growing things: poems 1205, 1206, 1214, 1228, 1236, 1238, 1239, 1240, 1246 and 1248.

513. Assistance vs. Obstruction: poems 1207, 1210, 1211, 1212, 1213, 1214, 1215, 1216, 1219, 1220, 1221, 1222, 1224, 1225, 1227, 1229, 1230, 1231, 1232, 1233, 1234, 1236, 1237, 1238, 1239, 1240, 1241, 1242, 1243, 1244, 1245, 1246, 1247, 1248, 1249, 1250, 1251, 1252, 1253, 1254 and 1255.

514. Equanimity vs. Confusion: poems 1204, 1205, 1217, 1219, 1223, 1229, 1230, 1231, 1232, 1234, 1235, 1237, 1240 and 1250.

515. Reality vs. Illusion: poems 1206, 1210, 1223, 1229, 1230, 1231, 1234 and 1250.

skill-set to choose a group of poems by other authors and arrange them to make such layered correspondences apparent. The latter is Shunzei's accomplishment: together these strategies cause the sequence to strongly cohere on levels that are simultaneously historical, intellectual, conceptual, sensual, and emotional.

It should be clear at this point in this study that the expenditure of effort necessary to compose court *waka* was, by this time in literary history, strongly identified with an analogous expenditure of effort necessary to attain enlightenment on the Buddhist path. This identification resulted in the formulation of the phrase *kadō soku butsudō*: the path of *waka* is none other than the path of the Buddha, of which the *shakkyō-ka* sequence in the *Senzaishū* is illustrative. Instead of alluding to the path, as other sequences had, this sequence *is* the path, a thorough conflation of Buddhist praxis and literary art.

SECTION 1   *KECHIEN* AND *SHUGYŌ* (POEMS 1202–1214)

(Corresponding to *Makashikan* Chapters 1 and 2

[*Hosshin* and *Shugyō*] and *Kegonji* and *Rokuonji* Periods)

[1202]

こゝに消えかしこに結ぶ水のあはの憂き世に廻る身にこそありけれ

koko ni kie / kashiko ni musubu / mizu no awa no / ukiyo ni meguru / mi ni koso arikere

ON THE ESSENCE OF THE METAPHOR "OUR BODIES ARE LIKE BUBBLES ON WATER" from the Ten Metaphors of the Yuima-kyō

> this body
> > keeps returning
> > > to the sad world
> > like foam
> > > on the water that
>
> disappears here
> > to be reborn
> > > over there

— Former Major Counselor Kintō

[1203]

定めなき身は浮雲によそへつゝはてはそれにぞ成り果てぬ
べき

*sadame naki / mi wa ukigumo ni / yosoetsutsu / hate wa sore ni zo / narihatenu
beki*

ON THE ESSENCE OF THE METAPHOR "LIKE FLOATING
CLOUDS"

    this brief body—

  often likened
  to floating clouds—
   in the end

    must become—that—

       — Kintō

[1204]

世の中は皆仏なりをしなべていづれの物と分くぞはかなき
yo no naka wa / mina hotoke nari / oshinabete / izure no mono to / waku zo hakanaki

ON THE ESSENCE OF CONTEMPLATING THE THREE BODIES OF THE BUDDHA

to ask "which body" is useless—

every body in the world

is Buddha

— Kazan-in Gyosei

[1205]

おほぞらの雨はわきてもそゝがねどうるふ草木はをのが
品／＼

ōzora no / ame wa wakitemo / sosoganedo / uruu kusaki wa / ono ga
shinajina

ON THE ESSENCE OF THE MEDICINAL HERBS CHAPTER
OF THE LOTUS SUTRA

    the vast sky
    doesn't choose where to rain
                    but
    each grass and tree gets wet
    with a difference

                    — Bishop Genshin

[1206]

求めてもかゝる蓮の露をおきて憂き世に又は帰るものかは
motometemo / kakaru hachisu no / tsuyu o okite / ukiyo ni mata wa / kaeru mono kawa

IN REPLY TO A REQUEST TO CUT SHORT A VISIT TO
BODAI-JI, where the author had come to hear sermons binding the
listeners with karmic affinity to the Buddhas

> having come this far
>> to find the real

>> do you think I'd run
>>> back to the sad world

>>> and toss away the blessing
>>>> dew on this lotus

— Sei Shōnagon

[1207]

月影の常にすむなる山の端をへだつる雲のなからましかば

tsukikage no / tsune ni sumu naru / yama no ha o / hedatsuru kumo no /
nakaramashikaba

ON THE ESSENCE OF THE LIFE-SPAN OF THE THUS
COME ONE CHAPTER OF THE LOTUS SUTRA,
                                                written when
retired Emperor Go-Reizei held a sūtra-copying ceremony at the
residence of the Empress

> that mountain ridge moon
>   always shines clear
>
>   (if only
>
>   there were no
>   interfering clouds)
>
>   — Fujiwara no Kunifusa

[1208]

入る月を見るとや人の思ふらん心をかけて西にむかへば

iru tsuki o / miru to ya hito no / omouran / kokoro o kakete / nishi ni mukaeba

ON THE ESSENCE OF THE VERSE "TURNING TO THE MOON BRINGS PARADISE TO MIND"

> people who think
> > I'm only watching
> > > moonset behind the mountain:

> > > when I face the West,
> > I'm composing
> my will

> > > — Horikawa no Nyūdō
> > > Minister of the Left
> > > (Minamoto no Toshifusa)

[1209]

薪尽きけぶりもすみて去りにけむこれや名残と見るぞかなしき

takigi tsuki / keburi mo sumite / sarinikemu / kore ya nagori to / miru zo kanashiki

WHEN THE AUTHOR MADE PILGRIMAGE TO TENNŌ-JI
TO WORSHIP THE BUDDHA'S RELICS

> the firewood exhausted—
> even the smoke dispersed—
>
> dead, then—
> and gone
>
> and sad to look
> on what little
> is left

> — Sensai Shōnin

[1210]

夢覚めむそのあか月を待つほどの闇をも照らせ法のともし火
yume samemu / sono akatsuki o / matsu hodo no / yami o mo terase / nori no tomoshibi

THE AUTHOR, PERFORMING AUSTERITIES TO PURIFY HIMSELF in preparation for a pilgrimage to Mount Kinpu, copied a Lotus Sutra in gold ink, which he intended to offer to the mountain. While making the pilgrimage—perhaps troubled in his heart?—he wrote this, and attached it to something ...

> while I pine for the dawn (will I wake
> 　　from the dream?)—
> shine in the dark, lamp
> 　　of the Law

... and then, after he died returning from the mountain, someone found the poem in his home village, or so it is said ...

— Fujiwara no Atsuie

[1211]

世を照らす仏のしるしありければまだともし火も消えぬな
りけり

*yo o terasu / hotoke no shirushi / arikereba / mada tomoshibi mo / kienu
narikeri*

WRITTEN WHEN THE AUTHOR SAW OIL OOZING OUT
OF THE EARTH at Tanikumi in Mino, while making pilgrimage to
the thirty-three sacred places of Kannon

> because the Buddha
> appeared as a shining
> on the earth
> this lamp too
> has never
> gone dark

— Former Grand Archbishop
Kakuchū

[1212]

見るまゝに涙ぞ落つる限りなき命に替る姿と思へば
miru mama ni / namida zo otsuru / kagirinaki / inochi ni kawaru /
sugata to omoeba

WHEN HE SAW THE KANNON AT ANŌ

> while I looked
> > I wept
>
> to remember
> > the limitless forms
> > > love took
> to change
> > one life

— Former Grand Archbishop
Kakuchū

[1213]

千歳までむすびし水も露ばかり我身のためと思ひやはせし
chitose made / musubishi mizu mo / tsuyu bakari / wagami no tame to / omoi yawa seshi

ON THE ESSENCE OF THE DEVADATTA CHAPTER OF
THE LOTUS SUTRA

the water
        I ladled for
                a thousand years
did I imagine
        even a dew-
                drop
was for my
        own body?

— Bishop Kakuga

[1214]

うれしくぞ名を保つだにあだならぬ御法の花に身をむすびける

ureshiku zo / na o tamotsu dani / adanaranu / minori no hana ni / mi o musubikeru

AFTER RECITING THE PASSAGE OF THE DHĀRANĪ CHAPTER OF THE LOTUS SUTRA that reads

> those who receive and keep the name of the Dharma Blossom, shall have happiness incalculable. How much the more so for protecting those who receive and keep it in its entirety,

and

after having understood the trustworthy bond for those who keep this Sutra, the author wrote this:

> even to preserve the name
> of the Noble Law

is not in vain—

> joined to the blossom,
> the body bears fruit

— Former Grand Archbishop Kaishū

The topics in this first sub-sequence of thirteen poems primarily concern the matters of actuating a relationship with the Buddhist teachings (*kechien*) and then engaging in religious practice (*shugyō*). These are topics that conform well to the first two Lesser Chapters of the *Makashikan* entitled "arouse the heart" (*hosshin*) and religious "practice" (*shugyō*), as well as the first two periods of the five-period systematization, the *Kegonji* and *Rokuonji* periods, during which the Avatamsaka Sūtra (Kegon-kyō) as well as the Mainstream Buddhist scriptures were preached. Confirmation that poems 1206–1214 match these topics comes partially from words and phrases that appear in the headnotes to the poems: Kechien kō (Kechien Lecture, 1206), Ipponkyō kuyō (Service to Present the Chapters of the Lotus Sutra, 1207), *tsuki ni yosete* (forging a relationship with the moon/Buddha, 1208), *Tennō-ji ni mairite* (making a pilgrimage to Tennō-ji, 1209), *Hokke-kyō kakite* (writing/copying the Lotus Sutra, 1210), *Sanjū sankasho Kannon ... tokorodokoro ni mairi* (making a pilgrimage to the thirty-three temples where Kannon is enshrined, 1211), *Anō no Kannon o mite* (seeing the Kannon statue at Anō, 1212), *jikyōsha no kechien* (actuating a relationship with the teachings for those who "hold" the Lotus Sutra, 1214).

However, the headnotes to the first four *waka* in this sub-sequence, 1202–1205—all of which are attributed to renowned poetic, religious, and imperial figures of the late tenth and early eleventh centuries—do not provide any such convenient verbal cues as to how these poems fit into the *Makashikan* and five-period systematization that I believe Shunzei had in mind. These poems are concerned with difficult concepts such as insubstantiality and impermanence as taught in the Vimalakīrti Sūtra, the three bodies of the Buddha (J: *sanshin*; S: *trikāya*), and the teachings of nondiscrimination as taught in the Parable of the Rain in the fifth (Medicinal Herbs) chapter of the Lotus Sutra.

But we may speculate, based on one primary factor, about why Shunzei felt these poems belonged in the first section. The teachings of the *Kegonji* period that precede the *Rokuonji* period did include concepts such as those I have just described, which were considerably more difficult to comprehend than the introductory teachings of the second period. Based upon the Mahāyāna Avatamsaka Sūtra, sometimes regarded as mystical in its expansiveness, the teachings of the *Kegonji* period were, as noted earlier, sometimes deemed inappropriate for the novice. Chih-i, however, did not agree, "Some [devotees enter the path] by means of [the teachings of] the *Avatamsaka Sūtra*, the *Vaipulya*, or the *Prajñāparamitā Sūtras*. ... These are no different from the original enlightenment [of the Lotus Throne by the Buddha]."[516] Kūkai concurred with Chih-i, and pointed to a story in the Avatamsaka in which Sudhana is led to (i.e., introduced to) the Buddhist path by the bodhisattvas Mañjuśrī and Samantabhadra. As well, the teachings of impermanence—one of the three marks of existence (*sanbōin*)—are found in the Āgamas (Mainstream Buddhist scriptures) and can be identified with the *Rokuonji* period, but their level of sophistication in the Vimalakīrti Sūtra places them instead in the *Kegonji* period.[517] Therefore, at least some authorities thought the teachings of the *Kegonji* period could actuate a relationship (*kechien*) with Buddhism, and that is also possibly why Shunzei considered them a suitable framework for the opening of the sequence, which addresses beginnings.

When we examine the internal strategies of these poems in relation to the texts or ideas in their headnotes, we find that the meditative mode of the first four poems is a logical poetic strategy by which to address the difficult concepts of the *Kegonji* period. In the first two *shakkyō-ka* on the impermanence of the body, Kintō operates in the soteriological/courtly modality, making meditative-lyric responses to metaphors which compare the body to foam on the water and floating clouds. Kintō's first poem (1202) foregrounds a philosophical statement of belief about how the universe operates: "this body / keeps returning ... to be reborn / over there." The subsequent image of foam on the water inflects the mode toward the lyric, but the result is a

---

516. Swanson, *Foundations of T'ien-t'ai Philosophy*, 249.

517. One could also make the argument that the teachings of the Vimalakīrti Sūtra belong to the third period when other major Mahāyāna sūtras were taught, but the argument for including them among the advanced teachings of the *Kegonji* period is, I think, equally valid.

wistful philosophical sentiment rather than a passionate one. Even further in the background of the poem is the narrative implication: rebirth has played out universally through eternity. The poem seems to point to a specific body, but merely as an example of the larger philosophical context. The primary gesture Kintō makes is to offer the smaller narrative about the foam as evidence in his larger argument about human rebirth. Kintō's second poem (1203) is similar, but focuses on the impermanence of the body, rather than rebirth through which the body cycles endlessly. Again the meditative mode, arguing that impermanence is the case, is in the foreground, to which the image of "floating clouds") adds an emotional-sensual layer.

The two poems that follow (1204–1205), by Retired Emperor Kazan and Bishop Genshin, keep this part of the sequence in the meditative mode; their modalities are closer to the soteriological/monastic than to the soteriological/courtly. The first poem carries forward the theme of the body, urging readers to interpret ("to ask 'which body' is useless") the religious teaching of the three bodies (*sanshin*) in relation to the actual human condition ("every body in the world / is Buddha"). This is an intellectual argument for which the evidence offered is general rather than specific; not surprisingly, given Genshin's vocation, the forceful declarative statement seems drawn from the rhetoric of monastic preaching. The meditative argument is also strongly in the foreground of Kazan's poem, but there is greater sensual specificity—imagery of rain, grass, and trees—in his rhetoric. Kazan's and Genshin's poems have in common the word *waku*: to discriminate or to distinguish. Kazan's argument is that if we discriminate among the three bodies, we do so in vain (*hakanaki*), while Genshin argues that "the vast sky / doesn't choose [discriminate]" upon what it will rain, the gist of the parable in the Medicinal Herbs chapter (5, *Yakusōyubon*) of the Lotus Sutra. Again the rhetorical approach of the latter poem, as well as the fact that the author was a priest in the Tendai tradition, characterizes it as belonging to a monastic modality. The project of both poems can be described as an argument *for* equanimity and *against* confusion about or struggle with concepts.

With their clear focus on *kechien* and *shugyō*, the nine poems that follow Genshin's move us into the *Rokuonji* period according to the *goji* system, while expressing the *hosshin/shugyō* division of the *Makashikan*. The poets use a variety of poetic strategies to express their relationship to the religious act, event, or text in (or alluded to in) the headnote. Deciding to dedicate oneself to the teachings of Buddhism and engaging in its practices requires emotional commitment and determination, which is confirmed by the predominance of lyric responses that express increasing emotional intensity. However, as we might expect, the narrative mode—how and where the connection was made and what or who is encountered during practice—is almost as strong as the lyric mode in this particular set of poems. The meditative response, often characterized by intellectual arguments such as those we found in the first four poems, is least represented here. The focus of all these poems, individually and as a set, is upon the path (*michi*), the journey. There are numerous words in both the headnotes and the poems such as *kaeru* (return), *hedatsuru* (apart from), the West(ern Paradise), and *mairite* and *mōde* (going and making a pilgrimage) that reinforce this focus, but in those poems in which such words do not appear, the emphasis is still upon internal journey, as words such as *omou* (think, feel) and *miru* (see, perceive, observe) indicate.

This sub-sequence (1206–1214) begins with a *waka* by Sei Shōnagon, quite different in tone from the previous four poems by Kintō, Kazan, and Genshin, in which the speaker expresses a strong sense of determination.[518] The narrative of this poem is both geographical and spiritual (a journey to the Kechien Lectures at Bodai Temple). The speaker's refusal to come home, expressed as a passionate rhetorical question ("do you think I'd run / back to the sad world"), is inflected even more deeply into the lyric mode by the sensual image of dew on the lotus. The poetic argument that one should never turn one's back on the chance "to find the real" (*motomete mo*) could have implications for the religious seeker in general, but the focus in this poem is on how

---

518. The speaker of the poem is most likely Sei Shōnagon herself, since the same poem with its short, though slightly different, narrative appears in Episode 34 of *Makura no sōshi*. Ivan Morris, trans., *The Pillow Book of Sei Shōnagon* (London: Penguin Books, 1967), 55.

this *particular* speaker will behave, a subjectivity that reinforces the lyric aspect. The search for salvation that occupies the core of the poem puts it in a soteriological modality, but the author's status, a lady-in-waiting at the court, indicates that the soteriological is paired with a courtly, rather than a monastic modality. The speaker may be determined to experience the absolute truth of the teachings, but there is no hint that she is about to leave the court to take the tonsure.

The two poems following Sei Shōnagon's are also by members of the court—Fujiwara no Kunifusa (dates unknown) and Minamoto no Toshifusa (1035–1221). With Kunifusa's *waka*, the sequence takes a step back from the urgency of the previous poem. Based upon Chapter 16 (The Life-Span of the Thus Come One) of the Lotus Sutra, the poem was written at the time of a memorial service (*kuyō*) where single chapters of the Sutra (*ippon-kyō*) were copied at the residence of Emperor Go-Reizei's Empress. The Life-Span of the Thus Come One is crucial to the teachings of the Lotus Sutra because it announces that the real nature of the Buddha is eternal, meaning that he will forever be a guide along the path. Kunifusa portrays the nature of the eternal Buddha as light: the "mountain ridge moon" that "always shines clear." This straightforward argument, which reiterates the central teaching of the chapter metaphorically, is coupled with a lyric gesture of frustration that the light, and thus the path, is not always visible because of the "interfering clouds" (of delusion).

Toshifusa's poem (1208) returns us to determination like Sei Shōnagon's, in this case as an apparent rejection of the courtly activity of moon viewing. The passage quoted in the headnote ("turning to the moon brings paradise to mind"), from the Amida Sūtra, reinforces the topic of *kechien* in the *kanbun* phrase *kigatsu* (read through the technique of *kundoku* as *tsuki ni yosete*). The word *yosu* means not only "to lean toward," but also "to make a connection or relationship with," in this case with the Buddha/moon. The passage also continues the image of light, as if rescuing it from its partial obscuration in Kunifusa's poem. Toshifusa makes a clarification that is at once intellectual and emotional: what may seem like moon viewing for aesthetic pleasure actually represents—"when I face the West"—an expression of resolute devotion ("I'm composing / my will") to Amida Buddha, and a longing to be reborn in Paradise. This meditative-lyric response primarily concerns the speaker, but implicitly directs a blunt critique toward those who waste their time in this world indulging their senses. From the point of view of Buddhist doctrine, this gesture indicates that he has acquired or is about to acquire a kind of Tendai *santai*, three-truth, realization whereby the provisional is transformed into the absolute through, in this instance, the middle practice of turning one's heart completely and fully in the direction of Amida's realm.

The four poems (1209–1212) that follow Toshifusa's were written on pilgrimages (a kind of *shugyō*)—to Tennō-ji, to Mount Kinbu, and to two temples of the thirty-three where statues of Kannon were enshrined. The presence of these poems in the *Senzaishū* marks the first time that *shakkyō-ka* on pilgrimages were included in an imperial anthology.

Such *shakkyō-ka*, addressing pilgrimages like the eighty-eight-temple pilgrimage in Shikoku and the thirty-three-Kannon-temple pilgrimage in western Japan (*Saikoku sanjū sankasho*), were sometimes called *goei-ka* ("imperial songs"), but were more commonly known as *junrei no uta* ("pilgrimage poems").[519] It is said that the origins of *goei-ka* date back to thirty-three such poems Retired Emperor Kazan composed on a pilgrimage to the Kannon temples sometime after his abdication in 986.[520] The custom of composing such poems and reciting them like prayers gained popularity among priests such as Saigyō, Jien, and Mujū Ichien, major contributors to the esoteric idea that *waka* were equivalent to the mystical *darani* in Buddhist texts. The equation of *waka* and *darani* expressed by the phrase *waka soku darani* (*waka* are none other than *darani*) may have begun with these three poet-priests, but became considerably more prevalent during the later medieval period. We do not find this particular formulation

---

519. *Bukkyō bungaku jiten*, 87–88, and Nakamura, *Bukkyō jiten*, 81.

520. Steven E. Gump, "Mythologies and Miracles: The Saikoku Kannon Peregrinogenesis," *Southeast Review of Asia Studies*, vol. 27 (2005): 147. Mark MacWilliams argues that none of these thirty-three poems were actually written by Kazan, but composed by ordinary pilgrims on the pilgrimage over the centuries. "Buddhist Pilgrim/Buddhist Exile: Old and New Images of Retired Emperor Kazan in the Saigoku Kannon Temple Guidebooks," *History of Religions* volume 34, no. 4 (May 1995): 313.

in Shunzei's writings, but it is similar to an expression he does use in the *Korai fūteishō*: *bonnō soku bodai,* mental *kleśas* are none other than enlightenment. Buddhist priests originally charged that the inspiration for writing poetry came from our attachment to sensual desires (*kleśas; bonnō*), but Shunzei's radical esoteric reformulation, equating those desires with enlightenment (*bodai*), gave strong support to the idea that composing poetry was enlightened practice: *bonnō/waka soku bodai/darani.* It is possible that Shunzei regarded the four pilgrimage poems as Buddhist *darani* because previous precedent had already conflated the secular aspect of pilgrimage *waka* with the religious uses to which such poems had been put.

Sensai Shōnin's poem (1209), the first of this group, returns to the emotional aspect of religious practice that was evident in the poems by Sei Shōnagon and Minamoto no Toshifusa.[521] The speaker makes a two-stage emotional response to his experience of the pilgrimage to Tennō-ji, and thus a pair of opposites structures the poem: what has gone vs. what is left. The first stage imagines the Buddha's cremation, and acknowledges his physical death as the cause of the separation (though there may also be a hint here of the separation caused by *mappō*). In this stage, it is as if this is the first moment in which the speaker became certain of the Buddha's death and is forced to accept it. In the second stage the speaker considers the Buddha's relics, which cause him sadness to see "what little / is left." (In moving from acceptance to grief, this speaker seems to have reversed two of Elisabeth Kübler-Ross's famous stages in reaction to death. But there is an emotional logic to this reversal: in order to grieve, he first had to accept. The order of the poem in the sequence also allows an interpretation of "If a superb spiritual athlete such as the Buddha can be reduced to these relics, how much more urgent for ordinary people

---

521. The Tendai monk Sensai Shōnin (d. 1127), founded Ungo-ji in the capital, where he held a number of poetry competitions, the most famous of which was the *Ungo-ji kechien-kyō kōen utaawase* of 1116 judged by Fujiwara no Mototoshi. There is no record that Sensai considered the composition of *waka* a detriment to Buddhist enlightenment; in fact, the fact that he sponsored *utaawase* is proof to the contrary. This particular *waka,* based upon a pilgrimage to Tennō-ji, originally appeared in the "Shakkyō" book of the *Shokushikashū* (1165). SKT, vol. 2, poem 469, 313.

to commit to spiritual practice.") Interestingly, the penultimate poem of the *shakkyō-ka* sequence (1254, by Abbot Meiun, also about the relics at Tennō-ji) uses an identical two-stage structure. An alternate version of Meiun's poem can be found in the *Tsukimōdeshū*, where the emotion expressed at viewing the "traces" is happiness rather than sadness; the *Senzaishū* version, in common with Sensai's poem, expresses sadness.

Poem 1210, by Fujiwara no Atsuie (1033–1090), has been given a tripartite "sandwich" structure by the anthologizer, by placing a strongly lyric poem in the middle of two narrative prose passages. This is one of a very few poems having both a headnote ("The author, performing austerities to purify himself in preparation for a pilgrimage to Mount Kinpu ...") and also an afterword recounting the discovery of the poem after the speaker died.[522] The poem returns to the imagery of light (from two poems back, in Toshifusa's poem), emanating in this case from a lamp (*tomoshibi*) that the speaker desires—in fact commands (*terase*)—to "shine in the dark." In the context of the poem it is clear that the speaker requires this light to sustain him in practice during his samsaric dream, but it is the narrative element Shunzei has supplied that amplifies the urgent context of the speaker's longing. The resident *kami* on Mount Kinpu—Zaō—was not only a manifestation (*gongen*) of the Buddha of the future, Miroku (S: Maitreya), but a protector of good health and a long life.[523] Therefore, Mount Kinpu was the logical goal of someone perhaps troubled by serious illness. The high stakes of this poem (not theoretical but actual) are a result, in part, of the threat and revelation of death in the headnote and the afterword.

Two poems (1211–1212) follow by the Tendai monk Kakuchū (1118–1177), brother of Jien.[524] The headnotes of each refer to a pilgrimage

---

522. For a discussion of *maikyō* (burying sūtras) in the Heian period see D. Max Moerman, "The Archeology of Anxiety: An Underground History of Heian Religion," 245–271. Relevance to Mt. Kinpu can be found on 258–265.

523. Ono Yasuhiro, et al., eds., *Nihon shūkyō jiten* (Tokyo: Kōbundō, 1985), 353.

524. Appointed abbot (*zasu*) of Enryaku-ji in 1162, in the end Kakuchū only held his post for two days: the monks from the head Tendai temple immediately protested his appointment to Go-Shirakawa because previously Kakuchū had been appointed head priest (*chōri*) at Onjō-ji, Enryaku-ji's lesser and much disparaged temple sibling. More-

that Kakuchū is believed to have made in 1161 to the thirty-three Kannon temples.[525]

The first of Kakuchū's poems makes a meditative-lyric response to the narrative material of the headnote ("Written when the author saw oil oozing out of the earth at Tanikumi in Mino, while making pilgrimage to the thirty-three sacred places of Kannon"). Kannon was

---

over, the Enryaku-ji monks said, Kakuchū, who had been ordained in Nara by monks belonging to the Mainstream Buddhist tradition, could not possibly become the head of a great Mahāyāna temple. Kakuchū may have been run out of this position on Mt. Hiei, but was later compensated with the abbotship of Hosshō-ji, which had been his father Tadamichi's temple. We also know that Kakuchū was involved in court poetry activities because he had held a poetry competition in 1169 at Onjō-ji. No matter how humiliated Kakuchū—and Go-Shirakawa—might have been as a result of this incident, there was apparently no stigma attached to either after Go-Shirakawa appointed Kakuchū to his position at Hosshō-ji, which left Shunzei free to include Kakuchū's *waka* in the "Shakkyō-ka" book. Adolphson, *The Gates of Power*, 139–140.

525. Gump, "Mythologies and Miracles," 148. Gump reproduces the names of the temples Kakuchū visited (see 158), based upon a compilation derived from the *Jimon kōsōki* (from which the information about Kakuchū's pilgrimage is confirmed) by Asano Kiyoshi in *Saikoku sanjūsansho reijō jiin no sōgōteki kenkyū* (Tokyo: Chūō Kōron Bijutsu Shuppan, 1990), 17–18. According to this list, Anaō-ji and Kegon-ji are the thirty-second and the nineteenth temples, different from what they are today.

The thirty-three temples on this pilgrimage reflect the belief that Kannon took thirty-three different forms (*sanjūsanjin*) in which to express limitless compassion to all sentient beings, a belief reflected in the miraculous tales about the Kannon images belonging to both temples. According to the *Genkō shakusho*, a history of Buddhism since its importation into Japan, by Kokan Shiren (1278–1346), the history of the Kannon statue at Anō-ji (sometimes called Tanikumidera) is that it was commissioned by Uji no Miyanari during the Ōwa era (961–964) and sculpted by Busshi Kansei (or Kanse, dates unknown). (It is also said that Busshi Kansei recited the Kannon-kyō—Chapter 25 of the Lotus Sutra—thirty-three times a day.) When the statue was found bleeding from the very spot where Miyanari had struck Kansei in a robbery attempt, this inspired Miyanari to repent, renew his friendship with Kansei, and take refuge in Kannon. (Manaka Fujiko, *Senzaishū Shinkokinshū shakkyō-ka no hyōshaku* [Tokyo: Mine Bunko, 1956]), 10–11; Ishihara, *Shakkyō-ka no kenkyū*, 218–219.) The Kannon at Kegon-ji, for its part, is thought to have been responsible for oil bubbling up like a spring from the ground. From that time on, it was believed, a fire lamp burned continually in front of the temple. (Ibid., 11–12, Ibid., 220–221.)

The statue in Mino was located at the Tanikumi Kannon at Kegon-ji—presently the thirty-third and final temple located in present-day Gifu Prefecture—while the Kannon at Anō was enshrined in the twenty-first temple (Anaōji) [again according to the pilgrimage as it is structured today] located in present-day Kyoto Prefecture. For the entire list of temples, see Nakamura, *Bukkyō jiten*, 363.

believed to have caused the oil to bubble from the earth, but Kakuchū is more interested in the lamp that, by implication, the oil has fueled. Kakuchū's response combines logical-rhetorical and emotional-sensual aspects: the lamp—an "eternal flame" linking this poem imagistically with Atsuie's—lights the way to this particular temple, and symbolizes the constant availability of the teachings there, "because the Buddha / appeared as a shining / on the earth."

Kakuchū's next poem is more overtly emotional, as the speaker weeps when he remembers "the limitless forms / love [compassion] took / to change / one life." The author alludes to the (at least) thirty-three forms Kannon was said to have taken to come to the aid of sentient beings, not to expound any such specific doctrine, but to offer gratitude—explicit in the parallel comparison of "limitless forms" to "one life"—for, in a larger sense, the guidance the Buddha has provided. Gratitude has been implied in several preceding *shakkyō-ka*, but here we find it explicitly paired with strong emotion, and the cause of it.

The subject of *shugyō* continues and comes to a close with the next two poems (1213 and 1214) respectively by Bishop Kakuga (1090–1146) and Former Grand Archbishop Kaishū (1100–1172), each based upon chapters of the Lotus Sutra.[526] The first poem alludes to the Devadatta chapter (12) of the Lotus Sutra, in which the Buddha serves Devadatta for many long years. References to this story are abundant in classical Japanese literature and must have been familiar to all: the headnote says the poem was composed on its "essence" (*kokoro*). The second poem refers to a section of text in the Dhāraṇī chapter (26) in the Lotus Sutra that reads, "… those who receive and keep the name of the Dharma Blossom [Lotus], shall have happiness incalculable. How much the more so for protecting those who receive and keep it in its entirety."[527] As a pair these poems emphasize, respectively,

---

526. Kakuga was a monk from Tōdai-ji—the head of the Kegon sect—in Nara, while Kaishū, Shunzei's elder brother, was a Tendai monk who served as the abbot of Enryaku-ji for a short time, before being expelled when the monks in the two main sections of Mt. Hiei, Tōtō and Saitō, realized they had not consented to his appointment. Adolphson, *The Gates of Power*, 137.

527. Hurvitz, *Scripture of the Lotus Blossom of the Fine Dharma*, 323–324; Sakamoto and Iwamoto, *Hokke-kyō*, vol. 3, 274.

service the Buddha provided to others, then service that it was felt ought to be extended to the Lotus Sutra itself. Thus the pair may be seen to continue the theme of generosity and gratitude. Both kinds of service can be regarded as a religious practice, but the poets respond to their material differently.

Kakuga's poem has narrative, meditative, and lyric elements. The compressed narrative—"the water / I ladled for / a thousand years"— would have caused readers at the time to recall the entire story in the Devadatta chapter, and made them aware the speaker is the Buddha himself. The Buddha's rhetorical question "did I imagine / even a dew- / drop / was for my / own body" implies an argument about the purpose of his service. The lyric inflection comes from the implication that a service so extreme and selfless requires a gratitude equally extreme. Imagistically, the dewdrop in this poem is linked with the dew of Sei Shōnagon's poem, as well as the tears in the poem of Kakuchū's that immediately precedes it.

Kaishū's *shakkyō-ka* is primarily a meditative response to the passage from the Dhāranī chapter, in which receiving and keeping the name of the Lotus Sutra is presented as equally valuable as keeping the Sutra (*jikyō*) itself. The poem and headnote imply that, first, there had been a period of time *before* reciting the verse when the speaker had not yet created an unbreakable bond (*kechien*) with the Lotus Sutra, and second, that he understood the importance of that bond *after* the recitation. This before/after dyad, while not explicit, seems to have been an organizing structure in the speaker's (and perhaps Shunzei's) mind. The poem inflects this abstract, intellectual element slightly toward the lyric by illustrating its point with blossom (*hana*) and fruit (the *kakekotoba* "*mi*" meaning both body and fruit). The authority of the Lotus text, as described in the headnote, is expressed in the poem itself by the word *minori*, the Dharma, or "Noble Law." It is this *minori* which makes it possible to actuate a bond (*kechien*) and to practice (*shugyō*), and which is the foundation for awakening (*satori*) and the awakened heart (*bodaishin*): the subject matter of the next sub-sequence of thirteen poems.

SECTION 2   *SATORI* AND *BODAISHIN* (POEMS 1215–1224)

(Corresponding to *Makashikan* Chapter 3 [*Kanka*] and the *Hōdōji* Period)

[1215]

わび人の心のうちをよそながら知るや悟りの光なるらん
wabibito no / kokoro no uchi o / yosonagara / shiru ya satori no / hikari naruran

ON THE ESSENCE OF THE BUDDHA OF WISDOM LIGHT,
one of twelve Buddhas of Light that appear in the Amida-kyō, which
the author was reading

> must he be the light? he
>
> who awoke, who knows
>
> every heart of despair
>
> from afar?

> — Minamoto no Shunrai

[1216]

誓ひをば千尋の海にたとふなりつゆも頼まば数に入りなん
chikai oba / chihiro no umi ni / tatou nari / tsuyu mo tanomaba / kazu ni irinan

When the Ex-Emperor asked that one hundred poems be composed, he himself wrote this
        ON THE ESSENCE OF THE PASSAGE
"THE VAST VOW IS DEEP AS THE SEA"
                from the Gateway to
Everywhere chapter of the Lotus Sutra

     it likens his
          vow to a sea

     a thousand
          fathoms deep:

     with even a dew-
            drop of trust

     I could be counted
            among that number

          — Sutoku-in Gyosei

[1217]

はかなくぞ三世の仏と思ひける我身ひとつにありと知らずて
hakanaku zo / miyo no hotoke to / omoikeru / wagami hitotsu ni / ari to shirazute

ON THE ESSENCE OF THE FLOWER GARLAND
SŪTRA,
from among the hundred poems mentioned in the preface
to the previous poem

> *foolish—*
> how I obsessed
> about Buddhas
>
> of the past, present, and future—
>
> not grasping
> they are one
> in my body

— Former Consultant Norinaga

[1218]

照る月の心の水にすみぬればやがてこの身に光りをぞさす
teru tsuki no / kokoro no mizu ni / suminureba / yagate kono mi ni / hikari o zo sasu

ON THE ESSENCE OF "ATTAINING BUDDHAHOOD IN
THIS VERY BODY"

> when the moon
>
> shines clear from
>
> the water
>
> of my heart—
>
> on this body
>
> just as it is
>
> *light is cast*

— Former Consultant Norinaga

[1219]

帰りても入りぞわづらふ真木の戸をまどひ出でにし心なら
ひに

*kaeritemo / iri zo wazurau / maki no to o / madoiidenishi / kokoro
narai ni*

ON THE ESSENCE OF THE BELIEF AND UNDERSTANDING
CHAPTER OF THE LOTUS SUTRA

even if I could go home
            it would grieve me—
                        to go in—
because
        when I went out that door
                    of precious wood

I had a heart accustomed
                to confusion

                — Former Grand Archbishop
                Kakuchū

[1220]

降る雪は谷のとぼそをうづむとも三世の仏の日や照らすらん
*furu yuki wa / tani no toboso o / uzumu tomo / miyo no hotoke no / hi
ya terasuran*

SENT IN THE WINTER WHEN THE LATER NYŪDŌ
HOSSHINNŌ WAS CONFINED AT MOUNT KŌYA

even if fallen snow buries
the way in and out
of the valley—the sun of Buddhas
past, present, and still to come
goes on shining—doesn't it?

— Sutoku-in Gyosei

[1221]

照すなる三世の仏の朝日には降る雪よりも罪や消ゆらん

terasu naru / miyo no hotoke no / asahi ni wa / furu yuki yori mo / tsumi ya kiyuran

A REPLY TO THE PREVIOUS POEM

> I hear it goes on shining—
> > the morning sun of Buddhas
> past, present, and still to come—
> > but it's our sin, not fallen snow,
> that must melt away—isn't it?

> — Ninna-ji Nochi no Nyūdō
> Hosshinnō Kakushō

[1222]

ふるさとをひとり別るゝ夕べにもをくるは月のかげとこそ
聞け
*furusato o / hitori wakaruru / yūbe ni mo / okuru wa tsuki no / kage to
koso kike*

ON THE VERSE FROM THE KEGON SŪTRA "ONLY THIS
WISH, THAT THE BODHISATTVA OF WISDOM NEVER
ABANDON ME,"
from among the poems on Dharma texts in a set
of one hundred poems

> on the night
> when I leave home
> forever—
>
> an out of this world trip—
>
> I hear it's moonlight
> will lead the way

— Shikishi Naishinnō

[1223]

人ごとに変るは夢の迷ひにて覚むればをなじ心なりけり
hitogoto ni / kawaru wa yume no / madoi nite / samureba onaji / kokoro narikeri

ON THE ESSENCE OF "THE WISDOM OF EQUAL NATURES," from a time when it was requested that a hundred poems be composed on Dharma texts about the *tathāgathās* of the five wisdoms

> by some delusion or dream
>> each person seems different
>
> when you awaken, though—
>> every heart is the same

> — Regent and Former Minister of the Left (Fujiwara no Kanezane)

[1224]

澄めば見ゆ濁れば隠るさだめなきこの身や水に宿る月かげ
sumeba miyu / nigoreba kakuru / sadame naki / kono mi ya mizu ni /
yadoru tsukikage

ON THE ESSENCE OF THE METAPHOR "THE BODY IS
LIKE THE MOON IN THE WATER," from the Ten Metaphors of
the Yuima-kyō

> when it is clear, it can be seen:
> when it is clouded, it is hidden:
>
> my inconstant body:
>   is moonlight
> reflected in water

— Kunaikyō Naganori

[1225]

いとゞしくむかしの跡や絶えなむと思ふもかなし今日の白雪
itodoshiku / mukashi no ato ya / taenamu to / omou mo kanashi / kesa no shirayuki

WHEN THERE WAS STUDENT DISCORD ON MOUNT HIEI and all the students had scattered,
                        Jien,
                                  having almost finished a thousand day retreat on the mountain and grieving that the teachings of the Saint were about to cease, stopped at a desolate mountain cave.
         Because it was winter, the next morning there was snow and he sent this to Son'en Hōshi:

    this morning's white
                    investiture—
    too sad to think

    the old tracks

    will disappear

                        — Hōin Jien

[1226]

君が名ぞ猶あらはれん降る雪にむかしの跡は埋もれぬとも
kimi ga na zo / nao arawaren / furu yuki ni / mukashi no ato wa /
uzumorenu tomo

A REPLY TO THE PREVIOUS POEM

> your name! will survive
>
>   after everything—
>
> even if the old tracks
>
> become buried
>
> in falling snow
>
>   — Priest Son'en

[1227]

ひとりのみ苦しき海を渡るとや底を悟らぬ人は見る覧
hitori nomi / kurushiki umi o / wataru to ya / soko o satoranu / hito wa miruran

ON THE ESSENCE OF THE PASSAGE "SECRETLY INSIDE
HE IS A BODHISATTVA"
                    from the Receipt of Prophecy by Five
Hundred Disciples chapter of the Lotus Sutra

before they realized
            you didn't need to cross—

were helping *others* across—

            did they think you crossed it alone,
                the ocean of suffering?

                — Sakon Middle Captain
                Yoshitsune

Having made a connection with the teachings (*kechien*) and engaged in the practices (*shugyō*) as illustrated in the previous sub-sequence of poems, the practitioner has created the potential to awake
out of confusion (*bonnō, yume*) into a more equitable (*byōdōshōchi*,
the wisdom of an equitable nature) stance toward the world and its
sentient beings. In these poems or their headnotes we find specific
words, significantly less common in the first sub-sequence of *shakkyō-
ka* than in this one, pertaining to these ideas, including *hotoke* (the
Buddha), *nyorai* (the *tathāgathā*), *sokushin jōbutsu* (Buddhahood in
this very body), *bodhisattva* (one destined for enlightenment), and
satori (awakening).[528] Other poems in this sub-sequence imply the
same concepts through contrast, example, or circumlocution: *madoi*
(confusion, *bonnō*), *tsuki no kage* (the rays of the moon, *satori*), *kono
mi suichū no tsuki no gotoshi* (this body is like the moon in the water,
sokushin jōbutsu), *chikai ... tanomaba kazu ni irinan* (counted among
the saved if one relies upon [Samantabhadra's] vow, *satori, bodhisattva*), and *kimi ga na* (the salvific power of a name, *satori*).

That this sub-sequence of poems turns from religious practice
towards its reward, enlightenment, is expressed distinctly by the
headnote to Minamoto no Shunrai's poem (1215) indicating that it
was written "on the essence of the Buddha of Wisdom Light [Chiekō
Butsu], one of the twelve Buddhas of Light [Jūnikō Butsu] that appear
in the Amida-kyō."[529] Shunrai's response to the Sūtra is primarily
meditative, in common with all the poems that contain explicit words
about Buddhahood and enlightenment in this sub-sequence. Shunrai
asks rhetorically if, in effect, the Buddha of Wisdom Light *is* the light,
and therefore capable of awakening everyone suffering in darkness.
This realization, the headnote tells us, arose from direct interaction
with the Amida-kyō scripture, and thus continues the theme of
gratitude, in this case toward both the scripture and the Buddha of

---

528. The word *hotoke*, for instance, appears only twice in the first sub-sequence of
poems, but six times in the second.

529. We avoided translating the word *satori* in the poem as enlightenment, but our
lines "must he be the light? he / who awoke ..." convey the presumption that the Buddha
of Wisdom Light shines the light of *satori* within "every heart of despair."

Wisdom Light. This gratitude, however, is expressed in a general and abstract manner rather than linked subjectively to the speaker of the poem, and thus not with the emotional emphasis we have seen in previous poems on that topic.

Shunrai's poem, as well as those from the sub-sequence that follow, correspond to the *Hōdōji* (Expanded and Equitable) period of the *goji* system and to Lesser Chapter 3 of Chih-i's *Makashikan* titled "Summon the Rewards" (*Kanka*). Since the complexities of the Mahāyāna sūtras, though not their full effect, were said to have been preached during the *Hōdōji* period, one can speculate that this might have been Shunzei's justification for introducing the topic of awakening. However, while matching the topic matter of these poems with the third era of the periodization system is easy, matching it with Chapter 3 of the Five Lesser Chapters of the *Makashikan* is slightly more difficult. Since this chapter was not expanded upon beyond a few sentences, we must speculate as to the significance of the rewards in the title. The opening sentences of the treatise read: "In chapter three we explain how calming and contemplation is expounded for the purpose of illumining the pure and great result (*kuo-pao*) [that is the true aim] of the bodhisattva ... if [the] practice [of the bodhisattvas] should conform to the middle way [*chūdō*], [the bodhisattvas] will earn the supreme and wondrous result."[530] In a footnote explaining the word *kuo-pao*, the translators write, "The binome *kuo-pao*, translated as 'result' or 'recompense,' can refer to the reciprocal effect of fruition of karma ... as well as to the fruition or result of the causal path of practice ... In this chapter the word primarily carries the latter sense of 'result,' as in the grand fruit of Buddhahood."[531] From this passage, it would seem that the translators have linked *kuo-pao* with the kind of enlightenment that arises when manifesting the middle truth (*chū*) of the three truths (*santai*). Consequently, such enlightenment is not that which arises from having comprehended the truth of the void (*kū*) or acknowledged the truth of the provisional (*ke*), but the specific enlightenment, taught in the Tendai sect, in

---

530. Stevenson and Donner, *The Great Calming and Contemplation*, 335.
531. Ibid.

which a complete ontological conflation occurs between the provisional and the void in the course of *chih-kuan* (*shikan*) meditation. It is with the truth of the middle that Shunzei concerned himself in the *Korai fūteishō*, and thus it is in relation to the truth of the middle that the *shakkyō-ka* sequence in the *Senzaishū* is best understood, since the entire sequence exemplifies the *bonnō/waka soku bodai/darani* formulation.[532]

Shunrai's poem illustrates the kind of enlightenment that is attained, not through one's own efforts (known as *jiriki*), but through the power of external guidance (known as *tariki*). The external guidance in this case comes from the Buddha of Wisdom Light, whose illuminative powers penetrate into and lead one out of samsāra, guiding the way to the Pure Land.

Retired Emperor Sutoku's poem (1216) focuses on Kannon's vow from the Kannon-kyō in the Lotus Sutra (25, The Gate to Everywhere chapter), through which the speaker is confident he will join the great crowd of the enlightened. The poem is structured by its primary gesture (another variation of the sequence's water imagery) which compares Kannon's vow to "a sea / a thousand / fathoms deep" and contrasts that with the "dew-drop of trust" the speaker requires. This gesture is emotional in the sense that it directly implicates the speaker, but intellectual to the extent that it speculates about the metaphor quoted in the headnote and reiterated in the first part of the poem.

A more corporeal form of enlightenment, focused upon Buddhahood within a single lifetime and in the body of all sentient beings, is the subject of two poems (1217, 1218) by courtier Fujiwara no Norinaga (1109–ca. 1180).[533]

Norinaga's poem was composed on the topic of "the essence of the

---

532. The phrase *bonnō soku bodai* appears in the headnote to poem 1237, which will be discussed later in this chapter.

533. Norinaga, a distant cousin of Shunzei's, was a retainer to Retired Emperor Sutoku, who was exiled to the province of Hitachi at the same time Sutoku was banished to Shikoku after the Hōgen Disturbance of 1156. Since Norinaga and Shunzei were active in the *waka* coterie of the Retired Emperor, they certainly interacted frequently at poetry events such as the commissioning of the *Kyūan hyakushu* that Shunzei categorized at Sutoku's behest in 1151. Kubota, *Shinkokin kajin no kenkyū*, 262.

Flower Garland Sūtra [Avatamsaka Sūtra; Kegon-kyō]." The phrase *miyo no hotoke* (or *sanzebutsu*), meaning the Buddhas of the three worlds—past, present, and future—occupies most of the second *ku*, and it seems to be this conceptual kernel that holds the truth of the Sūtra in the speaker's mind. This concept of the three worlds appears in numerous Buddhist texts, but an online search of the text of the Kegon-kyō reveals that it appears almost six hundred times, while the phrase "Buddha of the three worlds" appears almost seventy times. The number three as it relates to the Buddha recalls Kazan's poem (1204) based upon the three bodies of the Buddha (*sanshin nyorai*), but also foreshadows two more exact uses of the phrase *miyo no hotoke* in poems by Retired Emperor Sutoku (1220) and Kakushō (1221) later in the sequence.

Norinaga's poem, like Shunrai's, describes an interaction with a Buddhist sūtra, and, like Kazan's, is almost entirely in the meditative mode. The poet critiques a point of view apparently held by the inexperienced practitioner (by himself, before the quality of his realization deepened): that the three Buddhas of the past, present, and future are somehow separate, and perhaps unequal. In fact, the speaker concludes, such thoughts are "foolish" (*hakanaku*) since "they are one / in my body" (*waga mi hitotsu*). There is a slight lyric inflection in the speaker's regret for his misunderstanding, but as a whole the poem's project is to counter ignorance (*shirazute*) about ("not grasping") the truth.

It is interesting to compare Norinaga's first *shakkyō-ka* here, based upon the Kegon Sūtra, to a poem (1222) further along in the sequence, on the same Sūtra, by Shikishi Naishinnō (?–1201).[534] Despite the common scriptural basis, the poems differ in terms of content and modal response. Norinaga's poem makes a purely intellectual response to the concept of the Buddhas of the three worlds. This poem's strategy is almost identical with that of poem 1204, which also critiqued an unskillful spiritual opinion and suggested a more correct focus and interpretation. Shikishi's poem emphasizes both the narrative and

---

534. The daughter of Go-Shirakawa, Shikishi studied with Shunzei, and became a renowned poet, eventually regarded as one of the representative poets of the *Shinkokinshū*. It was for Shikishi that Shunzei wrote his poetic treatise *Korai fūteishō* in 1197.

emotional aspects of Samantabhadra's (Fugen's) vow to never abandon anyone at the moment of death. She makes clever use of the word *furusato* ([one's] old village) in reference to the present world, but read in the context of the Sūtra, it is clear that she means the moment when one leaves this world forever. The poem focuses on the assistance and encouragement given to the spiritual seeker along the path (for which the pilgrim must leave home, as in several previous poems). Here we have another variation, continued from three poems before Shikishi's, on the light/dark metaphor: the moon's light will guide the way to the West. Though a variety of feelings are implicit in the narrative predicament, the poem takes a surprisingly light and even witty touch—expressing no melodrama about a very serious topic, but rather a seemingly calm assurance.

Norinaga's second poem (1218) references another Buddhist concept that had penetrated aristocratic society and the world of *waka* composition: *sokushin jōbutsu*, or attaining Buddhahood in this very body. This concept played an important role in both the esoteric doctrine of the Shingon sect and the exoteric-esoteric doctrine (*taimitsu*) of the Tendai sect. While Kūkai's source for the concept came from an apocryphal treatise attributed to Nāgārjuna, Saichō's source was the story of the Nāga princess in the Lotus Sutra who changed into a male instantaneously, and reached enlightenment almost as quickly.[535] However, as Stone emphasizes, after the time of Annen (841–?), discussions about the concept within the Tendai sect "came increasingly to be associated with esoteric practices," and this, she says, "greatly influenced the development of medieval Tendai thought."[536] The concept eventually "transcended Tendai doctrine and emerged as a prominent theme in Japanese Buddhism more generally."[537]

"Realizing Buddhahood in this very body" does not have any apparent connection to the Lotus Sutra in Norinaga's poem and seems, therefore, to be more closely related to esoteric constructs in which

---

535. Stone, *Original Enlightenment and the Transformation of Medieval Japanese Buddhism* (Honolulu: University of Hawaii Press, 1999), 31.

536. Ibid., 32–33.

537. Ibid., 33.

realization comes through an identification of one's body and mind with that of Dainichi Nyorai (Mahāvairocana Buddha). Through his name—Great Sun Tathāgathā—this Buddha is related to the rays of the sun, but in Norinaga's poem it is the moon that casts its light.

Is this poem an expression of esoteric doctrine or an expression of *taimitsu* (Tendai exoteric) doctrine? The moon's reflection in the water, according to Chih-i, was a metaphor for the historical Buddha who represents the teachings (*shakumon*, "trace gate") in the first fourteen chapters of the Lotus Sutra. The moon shining in the sky, on the other hand, was likened to the eternal Buddha of the origin teaching (*honmon*, "origin gate") who represented the second fourteen chapters of the Sutra.[538] Eventually, this duality was refuted in a mid-twelfth-century Tendai text called the *Sanjū shika no kotogaki* (Notes on the thirty-four articles), and along with the refutation of the dualistic distinction between the trace Buddha and the original Buddha came the collapse of the metaphors: "To see the Buddha in his manifested trace (*suijaku-butsu*) is to see the Buddha in his original ground (*honji-butsu*). To see the moon in the water is to see the moon in the sky."[539] The metaphor in Norinaga's poem seems to be a product of this collapse, since the shining moon (*teru tsuki*)—in the sky, one presumes—casts its light (*hikari o sasu*) on this body (*kono mi ni*). Moreover, because the shining moon is clear (*sumeba*), it casts its reflection onto the water (the essential clarity of enlightened wisdom) of the speaker's heart (*kokoro no mizu*).

A very similar metaphor occurs in a subsequent poem (1224), by Fujiwara no Naganori (1100–1180). The headnote to that poem—"the body is like the moon in the water"—attributes that quote to the ten metaphors in the Yuima-kyō (Vimalakīrti Sūtra), but a search of the digital text of the Taishō Daizō-kyō reveals that this particular metaphor does not appear there or in any other Buddhist text. There are occurrences of the phrase "like the moon in the water" (*suichū no*

---

538. Ibid., 200.
539. Ibid.

tsuki no gotoshi) in the Yuima-kyō, but it is never preceded by the words "this body" (*kono mi*).[540]

Naganori argues that although the speaker's body is "inconstant" (*sadame naki kono mi*), it may serve as a vessel for enlightenment, just as, in the simile, the moon's rays "lodge" (are "reflected" in our translation) in the water (*mizu ni yadoru tsukikage*). This argument is similar to that of poem 1218 by Norinaga, in which the imperfect body was also seen as possible vessel of enlightenment. The body functions as such a vessel both "when [the moon] is clear" (*sumeba*) and "when it is clouded" (*nigoreba*), though when it is clear, "it can be seen" (*miyu*) and when it is clouded, "it is hidden" (*kakuru*). Here is another poem in which the speaker addresses a potentially emotionally charged topic with equanimity: he *notices* distinctions, conditions and states, rather than reacting strongly with either clinging or aversion.

The concept of the Buddhas of the three worlds (*miyo no hotoke*), the topic of Norinaga's poem (1217), continues to play a role in a pair of poems (*zōtōka*, 1220 and 1221) between Emperor Sutoku and the Ninna-ji priest Kakushō (1129–1169).[541] The phrase *miyo no hotoke* appears in both poems, further evidence that the twelve poems in this sub-sequence concern the theme of awakening and Buddhahood. However, while Norinaga's poem argued for the position that the three Buddhas "are one / in my body," Sutoku's argument is based upon the narrative predicament of the headnote (repeated in the poem): "Sent in the winter when the Later Nyūdō Hosshinnō was confined at Mount Kōya." Fearing Kakushō (the later Nyūdō Hosshinnō) might be trapped by snow on Mount Kōya (thus prevented from finishing the religious practices that would lead to enlightenment), Sutoku asks for confirmation that "the sun of

---

540. Despite this, many poets insisted that the metaphor did come from that group, including Fujiwara no Kintō who composed a poem on that topic and included it in his private anthology, *Kintō-shū*, and Koben, whose poem (1190) is included in the "Shakkyō" subsection of the *Goshūishū*. SKT, vol. 3, 306.

541. Kakushō, the fifth son of Emperor Toba, held poetry gatherings (*kakai*) at Shikindai-ji on the Ninna-ji temple grounds frequented by poets such as Saigyō and Norinaga. Matsuno Yōichi, *Torihaha: Senzaishū jidai waka no kenkyū* (Tokyo: Kasama Shobō, 1994), 404.

Buddhas / past, present and still to come / goes on shining." Kakushō's response, also in the form of a rhetorical question, assures the Emperor that the sun (the three Buddhas) in fact always shines. Making use of the *kakekotoba* "*tsumi*" (sin/accumulate), Kakushō asks Sutoku to reconsider his own question: "it's our sin, not fallen snow, / that must melt away—isn't it?"

This *zōtōka* between Kakushō and Sutoku is linked in the larger sequence to the image of a wooden door (*maki no to*) in the Kakuchū poem (1219) that preceded Sutoku's. The door (*toboso*) in Sutoku's poem refers to the entry into the valley below Mount Kōya, and thus metaphorically to the place from which the speaker of the poem will emerge after meditative practice; the door in Kakuchū's poem represented the place through which the speaker—the prodigal son in the "Belief and Understanding" chapter (4) of the Lotus Sutra—passed to wander the world of confusion. These two doors function as a pair of opposites: Kakuchū's represents *samsāra*, Sutoku's enlightenment.

Another meditative response to the topic of the enlightened wisdom of the Buddha can be found in a poem (1223) by Fujiwara (Kujō) no Kanezane (1149–1207), the Regent and former Minister of the Right during the latter half of the twelfth century.[542] In esoteric Buddhism, the five wisdoms (*gochi*), one of which Kanezane addresses in his poem, are represented by five tathāgatha (*gochi nyorai*). Kanezane's topic—the "wisdom of equal natures" (*byōdōshōchi*; S: *samatā-jñāna*)—is defined as "the wisdom that knows the conditions of equality" (*byōdō no sama o shiru chi*), "that understands the equal

---

542. Kanezane was the founder of the Kujō line, and the elder brother of Tendai abbot Jien whose poem (1225) comes almost immediately afterward in this sequence. After Kanezane fell from power in 1196, he is said to have taken refuge (*kie*) with Hōnen and spent his days in *nenbutsu* contemplation (*nenbutsu sanmai*). Despite his connection with the Pure Land teachings of Hōnen, Kanezane was commonly known by the name Gachirindono, a reference to the Shingon practice of *gachirinkan* discussed in Chapter 4 in relationship to a *shakkyō-ka* (1188) in the *Goshūishū* by the priest Kakuchō. Such diverse connections (to Tendai, Pure Land, and Shingon Buddhism) are not surprising in the religious environment of the late twelfth century, but it is from esoteric doctrine that Kanezane derives the topic of this poem in the *shakkyō-ka* sequence.

nature of self and others" (*jiko to tasha to no byōdōshō o rikai suru chi*), or "embodies the equality of self and others" (*jita no byōdō o taigen uru chi*).[543] Attaining such wisdom means not differentiating between dualities, a concept also expressed by the Tendai concept of the middle truth (*chū*).

Kanezane structures his explanation of the wisdom of equal natures as two parallel declarative statements: "by some delusion or dream / each person seems different" and "when you awaken, though— / every heart is the same." That he adds no subjective element to this argument renders the poem somewhat didactic.[544]

Ishida Mizumaro claims Kanezane's poem is only one of two in the *Senzaishū shakkyō-ka* sequence that makes reference to esoteric (*mikkyō*) doctrine (the other being the *sokushin jōbutsu* poem by Norinaga previously discussed)—by which he seems to mean Shingon doctrine.[545] Such an assessment downplays the expression of esoteric doctrine in other sects like the Kegon and the Tendai. Emperor Kazan's poem on the three bodies of the Buddha, as well as Bishop Genshin's on the rain pouring onto grass and trees both emphasize enlightened equanimity (*byōdō*), or radical nonduality, which is also Kanezane's topic. While Shunzei may have made only sporadic use of specific Shingon doctrines to construct his *shakkyō-ka* sequence, his inclusion of the poems by Emperor Kazan and Bishop Genshin is a clearly deliberate esoteric thread that runs throughout the entire fifty-four poems.

The pair of exchange poems (1225, 1226) by the Tendai abbot Jien (1155–1225) and the priest Son'en (dates unknown)—thought to be Shunzei's son—share snow imagery with the poems by Sutoku and Kakushō.[546] Jien's poem contrasts with the intellectual responses that

---

543. Nakamura, *Bukkyōgo daijiten*, 1147
544. Kanezane was not a preacher or a priest, and he apparently wrote the poem, not for a religious event, but for a *hyakushu* (*Jishō ninen udaijin Kanezane no ie no hyakushu*) which his son, Yoshitsune, compiled in 1178.
545. Ishida, *Nihon koten bungaku to Bukkyō*, 218–219.
546. Little is actually known about Son'en. Therefore, as Manaka Fujiko and Ishihara Kiyoshi have said, we cannot determine the veracity of this claim. Manaka, *Senzaishū Shinkokinshū shakkyō-ka no hyōshaku*, 25; Ishihara, *Shakkyō-ka no kenkyū*, 225.

have dominated this sub-sequence, instead making an emotional response to the narrative predicament recounted in some detail in the headnote. The student discord (*dōshū gakuto fuwa*) described there occurred in 1178, when Jien had almost finished a thousand-day retreat at Mudō-ji on Mount Hiei.[547] Fearing, or grieving, the potential loss of the Saint's (Saichō's) teachings due to this discord, Jien decided to remain where he was, alone, and presumably finish his retreat. The "Saint's tracks [teachings/doctrines]" (*hijiri no ato*) of the headnote are echoed by "ancient tracks" (*mukashi no ato*) in the poem; it is the possible erasure of these by the morning (*kesa,* a *kakekotoba* for religious vestments) snow (the student discord) about which Jien expresses sadness (*kanashi*). Son'en responds to Jien's emotion with reason, emphasizing that it will be Jien (expressed metonymically by his name [*kimi ga na*]) himself who will continue the tradition of study (*mukashi no ato*) even if everything is buried and destroyed by the snow. While there is no overt reference to enlightenment in his poem, Son'en implies that Jien is equal in enlightenment to Saichō, the founder of Tendai. Son'en's poem is the second in the sequence that has associated continuing power with a name; poem 1214 by Kaishū made a case for the salvific power of the name of the Lotus Sutra. This would seem to conflict with the idea of concepts needing to fall away, but in both cases it is said that the names are powerful and/or will survive because of their associations with the Buddhadharma itself.

Closing this sub-sequence of poems on *satori* and *bodaishin* is a *shakkyō-ka* (1227) by Kujō no Kanezane's son, Yoshitsune, compiler of the *Jishō ninen udaijin Kanezane no ie no hyakushu* for which Kanezane provided the topics. Yoshitsune's poem is based upon the Receipt of Prophecy by Five Hundred Disciples chapter (8) in the Lotus Sutra, and is a final reminder that everyone is already enlightened, the premise of "original enlightenment" (*hongaku*) thought. Here Pūrna appears to the Buddha's other disciples as a *śrāvaka* (J: *shōmon*), or voice-hearer, enlightened by hearing the

---

547. Katano and Matsuno, *Senzaiwakashū*, 372.

Buddha speak. The *śrāvaka* represents one of the three vehicles (*yāna*) by which a devotee can become enlightened, but according to the Mahāyāna teachings, a *śrāvaka* understands the Mainstream Buddhist teachings alone and not those found in the Lotus Sutra. In this chapter, however, the Buddha reveals that secretly (*naihi*) Pūrna is already a bodhisattva and teaches the Dharma from this high station.

The image of the "sea" (*umi*)—recalling all the water imagery in the sequence, but most recently the reflecting water in Naganori's poem (1224)—in the second *ku* implies through its modifier *kurushiki* (painful, suffering) that the other disciples to whom the Buddha preached have not yet crossed that sea to realize the highest teachings of the Lotus Sutra. Like several previous poems, this one makes distinctions and corrections in an unskillful view of things: Yoshitsune asks rhetorically, conversing with Pūrna himself, "did they [the Buddha's disciples] think you crossed it alone, / the ocean of suffering?" The answer, of course, is *no*: the disciples realized that "you [Pūrna] didn't need to cross" because, in fact, he was "helping *others* across." In fact, the poem might be glossed, "realize this, and feel gratitude." Though this is an intellectual argument, there is an emotional element in the poem's implication that everyone should be grateful for, in this case, the Buddha's prophecy of the secret bodhisattva in the Lotus Sutra.

SECTION 3 *KŪ (SŪNYATĀ)* [POEMS 1228–1238]

(Corresponding to *Makashikan* Chapter 3 [*Kanka*] and the *Hannyaji* Period)

[1228]

呉竹のむなしと説ける言の葉は三世の仏の母とこそ聞け
kuretake no / munashi to tokeru / koto no ha wa / miyo no hotoke no / haha to koso kike

ON THE ESSENCE OF THE PRAJÑĀPĀRAMITĀ SŪTRAS,
    from among poems on Dharma texts, composed when a hundred poems were called for by the Regent and former Minister of the Right

> those leaves of words
>   that teach "the emptiness
>
>   of bamboo"
>
> are mother to the Buddhas
>   of the three worlds:
>
>   thus have I heard
>
> — Fujiwara no Takanobu

[1229]

むなしきも色なるものと悟れとや春のみ空のみどりなるらん
*munashiki mo / iro naru mono to / satore to ya / haru no misora no /
midori naruran*

ON THE ESSENCE OF THE PASSAGE "FORM IS
EMPTINESS AND EMPTINESS ITSELF IS FORM,"
                                                          from
among the hundred poems mentioned in the preface to the previous
poem

      it says:

   wake up! things are empty! all the colorful forms!—

    is that why "empty" equals "sky"?

why the sky of spring shows green?

          — Tango of the Regent's Residence

[1230]

長き夜もむなしきものと知りぬれば早く明けぬる心地こそ
すれ

nagaki yo mo / munashiki mono to / shirinureba / hayaku akenuru /
kokochi koso sure

ON THE ESSENCE OF THE PASSAGE "THROUGH
THE LONG NIGHT / WE PRACTICED THE LAW OF
EMPTINESS" from the Lotus Sutra

    the long night, too,
was an empty thing—

    when I knew that—

I felt the light
    dawn quickly

— Former Middle Counselor
Moronaka

[1231]

鷲の山月を入りぬと見る人は暗きにまよふ心なりけり
washi no yama / tsuki o irinu to / miru hito wa / kuraki ni mayou /
kokoro narikeri

ON THE ESSENCE OF THE LIFE-SPAN OF THE THUS
COME ONE CHAPTER of the Lotus Sutra

> anyone to whom the moon
>
> appears to sink behind Vulture Peak
>
> has a heart
> > lost in darkness

— En'i Hōshi (Saigyō)

[1232]

いさぎよき池に影こそ浮かびぬれ沈みやせむと思ふわが身を
isagiyoki / ike ni kage koso / ukabinure / shizumi ya semu to / omou wagami o

WRITTEN WHEN THE HORIKAWA MINISTER OF THE RIGHT CAME TO THE PARADISE HALL OF SENSAI SHŌNIN'S UNGO-JI

> looking down into
> > the flawless pond
>
> > I saw my face
> > > reborn
>
> > when for so long
> > > I was sure
>
> > > I'd fall
> > > > into hell

— Jingi Haku Akinaka

[1233]

朽ちはつる袖にはいかゞ包まましむなしと説けるみ法なら
ずは

kuchihatsuru / sode ni wa ikaga / tsutsumamashi / munashi to tokeru /
minori narazu wa

ON THE ESSENCE OF THE EVER-WAILING BODHISATTVA
from the Larger Prajñāpāramitā Sūtra

> how could I keep anything
> in sleeves ruined as these—
>
> if there were no Law
> to teach (the heavens equal) emptiness?

— Priest Jakuchō

[1234]

見るほどは夢も夢とも知られねばうつゝも今はうつゝと思はじ
*miru hodo wa / yume mo yume tomo / shirareneba / utsutsu mo ima wa
/ utsutsu to omawaji*

ON THE ESSENCE OF THE METAPHOR "THIS BODY IS
LIKE A DREAM," from the Ten Metaphors of the Yuima-kyō

> because I can't know
> that dreams are dreams
> while I'm dreaming—
>
> I'm also likely never
> to believe
> that reality is real

— Fujiwara no Suketaka

[1235, no headnote]

おどろかぬ我心こそ憂かりけれはかなき世をば夢と見ながら
odorokanu / wa ga kokoro koso / ukarikere / hakanaki yo oba / yume to
minagara

> my ignorant heart!
> troubled while it dreams
> the dream of the always-
> disappearing world

— Priest Tōren

[**1236**]

あか月を高野の山に待つほどや苔の下にも有明の月
*akatsuki o / takano no yama ni / matsu hodo ya / koke no shita ni mo /
ariake no tsuki*[548]

WRITTEN WHEN MAKING A PILGRIMAGE TO KŌYA

    while I wait for first light
      on Kōya mountain

    already under the moss:
    the dawn moon

                — Priest Jakuren

---

548. The *furigana* on the fifth and sixth graphs in the SNKBT version of the
Senzaishū (375) are *takano*, but they can also be read *Kōya*.

[1237]

思ひとく心ひとつになりぬれば氷も水も隔てざりけり
*omoitoku / kokoro hitotsu ni / narinureba / kōri mo mizu mo /
hedatezarikeri*

ON THE ESSENCE OF THE PHRASE "MENTAL
AFFLICTIONS ARE THEMSELVES ENLIGHTENMENT"

after meditating, untangling, melting—
my heart became one—

ice was never different
from water, or water
from ice

— Chūjō of Shikishi Naishinnō's
Residence

[**1238**]

頼もしき誓ひは春にあらねども枯れにし枝も花ぞ咲きける
tanomoshiki / chikai wa haru ni / aranedomo / karenishi eda mo / hana zo sakikeru

WHEN THINKING ON KANNON'S VOW

> a promise so trustworthy—
> though it's not spring
>
> on the withered branches
> flowers bloom!

> — Former Major Counselor
> Tokitada

Three of the poems (1228, 1229, 1233) in this eleven-poem sub-sequence are based upon the Prajñāpāramitā, "perfection of wisdom," sūtras in which the teachings on emptiness (*kū;* S: *śūnyatā*) are prominent. Another four poems (1230, 1234, 1235, 1237) are based upon concepts like emptiness, insubstantiality, and radical nonduality that are found in sūtras other than the Prajñāpāramitā sūtras. The remaining four poems are connected indirectly to these seven poems. Jakuren's poem (1236) is related to the concept of emptiness and radical nonduality by virtue of its connection to Kūkai. Kūkai's teachings were firmly rooted in the principles of emptiness; he even composed a "secret key" (*hiken*) commentary on the Heart Sutra.[549] Two poems by Saigyō (1231) and Fujiwara no Akinaka (1232), and occasional *shakkyō-ka* like Jakuren's poem, seem at first to have no apparent relationship to the other poems in the sub-sequence, except perhaps by association—the first based on the Lotus Sutra (as is the poem preceding it); the second composed at Sensai Shōnin's temple, Ungo-ji.[550] Sensai Shōnin was the author of poem 1209, from the first sub-sequence of poems in the "Shakkyō-ka" book. The last poem (1238) in the sub-sequence, by Taira no Tokitada, acts as transition from the *shakkyō-ka* on emptiness to the next sub-sequence (1239–1249) of *Hokke-kyō-ka* based upon the Lotus Sutra.

According to the Tendai *goji* system, the Prajñāpāramitā sūtras were preached during the fourth period (Hannya [*prajñā*] period) that lasted twenty-two years of the Buddha's preaching life. Chegwan's *Tendai shikyōgi* that became influential in Japanese Tendai Buddhism states that these teachings "integrate [all the teachings so far] and wash away [all delusions by means of emptiness (*śūnyatā*) and wisdom (*prajñā*)]."[551] The teachings washed away by the Prajñāpāramitā sūtras were presumably those—both Mainstream Buddhist and Mahāyāna sūtras—that were taught and then recorded during the first and second periods.

---

549. Hakeda, *Kūkai: Major Works*, 262–265.

550. Akinaka participated in Sensai Shōnin's *Ungo-ji kechien-kyō no kōen utaawase* of 1116, but this poem does not appear there. SKT, vol. 5, 147–149.

551. Chappell, *T'ien-t'ai Buddhism*, 60.

In reality, however, scholars currently believe that "the earliest Mahāyāna *sūtras* [were] probably *Prajñāpāramitā sūtras*" and thus most likely precede many other sūtras that eventually became widespread throughout East Asia.[552] If this is in fact the case, it could help to explain the presence of their teachings—especially those about emptiness—in other Mahāyāna sūtras such as the Lotus Sutra and the Vimalakīrti Sūtra, both of which are represented in this sub-sequence.

The Prajñāpāramitā sūtras and their teachings date back to the Nara and early Heian periods when, according to Ryūichi Abe, the Heart Sutra "was one of the most popular Buddhist scriptures for both the ordained and lay, for their merit-producing acts of chanting and copying."[553] He argues that Kūkai's commentary on the Heart Sutra—*Hannya shingyō hiken* (The Secret Key to the Heart Sutra)—was instrumental in creating a "shift in the nature of scriptural reading from intellectual speculation to religious practice" by emphasizing the contemplative *darani* for which it is so famous.[554]

Chih-i (and eventually Japanese Tendai) adopts the concept of emptiness and provisionality into the three truths (*santai*) and three discernments (*sankan*) doctrines, but declares these truths to be "secondary derivations—false or, at best, provisional constructs (*ch'üan*) devised to convey the ultimate reality of the middle [*chū*] in a language consistent with the conventions of deluded experience."[555] Using such logic, Chih-i subsumes emptiness within the teachings of the Lotus Sutra (the next category and period to be discussed), where we discover it to be important too, but ultimately surpassed by a greater truth—that of the middle. Therefore, while the three truths are entirely dependent upon and essential to the truth of emptiness and provisionality, Chih-i gives them superior status to either one individually.

---

552. Williams, *Mahāyāna Buddhism*, 40.

553. Ryūichi Abe, "Scholasticism, Exegesis, and Ritual Practice: On Renovation in the History of Buddhist Writing in the Early Heian Period," in *Heian Japan: Centers and Peripheries* (Honolulu: University of Hawai'i Press, 2007), 179.

554. Ibid., 205.

555. Stevenson and Donner, *The Great Calming and Contemplation*, 12.

The three poems that begin the sub-sequence of *shakkyō-ka* on emptiness make use either of some form of the Japanese adjective *munashi* meaning "empty," or the Chinese character meaning sky (J: *sora*) that simultaneously doubles as the semantic marker for the adjective. The first of these poems, according to the headnote, was based upon the "essence of [all] the Prajñāpāramitā sūtras." Composed by Fujiwara no Takanobu (1142–1205) for the *Jishō ninen udaijin Kanezane no ie no hyakushu* of 1178, the poem makes a conceptual response, with almost no emotional component. The poem that follows by Tango (d. after 1208) was composed "on the essence of the passage 'form is emptiness and emptiness is form'" from the Heart Sutra (J: Hannya-shin-gyō; S: Prajñāpāramitā-hrdaya-sūtra). The poem argues for the truth of a particular passage (*shiki soku ze kū, kū soku ze shiki*) but includes sensual elements that balance the conceptual: the ending combines connotations of color, sky, spring, and green to suggest a state of physical, emotional and spiritual freshness, freedom and enjoyment. The poem constitutes a variation on the previous one, in that it seems to find delight, or even humor, in the idea that "all the colorful forms" are empty.

The third poem (1230) by Minamoto no Moronaka (1116–1172) is based upon a passage from Chapter 4 (Belief and Understanding, *Shingebon*) of the Lotus Sutra, "through the long night / we practiced the law of emptiness."[556] In the same way that poem 1218 by Norinaga in the previous sub-sequence warned against believing that the body is an unworthy vessel of the dharma, this poem seems to argue that *mappō* is no excuse for not continuing to strive on the path, as the darkness is also an empty concept and encouragement is available in that very realization. As such, Moronaka's poem is another variation on the idea of assistance across obstacles. The poem is a lyric-meditative hybrid: the understanding it achieves in the middle is intellectual and spiritual, but it also causes enormous relief, and is expressed in terms of *satori* ("felt the light/dawn quickly"). Interestingly, the poem also

---

556. This passage in Hurvitz's translation is "Throughout the long night of time / Having practiced and cultivated the dharma of emptiness ..." Hurvitz, *Scripture of the Lotus Blossom of the Fine Dharma*, 96; Iwamoto and Sakamoto, *Hokke-kyō*, vol. 1, 256.

downplays that development in a subtle way—however longed for, by its very nature dawn is an inevitable, rather than miraculous outcome.

Given the difficulty of the concept of emptiness, a strong meditative element might have been expected in this sub-sequence (as in the previous sub-sequence on awakening and the awakened heart), which would have subordinated the courtly lyric to a didactic impulse. That in fact the reverse is the case suggests Shunzei's allegiance to the project of traditional *waka*, though the "Shakkyō-ka" book as a whole demonstrates that he expanded the range of topics to which court *waka* in the imperial anthologies could respond.

It may be observed that the poets in this sub-sequence made a variety of different arguments in response to the concept of emptiness. Takanobu's poem places the concept in the foreground ("the emptiness / of bamboo"), comparing the teachings to the hollow inside of bamboo. "[T]hose leaves of words / that teach" (*koto no ha*), the sūtras themselves, he says, are nothing less than the "mother to the Buddhas / of the three worlds: / thus have I heard." These words echo those of Emperor Kōnin (r. 770–781) who said, "It is said that the *Prajñā-pāramitā* is the mother of all the Buddhas."[557] They also echo references in poems 1217, 1220, and 1221 in the previous sub-sequence to the Buddhas of the three worlds (*miyo no hotoke*). Takanobu's poem (1228) shifts emphasis away from the topics of the previous category and introduces the new one (emptiness). It also includes vocabulary from poems of the previous category, creates a bridge, or an "association"—to use Konishi Jin'ichi's word—between the new category and the *shakkyō-ka* that have preceded it.

Tango's poem (1229) on the phrase "form is emptiness and emptiness is form" is built cleverly upon the conceit that the Chinese character for "form" (*shiki*) is also the character for "color" (*iro*) in Japanese, while the Chinese character for "emptiness" (*kū*) is the same for "sky" (*sora*).[558]

Moronaka's poem (1230), based on a passage from the Lotus Sutra, emphasizes how the speaker felt (*kokochi koso sure*) about his realization

---

557. Abe, "Scholasticism, Exegesis, and Ritual Practice," 186.
558. Stevenson and Donner, *The Great Calming and Contemplation*, 12.

that the nature of the world is actually empty and nondualistic, a lyric element that recurs in poems 1232 and 1233 by Fujiwara no Akinaka (1059– 1129) and Jakuchō.[559]

Poem 1231, by Saigyō, is another variation on the theme of appearances vs. reality, and also on assistance vs. obstruction. The moon (the Buddhadharma), the speaker says, appears to sink, but only to the samsaric mind.

Akinaka's poem (1232), the fifth in the sub-sequence, turns away from the topic of emptiness entirely, returning to the device of the enlightened face (the moon in previous poems, his own face in this one) reflected in water. The words *uku* and *shizumu* (floating [up] and sinking [down]) express the contrast between salvation in Amida's paradise and damnation in hell. The poem is also a variation on the assistance/obstruction metaphor: the speaker's face is figuratively reborn in the temple pond, saving him from his previous samsaric state. He has brought himself to the temple (which reaches back to the earlier topic of pilgrimage practice), but the assistance he received there is expressed in terms of *satori*: one sees one's reflected face instantly, not by degrees.

The headnote of Jakuchō's poem (1233) that follows Akinaka's poem signals a return to the concept of emptiness, informing the reader that it is based upon "the essence of the Ever-Wailing Bodhisattva [Jōtai Bosatsu, S: Sadāprarudita] from the Larger Prajñāpāramitā Sūtra."[560] The Ever-Wailing Bodhisattva, the protector of this particular Sūtra,

---

559. A further connection of the Lotus Sutra with the Heart Sutra can be found in Saigyō's *Kikigakishū* where, Yamada Shōzen says, Saigyō added a poem on the Heart Sutra (and three other sūtras) to his twenty-eight poems on the Lotus Sutra (actually thirty due to the replication of two chapters, one of which was the Kannon chapter, 25). Yamada confirms Saigyō's involvement with the Shingon teachings—where the teachings of emptiness run deep—when he says that "[Saigyō] had thoroughly studied those texts that formed the fundamental doctrines of esoteric doctrine." Yamada Shōzen, "Poetry and Meaning: Medieval Poets and the Lotus Sutra," in Willa Jane Tanabe and George Tanabe, ed., *The Lotus Sutra in Japanese Culture* (Honolulu: University of Hawai'i Press, 1989), 106–107.

560. The Sūtra indicated here is the Mahāprajñāpāramitā Sūtra (Daibon hannyakyō, T 223). This poem was originally collected in the *Tsukimōdeshū* compiled by Kamo no Shigeyasu in 1178. SKT, vol. 2, 354, poem 1036.

is said to weep forever in compassion for the suffering of all sentient beings.[561] To explicate emptiness, Jakuchō makes use of one of the most common devices in classical Japanese literature: sleeves wet with tears. But his deployment of this image is complex, and the rhetorical question of which it is a part not easy to unpack: "my state is such (ruined sleeves) that I can keep nothing, but happily the Dharma teaches that the heavens (*munashi/sora*) consists in just such emptiness, therefore what I keep in ruined sleeves are the heavens itself." This logic is both emotional—"I'm empty and happy to be so"—and didactic in the sense that it encourages others to reach the same realization and the same liberated state.

As I have noted, the concept of emptiness and insubstantiality is found in other Mahāyāna sūtras than the Prajñāpāramitā sūtras. We have already seen an example of this in Moronaka's poem, based on the Lotus Sutra, but in the two poems that follow Jakuchō's, we find a further example based upon the same metaphor in the Vimalakīrti Sūtra—"this body is like a dream." The poem (1234) by Suketaka (?– after 1185) makes a purely meditative response to the material, while that (1235) by Priest Tōren (1126–1203) makes a purely lyric response. Though we have already encountered three poems (1202, 1203, 1224) in the *Senzaishū shakkyō-ka* sequence on the Vimalakīrti metaphors, this is the first poem on this particular metaphor, and the first time this metaphor appeared in any Buddhist *waka* in the imperial anthologies from the time of the *Shūishū*.

These two poems revive the device of "elegant confusion" used so often in the love poems in the *Kokinshū*.[562] There the confusion concerned whether the lover had visited in reality or in dream, but in the case of these two poems the confusion concerns the body. If dreams are indistinguishable from reality and the body is nothing but a dream—an unenlightened state—then how can we understand the reality of insubstantiality that is taught in the Sūtra? The problem, according to Suketaka, is the inability to discern the difference between

561. Nakamura et al., *Bukkyō jiten*, 533.

562. See *Kokinshū* 645, 646, and 658 by the Virgin Princess of Ise Shrine, Ariwara no Narihira, and Ono no Komachi. Arai and Kojima, *Kokinshū*, 199 and 202.

"not knowing" ("because I can't know / that dreams are dreams / while I'm dreaming—") and not believing ("I'll also likely never / to believe / that reality is real"). The speaker in this poem makes a declarative argument about the problem, without applying the problem to himself in an emotional way, unlike Priest Tōren's poem, in which the speaker is troubled by his own persistent misunderstanding ("my ignorant heart!"), continuing to dwell on the very dream that cements our attachments to the world and to our bodies. Both speakers realize that their inability to understand the truth of emptiness keeps them in the dream, but only the speaker of Suketaka's poem realizes that reality is no more truthful than the dream.

A lyric response continues to dominate this sub-sequence in three poems by Jakuren (1139–1202), Chūjō of Shikishi Naishinnō's Residence (dates unknown) [1237], and Taira no Tokitada (1130–1189) [1238], one of two members of the Taira clan to be represented in the *Senzaishū shakkyō-ka* sequence. The truth of emptiness in Jakuren's poem is located in the conflation of Kūkai (and his teachings) with the moon of enlightenment ("already under the moss: the dawn moon"). The speaker in Jakuren's poem waits on Mount Kōya in the dark, in *samsāra*. But he does so in confidence, as he knows light will come— interestingly, in two forms. Dawn will bring the sun's first light, but simultaneously the dawn moon will appear, the greater light and the lesser. Jakuren quietly anticipates his realization of emptiness—the same Kūkai addressed in his commentary on the Heart Sutra—that will be illuminated by the rays of the sun and the moon/Kūkai. That the moon is "already under the moss" presents the saint's grave as a kind of pregnancy metaphor: the saint's body has impregnated the earth, and will be (re)born from it at dawn to cast light again. As such, the poem is a variation on the assistance vs. obstruction theme: death obstructed the saint's work of assistance, but only temporarily (only in appearance).

In the case of Chūjō's poem, the truth of emptiness is expressed in the headnote by the conceptual phrase *bonnō soku bodai* (mental afflictions are nothing other than enlightenment), and in the poem itself as nondiscrimination between ice from water: "ice was never different / from water, or water / from ice." These are very abstract concerns, but the poem expresses them with the emotionally resonant metaphor of ice melting to become water, which by implication means to become fluid and free. The poem also has a didactic component: "if you look at this aspect of life as I have, you also will experience freedom." In the first *ku* Chūjō uses the associative word (*engo*) *toku* (to melt, solve)—in the verbal compound *omoitoku*—to foreshadow the words "ice" (*kōri*) and "water" (*mizu*), which serves to draw the upper (*kami*) and lower (*shimo*) sections of the poem together and, in a sense, to fuse the lyric and meditative gestures. Moreover, this fusion of the personal and didactic mirrors the conflation of mental attachments (J: *bonnō*; S: *kleśas*) with enlightenment (*bodai*), an experience that will effect true Mahāyāna realization. In these terms, the poem echoes others in the sequence that urge a different view of states that seem unsatisfactory or hopeless. Just as the night ends quickly for anyone who realizes it is empty (1230), and as the body in its imperfection may be the vessel of the dharma (1218), so in this poem mental afflictions are themselves enlightenment in a different form.

The final poem, by Taira no Tokitada, belongs equally to this sub-sequence and to the next sub-sequence of *Hokke-kyō-ka*. The headnote says it was composed "when thinking on Kannon's vow," presumably the vow in the Lotus Sutra,[563] which can be found in the Senju Darani-kyō (S: Nīlakanthaka Sūtra, T 1060).

As the bodhisattva of compassion, Kannon recalls the compassion of Jōtai Bosatsu, the Ever-Wailing Bodhisattva, from the Larger Prajñāpāramitā Sūtra in poem 1233 by Jakuchō. Moreover, because s/he appears as the principal character in the Heart Sutra, s/he also is linked with Tango's poem (1229) based on words spoken by Kannon: "form is emptiness, emptiness is form." However, Kannon is also the subject of the Kannon-kyō, or Kannon Sūtra, which serves double purpose as Chapter 25 of the Lotus Sutra. In the Lotus Sutra, Kannon's compassion allows appearance in numerous forms: the

---

563. The editors of the SNKBT version of the *Senzaishū* claim that the imagery for this poem comes from the Senju-darani-kyō (S: Nīlakanthaka Sūtra, T 1060), rather than imagery found in the Lotus Sutra. Katano and Matsuno, *Senzaiwakashū*, 376.

"body of a Buddha" (representing the Mahāyāna teachings) as well as in the "body of a pratyekabuddha" and the "body of a voice-hearer [śrāvaka]" (representing the Mainstream Buddhist teachings), to mention a few.[564] Through such versatility, the Kannon in Tokitada's poem belongs both to the category of poems on emptiness as well as to the category of Lotus Sutra poems to follow.

The image of the flowers blooming on withered branches in winter ("though it's not spring / on the withered branches / flowers bloom!") is also found in an *imayō* from the *Ryōjin hishō:* "even withered grass and trees, so / it is said, / blossom and bear fruit in a / moment."[565] It is impossible to say whether the *shakkyō-ka* influenced the *imayō* or vice versa, but the image expresses the curative powers of Kannon. It is also a variation on the image of the flowering plum common to court *waka*, a flower that blooms in late winter upon branches that seem dead, and which is thus a trope for fidelity: the poem transfers the fidelity to Kannon.

It may appear that the third section of *shakkyō-ka* on *kū* does not correspond to a chapter of the *Makashikan*. There is sufficient justification for connecting Lesser Chapter 3, "Manifesting the Great Result" (*Kanka*), with the second section on awakening and the awakened heart—but is the same justification applicable to the third section of poems on emptiness? If, in fact, the second section of *shakkyō-ka* is based upon enlightenment derived from the middle truth (*chū*) of the Tendai three truths, then it does not make sense to create a third sub-sequence of *shakkyō-ka* based entirely on the truth of the void (*kū*). The second sentence in Lesser Chapter 3 says, "If practice should deviate from the middle way, then [bodhisattvas] will experience recompense or results within the two extremes of [saṃsāra and nirvāna]."[566] Thus, Chih-i characterizes enlightenment (the recompense or results) that is based upon the middle truth as "the supreme and wondrous result," while practice that does not take root

564. Hurvitz, *Scripture of the Lotus Blossom of the Fine Dharma*, 314.

565. Kim, *Songs to Make the Dust Dance*, 74. Kim does not mention the Buddhist textual source for the *imayō*.

566. Stevenson and Donner, *The Great Calming and Contemplation*, 335.

in the middle truth is something that a bodhisattva will experience in a more limited way "within the two extremes."[567]

Is the doctrine of emptiness presented in the Prajñāpāramitā literature limited to the "two extremes," that is, to the two-truth doctrine of provisionality (*ke*) and void (*kū*)? Or is the doctrine of emptiness in this literature another expression of radical nonduality (three-truth doctrine) taught within the Tendai and Shingon sects? If the chapters of the *Makashikan* are an expression of the Tendai path to enlightenment (that which blossoms from the middle truth), and if the *shakkyō-ka* sequence in the *Senzaishū* is also a literary expression of this *mārga*, then it seems certain that the third section of poems on the teachings of emptiness conformed "to the middle way," at least as Shunzei perceived them, and would bring about "the supreme and wondrous result."

---

567. Ibid.

SECTIONS 4 AND 5   LOTUS SUTRA [1239–1248] AND NIRVĀNA SŪTRA [1248–1255]

(Corresponding to *Makashikan* Chapters 4 and 5 [*Retsumō* and *Kisho*] and the *Hokke-nehanji* Periods)

Lotus Sutra Poems

[1239]

春ごとに嘆しものを法の庭散るがうれしき花もありけり
harugoto ni / nagekishi mono o / nori no niwa / chiru ga ureshiki / hana mo arikeri

ON THE ESSENCE OF THE INTRODUCTION CHAPTER
OF THE LOTUS SUTRA

> every spring
> I grieved, but O
>
> in the garden of the Law
>
> the flowers are grateful
> when they fall
>
> — Fujiwara no Koretsuna

[1240]

水草のみ茂き濁りと見しかどもさても月澄む江にこそあり
けれ

*mikusa nomi / shigeki nigori to / mishikadomo / satemo tsuki sumu / e
ni koso arikere*

ON THE ESSENCE OF THE BESTOWAL OF PROPHECY
CHAPTER OF THE LOTUS SUTRA

> what I saw as
> water thick with weeds
>
> in truth is a cove
>
> where the moon lives
> clearly

> — Senior Assistant Minister of the
> Right Ward Sueyoshi

[1241]

武蔵野の堀兼の井もある物をうれしく水の近づきにける
musashino no / horikane no i mo / aru mono o / ureshiku mizu no /
chikazukinikeru

ON THE ESSENCE OF THE PASSAGE "BIT BY BIT HE SEES
THE SOIL GROW DAMP AND MUDDY / AND THEN HE
KNOWS FOR CERTAIN HE IS NEARING WATER," from the
Preachers of the Dharma chapter of the Lotus Sutra

> that Horikane well
> at Musashino? —
>
> *also* difficult to dig—
>
> but happily, water
> is close at hand

—Senior Assistant Minister
to the Empress Dowager, Shunzei

[1242]

谷水をむすべば映るかげのみや千歳を送る友となるらん
tanimizu o / musubeba utsuru / kage nomi ya / chitose o okuru / tomo to naruran

ON THE ESSENCE OF THE DEVADATTA CHAPTER OF
THE LOTUS SUTRA

when I ladled the valley water—

who
spent a thousand years
becoming my friend—

only my reflection?

— Priest Kenshō

[1243]

朽ちはててあやうく見えしをばたゞの板田の橋も今渡すなり
kuchihatete / ayauku mieshi / oba tada no / itada no hashi mo / ima watasu nari

ON THE ESSENCE OF THE FORTITUDE CHAPTER OF
THE LOTUS SUTRA

    nothing looks so rotted
       and risky as the

           bridge at Itada

              but if the aunt in that verse
                can become a Buddha

                    we can cross

                 — Hōkyō Taikaku

[1244, no headnote]

恨みけるけしきや空に見えつらん姨捨山を照す月かげ
uramikeru / keshiki ya sora ni / mietsuran / obasuteyama o / terasu
tsukikage

mustn't signs
of the grudge they bore
be seen in the heavens?

over "throw-the-old-woman-away" mountain
moonlight shines

— Fujiwara no Atsunaka

[1245]

日のひかり月のかげとて照しける暗き心のやみ晴れよとて

hi no hikari / tsuki no kage tote / terashikeru / kuraki kokoro no / yami hareyo tote

ON THE ESSENCE OF THE PASSAGE "THE LIGHT OF THE SUN AND MOON / CAN BANISH ALL OBSCURITY AND GLOOM," from the Supernatural Powers of the Thus Come One chapter from the Lotus Sutra

the sun has shone its light and
the moon has shone its light:

clear the dark away, I beg—
from my heart of darkness

— Priest Renjō

[1246]

さらに又花ぞ降りしく鷲の山法のむしろの暮れがたの空
sara ni mata / hana zo furishiku / washi no yama / nori no mushiro no / kuregata no sora

ON THE ESSENCE OF THE ENCOURAGEMENTS OF THE BODHISATTVA UNIVERSALLY WORTHY CHAPTER OF THE LOTUS SUTRA

> again and again,
> more and more flowers
> fall to cover
> > this ground:
>
> > Vulture Peak,
> where we met
> under the evening sky
> on the rush mats of the teachings

> > — Senior Assistant Minister to the
> > Empress Dowager, Shunzei

[1247]

待ち出でていかにうれしく思ほえむ二十日あまりの山の端の月
machiidete / ika ni ureshiku / omooemu / hatsuka amari no / yama no ha no tsuki

On the essence of the passage "WHEN THE TWENTY-ONE DAYS HAVE BEEN FULFILLED, I WILL BESTRIDE MY SIX-TUSKED WHITE ELEPHANT"

moon of twenty days and more—

how happy will I feel
waiting for you
            to appear
on the verge of the mountain—

— Nakahara no Ariyasu

[1248]

朝まだきみ法の庭に降る雪は空より花の散るかとぞ見る
asa madaki / minori no niwa ni / furu yuki wa / sora yori hana no / chiru ka to zo miru

ON THE ESSENCE OF THE LINE "LISTENING TO THE DHARMA ON A SNOWY MORNING"

> not-quite-morning, and
> over the garden
> of the Noble Law
>
> is it snow that falls?
>
> or are these
> the flowers they saw
> raining from the sky?

— Nakahara no Kiyoshige

Nirvāna Sūtra Poems

[1249]

望月の雲かくれけむいにしへのあはれを今日の空にしるかな

mochizuki no / kumo kakurekemu / inishie no / aware o kyō no / sora ni shiru kana

WHEN THINKING ABOUT THE BUDDHA'S PARINIRVANA
at dusk during a Nirvāna Service at Yamashinadera

    in today's sky I understand
       that grief of long ago:

    clouds must have
       hidden the fullness

    of the eighth month moon
       from sight

               — Priest Eshō

[1250]

清く澄む心の底を鏡にてやがてぞ映る色も姿も

kiyoku sumu / kokoro no soko o / kagami nite / yagate zo utsuru / iro mo sugata mo

ON THE ESSENCE OF THE PASSAGE "AS IF LOOKING AT VARIOUS COLORS AND SHAPES IN A MIRROR" from the Nehangyō

> deep in my heart
> immaculate clarity lives:
>
> a mirror in which
>
> colors and shapes reflect
> their truth

— Priest Shunshū

[1251]

煙だにしばしたなびけ鳥辺山たち別れにし形見とも見ん
keburi dani / shibashi tanabike / toribeyama / tachiwakarenishi /
katami to mo min

ON THE ESSENCE OF THE PASSAGE "THE FIRE RAGES
ON BUT DOES NOT BURN FOREVER"

> while I keep watch, smoke,
>   drift long
>
> over the burning ground
>   at Toribe:
>
> souvenir of the dead who
>   have risen

                    — Priest Jakuzen

[1252]

鳥の音も浪のをとにぞかよふなるをなじみ法を説けばなりけり
tori no ne mo / nami no oto ni zo / kayou naru / onaji minori o / tokeba
narikeri

ON THE ESSENCE OF THE AMIDA-KYŌ

alike, it says,

in the song of birds
and the sound of waves—

one hears
the same Noble Law

— Taira no Yasuyori

[1253]

世を救ふ跡はむかしに変らねどはじめ建てけむ時をしぞ思ふ
yo o sukuu / ato wa mukashi ni / kawaranedo / hajime tatekemu / toki o shi zo omou

WRITTEN WHEN THE EMPEROR CAME TO TENNŌ-JI, on the theme "Old Temples Arouse Poignant Thoughts of the Past"

> proof he saved the world—
>   is the same
>   as ever:
>
> recalling to me
>   the time this first
>   was built

>   — Fujiwara no Sadanaga

[1254]

常ならぬためしはよはの煙にて消えぬ名残を見るぞかなし
き

tsune naranu / tameshi wa yowa no / keburi nite / kienu nagori o / miru
zo kanashiki

WHEN WORSHIPPING THE BUDDHA'S RELICS ON
PILGRIMAGE TO TENNŌ-JI

> in the dead of night, smoke
>   is proof of brevity—
>
> how sad, to look
>   on the traces that remain

                    — Tendai Abbot Meiun

[1255]

みな人を渡さむと思ふ心こそ極楽に行くしるべなりけれ
mina hito o / watasamu to omou / kokoro koso / gokuraku ni yuku /
shirube narikere

COMPOSED WHILE THE AUTHOR WAS WRITING THE
ŌJŌKŌSHIKI

the heart that considers
how everyone might be helped
to cross over

is the guide
to the paradise
in the West

— Preceptor Yōkan

Arrangement of the Final Two Sections
of the "Shakkyō-ka" Book

Parts of the final two sections of *shakkyō-ka*—ten poems based upon seven chapters from the Lotus Sutra and two poems based upon the Nirvāna Ceremony (Nehan-e) and Sūtra (Nehangyō)—correspond to the final period, Hokke nehanji, which combined both Sūtras into one period in the *goji* system. Chegwan's *Tendai shikyōgi*, the influential text that enumerated the five periods and that was valued by the Japanese Tendai sect, provides evidence for the reason that the *Hokke* (Lotus) and *Nehan* (Nirvāna) periods were combined: "If we consider [the *Nirvāna Sūtra*] in terms of its period and the flavor [referring to the five flavors], then it is the same as the *Lotus Sūtra*."[568]

The concluding five poems in the "Shakkyō-ka" book, based upon the Zaigō ōhō kyōke jigoku-kyō (T 724), the Amida-kyō (T 366), two different pilgrimages to Tennō-ji, and a poem-song (*waka/kayō*) written when Yōkan (also Eikan, 1033–1111) was writing the *Ōjōkōshiki* in 1079, appear to fall outside of the *goji* periodization system. However, since they are based upon themes of death and rebirth, they create a natural coda to poems on the death of the Buddha.

The correspondence between the ten poems on the Lotus Sutra and the two poems on the Nirvāna Sūtra and Lesser Chapters 4 and 5 of the *Makashikan* are less obvious and with good reason: Chih-i barely sketched out Lesser Chapter 4 and provided only minimal text for Lesser Chapter 5. Moreover, he never wrote Greater Chapters 9 and 10 to which Lesser Chapters 4 and 5 correspond. Therefore, much of our understanding of these two chapters is guesswork. Lesser Chapter 4, "Rending the Great Net" (*Retsumō*), of the *Makashikan* corresponds to the Lotus Sutra poems by means of its chapter title. In this chapter "calming-and-contemplation is expounded for the purpose of rending the great net [of doubt that arises from the diversity] of the sūtras and treatises."[569] The translators of *The Great Calming and Contemplation* explain that

568. Chappell, *T'ien-t'ai Buddhism,* 67.
569. Ibid., 338.

> the image of the 'great net of doubt' and its 'rending' originates from the *Lotus Sūtra:* Because of their attachment to the earlier provisional vehicles, the śrāvakas and other individuals of the assembly are thrown into confusion over the Buddha's intention to preach the one Buddha vehicle. By revealing that all prior teachings of the three vehicles are expedients ... their 'network of doubt' is 'rent' and the arhats and śrāvakas are enlightened to the Buddha vehicle.[570]

In short, through a realization of the teachings expounded in the Lotus Sutra, a devotee's doubts about contradictions that may have arisen from reading other sūtras will be eliminated. Chih-i does not name the Lotus Sutra in the few sentences he wrote for this chapter, but if we accept its title as deriving from the Sutra, there is foundation for designating a schematic correspondence.[571]

A reading of Lesser Chapter 5, "Returning to the Great Abode" (*Kisho*), of the *Makashikan* reveals that there are also possibilities for its correspondence to the two *nehan* (*nirvāna*) poems (1249, 1250) in the "Shakkyō-ka" book. Unlike Lesser Chapter 4, Lesser Chapter 5 is a fuller text and therefore we can derive more information about what Chih-i may have intended to write in Greater Chapter 10, which was to be called "Returning of the Purport" (*Shiki*).[572] According to Stevenson and Donner, "the entire chapter [Lesser Chapter 5] centers around an important passage in the *Nirvāna Sūtra,* where the 'secret treasury' of the Buddhas is identified with three eternal and unchanging meritorious qualities (C: *san-te;* J: *santoku*) of the dharma-body, prajñā, and liberation."[573] After the "quiescence of the three qualities" is attained, the Sūtra says, "The path of speech is cut off.

---

570. Ibid.

571. A search of the text of the Lotus Sutra reveals that the phrase "great net of doubt" (*gidaimō; daimō o utagau*) appears numerous times, but I have not found any instances of it appearing directly with the word *saku* (to rend).

572. Sekiguchi, *Makashikan*, vol. 1, 122.

573. Stevenson and Donner, *The Great Calming and Contemplation*, 30.

The reach of discursive thought is annihilated. Eternally quiescent, it is like open space."[574] While this passage describes ultimate enlightenment (*nirvāna*), the phrase "eternally quiescent" also alludes to death (the Buddha's death)—the topic of the Sūtra as a whole.

The Nirvāna Sūtra did not hold a primary place of allegiance within any of the Japanese Buddhist sects. However, Chih-i quoted from it extensively in the *Makashikan* characterizing it as "subtle," that is, having the "concept of unity and integration."[575] In Japan, the Sūtra was most commonly chanted and copied during the ceremony called Nehan-e, which was held on the fifteenth day of the second month at Kōfuku-ji (Yamashinadera).[576] We should consider the first two *shakkyō-ka* that begin the *Nehanji* section (one based on the ceremony and the other on the Nirvāna Sūtra) as providing for the thematic space for the final five *shakkyō-ka* on death.

Lotus Sutra Poems (1239–1248)

Various factors, considered together, contribute to the skillful and intricate interweaving of these poems. The arrangement of *shakkyō-ka* by sūtra name occurred throughout the Buddhist *waka* sequences in the imperial poetry anthologies; we saw this arrangement in the *Goshūishū* (1189–1190, 1192–1196) for poems based upon the Vimalakīrti Sūtra and the Lotus Sutra and in the *Kin'yōshū* (634–639) for poems based upon the Lotus Sutra. In cases where the sūtra poems were grouped together, they were often arranged sequentially according to chapter number.[577] In the *Senzaishū shakkyō-ka* sequence, however, we find two kinds of Lotus Sutra poems: those that appear singly or in pairs prior to this sub-sequence, probably selected for their suitability to the

---

574. Ibid., 348.

575. Swanson, *Foundations of T'ien-t'ai Philosophy*, 127.

576. This ceremony was also a topic for poems 1181–1185 in the *Goshūishū shakkyō-ka* sequence.

577. One poem in this *Senzaishū* sub-sequence is out of sync with this arrangement: the last poem 1248 is based on the same chapter (1, "Introduction") as the first poem 1239.

section of poems in which they appeared, and those that were selected for this sub-sequence. This sequential ordering of poems highlights the Lotus Sutra as a single text (perhaps with a single teaching) that progresses in a systematic manner.

In addition to their sequential arrangement by chapter, the chapters that are represented often emphasize devotion to, and the teaching of, the Lotus Sutra. For example, poem 1239, based upon the first chapter and opens the sub-sequence, transports us to "the garden of the Law" (on Vulture Peak) where the Sutra was taught. Likewise in poem 1242, based upon the Devadatta chapter, the speaker's (the Buddha's) service (and devotion) to Devadatta occurred "when I ladled the valley water." And in poem 1245, based upon the chapter titled Supernatural Powers of the Thus Come One (21, *Nyoraijinrikihon*), the speaker asks to receive the teachings—moonlight and sunlight—so that they shine upon his "heart of darkness."

The poems in this sub-sequence are also organized to emphasize the teachings of emptiness as expressed in the Lotus Sutra. Kenneth Ch'en says that the Lotus Sutra teachings primarily concern "the absolute identity of contrast."[578] Tamura Yoshirō expresses the same idea a little differently: "Both attachment to self and attachment to things other than the self are exposed [through the teachings of the Lotus Sutra]; leaving only a realization of nonsubstantiality or emptiness of self and other."[579] Therefore, it is in the ontological conflation of opposites where we find the highest teachings of emptiness (cf. *bonnō/waka soku bodai/darani*). In the Lotus Sutra poems we see this expressed in terms of grieving and gratefulness (1239), "water thick with weeds" and "where the moon lives / clearly (1240), the "rotted and risky ... / bridge at Itada" where the devotee "can cross" (1243), and sun/moonlight in relation to darkness (1242).

Finally, the poems seem to be arranged figuratively to represent a place that either is, or is similar to, a garden. The two primary images

---

578. Ch'en, *Buddhism in China*, 307.

579. Tamura Yoshirō, "The Ideas of the Lotus Sutra," in George and Willa Tanabe, eds., *The Lotus Sutra in Japanese Culture* (Honolulu: University of Hawai'i Press, 1989), 39.

that support this and that dominate the sub-sequence are water and light. Poems 1240 to 1243 use either the word *mizu* (water) or imply water through images like *hashi* (bridge) and *niwa* (garden). In a similar way, the theme of light is woven through poems 1240, 1242, 1244, 1245, 1247 with images like *tsuki* and *tsukikage* (moon, moonlight), and *hi no hikari* (sunlight). In the same way that water is implied, light is also implied through its lack (1245, 1248) with images like *kuregata no sora* (sky at dusk) and *asa madaki* (morning has not yet arrived). The accumulated images of water and light seem to support a figurative representation of a garden. The sub-sequence is sandwiched between two poems (1239 and 1248] that use the Japanese word *niwa* for "garden" ("the garden of the Law" and "the garden / of the Noble Law") specifically, and many of the poems in between use images that are or can be associated with a Japanese garden: weeds (1240), moonlight and sunlight (1240, 1245), a well (1241), water (1242), a bridge (1243), flowers (1246), and the moon (1247).

An oddity about this sub-sequence of poems is that six of the ten Lotus Sutra *shakkyo-ka* were written by courtiers and priests about whom we know very little. We know that six poets were contemporary to Shunzei (who included two of his own poems in this section), and some, like Koretsuna, Atsunaka, and Ariyasu took part in *utaawase* in 1200, 1178, and 1191, respectively. Ariyasu is also famous for having taught Kamo no Chōmei to play the biwa. As for the priests, we know that Taikaku attained the position of *Hōkyō* (Master of the Dharma-bridge) in 1185 and Renjō took the tonsure in 1193. We have a little more information about Sueyoshi (a Fujiwara who lived from 1153–1211 and took the tonsure in 1210). The information we have about these poets contrasts sharply with what we know about Kenshō, on the other hand, who was one of the leading Rokujō poets (as contrasted with Shunzei's Mikohidari poets), and about whom numerous records attest to his involvement in poetry gatherings, competitions, and parties. And, of course our knowledge of Shunzei himself is substantial. We do not know if Shunzei picked these poets because they were not well known at the time, or because their poems were suitable for this sequence, but the poets' apparent obscurity makes this an unusual sub-sequence.

Another distinctive aspect of this sub-sequence of poems is that, except for the poem (1242) on the Devadatta chapter (12) by Kenshō, none are based on chapters of the Sutra that have appeared in any of the imperial anthologies preceding the *Senzaishū*.[580] Of the eighteen Lotus Sutra poems in the entire *shakkyō-ka* sequence, seven are based on chapters from the Sutra that have not appeared before the *Senzaishū*. Of course, there are many twenty-eight-poem Lotus Sutra sequences extant in private anthologies, so this finding does not apply to them. What this may indicate, however, is that the compilers of the imperial anthologies wished to widen the scope of topics and images they felt were appropriate for a public anthology.

More significant to our understanding of the poems in this sub-sequence of poems is that all but two make a lyric response to the material. A lyric response in a book of courtly *waka* is not unusual, but after two sections of poems in which the meditative mode was predominant, a sub-sequence that changes directions so completely is noteworthy. As we have seen previously, the defining characteristics of the lyric response is emphasis upon emotional states and deployment of sense-specific images. Positive emotional states are evident in the adjective *ureshi* (happy) that appears in three poems (1239, 1241, 1247) while negative states are evident in verbs such as *uramu* (to resent, regret, from poem 1244) and the noun phrase *kokoro no yami* (darkness of the heart, poem 1245); the sense-specific images are those of the garden that I have described.

To create this figurative garden in an independent and connected set of Lotus Sutra poems, Shunzei employed interwoven and overlapping strands of images (both explicit and implied), favoring the image over the fame of the poet who created it, and leading the reader away from the intellectual response that predominated in the

---

580. This is not true for the other Lotus Sutra poems that occur outside of this sub-sequence.

previous two sections of poems. Simultaneously he emphasized and enacted the teachings of emptiness in the Sutra through repeated conflation of pairs of opposites, whether of images drawn from nature or the speakers' emotional states. Individually, many of the Lotus Sutra poems may not stand out as poetic achievements, but as a set they are notable for their unity and the manner in which Shunzei caused their images, themes and emotions to interpenetrate.

Nirvāna Sūtra Poems (1249–1255)

The final group of seven poems does not match the Nirvāna period (*Nehanji*) entirely because only the first two poems are actually based upon the Nirvāna Ceremony (Nehan-e) or the Nirvāna Sūtra (Nehan-gyō). However, the death of the Buddha, commemorated at the Nirvāna Ceremony, and the Buddha's final extinction (*parinirvāna*) that lies at the core of the Sūtra, introduce the theme of death that is the topic of the last five poems.

Eshō's poem which opens this final sub-sequence was composed, the headnote says, at the Nirvāna Ceremony (Nehan-e) that took place at Yamashinadera (Kōfuku-ji). The poem recalls the opening three poems of the *Goshūishū shakkyō-ka* sequence by the priests Kōgen, Keisen, and Keihan, all of which were also based upon the same service. The images used there—"the long-ago garden / of goodbye" (1179), "the smoke of wood / that has been / consumed by the fire" (1180), and "the moon of evening" that goes "inside the veil / during the night's small hours"—became more common after the late eleventh century, and it is the final image that we see replicated in Esho's poem. However, here it is the image of *mochizuki* (the full moon of mid-autumn, or the eighth month), thought to be the fullest moon of the year, that Esho causes to disappear behind the clouds. Appropriately enough Esho says he "understand[s] / that grief of long ago" when the Buddha passed into extinction. But it is not only the loss of the historical Buddha which Esho grieves: there is a sense that he has only partial access to spiritual illumination in the present day, perhaps another reference to *mappō*.

The grief of Esho's poem is replaced by consolation in Shunshū's (1250), expressed with the reflected-light imagery we have seen in other *shakkyō-ka*. Based upon the final lines of the fifth chapter of the Nirvāna Sūtra ("On the Adamantine Body"), the poem quotes a section of text that reads, "Then the Buddha praised Bodhisattva Kāśyapa and said: 'Well said, well said! The body of the Tathāgata is adamantine and indestructible. You Bodhisattvas, now have the right view and right understanding. If you see clearly thus, you will see the adamantine and indestructible body of the Tathāgata just *as you see things reflected in a mirror.*"[581] The speaker of Shunshū's poem asserts confidence that the clarity of the enlightened heart ("deep in my heart / immaculate clarity lives") can skillfully interpret the data of the phenomenal world (perhaps the disappearing moon in the previous poem), and find "their truth." The truth of forms and the truth of emptiness of forms were similarly addressed by Tango's poem (1229) but the response this poem makes to the same material is far more intellectual.

Leon Hurvitz has said that the Nirvāna Sūtra "specifically declares [nirvāna] to be 'permanent, pleasant, personal, pure'."[582] Such a sensibility, however, does not match the current of sadness we find in most Japanese poetry. With Jakuzen's poem (1251), the sequence returns the reader to negative emotions, in a purely lyric response to the narrative of death and cremation that is only alluded to in the headnote: "On the essence of the passage 'the fire rages on but does not burn forever."[583]

Jakuzen's poem, from his private collection of *shakkyō-ka* called

---

581. Kosho Yamamoto, The Mahāyāna Mahāparinirvāna Sūtra, 47. <http://lirs.ru/do/Mahaparinirvana_Sutra,Yamamoto,Page,2007.pdf>. Accessed August 26, 2010. The italicized portion is that quoted in the headnote of Shunshū's poem.

582. Hurvitz, *Chih-i*, 194.

583. This passage is drawn from the Zaigō ōhō kyōke jigoku-kyō (T 724, Sūtra for the Retribution for Bad Karma Leading to Hell), a lesser-known Buddhist text in Japan.

Hōmon hyakushu, is a departure from Shunshū's meditative response to the death of the Buddha, making here a purely emotional response to death (based on a passage of sūtra text) as it was experienced and observed by the aristocracy in the Heian capital. The image of smoke to represent the impermanence of the body is also found in poem 1209 by Sensai Shōnin, but whereas that poem emphasized the sadness about the loss of the Buddha he experienced at Tennō-ji ("sad to look / on what little / is left"), here Jakuzen made the smoke emblematic of death in general—a "souvenir [*katami*] of the dead who / have risen." In spite of what the headnote suggests about "the fire … [that] does not burn forever," Jakuzen requests the smoke to linger—*shibashiba tanabike* ("smoke, / drift long")—seeming to express a reluctance to let go of the dead entirely.

While Jakuzen yearns, expressing his attachment to "this world," the world of samsāra, Taira no Yasuyori's (1252) poem brings consolation (much as Shunshū's poem did for Eshō's) in the form of an image of hope from "that world" (Paradise) where "in the song of birds / and the sound of waves— / one hears / the same Noble Law." The imagery Yasuyori provides is, according to Shunzei's headnote, the "essence of the Amida-kyō," in which we find descriptions of the Pure Land.[584] These images, very much a part of standard courtly *waka,* occur here in the context of Dharma (the Sūtra) and as such evoke a tone of hopefulness that provides an emotional counterbalance to Jakuzen's poem.

The two *waka* that follow Yasuyori's, on the topic of a pilgrimage to Tennō-ji, follow the alternating pattern of negative (1249, 1251) and positive (1250, 1252) emotions which began with the first poem by Eshō. The poem by Fujiwara no Sadanaga, was written, the headnote says, during the imperial pilgrimage of Go-Shirakawa on the topic "old temples arouse poignant thoughts of the past." The second, by the Tendai Abbot Meiun, was written upon a pilgrimage to worship "the Buddha's relics."[585] Both poems make an intellectual argument:

---

584. There are various birds depicted in the Sūtra, but in fact there is no image of a wave.

585. Meiun's poem can also be found in the *Tsukimōdeshū,* where the emotion expressed at viewing the "traces" is happiness rather than sadness. SKT, vol. 2, 354. While

Sadanaga's poem provides "proof he [the Buddha] saved the world—" in the form of the ancient Buddhist temple (Shōtoku Taishi's Tennō-ji), while Meiun's poem claims that, because the "smoke" is the "proof of [human] brevity," we cannot help but be sad looking upon the "traces [relics, *shari*] that remain." Meiun's expression of sadness tilts the poem slightly toward the lyric, but it is a general sadness that anyone might feel who would view such remains, not particular to the author.

Ending the Nirvāna Sūtra sub-sequence, as well as Shunzei's fifty-four poem literary representation of the Buddhist *mārga,* is a poem/song by Preceptor Yōkan, who, in addition to studying in the Sanron tradition and becoming temple administrator of Tōdai-ji in 1100, turned the Jōdo temple Zenrin-ji (also known as Eikandō) into a flourishing center for *nenbutsu* practice. Yōkan is also well known for having written a work called the *Ōjōkōshiki,* which describes a service to be held on the fifteenth of every month at the Lectures on Rebirth (Ōjō kō). The purpose of the lectures and service was to intone Amida's name (*Nenbutsu* rebirth/salvation) and request rebirth in *Gokuraku,* or the Pure Land. The lectures were divided into seven "gates" (*mon*) at the beginning of which verses from the Sukhāvatī sūtras were intoned. Yōkan's poem was originally referred to as a type of song, called a *kyōke* (song/poem for propagation of the Pure Land teachings), usually composed in the same 5-7-syllabic structure as *waka.* This particular song/*waka* was recited at the beginning of the fourth gate of teachings called Nenbutsu ōjō (*nenbutsu* rebirth/salvation) in front of the image of Amida. As a song, it was meant to arouse the emotions of the devotees, which it achieved by making a lyric response to the theme of rebirth. But layered into this emotional response is also an intellectual argument (foreshadowing the lecture to come) asserting that salvation for others is accomplished by means of one's compassionate "heart that considers / how everyone might be helped." Yōkan's song/poem leaves the reader of the *shakkyō-ka* sequence with assurance that the

---

we feel that the unexpected word "happy" makes the *Tsukimōdeshū* version more interesting in an aesthetic sense, we have preserved the word "sad" as it appears in the SNKBT version of the *Senzaishū.*

path, or *michi,* does indeed lead to salvation, not only for individuals, but for all. Assistance does not come (only) in the form of an external bodhisattva, but from the bodhisattva heart of every practitioner, which concerns itself with others and works on their behalf.

CONCLUSION

Behind the poetic scenes it was Shunzei, as anthologizer, who created the sense of hope one feels at the end of the sequence, through his skillful arrangement of fifty-four *waka* according to the *goji* periodization and *Makashikan* chapters schemata. This arrangement began with taking refuge in and practicing the initial teachings of the Buddha (represented by the Mainstream Buddhist view), led the reader through the Mahāyāna teachings of emptiness (*kū*) in the Prajñāpāramitā sūtras, radical nonduality in the Lotus Sutra, and concluded with the goal of enlightenment that is accomplished in the course of one's metaphorical death of self and in the course of one's actual death, rebirth, and salvation. The teachings of radical nonduality which permeate this sequence, eventually, with the help of Shunzei's *Korai fūteishō* of 1197, led to the view during the Kamakura and Muromachi periods that the writing of *waka* in this samsaric world (*bonnō*) is identical with (*soku*), the *darani* in the sūtras and, thus, with one's personal enlightenment (*bodai*). ✿

AFTERWORD

Not I, not I, but the wind that blows through me!
A fine wind is blowing the new direction of Time.
If only I let it bear me, carry me, if only it carry me!
If only I am sensitive, subtle, oh, delicate, a winged gift!
If only, most lovely of all, I yield myself and am borrowed
By the fine, fine wind that takes its course through the chaos of
    the world
Like a fine, an exquisite chisel, a wedge-blade inserted;
If only I am keen and hard like the sheer tip of a wedge
Driven by invisible blows,
The rock will split, we shall come at the wonder, we shall find the
    Hesperides.
                                        — D. H. Lawrence

The "wind from Vulture Peak" blew the Buddhist teachings from that elevation in India to China and Korea and then onward to Japan, where, continuously flowing over many centuries through every aspect of court culture, it transformed each obstacle it met into a new expression of itself. Encountering the long established *waka* tradition—the role of which in court culture it is hardly possible to overstate—that wind negotiated a channel through every formal and conceptual barrier that was presented, eventually inspiring a new topic, and a new category, within the old.

Just as the persistent pressure of this "fine, fine wind that takes its course through the chaos of the world" (to quote Lawrence) enlarged the potential of the *waka* tradition, the *story* of this enlargement has in turn breathed over my many years of study of Japanese language and poetry. This inspiration began with Professor Gordon Grigsby's seminar at Ohio State University on the influences of Buddhism in the Western poetry of Ralph Waldo Emerson, Gary Snyder, and Allen Ginsberg, and flowed to me variously through the *haiku* of Bashō, the poem-songs of Milarepa, and the Chan poems of Han Shan. Without the patience of innumerable language teachers and the assistance of the Japan Foundation, I would never have understood the myriad meanings of Japanese words, sentences, and books I wanted to read. Without *The Karma of Words* and the caring and solicitous concern of its author, William LaFleur, toward me and my topic, I would have written neither a Ph.D. thesis nor a book. Without my personal encounter with Chogyam Trungpa Rinpoche, I might never have had the opportunity to experience the practices of Buddhism and poetry in a single individual.

It has twice, over these years, been necessary for me to recalculate my estimation of the significance of the *waka* that are the focus of this study. Early on, discovering that Buddhist *waka* had been written in Japan but were of little interest to scholars of Japanese literature, I set out to learn why. After reading a few of these poems, I thought I shared some scholars' judgment that they were didactic in tone, thin in substance, and ambiguous in purpose. Later, after reading many more, I realized this was reader error: as is the case with reading any poetry or appreciating any art, there is a skill involved, a vocabulary and a context to learn, which at first I did not have. More recently, I made a similiar course-correction when poet Patrick Donnelly told me that he heard real people speaking in these poems (for him the *sine qua non* of poetry), and helped me to honor those voices in our translations.

As must be obvious, I eventually came to feel that these *waka*— though certainly they occupy a cul-de-sac of the incomparable achievement of Japanese poetry as a whole—ought not to be considered a lesser category of that achievement. They represent substantial artistic accomplishment, as well as daring cognitive enlargement, on the part of their authors and anthologizers, and reward the interest of readers by creating a world that is simultaneously historical, literary, intellectual, emotional, and spiritual.

"[F]inding / the Law fans / a wind of happiness," Ise no Tayū wrote when she found, a millennium ago, her father's fan in the sanctuary of Higashi Sanjō palace. For my own part, finding these poems and following their *michi* with so many splendid co-travelers, has also fanned a wind of great happiness.

Stephen D. Miller

APPENDIX

THE FIRST EIGHT IMPERIAL POETRY ANTHOLOGIES (*HACHIDAISHŪ*)

1. *Kokinwakashū* (*Kokinshū*): completed ca. 905, twenty books, 1,111 poems. Ordered by Emperor Daigo (year uncertain) and compiled by Ki no Tsurayuki, Ki no Tomonori, Ōshikochi no Mitsune, and Mibu no Tadamine.

2. *Gosenwakashū* (*Gosenshū*): completed in 951, twenty books, 1,426 poems. Ordered by Emperor Murakami in 951 and compiled by Ōnakatomi no Yoshinobu, Kiyowara no Motosuke, Minamoto no Shitagō, Ki no Tokibumi, and Sakanoe no Mochiki.

3. *Shūiwakashū* (*Shūishū*): completed early eleventh century (exact dates unknown), twenty books, 1,351 poems. Ordered (perhaps) by Retired Emperor Kazan and compiled (perhaps) by Fujiwara no Kintō and/or Kazan himself, though little is known about the circumstances of its compilation. It was based upon the text of the *Shūishō*, thought to have been completed in 999.

4. *Goshūiwakashū* (*Goshūishū*): completed in 1086, twenty books, 1,220 poems. Ordered by Emperor Shirakawa in 1075 and compiled by Fujiwara no Michitoshi.

5. *Kin'yōwakashū* (*Kin'yōshū*): three different versions presented between 1126 and 1127, ten books, 716 poems. Ordered by Retired Emperor Shirakawa in 1124 and compiled by Minamoto no Shunrai (Toshiyori).

6. *Shikawakashū (Shikashū)*: completed between 1151–1154, ten books, 411 poems. Ordered by Retired Emperor Sutoku in 1144 and compiled by Fujiwara no Akisuke.

7. *Senzaiwakashū (Senzaishū)*: completed in 1188, twenty books, 1,285 poems. Ordered by Retired Emperor Go-Shirakawa in 1185 and compiled by Fujiwara no Shunzei (Toshinari).

8. *Shinkokinwakashū (Shinkokinshū)*: completed in 1206, but there were revisions; twenty books, 1,981 poems. Ordered by Retired Emperor Go-Toba in 1201 and compiled by Fujiwara no Teika (Sadaie), Fujiwara no Ariie, Fujiwara no Ietaka, Minamoto no Michitomo, and Fujiwara no Masatsune. The Tendai priest Jakuren was also selected, but he died before compilation began.

A PARTIAL CHARACTER GLOSSARY OF CHINESE, JAPANESE, AND KOREAN WORDS

aishō-ka	哀傷歌	Dai-i	大意
ajari	阿闍梨	Daijō kishin ron	大乗起信論
Akazome Emon	赤染衛門	Dainichi nyorai	大日如来
Amaterasu Ōmikami	天照大御神	Darani-kyō	陀羅尼経
Amida	阿弥陀	Dōgen	道元
Annen	安然	Eiga monogatari	栄華物語
banka	挽歌	Eisai	栄西
Baramon Sōjō	婆羅門僧正	Enchin	円珍
Ben no menoto	弁乳母	En'i Hōshi	円位法師
Bifukumon-in	美福門院	Enkyō-ji	円教寺
Bodai-ji	菩提寺	Ennin	円仁
Bodai-kō	菩提講	Enryaku-ji	延暦寺
bodaishin	菩提心	Eshō Hōshi	恵章法師
Bodaishinron	菩提心論	eta	依他
bonnō	煩悩	Fūgashū	風雅集
bonnō soku bodai	煩悩即菩提	Fugen bosatsu	普賢菩薩
bosatsu	菩薩	Fujiwara (no)	藤原
Bukkyō-ka	仏教歌	Akimitsu	顕光
Bukkyō-kayō	仏教歌謡	Akinaka (Jingi Haku)	神祇伯顕仲
Bunkashūreishū	文華秀麗集	Akitada	顕忠
Butsumyō-e	仏名会	Akisue	顕季
Butsumyō-kyō	仏名経	Akisuke	顕輔
bussokuseki-ka	仏足石歌	Ariie	有家
byōdōshōchi	平等性智	Arikuni	有国
Chan-jan	湛然	Atsuie	敦家
Chegwan (J: Taikan)	諦観	Atsumitsu	敦光
Chiekō Butsu	智慧光仏	Atsunaka	敦仲
Chih-i	智顗	Fuhito	不比等
Chinkai Hōshi no Haha	珍海法師母	Ietaka	家隆
chōka	長歌	Kamatari	鎌足
chokusenshishū	勅撰詩集	Kanezane	兼実
chokusenwakashū	勅撰和歌集	Kanshi	寛子
Chōsei Hōshi	澄成法師	Kinshige	公重
Chōshū eisō	長秋詠藻	Kintō	公任
Chūjō (Shikishi Naishinnō		Kinzane	公実
no Ie no)	式子内親王家中将	Kiyosuke	清輔
dai	題	Koretsuna	伊綱
Daibon-hannya-kyō	大品般若経	Kunifusa	国房
daibon-ka	題品歌	Masatsune	雅経
daiei-ka	題詠歌	Masazane	雅実
Daigo-ji	醍醐寺	Michinaga	道長
Daigo tennō	醍醐天皇	Michinori	通憲
Daihatsu-nehan-gyō	大般涅槃経	Michitoshi	通俊

Michitsune	道経	Goryaku jikkō	五略十広
Morosuke	師輔	Go-Sanjō tennō	後三条天皇
Morozane	師実	Gosenshū	後撰集
Mototoshi	基俊	Go-Shirakawa tennō	後白河天皇
Munekane	宗兼	Goshūishū	後拾遺集
Munemasa	統理	Goshūishū mokuroku-jo	後拾遺集目録序
Naganori	永範	Go-Suzaku tennō	後朱雀天皇
Nagazane	永実	Go-Toba tennō	後鳥羽天皇
Naritoki	済時	Gyōki	行基
Norinaga	教長	Gyokuyō	玉葉
Onshi	温子	Gyokuyōshū	玉葉集
Sadanaga	定長	Gyōson (Sōjō)	僧正行尊
Sanekata	実方	hachidaishū	八代集
Saneyuki	実行	Haikai-ka (Haikai no uta)	俳諧歌
Shigeie	重家	Hamuro no Akiyori	葉室顕頼
Shunzei	俊成	hanka	反歌
Sueyoshi	季能	Hannyaji	般若時
Suketaka	師隆	Hannya-shingyō	般若心経
Tadamichi	忠通	Hannya shingyō hiken	般若心経秘鍵
Tadahira	忠平	Heian	平安
Tadanobu	斎信	Heian-kyō	平安京
Takamitsu	高光	Heiji no ran	平治の乱
Takanobu	隆信	Hen'en	偏円
Tametada	為忠	Henjō (Sōjō)	遍昭僧正
Teika	定家	Hieizan	比叡山
Toshitada	俊忠	Higan nenbutsu-e	彼岸念仏会
Tsunetada	経忠	Higashi Sanjō-in Senshi	東三条院詮子
Yorimichi	頼通	Higo (Kōgōgū no)	皇后宮肥後
Yorinaga	頼長	hijiri	聖
Yoshitsune	良経	Hirota-sha (no yashiro) no	
Yukinari	行成	utaawase	広田社歌合
Fumon-ji	普門寺	hitan	悲嘆
Fusō ryakki	扶桑略記	Hitomaro eigu	人丸影供
Ga no uta	賀歌	Hitomaru eigu-ki	人丸影供記
gachirinkan	月輪観	Hizō hōyaku	秘蔵宝鑰
Genji monogatari	源氏物語	Hizōki	秘蔵記
Genkō shakusho	元亨釈書	hōben	方便
Genpei	源平	Hōben	方便
Genshin (Sōzu)	僧都源信	Hōdōji	方等時
gochi	五智	hōen-ka	法縁歌
goei-ka	御詠歌	Hōgen no ran	保元乱
Gochi Nyorai	五智如来	Hoi-ka	補遺歌
Go-Ichijō tennō	後一条天皇	Hōjō-ji	法成寺
goji	五時	Hokke gengi	法華玄義
goji hakkyō hanjaku	五時八教判釈	Hokke hakkō	法華八講
Gokuraku rokuji	極楽六時	Hokke-ji	法花寺
Gokuraku rokuji sanka	極楽六時讃歌	Hokke-kyō	法華経
gomi	五味	Hokke-kyō nijūhappon-ka	
Gonki	権記	(Hokke-kyō-ka)	法華経二十八品歌
Go-Reizei tennō	後冷泉天皇	Hokke-nehanji	法華涅槃時

Hōmon hyakushu	法門百首	Kaijin (Hōshi)	懐尋法師
hōmon-ka (hōmon no uta)	法門歌	Kaishū (Saki no Daisōjō)	前大僧都快修
hongaku	本学	kakekotoba	掛詞
honji suijaku	本地垂迹	Kakuchō (Sōzu)	僧都覚超
honmon	本門	Kakuchū (Saki no Daisōjō)	大僧正覚忠
hōraku waka	法楽和歌	Kakuga (Sōzu)	僧都覚雅
Horikawa hyakushu	堀河百首	Kakuju Hōshi	覚樹法師
Horikawa tennō	堀河天皇	Kakushō (Ninna-ji Nochi	
Hōrin-ji utaawase	法輪寺歌合	no Nyūdō	
Hosshin	発心	Hosshinnō)	仁和寺後入道法親王覚性
Hosshin wakashū	発心和歌集	Kakuyo Hōshi	覚誉法師
Hossō	法相	kami	神
Hyakunin isshu	百人一首	Kamiasobi no uta	神遊歌
hyakushu-uta	百首歌	Kamo (no)	鴨
Ichihara no Ōkimi	市原王	Chōmei	長明
Ichijō tennō	一条天皇	Shigeyasu	重保
imayō	今様	Kamo Wakeikazuchi Jinja	賀茂別雷神社
Inari-sha (no yashiro) no		Kanajo	仮名所
utaawase	稲荷社歌合	Kanfugen-kyō	観普賢経
in-no-chō	院庁	Kangaku-e	勧学会
Insei (jidai)	院政(時代)	Kangaku-e ki	勧学会記
Ippon-kyō kuyō	一品経供養	kanjin	勧進
Ise no Chūjō	伊勢中将	Kanka	感果
Ise no Tayū	伊勢大輔	Kannon	観音
Izumi Shikibu	和泉式部	Kannon-kyō	観音経
Jakuchō	寂超	Kanchi hōgan utaawase	観智法眼歌合
Jakunen	寂念	kanshi	漢詩
Jakuren Hōshi	寂蓮法師	Kasa (no Iratsume)	笠（の郎）
Jakuzen Hōshi	寂然法師	Kataokayama	片岡山
Jien (Hōin)	法印慈円	Kazan tennō	花山天皇
jikaawase	自歌合	kechien	結縁
jingi-ka	神祇歌	Kechien-kō	結縁講
jiriki	自力	Kechien kuyō	結縁供養
Jishō ninen Kanezane no ie		Kegonji	華厳時
no hyakushu	治承二年兼実家百首	Kegon-kyō	華厳経
Jitsuban (Jippan)	実範	Keihan Hōshi	慶範法師
Jōdo	浄土	Keikokushū	経国集
Jōdo-ka	浄土歌	Keisen (Saki no Risshi)	前律師慶遷
Jōen (Sōjō)	僧正静円	Kenshō Hōshi	顕昭法師
Jōgon Hōshi	静厳法師	Kikyō	起教
Jōtai Bosatsu	常啼菩薩	Ki no Tsurayuki	紀貫之
jukkai(-ka)	述懐（歌）	Kintōshū	公任集
Jukkai hyakushu	述懐百首	Kin'yōshū	金葉集
Junikō Butsu	十二光仏	Kiryo no uta	羈旅歌
Junna tennō	淳和天皇	Kisho	帰処
junrei-ka (junrei no uta)	巡礼歌	Kishu	帰趣
kadō soku butsudō	歌道即仏道	Koben	小弁
Kagura uta	神楽歌	Kōfuku-ji	興福寺
Kahō	果報	Kōgen Hōshi	光源法師
Kaifūsō	懐風藻	Kojiki	古事記

Kokinrokujō	古今六帖	Moronaka	師仲
Kokinshū	古今集	Morotoki	師時
Kōki Tokuō Bosatsu	高貴徳王菩薩	Motoko	基子
Kokon chomonjū	古今著聞集	Narinobu	成信
kokoro	心	Sanekata	実方
Kōmyō tennō	光明天皇	Shitagō	順
Kongōbu-ji	金剛峰寺	Shunrai	俊頼
Kongōchō-kyō yuga chūhotsu		Sukekata	相方
anokutara sammyaku		Tamenori	為憲
sanbodaishinron		Tameyoshi	為義
金剛喩伽中発阿耨多羅三藐三菩提		Toshifusa	俊房
Kōnin tennō	光仁天皇	Toshikata	俊方
Konjaku monogatari	今昔物語	Tsunenobu	経信
Konoe tennō	近衛天皇	Yoshitomo	義朝
Korai fūteishō	古来風体抄	Yukimune	行宗
Kose no Shikihito	巨勢識人	Miroku bosatsu	弥勒菩薩
kotobagaki	詞書	Miyaki (Yūjo)	遊女宮木
kotodama	言霊	Mo-ho chih-kuan (See Makashikan)	
Kōya-san monjo	高野山文書	mono no aware	物の会われ
kū	空	Mono no na (Butsumei)	物名
k'uang-yen i-yu (See kyōgen kigo)		Mudō-ji	無動寺
Kuang-ting	灌頂	Mujaku	無着
Kudenshū	口伝集	mujō	無常
Kujō no Kanezane (See Fujiwara		Mujū Ichien	無住一円
no Kanezane)		Murakami tennō	村上天皇
Kūkai	空海	Myōe (Shōnin)	明恵上人
Kumano	熊野	Muryōju-kyō	無量寿経
Kūya Shōnin	空也上人	Myōson (Gon no Sōjō)	権僧正明尊
kyōgen kigo	狂言綺語	Nakahara (no)	中原
kyōhan (p'an chiao)	教判	Ariyasu	有安
Kyōkai	景戒	Kiyoshige	清重
kyōke	教化	Nakao Ō	仲雄王
kyōri-ka	教理歌	Nara	奈良
kyōshi-ka	経旨歌	nehan	涅槃
Kyūan hyakushu	久安百首	Nehan-e	涅槃会
maikyō	埋経	Nehan-gyō (See Daihatsu-nehan-gyō)	
Makashikan (Mo-ho chih-kuan)	摩訶止観	nenbutsu	念仏
Mansei (Shami)	沙弥満誓	Nenbutsu ōjō	念仏往生
Man'yōshū	万葉集	Nihongi (Nihon shoki)	日本紀／日本書紀
mappō	末法	Nihon ryōiki / Nihonkoku	
Meiun (Tendai Zasu)	天台座主明雲	genpō zen'aku	日本霊異記／
michi	道	ryōiki)	日本現報善悪霊異記
Michitsuna no Haha	道綱母	Nijō tennō	二条天皇
Miidera no Shiragi no		Ninna-ji	仁和寺
yashiro no utaawase	三井寺新羅社歌合	Ninnō-kyō	仁王経
Mikohidarike	御子左家	nori	法
Mimosusogawa jikaawase	御裳濯川自家合	Ochikubo mongatari	落窪物語
Minamoto (no)	源	Ōhara sanjaku	大原三寂
Michitomo	通具	ōjōden	往生伝

Ōjō kō	往生講
Ōjōkōshiki	往生講式
Ōkagami	大鏡
Ōnakatomi no Yoshinobu	大中臣能宣
Ono (no)	小野
Komachi	小町
Minemori	峯守
Nagami	永見
Ōtomo no Tabito	大伴旅人
p'an-chiao (*See* kyōhan)	
Po Chü-i	白居易
rekishi monogatari	歴史物語
Renjō Hōshi	蓮上法師
Retsumō	裂網
Ribetsu no uta	離別
rissha	堅者
rōei	朗詠
Rokujō	六条
Rokuonji	鹿苑時
rongi	論議
Ryōgen	良源
Ryōjin hishō	梁塵秘抄
Ryōunshū	陵雲集
Saga tennō	嵯峨天皇
Saichō	最澄
Saigyō	西行
Saiin	斎院
Saikoku sanjū sankasho	西国三十三カ所
Saishō-ō-kyō	最勝王経
Sanbō ekotoba	三宝絵詞
sanbōin	三法印
Sanboku kikashū	散木奇歌集
sankan	三觀
Sanka utaawase	山家歌合
Sannomiya (*See* Sukehito Shinnō)	三宮
sanshin	三身
santai	三諦
san-te (*See* santoku)	
santoku	三徳
Sasamegoto	ささめごと
satori	悟
sedōka	旋頭歌
Seireishū	性靈集
Sei Shōnagon	清少納言
Senju Darani-kyō	千手陀羅尼経
Senkei Hōshi	仙慶法師
Sensai Shōnin	瞻西上人
Senshi Naishinnō	選子内親王
Senzaishū	千歳集
Seppō	摂法
shakkyō-ka (shakkyō, shakkyō waka)	釈教歌 / 釈教 / 釈教和歌
shakkyō-shi	釈教詩
shakumon	迹門
Shakumyō	釈名
Shaku Tsūkan	釈通観
Shari-e	舎利繪
Shari-kō	舎利講
Shasekishū	沙石集
shih	詩
shikan	止観
shikashū	私家集
Shikashū	詞花集
shiki	色
Shikishi Naishinnō	式子内親王
shinbutsu shūgō	神仏習合
Shinchokusenshū	新勅撰集
Shingon	真言
Shinkei	心敬
Shinkokinshū	新古今集
Shinsei	真静
Shinzokukokinshū	新続古今集
Shirakawa tennō	白河天皇
shisenshū	私撰集
Shōchō Hōshi	勝超法師
Shōdaijōron	摂大乗論
Shōkai Shōnin	清海上人
Shokugosenshū	続後撰集
Shoku Nihongi	続日本紀
Shokushikashū	続詞花集
Shōkū Shōnin	清空上人
shōmon	声聞
Shōmu tennō	聖武天皇
Shosha-san	書写山
Shōshi-kai	尚歯会
Shōshū shikan	正修止観
Shōtetsu	正徹
Shōtoku Taishi	聖徳太子
shugyō	修行
Shugyō	修行
Shūgyokushū	拾玉集
Shūishō	拾遺抄
Shūishū	拾遺集
shukke	出家
Shunshū Hōshi	俊秀法師
sugata	姿
sokushin jōbutsu	即身成仏
Son'en Hōshi	尊円法師

Sonshi (Naishinnō)	尊子内親王
Sosei Hōshi	素性法師
Sukehito Shinnō	輔仁親王
Sumiyoshi-sha	住吉社
Sumiyoshi-sha (no yashiro) no utaawase	住吉社歌合
Susano-o no Mikoto	須佐之男命
Sutoku tennō	崇徳天皇
Tachibana (no) Narisue	橘 成季
Taguchi Shigeyuki	田口重如
Taikaku (Hōkyō)	法橋泰覚
Taikenmon-in	待賢門院
taiken-ka	体験歌
Taiki	台記
Taira (no)	平
Kiyomori	清盛
Tadamasa	忠正
Tokitada	時忠
Yasuyori	康頼
Taishō Shinshū Daizō-kyō	大正新修大蔵経
Taisō	体相
Takamitsu nikki	高光日記
takusen-ka	託宣歌
Tango (Sesshō no Ie no)	摂政家丹後
tanrenga	短連歌
tao	道
tariki	他力
Tendai Bukkyō	天大仏教
Tendai mikkyō	天大密教
Tendai shikyōgi	天台四教儀
Tennō-ji	天王寺
T'ien't'ai ssu-chiao (See Tendai Shikyōgi)	
Toba tennō	鳥羽天皇
Tōdai-ji	東大寺
tokoyo	常世
Tōnomine shōshō monogatari	多武峯少将物語
Tōren Hōshi	澄蓮法師
Tsui yeh ying pai chiao hua ti yü ching (See Zaigō ōhō kyōke jigoku-kyō)	

Tsukimōdeshū	月詣集
Udaijin no ie no hyakushu	右大臣家百首
Uda tennō	宇多天皇
Unji gi	吽字義
Ungo-ji	雲居寺
Ungo-ji Shōnin zan kyōgen kigo wakajo	雲居寺上人懺狂言綺語和歌序
uta	歌
utaawase	歌合
utamonogatari	歌物語
waka	和歌
Waka Mandara	和歌曼荼羅
waka soku darani	和歌即陀羅尼
Wen hsüan	文選
wu-shih (See goji)	
Yakushi-ji	薬師寺
Yakushi Nyorai	薬師如来
Yamanoue Okura	山上憶良
Yamashinadera	山階寺
Yamato	倭 / 大和
Yasusuke no Ō no Haha	康資王母
Yōen (Gon no Sōjō)	権僧正永縁
Yōkan (Risshi)	律師永観
Yōmei tennō	用明天皇
Yoshishige no Yasutane	慶滋保胤
yūgen	幽玄
Yuiishiki	唯意識
Yuima-e	維摩会
Yuima-kyō	維摩経
yūzu nenbutsu	融通念仏
Zaigō ōhō kyōke jigoku-kyō	罪業応報教化地獄経
Zaō	蔵王
zazen	座禅
Zengen hōin-bō utaawase	全玄法印坊歌合
Zenrin-ji	禅林寺
zōka	雑歌
zōtōka	贈答歌

BIBLIOGRAPHY

Abe, Ryūichi. *The Weaving of Mantra: Kūkai and the Construction of Esoteric Buddhist Discourse*. New York: Columbia University Press, 1999.

———. "Scholasticism, Exegesis, and Ritual Practice: On Renovation in the History of Buddhist Writing in the Early Heian Period." Chapter 8 in *Heian Japan: Centers and Peripheries*. Honolulu: University of Hawai'i Press, 2007.

Adolphson, Mikael. *The Gates of Power: Monks, Courtiers, and Warriors in Premodern Japan*. Honolulu: University of Hawaii Press, 2000.

———. *The Teeth and Claws of the Buddha: Monastic Monks and Sōhei in Japanese History*. Honolulu: University of Hawaii Press, 2007.

Andrews, Allan. "Genshin's 'Essentials of Pure Land Rebirth' and the Transmission of Pure Land Buddhism to Japan. Part 1. The First and Second Phases of Transmission of Pure Land Buddhism to Japan: The Nara Period and the Early Heian Period." *The Pacific World* 5 (Fall 1989): 20–31.

Arita Shizuaki. "*Man'yōshū* ni arawareta mujōkan," *Bukkyō bungaku* (1978): 3–8.

Ariyoshi Tamotsu. "Hachidaishū to kadan." *Kokubungaku*, vol. 32, no. 5 (April 1987): 48–55.

Asano Kiyoshi. *Saikoku sanjūsansho reijō jiin no sōgōteki kenkyū*. Tokyo: Chūō Kōron Bijutsu Shuppan, 1990.

Aso Mizue. "*Man'yōshū* to Bukkyō," *Kokubungaku: kaishaku to kanshō* vol. 48, no. 15 (December 1983): 120–122.

Aston, W. G., trans. *Nihongi: Chronicles of Japan from the Earliest Times to A.D. 697*. Rutland and Tokyo: Charles E. Tuttle Co., 1972.

Augustine, Jonathan Morris. *Buddhist Hagiography in Early Japan: Images of Compassion in the Gyōki Tradition*. London and New York: Routledge-Curzon, 2005.

Boisvert, Mathieu. *The Five Aggregates: Understanding Theravāda Psychology and Soteriology*. Delhi: Sri Satguru Publications, 1997.

Bowring, Richard, trans. *The Diary of Lady Murasaki*. London: Penguin Books, 1996.

———. *The Religious Traditions of Japan 500-1600*. Cambridge: Cambridge University Press, 2005.

Brower, Robert and Earl Miner. *Japanese Court Poetry*. Stanford: Stanford University Press, 1961.

Bukkyō bungaku jiten. Takeishi Akio and Suganuma Akira.

Bukkyō jiten. See Nakamura Hajime.

Bukkyōgo daijiten. See Nakamura Hajime.

Chappell, David W. *T'ien-t'ai Buddhism: An Outline of the Fourfold Teachings.* Tokyo: Daiichi Shobō, 1983.

Ch'en, Kenneth. *Buddhism in China: A Historical Survey.* Princeton: Princeton University Press, 1964.

Cleary, Thomas, trans. *The Flower Ornament Scripture: A Translation of the* Avatamsaka Sutra. Boston and London: Shambhala Publishing, 1993.

Como, Michael. *Shōtoku: Ethnicity, Ritual, and Violence in the Japanese Buddhist Tradition.* Oxford: Oxford University Press, 2008.

Crane, Mary Thomas. *Shakespeare's Brain: Reading with Cognitive Theory.* Princeton and Oxford: Princeton University Press, 2001.

Cranston, Edwin. *A Waka Anthology,* vol. 1. Palo Alto: Stanford University Press, 1993.

Davidson, Ronald M. "Studies in Dhāraṇī Literature I: Revisiting the Meaning of the Term Dhāraṇī." *Journal of Indian Philosophy* 37 (2009): 97–147.

Deal, William Edward. "Ascetics, Aristocrats, and the Lotus Sutra: The Construction of the Buddhist University in Eleventh Century Japan." Ph.D. dissertation, Harvard University, 1988.

de Bary, W. M. Theodore, ed. *The Buddhist Tradition in India, China, and Japan.* New York: The Modern Library, 1969.

Donnelly, Patrick. "How the Narrative, Lyric, and Meditative Modes of Poetry Combine in Hybrid Modes—and Why," unpublished manuscript.

———. "The Reverse Side," poem by Stephen Dunn. http://www.answers.com/topics/the-reverse-side-poem-6>. 2004.

Donner, Neal. "The Great Calming and Contemplation of Chih-i, Chapter One: The Synopsis." Ph.D. dissertation, University of British Columbia, 1976.

Dykstra, Yoshiko, trans. *Miraculous Tales of the Lotus Sutra from Ancient Japan.* Honolulu: University of Hawai'i Press, 1983.

Ebersole, Gary. *Ritual Poetry and the Politics of Death in Early Japan.* Princeton: Princeton University Press, 1989.

Eckel, Malcolm David. *To See the Buddha: A Philosopher's Quest for the Meaning of Emptiness.* New York: Harper Collins, 1992.

Farris, William Wayne. "Famine, Climate, and Farming in Japan, 670–1100." Chapter 11 in *Heian Japan: Centers and Peripheries.* Honolulu: University of Hawai'i Press, 2007.

Fujimoto Kazue, ed. and trans. *Goshūiwakashū zen'yakuchū,* 4 vols. Tokyo: Kōdansha, 1983.

Fukaura Masafumi. "Kokubungaku no oyoboseru Bukkyō shisō no eikyō—toku ni *Man'yōshū* ni tsuite." *Bukkyōgaku kenkyū* (The Studies in Buddhism), vol. 18–19 (January 1967): 138–147.

Fukui Kyūzō. "Shakkyō Waka ni tsukite," *Tanka kenkyū* (April 1934): 316–322.

Gatten, Aileen. "Fact, Fiction, and Heian Literary Prose: Epistolary Narration in Tōnomine Shōshō Monogatari," *Monumenta Nipponica,* vol. 53, no. 2 (Summer, 1998): 153–195.

Gibbs, Jr., Raymond W. *Embodiment and Cognitive Science.* Cambridge: Cambridge University Press, 2006.

Groner, Paul. *Saichō: The Establishment of the Japanese Tendai School.* Honolulu: University of Hawai'i Press, 2000.

———. *Ryōgen and Mount Hiei: Japanese Tendai in the Tenth Century.* Honolulu: University of Hawai'i Press, 2002.

Gump, Steven E. "Mythologies and Miracles: The Saikoku Kannon Peregrinogenesis." *Southeast Review of Asia Studies,* 27 (2005): 141–158.

Hakeda, Yoshito S., trans. *The Awakening of Faith: Attributed to Aśvaghosha.* New York: Columbia University Press, 1967.

———. *Kūkai: Major Works.* New York: Columbia University Press, 1972.

Hamilton, Sue. *Identity and Experience: The Constitution of the Human Being According to Early Buddhism.* London: Luzac Oriental, 1996.

Harper-Collins Dictionary of Religion. See Jonathan Z. Smith.

Hashimoto Fumio. "Shūishū." In *Man'yōshū to chokusenwakashū.* Vol. 4 of *Waka bungaku kōza.* Tokyo: Ōfūsha, 1972.

Hashimoto Fumio, et al., eds. *Karonshū.* Vol. 87 of *Shin Nihon koten bungaku zenshū.* Tokyo: Shōgakkan, 2006.

Hayami Tasuku. *Nihon Bukkyōshi: Kodai.* Tokyo: Yoshikawa Kōbunkan, 1986.

Higuchi Yoshimaro. "Shikashū." In *Man'yōshū to Chokusenwakashū.* Vol. 4 of *Waka bungaku kōza.* Tokyo: Ōfūsha, 1972.

Hirota, Dennis, trans. "In Practice of the Way: Sasamegoto, An Instruction Book in Linked Verse." *Chanoyu Quarterly* 19 (Kyoto, 1977): 31–46.

Hogan, Patrick Colm. *Cognitive Science, Literature, and the Arts: A Guide for Humanists.* New York and London: Routledge, 2003.

Hongō Masatsugu, "State Buddhism and Court Buddhism: The Role of Court Women in the Development of Buddhism from the Seventh to the Ninth Centuries." Chapter 3 in *Engendering Faith: Woman and Buddhism in Premodern Japan.* Ann Arbor: The Center for Japanese Studies, 2002.

Hori Ichirō. "Shakkyō-ka seiritsu no katei nit suite." *Indogaku Bukkyōgaku kenkyū* vol. 3, no. 2 (March 1955).

Huey, Robert. "The Medievalization of Poetic Practice." *Harvard Journal of Asiatic Studies* vol. 50, no. 2 (December 1990): 651–668.

Hurst, G. Cameron. *Insei: Abdicated Sovereigns in the Politics of Late Heian Japan*

1086-1185. New York: Columbia University Press, 1976.

———. "Insei." Chapter 9 in *The Cambridge History of Japan*, vol. 2 *Heian Japan*. Cambridge and New York: Cambridge University Press, 1999.

Hurvitz, Leon. *Chih-i (538–297): An Introduction to the Life and Ideas of a Chinese Buddhist Monk*. Brussels: Mélanges chinois et bouddhiques, vol. 12, 1962.

Hurvitz, Leon trans. *Scripture of the Lotus Blossom of the Fine Dharma*. New York: Columbia University Press, 1976.

Ichiko Teiji, et al., eds. *Nihon koten bungaku daijiten (kan'yaku ban)*. Tokyo: Iwanami Shoten, 1986.

Ikeda Tomizō. *Minamoto Shunrai no kenkyū*. Tokyo: Ōfūsha, 1973.

Imano Atsuko. "'*Shūishū*' maki dai-nijū aishō no shakkyō-ka gun e no isshiten: '*Makashikan*' to hairetsu kōsei." *Waka bungaku kenkyū*, vol. 81 (Dec 2000): 11–20.

Inoue Kaoru. *Gyōki*. Tokyo: Yoshikawa Kōbunkan, 1959.

Inoue Mitsusada. *Nihon Jōdokyō seiritsushi no kenkyū*. Tokyo: Yamakawa Shuppan, revised edition 1989.

Inukai Kiyoshi, et al., eds. *Waka daijiten*. Tokyo: Meiji Shoin, 1989.

Ishida Mizumaro. *Nihon koten bungaku to Bukkyō*. Tokyo: Chikuma Shobō, 1975.

Ishihara, Kiyoshi. *Shakkyō-ka no kenkyū*. Kyōto: Dōhōsha, 1980.

———. "*Hōmon hyakushu kō*." *Ryūkokudaigaku ronshū* 419 (Oct 1981), 23–46.

———. "Jōdai Nihon bungaku ni tōei shita Bukkyō," unpublished manuscript.

———. *Hosshin wakashū no kenkyū*. Osaka: Izumi Shoin, 1983.

Itō Hiroyuki, et al., eds. *Bukkyō bungaku no genten*. Vol. 1 of *Bukkyō bungaku kōza*. Tokyo: Benseisha, 1994.

Jewell, Elizabeth J. and Frank Abate, eds. *The Oxford American Dictionary*. Oxford: Oxford University Press, 2001.

Johnson, Mark. *The Meaning of the Body: Aesthetics of Human Understanding*. Chicago and London: The University of Chicago Press, 2007.

Kamens, Edward, trans. *The Three Jewels: A Study and Translation of Minamoto Tamenori's* "Sambōe." Ann Arbor: Center for Japanese Studies, 1988.

———. *The Buddhist Poetry of the Great Kamo Priestess: Daisaiin Senshi and Hosshin wakashū*. Ann Arbor: The Center for Japanese Studies, University of Michigan, 1990.

Kamijō Shōji. "Fujiwara no Shunzei." In Ōchō no waka. Vol. 5 of *Waka bungaku kōza*. Tokyo: Benseisha, 1993.

Katano Tatsurō and Matsuno Yōichi, eds. *Senzaiwakashū*. SNKBT vol. 10. Tokyo: Iwanami Shoten, 1993.

Katō, Bunnō, et al., ed. and trans. *The Threefold Lotus Sutra*. Tokyo: Kosei Publishing Co., 1988.

Kawakami Shin'ichirō. "'*Hōmon hyakushu*' no kōsatsu." In *Ōchō no uta to monogatari*. Tokyo: Ōfūsha, 1980, 26–55.

Kawamura Kōshō, ed. *Tendaigaku jiten*. Tokyo: Kokusho kankōkai, 1990.

Kawamura Teruo, ed. *Goshūiwakashū*. Vol. 5 of *Izumi koten sōsho*. Osaka: Izumi Shoin, 1991.

———, et al., ed. *Kin'yōwakashū Shikawakashū*. SNKBT vol. 9. Tokyo: Iwanami Shoten, 1989.

Kawamura Teruo and Kubota Jun. *Chōshū eisō Toshitada-shū*. Tokyo: Meiji Shoin, 1998.

Kawasaki Mochiyuki, et al. *Yomeru nenpyō: Nihonshi*. Tokyo: Jiyū Kokuminsha, 1998.

Kikuchi Hitoshi. "Setsuwa: Denshō to Izumi Shikibu." *Kokubungaku* vol. 35, no. 12 (October 1990): 100–102.

Kikuchi Ryōichi. *Kodai chūsei Nihon Bukkyō bungaku ron*. Tokyo: Ōfūsha, 1976.

Kim, Yung-Hee. *Songs to Make the Dust Dance: The* Ryōjin hishō *of Twelfth-Century Japan*. Berkeley and Los Angeles: University of California Press, 1994.

Kitagawa, Joseph M. *Religion in Japanese History*. New York: Columbia University Press, 1966.

Kojima Noriyuki and Arai Eizō, eds. *Kokinwakashū*. SNKBT vol. 5. Tokyo: Iwanami Shoten, 1989.

Kojima Noriyuki, Kinoshita Masatoshi, Satake Akihiro, eds. *Man'yōshū*. Vol. 1 of *Nihon koten bungaku zenshū*. Tokyo: Shōgakkan, 1989.

Komachiya Teruhiko. *Fujiwara Kintō*. Tokyo: Shūeisha, 1985.

———, ed. *Shūiwakashū*. SNKBT vol. 7. Tokyo: Iwanami Shoten, 1990.

Komatsu Shigemi. *Fujiwara no Tadamichi hitsu Kangaku-e ki kaisetsu*. Tokyo: Kodansha Publishing, 1984.

Konishi Jin'ichi. *A History of Japanese Literature, Volume One: The Archaic and Ancient Ages*. Aileen Gatten and Nicholas Teele, trans. Princeton: Princeton University Press, 1984.

———. *A History of Japanese Literature, Volume Two: The Early Middle Ages*. Aileen Gatten, trans. Princeton: Princeton University Press, 1984.

———. *A History of Japanese Literature, Volume Three: The High Middle Ages*. Aileen Gatten and Mark Harbison, trans. Princeton: Princeton University Press, 1991.

Kotas, Frederick J. "Ōjōden: Accounts of Rebirth in the Pure Land." Ph.D. dissertation, University of Washington, 1988.

Kubota Jun. *Shinkokin kajin no kenkyū*. Tokyo: Tokyo Daigaku Shuppan Kai, 1978.

———. *Chūsei*. Vol. 3 of *Nihon bungaku zenshi*. Tokyo: Gakutōsha, 1990.

———. "Hōmon-ka to shakkyō-ka." In *Kyōten*. Vol. 6 of *Nihon bungaku to*

Bukkyō. Tokyo: Iwanami Shoten, 1994.

Kubota Jun, et al., ed. *Waka.* Vol. 6 of *Kenkyū shiryō Nihon koten bungaku.* Tokyo: Meiji Shoin, 1983.

Kubota Jun and Hirota Yoshinobu, eds. *Goshūiwakashū.* SNKBT vol. 8. Tokyo: Iwanami Shoten, 1994.

Kudō Shigenori, et al., ed. *Kin'yōwakashū Shikawakashū.* SNKBT vol. 9. Tokyo: Iwanami Shoten, 1989.

Kunieda Toshihisa. "*Hōmon hyakushu* shichū: Shakkyō-ka kenkyū no kisoteki sagyō (2)." *Shinwa kokubun* 8 (Feb. 1974), 75–88.

———. "*Hōmon hyakushu* shichū (2)." *Shinwa kokubun* 9 (Feb. 1975), 36–45.

———. "Tendai no goji hakkyō to waka: Shakkyō-ka kenkyū no kisoteki sagyō (1)." In *Kokugo kokubungaku ronshū: Taniyama Shigeru kyōju taishoku kinen.* Tokyo: Hanawa Shobō, 1976.

———. "Yuima-kyō jūyu to waka: Shakkyō-ka kenkyū no kisoteki sagyō (6)." *Bukkyō daigaku kenkyū kiyo,* vol. 64 (March 1980): 62–67.

———. "Tendai no goji hakkyō to Ōkagami." *Bukkyō bungaku,* vol. 8 (March 1984): 49–57.

LaFleur, William R. *The Karma of Words.* Berkeley and London: University of California Press, 1983.

Lakoff, George. *Women, Fire and Dangerous Things: What Categories Reveal About the Mind.* Chicago and London: The University of Chicago Press, 1987.

Lakoff, George and Mark Johnson. *Philosophy in the Flesh: The Embodied Mind and Its Challenge to Western Thought.* New York: Basic Books, 1999.

Levy, Ian Hideo. *The Ten Thousand Leaves: A Translation of the Man'yōshū, Japan's Premier Anthology of Classical Poetry: Vol. 1.* Princeton: Princeton University Press, 1981.

Luk, Charles. *The Vimalakīrti Nirdeśa Sūtra.* Boston and London: Shambhala Publications, Inc., 1972.

MacWilliams, Mark. "Buddhist Pilgrim/Buddhist Exile: Old and New Images of Retired Emperor Kazan in the Saigoku Kannon Temple Guidebooks." *History of Religions* 34.4 (May 1995): 375–411.

Manaka Fujiko. *Senzaishū Shinkokinshū shakkyō-ka no hyōshaku.* Tokyo: Mine Bunko, 1956.

———. *Kokunbungaku ni sesshu sareta Bukkyō.* Tokyo: Bun'ichi Shuppan, 1972.

Marra, Michele. "The Development of Mappō Thought in Japan (I)." *Japanese Journal of Religious Studies,* vol. 15, no. 1 (March 1988): 25–54.

Masuda Shigeo. *Kuraki michi.* Kyoto: Sekai Shisōsha, 1987.

Matsuda Takeo. *Kin'yōshū no kenkyū.* Tokyo: Parutosu-sha, 1988.

Matsunaga, Daigan and Alicia. *Foundation of Japanese Buddhism,* vol. 1. Tokyo: Buddhist Books International, 1974.

Matsuno Yōichi. *Fujiwara Shunzei no kenkyū.* Tokyo: Kasama Shoin, 1973.

——, ed. *Shikawakashū.* Vol. 7 of *Izumi koten sōsho.* Osaka: Izumi Shoin, 1988.

——. *Torihaha: Senzaishū jidai waka no kenkyū.* Tokyo: Kazama Shobō, 1994.

McCullough, Helen Craig. *Ōkagami: The Great Mirror.* Princeton: Princeton University Press, 1980.

McCullough, William H. and Helen Craig McCullough, trans. *A Tale of Flowering Fortunes.* (Stanford: Stanford University Press, 1980.

McKinney, Meredith. *The Pillow Book.* New York: Penguin Books, 2006.

Mezaki Tokue. *Suki to mujō.* Tokyo: Yoshikawa Kōbunkan, 1988.

——. *Saigyō.* Tokyo: Yoshikawa Kōbunkan, 1989.

Mikoshiba Daisuke. "Empress Kōmyō's Buddhist Faith: Her Role in the Founding of the State Temple and Convent System." Chapter 2 of *Engendering Faith: Women and Buddhism in Premodern Japan.* Ann Arbor: The Center for Japanese Studies, 2002.

Miller, Roy Andrew. *Footprints of the Buddha.* New Haven: American Oriental Society, 1975.

Mitchell, Donald W. *Buddhism: Introducing the Buddhist Experience.* New York: Oxford University Press, 2002.

Moerman, D. Max. "The Archaeology of Anxiety." Chapter 10 in *Heian Japan: Centers and Peripheries.* Honolulu: University of Hawai'i Press, 2007.

Morrell, Robert, trans. *Sand and Pebbles (Shasekishū).* Albany: State University of New York Press, 1985.

Morris, Ivan, trans. *The Pillow Book of Sei Shōnagon.* London: Penguin Books, 1967.

Muraishi Esho. "Buddhism and Literature in Japan." Chapter 1 in *Understanding Japanese Buddhism,* ed. Hanayama Shōyū. Tokyo: Japan Buddhist Federation, 1978.

Nakamura Hajime, et al., eds. *Bukkyō jiten.* Tokyo: Iwanami Shoten, 2006.

——, ed. *Bukkyōgo daijiten.* Tokyo: Tokyo Shoseki, 1985.

Nihon kokugo daijiten, 2nd edition, vol. 6. Tokyo: Shogakkan, 2001.

Nihon koten bungaku daijiten (kan'yaku ban). See Ichiko Teiji.

Nishida Masayoshi. *Mujō no bungaku.* Tokyo: Hanawa Shobō, 1975.

Nishizawa Makoto. "Shakkyō bu no hairetsu kōsei." Chapter 8 of Ariyoshi Tamotsu ed., *Senzaiwakashū no kisoteki kenkyū.* Tokyo: Kasama Shoten, 1976.

Nishizawa Yoshihito, Utsugi Genkō, Kubota Jun, eds. *Sankashū Kikigakishū Zanshū.* Vol. 21 of *Waka bungaku taikei.* Tokyo: Meiji Shoin, 2003.

Okazaki Kazuko, "'Shakkyō-ka kō: hachidaishū o chūshin ni." In *Bukkyō bungaku kenkyū (1).* Kyoto: Hōzōkan, 1963, 79–118.

Olinyk, Christina. "Poems of the Gods of the Heaven and the Earth: An Annotated Translation of the Jingi-ka Book of the *Senzaishū*." M.A. thesis, University of Massachusetts Amherst, 2010.

Ono Yasuhiro, et al., eds. *Nihon shūkyō jiten.* Tokyo: Kōbundō, 1985.

Ōsone Shōsuke, et al., eds. *Honchō monzui.* SNKBT vol. 27. Tokyo: Iwanami Shoten, 2007.

Ōsumi Kazuo. "Historical Notes on Women and the Japanization of Buddhism." Forward in *Engendering Faith: Women and Buddhism in Premodern Japan.* Ann Arbor: Center for Japanese Studies, 2002.

Paden, William E. *Religious Worlds: The Comparative Study of Religion.* Boston: Beacon Press, 1994.

Pandey, Rajyashree. *Writing and Renunciation in Medieval Japan: The Works of the Poet-Priest Kamo no Chōmei.* Ann Arbor: The Center for Japanese Studies, University of Michigan, 1998.

Phillipi, Donald L., trans. *Kojiki.* Princeton and Tokyo: Princeton University Press and the University of Tokyo Press, 1968.

Piggott, Joan. *The Emergence of Japanese Kingship.* Stanford: Stanford University Press, 1997.

Rabinovitch, Judith N. & Timothy R. Bradstock. *Dance of the Butterflies: Chinese Poetry from the Japanese Court Tradition.* Ithaca: Cornell East Asia Series, 2005.

Rimer, J. Thomas and Jonathan Chaves, eds. and trans. *Japanese and Chinese Poems to Sing: The* Wakan Rōeishū. New York: Columbia University Press, 1997.

Rodd, Laurel Rasplica with Mary Catherine Henkenius. *Kokinshū: A Collection of Poems Ancient and Modern.* Princeton: Princeton University Press, 1984.

Rouzer, Paul. "Early Buddhist Kanshi: Court, Country, and Kūkai." *Monumenta Nipponica,* vol. 59, no. 4 (Winter 2004): 431–459.

Royston, Clifton W. "The Poetics and Poetry Criticism of Fujiwara Shunzei (1114–1204)." Ph.D. dissertation, University of Michigan, 1974.

Sakaguchi Genshō. *Nihon Bukkyō bungaku josetsu.* 1935. Tokyo: Kokusho Kankōkai, 1972.

Sakamoto Tarō. *The Six National Histories of Japan,* John S. Brownlee, trans. Vancouver and Tokyo: University of British Columbia Press and the University of Tokyo Press, 1991.

Sakamoto Yukio and Iwamoto Yutaka, eds. *Hokke-kyō,* 3 vol. Tokyo: Iwanami Bunko, 1989.

Sansom, George. *A History of Japan to 1334.* Stanford: Stanford University Press, 1958.

Sekiguchi Shindai. *Makashikan: Zen no shisō genri,* vol. 1. Tokyo: Iwanami Shoten, 1989.

Sekiguchi Sōnen. "Shakkyō-ka ron." *Bungei kenkyū,* vol. 6, no. 10 (June 1952): 20–26.

Sekine Yoshiko and Furuya Takako, eds. *Sanboku kikashū—shūchūhen gekan.* Tokyo: Kazama Shobō, 1999.

Shigematsu, Akihisa. "An Overview of Early Japanese Pure Land." In *The Pure Land Tradition: History and Development.* Berkeley: Berkeley Buddhist Studies Series, 1996, 267–312.

Shin kokka taikan. Shikashū hen, vol. 3. Tokyo: Kadokawa Shoten, 1987.

Slingerland, Edward. *What Science Offers the Humanities: Integrating Body and Culture.* Cambridge: Cambridge University Press, 2008.

Smith, Jonathan Z. *Harper-Collins Dictionary of Religion.* San Francisco: Harper-Collins, 1995.

Stevenson, Daniel B. and Neal Donner. *The Great Calming and Contemplation: A Study and Translation of the First Chapter of Chih-i's* Mo-ho chih-kuan. Honolulu: Kuroda Institute and the University of Hawaii Press, 1993.

Stone, Jackie. "Seeking Enlightenment in the Last Age: *Mappō* Thought in Kamakura Buddhism, Part One." *The Eastern Buddhist,* vol. 18, no. 1 (Spring 1985): 28–56.

Stone, Jacqueline. *Original Enlightenment and the Transformation of Medieval Japanese Buddhism.* Honolulu: University of Hawai'i Press, 1999.

Sueki Fumihiko. "*Man'yōshū* ni okeru mujōkan no keisei." *Tōyō gakujutsu kenkyū,* vol. 21, no. 1 (Tōyō tetsugaku kenkyūjo, 1982): 62–63.

Suzuki Hideo. "Goshūishū." *Inseiki bungaku-shi no kōsō tokushu* in *Kokubungaku kaishaku to kanshō,* vol. 53, no. 3 (March 1988): 82–83.

Swanson, Paul. *Foundations of T'ien-t'ai Philosophy.* Nagoya: Asian Humanities Press, 1989.

Takagi, Yutaka. *Heian jidai Hokke-kyō Bukkyōshi kenkyū.* Kyoto: Heirakuji Shoten, 1978.

Takakusu Junjirō. *The Essentials of Buddhist Philosophy.* Honolulu: University of Hawaii Press, 1947.

Takakusu Junjirō, Fukui Kyūzō, et al., eds. *Shakkyō kaei zenshū.* 1934. Tokyo: Tōhō Shuppan, 1978.

Takatsuka Zonkei. "*Senzaiwakashū* 'Shakkyō' bu ni tsuite." *Bukkyō bunka kenkyūjo kiyō* 8 (June 1969), 89–93.

Takeishi Akio. *Wasan: Bukkyō no poejii.* Kyoto: Hōzōkan, 1986).

Takeishi Akio and Suganuma Akira, eds. *Bukkyō bungaku jiten.* Tokyo: Tokyodō Shuppan, 1980.

Takeshita Yutaka. "Shinpū e no taidō." In *Wakashi: Man'yō kara gendai tanka made.* Osaka: Izumi Shoin, 1996.

Takeuchi, Rizō. "The Rise of the Warriors." *The Cambridge History of Japan: Heian.* Cambridge: The Cambridge History of Japan, 1999.

Takusu Yōko. "Shakkyō-ka o meguru kōsatsu." *Kokubun* 37 (June 1972): 11–25.

Tamura Yoshirō. "The Ideas of the *Lotus Sutra.*" In *The Lotus Sutra in Japanese Culture.* Honolulu: University of Hawai'i Press, 1989, 37–51.

Tanaka Yutaka and Akase Shingō, eds. *Shinkokinwakashū.* SNKBT vol. 11. Tokyo: Iwanami Shoten, 1992.

Taniyama Shigeru. *Fujiwara Shunzei: Hito to sakuhin.* Vol. 3 of *Taniyama Shigeru chosakushū.* Tokyo: Kadokawa Shoten, 1982.

———. *Senzaiwakashū to sono shūhen.* Vol. 5 of *Taniyama Shigeru choshakushū.* Tokyo: Kadokawa Shoten, 1982.

Tendaigaku jiten. See Kawamura Kōshō.

The Oxford American Dictionary. See Jewell, Elizabeth J. and Frank Abate.

Thurman, Robert A. F., trans. *The Holy Teaching of Vimalakīrti.* University Park and London: The Pennsylvania State University Press, 1976.

Toury, Gideon. *Descriptive Translation Studies.* Amsterdam and Philadelphia: The John Benjamins Publishing Company, 1995.

Tsuji Zennosuke. *Nihon Bukkyō-shi,* vol. 1. Tokyo: Iwanami Shoten, 1944.

Turner, Mark. *Reading Minds: The Study of English in the Age of Cognitive Science.* Princeton: Princeton University Press, 1991.

Ueda Masaaki, et al., eds. *Nihon jinmei jiten.* Tokyo: Sanseidō, 1990.

Ueno Osamu. "Goshūishū." In *Man'yōshū to chokusenwakashū.* Vol. 4 of *Waka bungaku kōza,* Hisamatsu Sen'ichi et al., ed. Tokyo: Ōfūsha, 1970.

Waka daijiten. See Inukai Kiyoshi.

Watanabe Yasuaki. *Chūsei waka no seisei.* Tokyo: Wakakusa Shobō, 1999.

———. "*Kokinshū* to shinkō: Mujōkan o megutte." *Kokubungaku: kaishaku to kanshō,* vol. 65, no. 10 (October 2000): 33–39.

Watson, Burton, trans. *The Lotus Sutra.* New York: Columbia University Press, 1993.

Williams, Paul. *Mahāyāna Buddhism: The Doctrinal Foundations.* London: Routledge, 1989.

Yamada Shōzen. "Kyōshi-ka no seiritsu." *Buzan gakuho* 2 (November 1954): 131–142.

———. "Kakinomoto no Hitomaro eigu no seiritsu to tenkai: Bukkyō to bungaku to no sesshoku ni shiten o oite." *Taishō Daigaku kenkyū kiyō* 51 (1966): 83–124.

———. "Mikkyō to waka bungaku." *Mikkyōgaku kenkyū.* (March 1969): 151.

———. *Saigyō no waka to Bukkyō.* Tokyo: Meiji Shoin, 1987.

————. "Poetry and Meaning: Medieval Poets and the *Lotus Sutra*." In *The Lotus Sutra in Japanese Culture*. Honolulu: University of Hawai'i Press, 1989, 95–117.

————. "Shakkyō-ka no seiritsu to tenkai." In *Waka, Renga, Haikai*, vol. 4 of *Bukkyō bungaku kōza*. Tokyo: Benseisha, 1995.

Yamagishi Tokuhei, ed. *Hachidaishū zenchū*. Tokyo: Yūseidō, 1960.

Yamamoto Akihiro. *Jakuzen Hōmon hyakushu zen'yaku*. Kyoto: Kazama Shobō, 2010.

Yamamoto, Kosho. *The Mahāyāna Mahāparinirvāna Sūtra*. <http://lirs.ru/do/Mahaparinirvana_Sutra,Yamamoto,Page,2007.pdf>.

Yamasaki, Taizō. *Shingon: Japanese Esoteric Buddhism*. Boston: Shambhala Publications, Inc., 1988.

Yomeru nenpyō: Nihonshi. See Kawasaki Mochiyuki.

Zunshine, Lisa. *Why We Read Fiction: Theory of Mind and the Novel*. Columbus: Ohio State University Press, 2006.

INDEX OF AUTHORS

463

INDEX TO FIRST LINES OF WAKA

MAIN INDEX

STEPHEN D. MILLER is associate professor of Japanese language and literature at the University of Massachusetts, Amherst. He was educated at the Ohio State University (B.A. 1971), Columbia University (M.A. 1983), and the University of California at Los Angeles (Ph.D. 1993). Miller is translator of *A Pilgrim's Guide to Forty-Six Temples* (Weatherhill Inc., 1990), and editor of *Partings at Dawn: An Anthology of Japanese Gay Literature* (Gay Sunshine Press, 1996), as well as translator of one of the items in that anthology. He lived in Japan for nine years between 1980 and 1999, in part as the recipient of two Japan Foundation fellowships for research abroad in Japan.

PATRICK DONNELLY is the author of *The Charge* (Ausable Press, 2003, since 2009 part of Copper Canyon Press) and *Nocturnes of the Brothel of Ruin* (Four Way Books, 2012). He is an associate editor of *Poetry International*, director of the annual Poetry Seminar at The Frost Place, and has taught writing at Smith College, Colby College, the Bread Loaf Writers' Conference, and elsewhere. His poems have appeared in many journals, including *American Poetry Review, Ploughshares, The Yale Review, The Virginia Quarterly Review*, and *The Massachusetts Review*. With Stephen D. Miller he has translated the sixteenth-century Japanese Nō play *Shunzei Tadanori* for *Like Clouds or Mists: Studies and Translations of Nō Plays of the Genpei War* (Cornell East Asia Series, 2013).

First front matter epigraph: Twichell, Chase. Excerpted from "Work Libido," *Dog Language*. Port Townsend: Copper Canyon Press, 2009, 105.

Second front matter epigraph: Whitman, Walt. Excerpted from "Continuities," *Whitman: Poetry and Prose*. New York: The Library of America, 1982, 626.

Third front matter epigraph: Sōjō Jōen, *Kin'yōshū* 635/677, translation by author with Patrick Donnelly.

Afterword epigraph: Lawrence, D. H., excerpted from "Song of a Man Who Has Come Through," *D. H. Lawrence: Complete Poems*, New York: Penguin Books, 1993, 250.

CORNELL EAST ASIA SERIES

CORNELL East Asia Series

eap.einaudi.cornell.edu/publications